It Takes a
Family

It Takes a Family

CONSERVATISM AND THE COMMON GOOD

RICK SANTORUM

WILMINGTON, DELAWARE

Santorum, Rick, 1958–

    It takes a family : conservatism and the common good /
Rick Santorum. — 2nd ed. — Wilmington, Del. : ISI
Books, 2006.

        p. ; cm.
        ISBN-13: 978-1-932236-83-5
        ISBN-10: 1-932236-83-X
        Includes bibliographical references and index.

        1. Christian conservatism—United States. 2.
Family—United States. 3. Politics and culture—United
States. 4. United States—Politics and government—2001–
5. United States—Economic policy—2001– I. Title. II.
Conservatism and the common good.

JC573.2.U6 S26 2006   2006921515
320.5/5—dc22   0604

Published in the United States by:

    ISI Books
    Intercollegiate Studies Institute
    3901 Centerville Road
    P.O. Box 4431
    Wilmington, DE 19807-0431

Interior design by John M. Vella

For Karen Anne – my wife – my Song of Solomon

Non nobis Domine non nobis,
Sed Nomini tuo da gloriam

Table of Contents

Preface   *ix*

Part One: IT TAKES A FAMILY
    I. The Task of Stewardship   3
   II. The Liberal Vision: No-Fault Freedom   13
  III. Families and the Common Good   21
  IV. The Meaning of Family   28

Part Two: SOCIAL CAPITAL AND THE TIES THAT BIND
    V. What Kind of Freedom?   43
  VI. Habits of Association   50
 VII. Trust and Civic Connection   58
VIII. Subsidiarity vs. Central Control   65
  IX. Changing Lives, Building Families   73
    X. Parents and Children   93
  XI. Religion and Social Capital   101
 XII. Where Social Capital Is Weakest   109

Part Three: THE ROOTS OF PROSPERITY
XIII. Abundant Families in the Land of Plenty   119
 XIV. Economic Responsibility   127
  XV. Work and Human Dignity   135

XVI.	Wealth and Ownership	143
XVII.	The Power of Knowledge	163
XVIII.	Faith-Based Transformations	168
XIX.	Smart Reinvesting	176
XX.	Wealth and Race	189

Part Four: MORAL ECOLOGY
XXI.	Liberty and Virtue	197
XXII.	Moral Capital and the Moral Environment	210
XXIII.	The Rule of Judges	220
XXIV.	Abortion: A Personal Aside	239
XXV.	The Impact of Partial Birth Abortion	248
XXVI.	How Abortion Affects Our Moral Ecology	258

Part Five: CULTURE MATTERS
XXVII.	The Good, the True, and the Beautiful	271
XXVIII.	The Good, the Bad, and the Ugly	278
XXIX.	Culture: Ally or Adversary?	288
XXX.	Violence and a Coarsened Society	304
XXXI.	Sex, Drugs, and Rock 'n' Roll: Mostly Sex	313
XXXII.	Not Withdraw, but Engage	320
XXXIII.	Culture-Makers, Culture-Mongers, Culture-Consumers	326
XXXIV.	Culture and Public Policy	340

Part Six: EDUCATIONAL EXCELLENCE
XXXV.	Knowledge, Truth, and Education	351
XXXVI.	Who Rules the Schools?	360
XXXVII.	Not Raising Children, but Raising Adults	371
XXXVIII.	Bringing the Lessons Home	383
XXXIX.	Moral Truth and the End of Man	388
XL.	Higher Education and Liberal Education	403

Conclusion	421
Bibliographical Note	429
Index	439

Preface

A large part of the district I represented as a freshman
congressman in 1993–1994 was the old steel valley southeast of Pittsburgh. Unlike, say, Silicon Valley, this was not an
area bursting with new jobs and economic opportunity. The
little mill towns along the Monongahela River looked more like
ghost towns. Unlike most congressional Republicans, I represented a lot of people who were poor, but with rich traditions;
bitter, but still proud. They also, increasingly, didn't have much
hope. My main district office was in the heart of one of those
mill towns, McKeesport. Almost every day my staff and I dealt
with chronic problems of poverty and despair that were the
result of economic dislocation that was only made worse by a
liberal vision of how to return these areas to their former glory.
The liberal vision wasn't working. So what was the conservative vision? What was *my* vision?

I came to the uncomfortable realization that conservatives
were not only reluctant to spend government dollars on the poor:
they hadn't even thought much about what might work better. I
often described my conservative colleagues during that time as
simply "cheap liberals." My own economically modest personal

background and my faith had taught me to care for those less fortunate, but I too had not yet given much thought to the proper role of government in this mission.

It happened that at the very same time I was trying to help the people of the Mon Valley, I was assigned the task of responding to President Clinton's call to "end welfare as we know it." I led a team in drafting a welfare reform bill for the Republicans on the House Ways and Means Committee. My district and that bill started me down the road to building up a conservative philosophy within which we could use government policies and dollars as a catalyst to renew and re-form the poor families and communities in our country. After I was elected to the Senate in 1994, I met up with someone who was already well down that road of reform, Senator Dan Coats of Indiana. We became the heart of a conservative group who shared a concern for the poor and who wanted to reverse the ill effects that decades of liberal policies had inflicted on the least well off.

While we had some successes in adding many of our ideas to the 1996 Welfare Reform Act and the American Community Renewal Act, our ideas were nonetheless vilified by the liberal architects of the existing system and largely ignored by the vast majority of traditional conservatives. Our fortunes changed with the election of George W. Bush and his "Compassionate Conservative" agenda. His faith-based program, reflecting his sincere belief that faith-based and community organizations can change people's lives, brought our efforts into the mainstream of political debate.

In spite of the president's good work in this area, I have long believed that no one has yet laid out a coherent and comprehensive theoretical argument for this apparently new type of conservatism. This book is not a public policy agenda—although there are plenty of new initiatives proposed. Nor is it the book that I originally conceived, which would have focused exclusively on the poor in America—although the poor are at the heart of my arguments. No, this book has turned into something more ambitious. It is an attempt to sketch the past forty years of American history in light of our founders' vision for the pursuit of the common good in a civil society. Just what was our founders' vision? Are we still the country we were born to be? How did we arrive at this state? Where is our destination, if we do not change? And how can we reclaim our rich inheritance from generations past and with it build up a society our founders would revere?

BEFORE I THANK ALL WHO ASSISTED ME in the writing of this book, I want to thank those who brought me to the dance—people without whom I would have had very little to say. First among these are my wife Karen and our six children, the family for whom I live.

Karen is so much of who I am and what I do that it is hard to give her enough credit in a book, much less a few lines. She is truly my soul mate. There could be no more loving, faithful, honest, and supportive spouse to have accompanied me through the last fifteen years of campaigns, legislative and home-state crises, and most importantly, parenthood. Our hours are long, the pace intense, and the stress high, but she not only helps hold me together, she is often single-handedly the steady guiding light for our six children, ages 3 to 14, too. Karen's wisdom and her actions in our own family permeate my discussion of family in this book. She is my refuge, strength, and inspiration. And aside from all that, she is a twice-published author, having written and edited *Letters to Gabriel* and *Everyday Graces: A Child's Book of Good Manners,* respectively. (I realize that I married up!)

I want to thank my terrific children for having patience with me. Putting up with the schedule of a father who is a U.S. senator is tough enough, but for the last few months they have been doubly understanding as I spent hours squirreled away writing. Karen and I have been abundantly blessed with the privilege of raising six magnificent souls. In fact, our lives were incomplete until we had each and every one of our children. My prayer is that the time I poured into this book will result in a somewhat better America in which they may grow and serve their fellow citizens.

When I was growing up, my whole life seemed to be spent around family. There was the occasional lecture about its importance, but I learned about the centrality of family mostly because family was simply what we did. I was blessed with a terrific father and mother who planted seeds that eventually took root. They, like Karen's parents, were very much of the "old school." While I didn't appreciate it at the time, I certainly do now, as Karen and I try to raise our children with those same traditional values.

I extend my heartfelt gratitude to my father- and mother-in-law, Ken and Betty Lee Garver, for all of their encouragement and support through the years; but most of all, for giving me Karen.

I also want to thank the people I grew up with in the small, blue-collar town of Butler, Pennsylvania. It was a place where family togetherness, being a good neighbor, and civic participation were on display every day, without complaint or apology. I had so many good role models as a kid: I could not have been more blessed.

THIS BOOK HAS TRULY BEEN a collaborative effort. I want to thank Jeff Nelson, the publisher of ISI Books, for pitching to me the idea of tackling so large a subject. I never thought I would have the time to take on such a project, and I wouldn't have without the help of Jeff Rosenberg and the "Marks Brothers"—Mark Henrie, Mark Rodgers, and Mark Ryland. Jeff Rosenberg helped immensely by working with me to interview many of the people you will meet in this book and by writing many of the chapter first drafts. Mark Henrie was an outstanding editor and counselor who drew out of me in countless conversations the philosophical basis for my actions in Washington and made sure this was woven throughout the book. I thank him for all of his excellent advice and contributions. He also had his work cut out for him in keeping me from running down numerous rabbit trails.

Mark Rodgers is the chief of staff for the Senate Republican Conference, which I chair. We have been a team since he appeared in September 1990 to help engineer my somewhat miraculous first congressional race. Mark is a great blessing to me. Without a doubt, much of my political and public policy success is attributable to his superb planning, management, and creative skills. One of Mark's interests is in shaping the popular culture to be a more positive influence in our society, and in this regard he has led many efforts on and off the Hill that are having a positive impact. I want to thank him especially for everything he put into the cultural capital section of the book.

Thanks, too, to Mark Ryland, who has been a teacher, lawyer, and Microsoft executive, and who now works at a think tank in Washington. He is also a homeschooling father of nine. He helped tremendously in laying out the framework of this volume and added greatly to the discussion on intellectual capital and our public education system. I am extraordinarily grateful for his valuable contributions.

I COULD NOT FINISH without also thanking the good people of Pennsylvania, for two reasons. First, as you will soon read, many civic leaders in our state contributed to this book by standing out as examples of what we all should strive to be. Through their self-sacrifice and care for others, they give hope to the people they serve and inspiration to us all.

Second, and finally, I would not have had the opportunity to share in this book my vision for America were it not for the honor the people of Pennsylvania have given me to represent them in the United States Senate. It has been a great privilege. Thank you.

Part One

IT TAKES A FAMILY

I

The Task of Stewardship

On my right wrist, every day, I wear a royal blue piece of cloth, a bracelet of sorts. Stitched in white are the letters F.A.M.I.L.Y. That is a word, of course, but it is also an acronym. The word is what's most important in the choices we face together as a country. The acronym is what is most important for me as I confront the choices I must make in my own life—as a husband, father, citizen, and lawmaker.

I'll explain F.A.M.I.L.Y., the *acronym*, a bit later. But the word, *family*, is where I want to start. It is where we have to start, because it is where we all *do* start—a fact that many in Washington often overlook.

The liberal news media, Hollywood, and the educational elite in America tend to portray political liberals as the courageous champions of the average guy—and, of course, the poor. It is simply assumed that their more "enlightened" economic policies are all about helping the poor and middle class. Conservatives, on the other hand, are portrayed as fundamentally selfish, self-interested individuals, whose economic policies are crafted to protect or advance their (or their golf partners') "special interests." I will argue in this book that liberal economic policies have not only been devastating to the poor and the middle class economically, but have actually undermined the basic structures of our society. I will also argue that both conservative economic policy and conservative efforts to help the poor help themselves are more genuinely compassionate—and effective—than the liberal alternative. These policies are already beginning to work, for all Americans.

Another view the media echo chamber promotes is that liberal social policies are rational, tolerant, progressive, and caring. Social conservatives, on the other hand, are portrayed as irrational, ignorant, rigid Bible-thumpers obsessed with prophesying woe. In this book, I hope to show that this all-too-common caricature of conservatives and their social policies by the liberal elite can be attributed to liberals' fundamentally different vision for America—a vision that is completely at odds with that of our nation's founders, and with the views of most Americans today. Liberalism is an ideology; conservatism is common sense.

By almost any measure, the political, economic, and social achievements of this nation in just over two centuries are astounding, and American accomplishments in our own lifetime are no less extraordinary. We all recognize the progress we have made through a sustained effort over the course of the last few decades: we have faced down Soviet communism, the greatest tyranny the world has ever seen; through an effort of moral self-examination and reform, we have made extraordinary strides in overcoming the legacy of racial prejudice; we have committed ourselves to programs that have made our natural environment cleaner for future generations; we have remained in the forefront of scientific investigation in virtually every field; and through it all, America has remained a land of economic opportunity unmatched in human history. Nevertheless, just as personal success can lead to pride, avarice, extravagance, and self-absorption, history has shown that great civilizations can also go astray.

The simple truth is, as the voters in the 2004 elections indicated, not everything is well in America. If, over the past generation, we have made great strides in some areas, it is also the case that in the same generation we have seen alarming trends in American society as well: an epidemic of promiscuity and sexually transmitted diseases among the young; crime rates that are still much too high; extreme violence and offensive sexual content on everything from video games to the Internet; 3,500 healthy expectant mothers carrying healthy children exercising a "choice" to end the lives of their children every day; religion under assault by the media and liberal activists and then booted from the public square by court order; our schools failing the poor in providing the basics for life and indoctrinating both rich and poor with politically correct dogma instead of virtue and truth; the foundational institution of every civilization known to man—marriage—under siege; and millions retreating from our neighborhoods and the civic and fraternal organizations that bind us together. Across America, when they gather at backyard barbecues or Little League games, parents share with each other their deep concerns about how *hard* the world around us makes it to raise children the right way today.

Once, our social, governmental, and educational institutions, along with the popular culture, seemed to work together to aid parents in raising their children. Today, many feel that these same institutions are somehow conspiring *against* them. The media missed the impact of the "values voter" in the 2004 election, in part because they didn't know what to look for. These values voters may not be pro-life or favor a constitutional amendment to define traditional marriage, they may not think of themselves as conservatives, and they may not be registered Republicans, but they can feel in their bones that *something is wrong*, and they sense that the institutions dominated by liberals are a big part of the problem. I believe these voters decided one of the most critical elections in recent times in favor of President Bush and the Republicans because they see these values issues as a bigger problem in their lives than either terrorism or the economy. They are looking to something or someone for answers.

That points to a problem facing postmodern America. We too readily look to those wielding power and influence to solve society's big problems for us—in particular, we look to the government. And why not? They are "society's" problems, and the government is society's representative. But over the past generation we have been learning that governmental, cultural, social, moral, and intellectual power brokers in far too many cases have made our problems worse. This has created a vicious downward spiral in which the more the public relies on the powerful elite, the worse it gets, which leads to the public relying on these elites even more.

Who are these big, powerful forces upon which so many rely to shape our economy, culture, society, values, and learning? They are what I call the "Bigs"—big news media, big entertainment, big universities and public schools, some big businesses and some big national labor unions, and of course, the biggest Big of all, the federal government. When I hear that catchphrase of the liberals, "It takes a village to raise a child," I hear *Big*. It's a homely image, a village, but when you get past the metaphor, what do you really see in the details? Top-down, elitist prescriptions imposed by those who believe they are the postmodern kings of the masses—particularly of the supposedly ill-informed "peasants" of red-state America.

The people who run the Bigs I like to call the "village elders." They are the liberal elite who think they know what is best for individual Americans and how best to order (or rather, re-order) our society along the lines of their ideological abstractions. They see any institution that stands between the Bigs and the isolated individual as an annoyance or hindrance. In fact, in the view of the Bigs, it is often just these intermediary associations that are responsible for what the Bigs understand to be our social problems. The liberal answer to the "problem" of intermediary institutions is to "liberate" individuals from them—whether individuals want that or not.

And what are these problem-creating associations that liberals believe harm people? They are the "Littles": local government, civic and fraternal associations, clubs, small businesses, neighborhoods, local school districts, churches and church ministries—and of course, the greatest offender of all and the greatest thorn in the liberals' side, the iconoclastic traditional family. Liberal ideology promises a utopia of freedom and equality, if only the Littles can be engineered out of existence.

So where do we conservatives look for answers to the social issues of such widespread concern to Americans today? Why, to the very associations that the village elders distrust. And we ought to start with what has been the foundation of every successful civilization in history: the traditional family.

LET ME START by defining the conservative mission in the broadest terms.

One twentieth-century American conservative thinker, Russell Kirk, argued that the fundamental conservative disposition in politics is the "stewardship of a patrimony." Those are two words we don't use every day. A patrimony is simply an inheritance. A steward is a caretaker, like the Steward of Gondor in the movie The Return of the King, who does not truly possess but simply

administers on behalf of something or someone more important. Conservatives are the caretakers of a precious inheritance.

Our inheritance, as we will see in a moment, isn't stocks
and bonds. What's more, to be stewards of an inheritance does
not mean sitting back and enjoying our dividends. Think about
someone who inherits a family business. She knows that her
parents or even grandparents built up the business with years of
hard work cultivating clients, increasing productivity through
new techniques, and improving the business's products or services. In the spirit of *stewardship*, she knows that she will also
have to invest years of hard work and much capital, so that her
own children will be able to inherit a thriving business. That is
what stewardship means. All of us naturally want to bequeath
to our children something more, something better, than we received from our own parents, and so we naturally want to be
good stewards of whatever inheritance we may have had.

That is how a conservative approaches social and political
life. We know that the good things in American life that we are
tempted to take for granted are not necessarily ours by nature
or by chance, but are the result of the constant efforts of those
who came before us. We don't think that it is necessary to rein-
vent the wheel just because it's our turn to run the business. We
don't believe we are free to experiment with the inheritance we
have been given just because it's the fad of the day. No, govern-
ing America is serious business, for we have been entrusted with
the greatest enterprise in the history of the world. America not
only provides for us, but also is the beacon of hope for much of
the world. As stewards, our task is to secure and increase this
patrimony for our children.

Speaking in terms of our "inheritance" has a special advantage, because it helps us think, symbolically, about "capital." In
a business, capital (money) must constantly be invested to keep

things going. Machines wear out and have to be replaced; money must be spent to train workers in new techniques; if the business is to grow, whole new buildings must sometimes be built. There must be constant reinvestment for the business to remain productive—investments not just in buildings and equipment, but in salespeople, marketing, distribution, accounting, and management. And something like this is true about our civilization as well. We need to invest not only in our economy, but in our culture, our social interactions, our values, and the methods by which we pass all these good things on to the next generation. That is what is meant by the *stewardship* of a patrimony: in society as a whole, various kinds of capital, not just money, must be *replenished* in every generation. I will argue that the unit that most efficiently, effectively, and naturally builds and replenishes capital in every aspect of our civilization is the family.

Throughout this book, therefore, I will be discussing different types of "capital" and how family breakdown—out-of-wedlock births, divorce, cohabitation, and absentee parenthood—has depleted that capital in recent decades. For it sometimes happens that the patrimony we inherit has not been well cared for by the immediately previous generation. I will also show how strong families can help build up our common capital, for this and for future generations.

I group American civilization into five distinct but interrelated pieces. These pieces represent the forces that determine who we are collectively as a people, and, at once, constitute the environment in which our lives and the lives of the next generation are shaped. Our task as stewards of this great land is to enhance the richness of these five pillars of American civilization: social capital, economic capital, moral capital, cultural capital, and intellectual capital.

I will argue that the key to building capital in all of these areas is fostering the formation, stability, and success of the traditional family. This conviction of mine is not born from a desire to return to an idyllic bygone era that liberals insist never existed, but from a basic understanding of how America can fulfill her promise to her people. This stands in sharp contrast to those who believe that America's promise lies with the village elders redesigning America from on high.

The first kind of capital I will be talking about is social capital. Social capital comprises all the habits and forms of trust, mutual responsibility, and solidarity and connectedness that make it possible for us to get along together. That sounds rather simple, until you realize that there are large parts of America where social capital has eroded badly, with disastrous results especially for the poor. Where social capital has disappeared, the breakdown of the traditional family usually was a huge factor in that calamity.

I'll also be talking about economic capital. Here, I don't mean millionaire capitalists. Rather, I mean the *wealth* of *families*. Too often, "village" economic policy looks only at income transfers as a solution to poverty—which can lead to making families dependent on the government, year after year. But financially secure families, standing on their own two feet, are the basis of any good society. Therefore, our economic policies need to aim at creating economic growth, and importantly, building up family savings, especially among those who are struggling at the margins of our society. With even modest wealth comes more opportunity, and also more family stability. But as we all know, wealth alone does not create strong families and build strong communities. There are too many "wealthy" families and communities that are far from healthy.

That leads me to moral capital and the key roles religious institutions and the family play in transmitting virtue. Moral capital refers to the virtue, proper conduct, and respect for human life that build trustworthiness and bind us together in a common mission. When moral capital is high, we feel that our common life is a moral and ethical endeavor, and we strive to live *up* to high standards. Too often today, however, we have a public standard of moral neutrality, which amounts to moral relativism. As a result, we become de-moralized, and thus we live *down* to our lowest selves.

There's also cultural capital. This includes all the stories, images, songs, and arts that explain to us, and in particular our children, who we are. The arts and entertainment industry is producing a flood of content so pervasive that the sheer quantity of images is overwhelming. The messages in these "artifacts" of the culture are too often more interested in sizzle and shock than truth and meaning. I believe that bad culture is culture that lies; good culture, even if it may be ugly, tells the truth. There is hope here, however, and I will explore how families influence the culture and how they can be protected from its destructive effects.

Finally I'll have something to say about what I call intellectual capital. That's a fancy way of talking about our traditions of education and schooling. The most essential thing any society does is to help parents raise the next generation. How are our schools and families doing at this vital task today? Let's just say we can do better.

We must be good stewards of each of these stores of "capital" so that our children will inherit a strong, vibrant country. That requires every generation to put forth the effort to renew and restore the capital of their patrimony, just as in a family business. If even one part of our inheritance becomes depleted, we will have failed the test of our generation, to the detriment of our children. And let's be honest with ourselves: have we been good stewards of our inheritance on all these fronts?

Here is the good news. America has faced such challenges in the past and has risen to meet them. We have overcome declines in capital during the Great Depression (economic), Civil War (social), slavery and racism (moral), the Roaring Twenties (cultural), and the era after Sputnik (intellectual). In many respects, the problems we now face represent a more complex challenge, because almost all aspects of our civilization seem to be at tipping points. The good news is that capital *can* be replenished. But just as with any other problem, we must first admit it exists before we can work together to solve it. Then we must determine the reason for its depletion and the sources of rejuvenation.

I do not want to exaggerate and claim, like Chicken Little, that the sky is falling. But I do want to be honest in laying out in detail the challenges that face us on these five fronts—social, economic, moral, cultural, and intellectual. I will then step back and analyze the reason for the decline, and try to offer some ideas to turn back the tide. It will come as no surprise that I believe the place to start in restoring these pillars of our society is with the family—because the family is at the center of all the types of capital I've just described.

As the fundamental building block of society, the family creates, strengthens, nurtures, and replenishes each of these stores of capital. And each of these kinds of capital directly affects the strength and stability of families. In other words, if any of these stores of capital are weakened or depleted, it harms families, especially low-income families.

II

The Liberal Vision: No-Fault Freedom

I have been involved in one way or another in politics since I was a bleeding-blue-and-white, Joe Paterno–loving freshman at Penn State University. From the time I arrived in State College, I joined the conservative ranks and fought against the liberals on campus and in government. It wasn't until recently that I discovered that one of my fundamental beliefs about American politics was wrong. You see, I always believed—and publicly stated—that conservatives and liberals had the same vision of America, but just had different ways of getting there. For example, I believed that everyone wanted the poor to achieve economic self-sufficiency, but that the two parties had different approaches to achieve that goal. I don't believe that anymore. That is not to say that there are no commonalities, but they are becoming fewer and fewer as the liberals go farther left. The liberal vision of America-the-beautiful is different from mine and, more importantly, different from that of most Americans. The basis of that difference can be found in the concept of freedom, and it is manifest in the ways each would order American society—that is, in how we see the role of its essential elements: faith and the traditional family.

So what is the liberal definition of freedom? It is the freedom to be and to do whatever we want—freedom to choose, irrespective of the choice, freedom without limits (with the obligatory caveat that you can't hurt anyone else *directly*). But someone always gets hurt when masses of individuals do what is only in their own self-interest. That is the great lie of liberal freedom, or as I like to say, "No-Fault Freedom" (all the choice, none of the responsibility). When I listen to the rock group U2's latest hit "Vertigo," which criticizes the dizzying culture surrounding us, a chill goes through me when Bono sings, in a satanic voice, "All of this, all of this can be yours—just give me what I want and no one gets hurt."

No one gets hurt? Believers in No-Fault Freedom turn a blind eye to the damage such a notion of freedom causes not to this or that individual but to society as a whole. We have sexual freedom: and the resulting debasement of women, mental illness, and an epidemic of sexually transmitted diseases causing infertility, cancer, even death. Adults have freedom to divorce (No-Fault) when it suits them: and too many children end up being scarred for life. This is but a taste of the collateral damage inflicted on society, families, and individuals by No-Fault Freedom.

The goal of "freedom" understood as maximum choice for personal satisfaction (within the latest new guidelines set by the politically correct village elders) is not the *liberty* envisioned by our founders. Ironically, Judeo-Christian thinkers have, over the centuries, called the liberal kind of freedom by its real name: slavery to sin, with all the consequences such actions have on one's No-Fault Freedom.

And what is the conservative view of freedom? It is the *liberty* our founders understood. Properly defined, *liberty* is freedom coupled with responsibility to something bigger or higher than the self. It is the pursuit of our dreams with an eye toward the common good. Liberty is the dual activity of lifting our eyes to the heavens while at the same time extending our hands and hearts to our neighbor. In other words, our founders' understanding of liberty ordered the individual toward a higher good, defined in part by our Judeo-Christian roots.

The foundational social unit that instills a devotion to such liberty and that stands against No-Fault Freedom's toxic effects is the traditional family. Strong families generate values and virtues. They are moralistic, and so they are moralizing. They teach right from wrong. Healthy families are our first strike for what is right and our first defense against what is wrong in America today.

When an architect designs a skyscraper he knows the most crucial part of his plan is something that no one notices and few appreciate: the foundation. None of the elite architectural critics will even mention it or its importance. Yet without a strong foundation, even the grandest structure will eventually crumble, and sooner rather than later. Likewise, the family is the foundation of our civilization. Without it America will crumble. It is essential that we strive to build the strongest foundation possible, one that will support the most stable and lasting structure of the common good. When I say "it takes a family," I don't mean to exclude single-head-of-household families. Nonetheless, our focus should be on trying to build a foundation that all the research and thousands of years of human history say is the best for our country and our children. That foundation is the family headed by a married mother and father.

We all know that not all two-parent families are healthy families. There are many families in America today with absentee mothers and fathers, or with parents who don't take the time to instill virtue or build character in their children. As Mary

Eberstadt's recent book *Home-Alone America* points out, married parents can be as self-centered and absent from their children's lives as divorced or unmarried parents, and such absence can have the same devastating effect on their children. So I will not just be advocating for traditional families, but for healthy traditional families: in other words, families in which selfless regard for others is the rule, not self-centeredness. As I will argue later, selflessness in the family is the basis for the political liberty we cherish as Americans.

I have to say that up until now there hasn't really been a coherent conservative agenda for low-income Americans. The village elders have been very clear and coherent about their agenda and in many cases, unfortunately, they have managed to implement it. In this book I don't want to spend a lot of time attacking liberal policies, but the truth is that liberal social policy has helped to dismantle the traditional family and failed the poor individuals it aimed to liberate.

Liberal social policy has never put an emphasis on the family because the village elders, frankly, don't believe in the importance of strong, traditional families. For a raft of reasons, the village elders view the strong, traditional, married-mother-and-father family as contrary to their social agenda. They think of society as fundamentally made up of *individuals* guided by elite and "expert" organizations like government, not the antiquated, perhaps uneducated, independent family. The village elders *want* society to be individualistic, because a society composed only of individuals responds better to "expert" command and control. Your father or your grandmother (or your priest or rabbi) may give you advice that contradicts the latest "expert" wisdom. The village elders just don't want such competition.

This reminds me of a bit of African wisdom about the best way to raise children—one with a moral that is right on. It is the Kenyan story of the father who gave each of his many children a stick and asked them to break it. They each do so easily. Then he gathers up a stick from each of his children, puts them together in a bundle and asks them to break the bundle. Of course they cannot. The message is easy enough for a child to understand. When families stick together—that is, lovingly give of themselves to each other, mothers, fathers, and children—the family is stronger, each member of the family is more secure, and society has a strong foundation upon which to build. It takes a family.

Aside from seeing families as a barrier between the Bigs and atomized individuals, the village elders dislike the traditional family because of what it instills in children and society—traditional values. In the liberals' ideal world there is no right or wrong; there is only tolerance and intolerance, diversity and narrow-mindedness. These two words—tolerance and diversity—are holy writ to liberals, because they believe that traditional morality and virtue represent the imposition of someone else's rigid worldview and are therefore somehow unfair. Theirs is a world in which ideally nobody, not even mothers and fathers, ever judges anyone's actions. The liberal world of No-Fault Freedom is a completely de-moralized world, and such a world can only be achieved either by eliminating the family or rendering it meaningless.

About now, you may be thinking: "I know some liberals who are in good marriages and have strong families. They aren't anti-family." And you would, of course, be right. There are many liberals who are selfless mothers and fathers. What they are doing is not practicing what their village elders preach. They are following common sense rather than ideology.

When I use the terms "liberals" and the "village elders" I am talking about the intellectual as well as practical leaders of the liberal movement in America. And let me stress here how influential these rather small, well-positioned groups of people are in our society. They completely dominate the academy. We all see how they dominate the mainstream news media: over 90 percent of the elite news media voted for Senator John Kerry in 2004. And that percentage may be even higher when it comes to Hollywood. While the village elders control the national labor unions—particularly the AFL-CIO, which is increasingly being run by the public-sector big-government unions—their influence is waning with the locals, some of the private-sector unions like the building trades, as well as among the rank-and-file workers. No, I am not talking about your liberal next-door neighbors: I am talking about the Bigs. These village elders have pushed American society for forty years toward a no-fault view of freedom, and we are all suffering the consequences.

LET'S LOOK AGAIN at how families work, and how they contribute to a free society. Families—and that is to say, *moms and dads*—set standards and demand that their children live up to them. Strong families are grounded in a code of conduct, morality, values, and, much more often than not, a shared faith, plus judicious use of the age-old sanctions of shame and stigma. And that last part, by the way—parental *enforcement* of standards—is one reason why liberals view the traditional family with suspicion. After all, they say, children did not *consent* to their parents' values. Shouldn't children be free to discover and create their own values? Who are you to enforce your values on another individual—even your own child? (If you are like me, you may wonder sometimes whether liberals who think this way have ever had any children of their own! Not surprisingly, many do not—see below.)

Beyond "enforcement," however, healthy families are bound by a unique mixture of unconditional love, commitment, and support, a mixture that is literally irreplaceable. Children who grow up in an intact family with a mother and a father approach the world with a profound security. And that security isn't a matter of household income or anything else for which the government can provide a substitute. The village elders don't seem to understand that a stable marriage is the greatest protection for children and the most powerful energizer of their success. The research on this point has found that children living with their married mother and father, as compared to other children, are less likely to get into trouble or use alcohol and drugs. They do better in school and are more likely to obtain a postsecondary education. As a result, they get better jobs. No surprise, they also have happier marriages. Another study revealed that children whose parents are happy in their marriage have higher grades and, according to their teachers, are better students than kids whose parents are not happily married. You may think it sounds trite when you tell one of your children, "I love you and I'll always be here for you, buddy." But to a child, that message is the very foundation for a life of self-confidence, achievement, and happiness.

Young people understand that the married, two-parent family is vital. They understand because most have experienced the opposite in their own lives or in the lives of their friends. Young people today, from teenagers to those in their late thirties, have experienced the highest divorce rates in history, and they will tell you how much it hurts and has affected them and their ability to form stable families of their own. Maybe that is why for the last few years the divorce rate has actually begun to decline: because these "kids" are trying not to do to their children what their parents did to them.

A few years ago, I met with the editors of the college newspaper at Penn State, my alma mater. We were having a very frank discussion about all kinds of issues, and then I asked them, "What do you believe is the biggest problem in our society today?" Now mind you, by this point we had been talking for at least a half-hour, and they hadn't agreed with me on a thing, not one single issue. So it was not as if I was talking to a group of College Republicans. But I asked that question, and one man in the back raised his hand and said, "The breakup of the family." *Every one of those students agreed.* They were unanimous. Immediately, these mostly liberal college students started talking about the harm being caused by divorce and by kids growing up without fathers. I was stunned. (In fact, I told them they could all be Republicans, but none of them took me up on the offer.) One thing is certain—at least when it comes to their view of the family, none of these young people was a liberal.

Here's more proof that kids today get it. In 1977, 55 percent of American teenagers thought divorce should be harder to get. By 2001, fully 75 percent of all teenagers wanted divorce to be harder to get, not easier.

Kids get it. Conservatives get it. The village elders don't. Because if we boil this down, families are about selfless love, right and wrong, commitment and the security children feel from it, imparting faith and its virtues, and developing character. These things are something the village elders just can't embrace. Can you imagine Hollywood, the media, and university faculty communicating the value of selflessness, commitment, faith, virtue, and a keen sense of right and wrong?

III

Families and the Common Good

It is an open and shut case: the best place for kids to grow up is with a happily married mom and dad, and the more of these families there are in a community, the better it is for everyone.

Crime, for example, is directly related to family structure. We should *know* this from common sense and our own life experiences. But for those who need a study to prove what is obvious, I have a bunch. In one study of more than 6,000 young men ages 14 to 22, it was found that boys who grew up without a married mother and father were more than *twice* as likely to end up in jail as boys who did. This proved true even after taking into account factors such as a mother's education level, race, family income, and community unemployment rates and median income.

Other studies have shown that broken homes can increase the delinquency in a community by 10 to 15 percent, and the proportion of single-parent households in a community predicts the rate of violent crime and burglary much better than a community's level of poverty.

Recent research has also shown that healthy communities and healthy families support each other and make it more likely that kids will do well. Good communities are more able to benefit from the value of healthy families, and healthy families are more able to benefit from the value of good communities. For example, teenage boys who come from strong families living in a good neighborhood are less likely to get into fights than boys who come from a good family or a good neighborhood but not from both.

Having said all that, I have to say two more things. First, lots of single parents do a wonderful job raising children. It's not only possible that children can experience positive outcomes growing up in a single-parent household; depending on the neighborhood and the single parent's own family history, it is more likely than not. But, as Dr. Wade Horn, an assistant secretary at the U.S. Department of Health and Human Services and one of the Bush administration's foremost experts on family life, points out, the risks for children are simply greater when they grow up in a single-parent home. Dr. Horn often compares it to two airplanes. One nearly always gets you to your destination safely. The other gets you there most of the time, but significantly less often than the first. Both planes offer at least pretty good odds, but every one of us would choose the first plane. Well, when it comes to children, the first plane is a family headed by a mother and father in a healthy marriage. The second plane is the single-parent home.

Second, I want to be sure that we avoid the trap of somehow presenting father absence as an inner-city, minority problem. It is not. In absolute numbers, there are more white than black children growing up without fathers today. And father absence isn't just about men who get women pregnant and then abandon them. It is about emotional detachment as well: middle-class men whose lives center around work and the golf course instead of around their wives and children, for example. And as

I just said, it's about divorce: very much about divorce. Divorce leads to father abandonment much more often than people recognize, despite the constant attempts by the popular culture to paint a picture of the "happily" divorced. (I don't mean to browbeat divorced men and women, but I do think that they will agree that at the heart of every divorce there is a tragedy—one which the popular culture pretends does not exist.) In a childless marriage, it is conceivable that the No-Fault Freedom caveat may be true, (i.e., "as long as no one gets hurt"), but this is virtually impossible when children are involved. In disrupted families, only about one child in six sees his father as much as once a week. Ten years after a marriage breaks up, research has shown that approximately two-thirds of children report that they haven't seen their father for over a year.

I have met with my share of fatherhood-rights groups, so I know that the divorce courts are often not kind to fathers. I also know that divorced wives can make it difficult for the fathers of their children to visit. Personally, I cannot imagine the pain of not being able to be a part of my children's formative years. But fathers, let's be honest with ourselves: decisions have consequences—for us, and for our children.

Marriage matters because children matter. Without marriage, children suffer. There is simply no better investment parents can make in their children's future than a healthy marriage. For my wife Karen and me, marriage is a sacred vocation. We give ourselves to each other: mind, body, and soul. Nothing in this world is more important to me than the happiness and well-being of my wife and children. It is my most important job. All of my strength comes from my love for them and God's love for me. When children live with parents who love each other, sacrifice for each other, and are committed to each other, they are given a real head start on life.

Children living outside of wedlock get hurt. And here are some more hard numbers:

One study analyzing the outcomes of over one million children ages one to four found that children born to unmarried parents are at greater risk of dying from an injury, even after taking into account differences in income, education, race, and age.

Children living in single-parent homes are as much as twice as likely to suffer physical, emotional, or educational neglect. The overall rate of child abuse and neglect in single-parent homes is 27.3 per 1,000 children, while in two-parent households it is 15.5 per 1,000. It is lower still in two-parent *married* households.

According to one large national study, teenagers in single-parent households or households with a stepparent are at 1.5 to 2.5 times the risk of using illegal drugs as are teens living with their mother and father.

Children who live with only one parent have poorer grades, poorer attendance records, and higher dropout rates at school than students who come home to a two-parent household.

Finally, children in single-mother families are 1.5 to 2 times more likely to have behavioral or emotional problems than kids living with a married mother and father.

I could go on. The research making this point could fill a book bigger than this one. Every statistic that I am aware of—and I would be eager to hear if there is even *one* on the other side—indicates that marriage is better for children, and usually by a very large margin. Back in the 1960s and 1970s when the village elders pressed to make divorce easier through no-fault divorce laws and championed the legitimacy of "alternative lifestyles," we didn't really have evidence about the effect of these revolutions on children. Now we *know*.

That's why there should really be no family "debate," no

marriage "debate." The social science evidence, four thousand years of human history, and common sense have long settled the question. In a decent society, every child should have the best shot at growing up to be a healthy and successful adult. That opportunity is found in healthy, married, mom-and-dad families. The traditional family is not about some "special interest." It's about the rights of parents and children, and ultimately it's about the common good.

THERE SHOULD BE no argument that a married mother-and-father household is the best place for raising kids. The problem is, we don't do anything about it. And part of the problem is that our government and many social service agencies often do a lousy job of supporting healthy marriages and repairing unhealthy ones.

The common myth is that the reason high percentages of children in low-income, minority communities are living without a father is because men get women pregnant and, if the women are not convinced by the fathers and their peers to abort the children, the men disappear from their lives. But the truth is more complicated. Eighty-two percent of urban, low-income fathers and mothers are in a romantic relationship at the time their child is born. The vast majority of these expect that they will get married. One major study of urban parents found that, of those who were not living together but were romantically involved at the time their baby was born, more than 80 percent of both the mothers and the fathers expected that they would marry or, at the least though certainly not as good, live together. But a year later, in this study, just 11 percent of these couples had actually married. We know that over time, fathers who are not married to their children's mother begin to disappear. So what is happening here? What is going wrong so that couples that have a baby, who want to get married and think they will get married, end up not getting married?

"When low-income couples have a child out of wedlock and they are considering marriage, they are met with a deafening silence from the existing social services delivery network," is how Dr. Horn explains it. "Instead of a social services system that supports and encourages them to pursue their choice of marriage, they are told that, rather, the goal is for the father to simply sign a paternity establishment paper."

In other words, the government in the form of the social worker communicates loud and clear that it doesn't believe low-income, minority couples can maintain a marriage. It effectively says: don't bother trying, just be sure the father establishes paternity so we can come after him for child support. But where are the churches, the civic groups and community organizations? Have they given up hope as well? Sadly, the answer is, with a few notable exceptions, yes. We've gone from the days of shotgun marriage (which I'm not sure in some cases was all that bad) to the days of shotgun paternity establishment. As communities facing out-of-wedlock pregnancy, we've gone from common concern to common indifference.

Jason Krofsky works for Families Northwest, a pro-family organization based in Washington State and founded by former pro football player Jeff Kemp. Jason heads up the work they do in communities throughout the Pacific Northwest to build partnerships among government, businesses, religious institutions, and community- and faith-based organizations to support healthy families and strong marriages. Invariably, he says, he finds that most religious leaders are just as guilty as the government when it comes to believing the institution of marriage is beyond repair, especially in inner-city communities.

Further evidence that our society is somehow having a terrible effect on family ties comes in a study of the experience of immigrant Latino families versus Latino families who have been in this country more than one generation. Immigrant Latino teenagers—that is, youth who came to this country with their families—are less likely to engage in unhealthy risk behaviors, such as violence and fighting, than Latino teenagers who were born in this country. This is true even though immigrant Latino teenagers tend to live in families and neighborhoods that are poorer than those of later-generation Latino youths.

Why is this? What does this country do to families that chips away, even tears down, the foundation that kids need to grow up healthy and secure? I think the answer lies in the erosion of the kinds of capital I discussed earlier. A society rich in social, cultural, and moral capital—like America in previous generations—supports and nurtures families. A society in which those kinds of capital have eroded creates something like a vacuum, sucking the life out of families.

We've wasted decades and countless lives under the direction of the village elders trying to build bureaucracies to aid the poor and marginal in our society, while ignoring the central importance of the traditional family. We must stop pretending that the health of the mom-and-dad family isn't really important. Conservatives always knew this was a mistake, but, to be quite candid, failed to offer an alternative vision; now, thanks to the social science evidence, we *all* know that this was a mistake. We need to spend the coming decades working to build up traditional families. What is it that stands against us in this effort? The village elders and their well-funded special interests—and they will not go away quietly.

IV

The Meaning of Family

I have been talking about the "traditional" family. By that, I mean a family constituted by a mother and a father who have committed themselves to each other in lifelong marriage, together with their children. This is "traditional," but the reason it is a traditional relationship is because it is fundamentally *natural*. But it is just there that the village elders dig in their heels and cry "Foul!" To the liberal mind, such a definition is "restrictive." It limits our "freedom" to choose who and how we will love. It "excludes" what liberals like to think of as simply "different kinds of families," no better and no worse than the natural family. Liberals get nervous at the very word *natural*, since nature is what we are as human beings, which we cannot change or choose otherwise.

In the tradition of my own faith community, the Catholic Church, we speak about the *natural law*, which we might think of as the operating instructions for human beings. The promise of the natural law is that we will be happiest, and freest, when we follow the law built into our nature as men and women. For liberals, however, *nature* is too confining, and thus is the enemy of *freedom*. Consequently, when liberals think about society, they see only "individuals"—*not* men and women and children. Men and women and children have natures, but liberal "individuals" are abstractions, free to choose anything at all and unconfined by purportedly illusory factors like gender. At first, the liberal vision may sound attractive—because freedom is attractive. The only problem is that it is a false vision, because nature is nature, and the freedom to choose against the natural law is not really freedom at all.

That all sounds pretty philosophical. But take cohabitation, or living together outside of marriage, as an example. Today's conventional wisdom holds that it is better than harmless, that it is a healthy way for a couple to "test drive" marriage. Some even say that cohabitation is better than marriage, since people should be together only when they are in love with one another, and we can never know how and whom we will love in the future: a vow of lifelong love, they say, is unrealistic. Today, the majority of men and women under the age of 30 believe that living together before marriage is a good way to avoid an eventual divorce. About half of all unmarried women between the ages of 25 and 39 have lived with a man whom they were not married to at some point in the past, and about one-quarter are currently living with a man without the benefit of marriage.

The problem is that the myth that living together leads to better marriages is wrong. The opposite is true. One study found that marriages preceded by cohabitation have nearly a 50 percent greater chance of ending in divorce than marriages that were not preceded by cohabitation. Furthermore, children born to parents who are just living together instead of married do not fare very well. Teenagers, for example, growing up with unmarried, cohabiting parents have more emotional and behavioral problems than do teenagers living with their married mother and father.

Despite all the evidence, as a society today we will go to almost any length to avoid telling ourselves, and others, the truth: marriage is better than living together. Too few of us dare say living together without the benefit of marriage is *wrong*. We are afraid to make any such "value judgment." But that is exactly what we need to do. We parents owe it to our children to be honest, to give them a vision of the highest good. Failure to affirm a moral vision to our children is a form of *abandonment* by parents and by society. It leaves our children defenseless against the endless parade of influences the popular culture has in store for them.

And we need to be honest about the latest liberal assault on our marriage tradition as well. Even a year or two ago, few Americans imagined that we would be facing the issue of same-sex marriage today. Thanks to a few activist justices on the U.S. Supreme Court and to even more activist judges in Massachusetts, however, America is on the verge of undergoing a social revolution simply without any historical precedent. There are few places where the clash between what freedom means and its impact on families is clearer than when it comes to transforming the definition of marriage.

Liberals believe that the traditional family is neither natural nor vital, that it's an antiquated social convention which has not only outlived its usefulness, but is now inherently discriminatory and repressive toward legitimate alternative "families." As the Massachusetts high court said to the legislature of Massachusetts concerning the *Goodrich* case, "For no rational reason the marriage laws of the Commonwealth discriminate against a defined class (homosexuals); no amount of tinkering with language will eradicate that stain." So traditional marriage is a stain on the fabric of America that needs to be "Shouted out." How have we come to this?

It may come as a shock to some, but marriage is not, and never has been, just about the sex life of consenting adults. However, given the self-centeredness of our popular culture, it is not surprising that many adults today see marriage as about them being happy as *individuals*. This is one of the reasons our divorce rate is so high. Since marriage has become more and more about adult happiness, and less and less about children and their well-being, it is no wonder other groups in society want to use marriage for the same purpose. In fact, one of the criticisms I often hear when I speak with proponents of same-sex marriage is that heterosexuals have so deconstructed marriage through no-fault divorce that today marriage is only about adults, so why shouldn't it include them too? Touché! But do I need to say in response that two wrongs don't make a right?

Society's interest in protecting marriage goes beyond the public recognition of a romantic relationship and making people feel accepted. I've made the case that the reason our society has such a strong interest in strengthening the institution of marriage is because marriage as we traditionally understood it is far and away the best place for raising children—who happen to be the future of any society. All of the "legal incidents" of marriage built up over the years aim to secure a stable family in which to welcome children. Every known society has some form of marriage. And it's always about bringing together a male and female into the kind of sexual union where the interests of children under the care of their own mother and father are protected. Marriage is the word for the way in which we connect a man, a woman, and their children into one loving family. It represents our best attempt to see that every child receives his or her birthright: the right to know and be known by, to love and be loved by, his or her own mother and father.

When liberals, through unelected judges, order us to change

this understanding of marriage into something radically different, the result is likely to be dangerous for children and for society. When the state declares two men marrying is just as valuable to society as the union of husband and wife, this is not neutrality, it is radical social engineering. It commits the government to the position that family structure does not matter; that children don't need fathers (or mothers for that matter), just abstract individual "caregivers." It shifts marriage further away from its core purpose of protecting the needs of (and the need for) children. It would transform our public understanding of marriage so that marriage would mean something like mere cohabitation, an adult relationship to be formed as adults please, rather than as children need.

Do we need to confuse future generations of Americans even more about the role and importance of an institution that is so critical to the common good? It is because children have a right to a faithfully married mother and father that we must oppose this radical redefinition—not because we are mean-spirited.

Moreover, once the government commits to same-sex marriage as a civil right, it will use the power of the state to enforce this new vision of marriage. Public schools will teach it, of course. But the logic of same-sex marriage will lead inevitably to even more government intrusion on the freedom of people and faith communities who continue to define marriage as the union of husbands and wives. What do I mean? When in *Loving v. Virginia* the Supreme Court ruled that state laws banning interracial marriage were unconstitutional, that ruling seemed at first to affect only private individuals. But sixteen years later, the IRS ruled that religious groups that opposed interracial marriage could be stripped of their tax-exempt status, because they were not operating for the public good. The Supreme Court ruled furthermore that the First Amendment's protection of the free exercise of religion provided no defense. Of course, I agree that laws against interracial marriage were unjust. My point is this: If we apply the logic of a civil right to same-sex marriage, people who believe children need mothers and fathers will be treated in the public square like racists, and churches that persist in teaching the traditional norm will risk the loss of their tax-exempt status. In other words, such churches will be treated as outlaws. How can we turn boys into good family men in a society that treats the idea that fathers matter as a form of bigotry?

Same-sex marriage is really "liberal marriage." That is, the "right" of homosexuals to "marry" one another is a logical result of what *must* happen to the definition of marriage if we view society as composed of nothing but abstract, autonomous *individuals*, rather than of men and women with their given natures. Abstract individuals, after all, are completely interchangeable and completely "free" to define who and what they are. To the liberal mind, therefore, there is no "rational basis" for limiting marriage only to people of opposite sexes: and that is what the four left-wing judges in Massachusetts held. Our village elders now declare that those holding to the traditional understanding of marriage are simply irrational.

But there is one more thing about these abstract, autonomous individuals that the left say are the real basis of society. Call it the liberal's marriage paradox. Individuals are free to do anything they want, including to redefine marriage, gender, and basic social institutions in pursuit of individual desire and preference. There is only one thing that individuals cannot do if they are to remain autonomous: they cannot commit themselves permanently to another human being. To do so would be a kind of slavery. As a result, the left's view of any marriage contract is that it is really only a kind of cohabitation, the choice of two people, each day, to continue together, but always with the perfect freedom to leave whenever either chooses. Of course, all too many marriages today end in divorce, and to most Americans that is a tragedy. But in "liberal marriage," there can never be any real expectation of permanence. In a society in which the liberal understanding of marriage becomes the law of the land, divorce would not only be the norm rather than the exception, but the institution of marriage would disappear altogether.

Just imagine two or three generations from now, if we legalize same-sex marriage today, what young adults will understand about marriage. Keep in mind that they will have been raised in a society that considers marriage nothing more than a romantic and sexual coupling between men and men, women and women, and men and women. The law will have declared it so, dissenters will be pressured into silence, and public schools will embrace and teach same-sex marriage as the law of the land. Laws have meaning, and therefore, laws *teach*. When something is legal it has the presumption that it is moral and right. If the sexual unions of men with men and women with women have equal dignity with the union of men and women, then marriage cannot be understood as having anything intrinsically to do with children. Society will teach the next generation that marriage is a self-centered endeavor primarily about adult satisfaction, not children's well-being.

What happens to a society that disconnects marriage from babies in this way? The connection has already been strained by the consequences of children being born out of wedlock and the damage wrought by our divorce culture. Same-sex marriage severs this connection completely. Once same-sex marriage becomes firmly entrenched as the law of the land, we can expect to get even more children being raised outside of marriage. And we will also have fewer children, period.

We don't need to hypothesize about what would happen if America definitively adopted the liberal conception of marriage: all we need to do is look to Europe today. European law has begun not only to acknowledge same-sex unions as marriages but also to treat cohabiting couples just the same as married couples. America, a mobile society, has always had somewhat higher divorce rates than Europe, but today European countries are catching up fast. And Europeans appear firmly committed to the most disastrous family trend of all: they are simply not having children.

The Council of Europe's Demographic Yearbook 2003 reports,

> In all European countries, except Turkey, the total fertility rate is currently below replacement level. . . . The main features of nuptiality are the declining number of marriages, the rise in the number of separations, and the appearance of other forms of union, particularly cohabitation. There has also been a widespread parallel increase in the number of births outside marriage. In certain countries, such as Iceland, Norway, Sweden, Estonia, and the former German Democratic Republic, such births represent more than 50 percent of the total.

The report goes on to state, "Generally speaking, natural growth (the excess of births over deaths) is declining in Europe, and in more and more cases is negative or only marginally positive. In 1990, three countries—Germany, Bulgaria and Hungary—had negative natural growth for the first time. By 2002, it was negative in fifteen countries. . . ."

Relatively few Americans are aware of this dramatic change. "Very low fertility" is a birthrate below 1.5 children. Europe's *total* fertility rate from 1995 to 2000 was 1.42 children per woman. In 2002, 28 nations experienced very low fertility, including Switzerland (1.4), Germany (1.3), Austria (1.3), Italy

(1.3), Spain (1.2), Greece (1.3), Japan (1.3), Russia (1.3), the Czech Republic (1.1), and most other Eastern European nations.

WHAT ARE THE CONSEQUENCES of low fertility rates? At the April 2, 2004, meeting of the Population Association of America, United Nations demographer Joseph Chamie warned, "A growing number of countries view their low birth rates with the resulting population decline and aging to be a serious crisis, jeopardizing the basic foundations of the nation and threatening its survival. Economic growth and vitality, defense, and pensions and health care for the elderly, for example, are all areas of major concern."

Scholars do not agree on all the causes of low fertility, but the increasing disconnect between marriage and childbearing plays a clear role. At the Expert Group Meeting on Policy Responses to Population Aging and Population Decline in New York in October 2000, demographer Patrick Festy observed:

> Low fertility can also be linked to the movement away from marriage, which many western European countries have experienced for the recent decades. Of course, marriage is no longer a pre-condition for childbearing in most of these populations, but it remains true that married couples have a higher fertility than non-married people, even those who live in a "marriage-like" cohabitation.

What all of this means is that the nations of Europe are slowly dying off—sometimes not so slowly. Today, European governments are struggling with an increasingly aging population, large-scale immigration challenges, a rise in disturbing ultranationalism, and all of the individual and community issues that arise when children grow up without fathers. And not surprisingly, Europeans seem incapable of making the changes in their welfare and pension systems that are absolutely necessary to prevent a future fiscal crisis. Why not? Because without children, they have no future. They are failing in their responsibility to be stewards of their inheritance—because they do not see anyone after them who will inherit.

Irving Kristol once wrote that the most subversive question that can be posed to civilization is: Why not? Thanks to the decision of four activist liberal judges in Massachusetts, that is a question we now must face as Americans. In order to answer the question of "Why not?" with respect to same-sex marriage, we have to come to a fuller understanding of what marriage is. Is it simply about publicly honoring a romantic attachment? That's what the highest court in Ontario, Canada, believes. Just in time for the June wedding season of 2003 that court wrote, as it ruled in favor of same-sex marriages:

> Marriage is, without dispute, one of the most significant forms of personal relationship. . . . Through the institution of marriage, individuals can publicly express their love and commitment to each other. Through this institution, society publicly recognizes expressions of love and commitment between individuals, granting them respect and legitimacy as a couple.

Marriage in this view means nothing more to society, to what we are as a people, and to our future, than making people feel accepted. The state's interest in promoting and stamping approval upon a marriage starts and stops with tolerance, and is therefore meaningless.

When we think about it for just a minute, Americans with loving hearts may be tempted to agree with Ontario's highest court. But if we think about it for ten minutes or longer, I think Americans will come to recognize that traditional marriage is what it is for good reasons. Who could have imagined that it would take courage to say: there *is* a rational basis for limiting marriage only to persons of the opposite sex? But we need that courage today. In a compassionate society, adult interests and agendas cannot be allowed to trump the basic needs and rights of children. A forward-thinking society reaches out to children in every family form, but it never deliberately endorses or encourages adults to deprive their children of a mother or a father. Men and women marry for many reasons. But the reason the law is involved in marriage is to protect society's future.

Unfortunately, as I will discuss in detail later, our courts are changing the landscape of the family by de facto amending our Constitution. Starting its campaign with the line of cases establishing the so-called right to privacy, the shock troops of the village elders are now battering at the gates of the fortress of marriage. The gates will not long hold. The fortress is but a few years away—at most!—of being laid to ruin, unless we, like the apparently doomed warriors at Helms Deep in the movie *The Two Towers*, make that last charge against the foe. Like them, it will take all of our effort, and the help of forces unseen, but it is a fight that must be waged.

That is why I support the Marriage Protection Amendment and commend President Bush for doing likewise. The amendment would spell out in our Constitution what our founding fathers could not have fathomed would someday need to be said: that marriage is the union of one man and one woman. I fully understand that amending the Constitution is the most solemn of legislative changes and therefore should only be used as a last resort. But I fear we have reached the moment of last resort. Unlike the courts, Congress does not have the power to change the Constitution through a simple majority of one body. Congress must amend the Constitution as our founders provided for in that Constitution. The amendment must pass the House and the Senate with a supermajority of two-thirds and then be ratified by a supermajority of three-fourths of the states. It is a long and difficult process.

In 2004, thanks to the tremendous work by citizen groups led by, among others, Dr. James Dobson and Maggie Gallagher, the fine scholarship of Stanley Kurtz, and the leadership in the Senate of Senator Bill Frist, the Marriage Protection Amendment was brought to the floor for a vote. The Senate Democrat leadership refused to allow the amendment to be debated, amended, and voted upon. Senator Frist was forced to file cloture to end the Democrats' filibuster. But the vote failed to get even a simple majority. This is going to be a tough fight. But I am heartened by the fact that in the eleven states that held referendums on marriage in 2004, the supporters of traditional marriage won every time, and almost always by a large margin.

Like so many important issues in our nation's history, it may take years for the Marriage Protection Amendment to pass. But like many other great struggles to ensure the common good, I am confident that it will one day become law.

Part Two

SOCIAL CAPITAL
AND THE TIES THAT BIND

V

What Kind of Freedom?

I t's not your founding fathers' freedom.
As Americans, we enjoy historically unparalleled personal
freedoms guaranteed in our Constitution, and we take great
pride in understanding our country, correctly, as "the land of
the free." In our judgments of other nations, we make respect
for liberty and human rights our priority. But too often, the
freedom we boast of in America is not the freedom envisioned
by the likes of Washington, Adams, Madison, and Jefferson. It
is different today, in tone and substance.

The freedom enshrined constitutionally by our founding fathers was a freedom that both gained its vitality from and was
limited by the social bonds between fellow citizens. America's
founders understood the securing of freedom as the ultimate aim
of politics: but they also saw the promotion of virtue as the ultimate aim and the indispensable support of freedom. As Samuel
Adams wrote, "We may look up to Armies for our Defence, but
Virtue is our best Security. It is not possible that any State should
long remain free, where Virtue is not supremely honored."

To the remarkable generation that made the American Revolution and framed a government that has lasted now for more

than two centuries, virtue wasn't the special property of rabbis and priests; it didn't have those Victorian overtones of prim chastity, either. Virtue consists in the decency, fairness, and respect for others that we're all capable of, the sort of goodness that makes walking through your neighborhood a pleasant experience rather than an ordeal. It's our private morality put into public practice, and selflessness is at its center.

Another way of saying this is that the freedom talked about at our Constitutional Convention did *not* mean the village elders' self-centered, No-Fault Freedom. It wasn't a freedom that celebrated the individual above society. It wasn't a freedom that gave men and women blanket permission to check in and out of society whenever they wanted. It wasn't the freedom to be as selfish as I want to be. It wasn't even the freedom to be left alone, with no obligations to the people we know and to the people we don't yet know. The Constitutional Convention's freedom, America's traditional freedom—or the better word, as I defined it earlier, *liberty*—was a selfless freedom, freedom for the sake of something greater or higher than the self. For our founders, this liberty was defined and defended in the context of our Judeo-Christian understanding of humanity. Often, in fact, American liberty meant the freedom to attend to one's duties—duties to God, to family, and to neighbors. Our founders were in the business of constructing a nation, a political community. No-Fault Freedom, a freedom from every tie and duty, provides no basis for that project: it is a principle of division and social deconstruction.

John Adams predicted that the United States would rise to become the greatest nation on earth. He had two reasons for this confidence: on the one hand, the vast natural resources of his new country; but on the other hand, and more importantly, the fact that Americans, no matter how different, from New England to the Carolinas, shared a sense of justice and morality. Think about it. It was hard enough to craft a nation out of thirteen colonies. It would have been downright impossible if these colonies were filled with men and women who wanted nothing more than the freedom to be selfish individualists—and who shared no common vision for society.

Every society must have its share of rugged individualists, who are often in the forefront of entrepreneurship. But a healthy society first needs a strong foundation, a foundation based on selflessness, a common moral vision, everyday virtues and everyday graces. That foundation is the natural family. And from that common foundation, in turn, spring the ties that bind us to one another in mutual obligation and respect.

It is no surprise that in an increasingly self-centered culture the American family is suffering. It is suffering most acutely in our poorest neighborhoods. Yet in these communities, poverty did not cause the breakup of the family: rather, poverty is the result of myriad factors, including family breakup itself. If we are to be good stewards of our inheritance as Americans, we must begin rebuilding the foundation of the family across America, and particularly in our distressed neighborhoods, for the same reason we would first work on the foundation of a crumbling home: foundations come first.

Liberals tried for forty years to help low-income Americans through Great Society welfare programs. I have to give them credit for trying, but their experiment has failed. And the worst part of their failure is *not* that trillions of tax dollars have barely budged the poverty rate. No, the worst part of their failure is that their welfare policies fractured families and pulled apart communities, pulverizing the foundation both of individual success and of the common good.

For our part, conservatives, with respect to the poor, haven't tried hard enough. We have long held that if the economy is strong, Americans will be too. "A rising tide lifts all boats." What we have sometimes failed to realize is that the "boats" of far too many American families have holes in the hull. While conservatives have always recognized the difficulties facing low-income families, we also resisted government involvement. That resistance has meant, in practice, that we simply allowed the liberals to design our nation's social policies, and that has hurt the poor even more. The real solution, the conservative solution to the problems of low-income America, is to structure all our programs around the family, to work with the family rather than against it.

I am immensely proud that I helped author the first major attempt to infuse conservative solutions into the American social welfare system in the 1996 Welfare Act. That law has resulted in the greatest social welfare success in American history. But even that great success focused mostly on getting single mothers—who were and are the overwhelming majority of welfare clients—back to work. We all knew that was essential, but we also knew it was just a start. We need to improve not only the welfare mother's balance sheet, but her family and social environment. We need to build up the ties that bind, because the ties that bind are also the ties that support, the helping hands of neighbors, friends, and family who care—in ways that government bureaucrats never can.

Back to freedom.

THE AMERICAN DREAM, which motivated the founding fathers in a hot, humid, and at times cholera-plagued Philadelphia in 1787, shaped our purpose as a people. That purpose is explained in our Constitution, quite specifically and succinctly, in the Preamble. (And if I may be allowed a parochial pitch for my home state here: Please take your children to the National Constitution Center in Philadelphia. It will create a yearning to understand the part we must all play in the future of our country.)

The Preamble reads:

> We the People of the United States, in order to form a more perfect union, establish justice, insure domestic tranquility, provide for the common defense, promote the general welfare, and secure the blessings of liberty to ourselves and our posterity, do ordain and establish this Constitution for the United States of America.

Notice that of all the verbs used in the Preamble, "promote" stands out as something different from the rest. The other words—establish, insure, provide, and secure—place responsibility mostly on the government: for justice, domestic tranquility, defense, and liberty. This isn't the case when it comes to the general welfare, because the government's role with respect to the general welfare is an *indirect* one. Our founding fathers never believed the government could "secure" or "establish" the general welfare. The responsibility for the achievement of the general welfare, the common good, does not reside with the *government* but with *We the People*. It is up to us.

The Bill of Rights, the first ten amendments to the federal Constitution, enshrines our inalienable rights as a free people. Through the responsible use of these rights we can seek truth and the Truth Giver, marry and raise a family, pursue our dreams, and influence the government and each other. These are opportunities that every American inherits from the great document that is our Constitution. Yes, these are rights that belong to us as individuals. But these rights were never intended solely for individual gain or for "the *individual* welfare." The framers clearly stated that the purpose of the Constitution—and, therefore, of all these individual rights—is to promote the *general welfare*, *not* simply the welfare of the individual. The men who wrote the Constitution gave us, in the Preamble, a purpose for these personal freedoms—a purpose greater than the needs, wants, or dreams of any one person. Freedom's goal in their mind was not individuals pursuing whatever end fits an individual's desire, but the general welfare, *the common good*.

In 1787, Americans understood what was meant by the general welfare. This understanding was based on the Judeo-Christian tradition of order established by the Ten Commandments and the justice and equality of the Golden Rule. As John Adams said, "Our Constitution was made only for a moral and religious people. It is wholly inadequate to the government of any other."

Adams's insight remains true today. While our society is increasingly self-absorbed, and individual welfare too often outweighs the general welfare, we need to be reminded today of the responsibility our founders placed upon *We the people* to use our freedom in service to others. And despite the self-centered messages that blare at us in the popular culture, I believe that Americans still do resonate and respond to our founding vision of a free people pursuing a common good.

At his 1961 inaugural, President Kennedy exclaimed, "Ask not what your country can do for you—ask what you can do for your country." You may not know that this famous statement was actually an echo from a talk given in 1843 by a great American thinker who deserves to be better known, Orestes Brownson. Brownson said:

> Ask not what your age wants, but what it needs; not what it
> will reward, but what, without which, it cannot be saved; and

that go and do; and find your reward in consciousness of having done your duty, and above all in the reflection that you have been accounted to suffer somewhat for mankind.

President Kennedy understood duty and suffering. They are not popular concepts in America today. The word duty has fallen out of favor and even out of our public lexicon, except when talking about our outstanding men and women in uniform. However, generations past always felt a duty to our country, which is really a duty to tomorrow, to our posterity, to our children. As for suffering? Frankly, too many people are suffering in this country today. But many are not suffering voluntarily—that is, sacrificing—for the sake of their neighbors; they are suffering without purpose. Even the successful who enjoy great blessings are often bound on a joyless quest for joy, equally without purpose. To repair the American promise, we must start with a correct understanding of freedom—*liberty*—and then work to create a society that strengthens families, with the *common good* as our aim.

VI

Habits of Association

It is the pursuit of the common good, of using our freedoms to promote the general welfare, that makes the Great Experiment of American democracy so remarkable. But today, it must be said, we have not always been good stewards of our founding fathers' freedom. We are free, of course. But it seems we are increasingly comfortable with the village elders' view of freedom: No-Fault Freedom. The Preamble has been long forgotten; freedom is increasingly just about the individual and his choices. Freedom has become its own end, and virtue has fallen out of the equation. No-Fault Freedom serves no common good, only the pursuit of one's own happiness. Promoting the general welfare is no longer considered a duty of citizens—after all, that's why we have the government, right?

Today, No-Fault Freedom may even be the dominant view of freedom in America. The village elders are winning. So much so that they typically mock the very notion of a common good: the multiculturalist village elders deny there is such a thing as "common," and the relativist village elders deny there is such a thing as an absolute "good." As a result, families trying to live and to raise children as decent citizens suffer. When, in the name of "freedom," public virtue is sunk so low that families must swim against a toxic tide to raise children to be decent and public-spirited adults, something has gone terribly wrong with our understanding of freedom. This is not just one issue among many facing politicians in Washington; it is a problem that cuts to the heart of American democracy.

Alexis de Tocqueville was a French statesman and social thinker who came to the United States in the first half of the nineteenth century. The French Revolution of 1789 had turned out disastrously—spawning revolutionary terror, war, and seemingly perpetual political instability—while America after her revolutionary founding prospered in peace and freedom. The Great Experiment of democracy in France seemed a nightmare, but the Great Experiment of democracy in America seemed, to the French observer, a paradise. Tocqueville wanted to understand why this was so, and so he traveled widely, thought deeply, and wrote *Democracy in America*, a book that Harvard professor Harvey Mansfield calls both the best book ever written about democracy and the best book ever written about America.

Tocqueville didn't credit America's success to geography, to its abundant natural resources, or even to its laws and political leaders. Rather, he largely credited what he saw as Americans' unique ability to form *associations*, a habit of building bonds between citizens to both achieve something beyond ourselves and to find a fulfillment unavailable to us as individuals.

In France, freed from monarchic rule and the dictates of the church, which the revolutionaries saw as the root of tyranny against the people, the French were intent on looking to their newly "democratic" government to solve all their problems and on secularizing their institutions and customs. The French ended up frequently rebelling against both when they didn't get their way. Unlike the French, America's common vision for the order and structure of society was grounded in the Judeo-Christian ethic and implemented not by the centralized state, but through citizens associating together to achieve the common good. The American habit of coming together for common purposes, with faith as a prime motivator, was the key to the success of American democracy. Intermediary associations were not an impediment to democracy, Tocqueville discovered: they were indispensable to democracy.

Tocqueville also worried about the future, however. He wondered if it would be possible for Americans to maintain this virtuous habit of association for very long under the conditions of democracy. If the habit of association was the key to democracy working, then the great threat to democracy lay in the temptation to what Tocqueville called *individualism*.

Tocqueville didn't mean by that what we call "rugged individualism," the habits of self-reliance that built the American frontier. In fact, Tocqueville was especially impressed by the way that our "rugged individualists" on the frontier came together to help each other in the face of a harsh natural environment. Rather, Tocqueville's individualism was a temptation to withdraw into a private realm of personal interests, entertainments, and satisfactions, and to leave the public realm (and the common good) to others—especially the government. Just as original sin is man's inclination to try to walk alone without God, individualism is man's inclination to try to walk alone among his fellows. Under the spell of individualism, we splinter into pursuing what each of us considers important for ourselves and think little if anything about what might be important for our communities. And we do so not necessarily for any grand reason or purpose, but merely because it is more convenient, merely because it is easier.

What Tocqueville warned us about in *Democracy in America* is what we see around us so often today. Freedom has become the freedom simply to check out from the pursuit of the common good and to do what feels right for me, without regard to those around me. The United States Supreme Court practically put this into law in its 1992 decision on the Pennsylvania Abortion Control Act, *Planned Parenthood v. Casey*. In a passage that I will quote again later, the Court wrote, "Our obligation is to define the liberty of all, not to mandate our own moral code." But then they did just that, defining liberty in the most individualistic way imaginable: "At the heart of liberty is the right to define one's own concept of existence, of meaning, of the universe, and of the mystery of human life."

Had Tocqueville been told of this by a time traveler, he would have shuddered at his unfortunate prescience. The problem with what the Supreme Court wrote—or I should say, one of the problems—is that you cannot build a community that is healthy for families and individuals if you understand society only as an unconnected group of individuals, each pursuing his own idiosyncratic vision of his self-centered good. That isn't our founders' vision of a community with a common good; it's an image of society as a pile of sand, each grain unconnected to all the others. And the common good, like a house built on sand, sinks and fractures. No, No-Fault Freedom is *not* American liberty.

TOCQUEVILLE'S INSIGHT that the continuing success of democracy depends on the habit of association is not some old philosophical notion that you learn about in college but doesn't have a clear application today. Quite the contrary, Tocqueville's insight is at the basis of some of the most significant developments in social science of the past decade, developments that have been put to use, for example, in American efforts to help the new democracies in Eastern Europe as they emerge from communism. The term the social scientists use to explain what Tocqueville was talking about is *social capital.*

Robert Putnam is a Harvard political scientist who completed one of the most important studies on social capital, published in 2000 as the book *Bowling Alone.* That title refers to one of the many small findings of his book that together add up to something of huge significance for all Americans. The small finding is the fact that while the number of Americans who went bowling for recreation was higher in the 1990s than in the 1950s, the number of Americans participating in bowling leagues had declined markedly over the same period.

Now, that may sound trivial, but think what that kind of statistic means. A bowling league is an association; *joining* means agreeing to change your personal, individual life—for example, by agreeing to show up for games every Monday night, whether it is convenient or not—for the sake of others, who rely on you to show up. It's one thing to tell a friend, "I'll always be there for you," but when you join an association like a bowling league, that promise is delivered on, week after week. And finding that we can rely on our friends in a small matter—showing up for bowling—we often expand our reliance, building up ties of mutual obligation and solidarity. We "look out" for one another. The thing of huge significance to all Americans is that the decline of bowling leagues is but one of countless examples revealing that Americans over the past generation have given up on the habit of joining, the habit of association. Now, we still sometimes go bowling, but only on our terms, as the fancy strikes us—which means we go bowling alone. Most often, however, we just stay home and watch TV, alone. We have gone from being a nation of reliable joiners to a nation of individuals jealously guarding their "free time," the time when no one has a claim on them. We are not renewing our social capital.

Putnam writes, "The core idea of social capital theory is that social networks have value [and] . . . social contacts affect the productivity of individuals and groups." He offers this definition of social capital: "Whereas physical capital refers to physical objects and human capital refers to properties of individuals, social capital refers to connections among individuals—social networks and the norms of reciprocity and trustworthiness that arise from them."

In other words, society *isn't* an unconnected pile of sand. If we really want to understand a society, we have to see the bonds that "connect the dots." Those bonds are part of society too. What is more, Putnam shows that a society which is high in social capital—with lots of connections—is healthier in almost every way than a society that is low in social capital. It's just as Tocqueville would have predicted. Any attempt at social progress that pays attention only to individuals but neglects the bonds between them is destined to fail.

Putnam's very sophisticated social scientific findings, by the way, created something of a revolution in academic political science. So much so that canny politicians and publicists among the village elders have since tried to tie their agendas to Putnam's insights. But the truth is that Putnam's work merely provides conclusive evidence for a tradition of *conservative* argument that includes such thinkers as the economist Wilhelm Röpke (1899–1966) and the sociologist Robert Nisbet (1913–1996). And both of these men were themselves writing in the spirit of Tocqueville.

Why is social capital important for the common good? Well, one reason, though not the most important, is that high levels of social capital reduce "transaction costs." That's a very social-scientific way of putting it, so here is something a bit more concrete. Think of a community as a bicycle chain. If well oiled, each link moves along the sprocket easily. The oil is social capital. The oil is the trust, norms for behavior, social relations, shared values, and the give and take of countless little negotiations that make us social beings. Without oil, a bicycle chain gets mucked up and doesn't travel over the sprocket smoothly. That's what happens to a community without social capital. At best it can only grind along, no matter how furiously the cyclist is pedaling.

I started this section about social capital discussing freedom because we need an abundant store of social capital to create and sustain the kind of freedom that our founding fathers envisioned, the kind of freedom that promotes the common good and supports families. It's a freedom requiring a certain degree of selflessness and virtue. You can't have social capital without people being willing to be selfless. And I'm not talking about a Mother Teresa kind of selflessness. I mean, there's a touch of that, yes. But it's really the kind of selflessness that gets repaid many times over. Sometimes immediately, sometimes down the road, by creating a community that we want to live in and that makes our lives more pleasant.

But let me link social capital to freedom even more directly. Take No-Fault Freedom. It's about me, or as the Supreme Court wrote in *Casey*, "the right to define one's own concept of existence." When No-Fault Freedom reigns, trust and selflessness are rare commodities because we each know that others in our community are simply out for themselves. And isn't that what the *Casey* decision really says—that life is all about being out for ourselves, and there really aren't any ties that bind individuals to each other (except, perhaps, the laws alone)? With No-Fault Freedom, social capital decreases and the stress of daily life increases, and we look at our fellow citizens with suspicion rather than with neighborliness and trust. In the next chapter I will discuss how the work requirement in the welfare reform law has led formerly dependent mothers to achieve unprecedented economic success. But these women have grown up, and still live in, communities that have very little social capital. Continued economic success is going to be hard to sustain for them unless we improve all forms of capital, but especially the social kind. Republicans need to realize that as great as welfare reform has been in creating economic opportunities and instilling the work ethic in those who were dependent, a good deal of work is yet to be done. That work begins with rebuilding social capital in those parts of America that are in distress: and the place to begin in building up social capital is with the family.

Remember the founding vision of the Constitution: freedom *for* the common good. In that vision, trust is more abundant and people are more willing to be selfless because they understand and expect that their fellow citizens are concerned about the common good, not just themselves. People can actually rely on each other, because they have themselves built up the habit of being reliable. Communities like this—healthy communities—make for healthier families, and healthier families make for better communities and a better country.

VII

Trust and Civic Connection

Two examples may help to make this concept of social capital clearer. The first concerns a place where social capital
is plentiful. The second comes from a community where it is
quickly drying up.

In the New York Diamond Market, it is not uncommon for
a merchant to leave a bag of diamonds worth hundreds of thousands of dollars with a neighboring merchant while he runs an
errand. The errand-running merchant doesn't ask for a receipt.
No paperwork records the fact that he has just given a bagful of
diamonds to one of his *competitors*. Why not? There are no
hidden cameras recording every move. The diamonds haven't
been secretly marked. No, it's just that the merchant trusts his
competitor not to steal from him. And why does he trust him?
He trusts because the two of them together, and the merchants
in the New York Diamond Market as a group, have a full store
of social capital amongst them. They share customs, relations,
and informal norms that bind them together in ways that make
stealing from one another unthinkable.

The merchants in the New York Diamond Market are all
members of an Orthodox Jewish community that traces its roots

back to the same neighborhood in Poland. At least as much as fearing the police if they stole from one another, they would suffer from shame and the disapproval of people with whom they share values, relationships, and a way of life. Theirs is a story of a community extremely rich in social capital.

Kelly Bourque's community is one suddenly running a severe social capital deficit.

Kelly Bourque is about 40 years old, married, and the father of two, a daughter in nursing school and a son who is fourteen. The Bourques live in Germantown, Maryland, which sits in the northern half of Montgomery County, a suburb of Washington, D.C., and one of the wealthiest counties in the United States. Kelly works in management at a company that sells automatic garage doors for residences and businesses. For years, he's been saving to retire to his native Louisiana where, he likes to say, land and mosquitoes are easy to find. He and his wife Karen had planned to stay in their modest single-family house until their youngest was off to college, and then retire. But their plans have changed—at least for the moment—quite significantly.

Kelly and Karen's neighborhood has never been one where lawyers and doctors lived. But it was filled with solid families who worked at places like Verizon or for the federal government. Down the street are several rows of small townhouses and a couple of apartment buildings where people of limited means could live.

Outside the Bourques' front door the grass is worn bare. For years, kids from throughout the neighborhood gathered in their front yard for pick-up baseball games. If the kids weren't playing ball, they were out riding their bikes together. The neighbors knew each other. Mostly, they liked each other. And Kelly, who works long hours starting each day at 5 a.m. with a 40-mile commute, and who volunteers even more hours, knew he could

rest on his couch, watch TV, and not worry about his son playing outside. He and Karen knew there were plenty of adults to
keep an eye on things. Now things are different.

It only took about three years, but kids don't play much in
Kelly's neighborhood anymore. The young people hanging around
are just hanging around, smoking, drinking beer, and sometimes
selling drugs. Kelly suspects gang activity. The county police
had to open a new sub-station just a couple of blocks down the
road. Kelly and Karen's son doesn't want to go outside.

The social capital has been drained right out of this neighborhood. Why? It's not that the kids who used to play baseball
are now into drugs. Rather, different kids now occupy the streets
of Kelly's neighborhood. And those are the kids who grew up in
the low-income housing next door. Kelly is quick to point out
that this isn't about race or about income. The kids who hung
out in Kelly's front yard were of all racial and ethnic backgrounds. This has always been a very racially integrated neighborhood. And plenty of the old kids had very modest means.

What it is about is *family*. Kelly reports that more and more
of the families that have moved into his neighborhood over the
past few years are missing one thing: a dad. Indeed, drive around
the neighborhood on a Saturday afternoon and you see star-
tlingly few fathers.

As I write this, a "For Sale" sign stands in Kelly and Karen's
worn front yard. Kelly and his family are moving out, to
Frederick, Maryland. The awful part of this story is that it's the
depletion of social capital that is driving them from their long-
time neighborhood. Kelly has done more to build social capital
throughout Germantown than almost anybody. He helped create a youth sports program, sat on its board for four years,
busted his back to build new ballfields in the community, and
was active in community politics.

Now he, Karen, and their children are leaving. The social capital in that neighborhood will be taking another hit.

SO WHAT'S THE STATUS of America's social capital account? Are we more like the diamond merchants or leaning more toward Kelly's "For Sale" sign?

Choosing just a few data items from Putnam's 513-page *Bowling Alone* paints a jarring picture of our loss of social capital. Public opinion polls over the past two decades reveal that every measure of civic engagement, from simply signing a petition to running for office, has steadily declined. In the twenty years between 1973 and 1994, the number of Americans who attended just one public meeting about neighborhood or school issues dropped 40 percent.

Church membership in this country rose steadily from the 1930s to about 1960. Since then, it has dropped about 10 percent from the 1960s to the 1990s.

We are also less likely to have friends over to our house today than in past years. In the mid to late 1970s, Americans entertained friends at home an average of 14 to 15 times per year. By the end of the 1990s, that was down to eight times per year. In other words, from 1974 to 1998 the number of times Americans spent an evening with a neighbor or friend dropped by about one-third.

These trends hold true for our generosity, as well. As a percentage of our income, Americans' donations to charity steadily increased from after the Depression until 1960. But since then they have steadily declined. As of last year, we gave only one and one-half cent of every dollar made in America to charity, down from over two cents several decades ago. And on this score, I have joined Congressman George Radanovich in an effort he calls the One Percent Solution, to increase the charitable giving rate to 2.5 percent.

Of course, the instance where the depletion of social capital is most clear is crime against the person: what, after all, could express greater contempt for the ties that bind than directly harming a neighbor and fellow citizen? Robert Woodson, president of the National Center for Neighborhood Enterprise and one of the most creative African-American leaders we have, would say that one of the worst and most painful indicators of our social capital drain is "black-on-black" crime. "Each year more blacks are killed in urban violence by other blacks than the total number of the blacks who died in service throughout the nine years of the Vietnam War," he writes.

African-American communities are hard hit by crime in another way: the large percentages of black men who become involved in the criminal justice system. The U.S. Department of Justice estimates that 16.2 percent of blacks will go to prison at some point in their lives, compared to 2.5 percent of whites. For black males, the number is 28.5 percent. The impact of these figures upon the community is staggering. Just think what these percentages mean to marriage, to families, and to children. Plus, in many states, convicted felons can never vote, practically ensuring that large numbers of black men are permanently disengaged from civic life. That is why I have supported state laws and even voted for federal laws allowing felons to vote again, provided they have been crime-free for five years.

A few years ago I visited William Penn High School in inner-city Philadelphia. Many of the children who attend that school live in and around the Richard Allen Public Housing Project, one of the toughest neighborhoods in the city. Of the young people who enter the school in the ninth grade, only 5 percent will go on to college. In the entire school, there is just one class of college-bound students. I was asked to speak with that class. When I entered the room someone was speaking on behalf of a local college telling them about all of their financial aid options, which were plentiful. Following such a positive moment, I expected to see a classroom where hope was present and the future looked bright. Instead, I found a classroom as depressed and tense as any other. The faces of the students weren't cheerful and optimistic. They ranged from anxious to somber.

Each and every one of the students complained about how they were singled out by their peers for criticism. Their success was discouraged by both mental and physical harassment. When I asked them what they felt was the greatest challenge they faced at school, one of them said, "Getting to school alive every day." The rest of the students nodded their heads and sounded off in strong agreement.

I stood at the front of that class and looked at these children who had survived the gangs, the drugs, the violence, and had suffered for being the best and brightest. My heart was at once full of admiration and sadness. What a portrait of courage, but so few, so very few, and at what cost to them?

I returned to that school a few years later at the request of an organization that was trying to rekindle the flame of hope through mentoring: City Year. I was pleasantly surprised to see AmeriCorps workers seeded throughout the City Year program. I say surprised, because early on I was not a supporter of AmeriCorps. When I ran for the U.S. Senate in 1994, I said it was a waste to spend precious federal dollars on "volunteers" so that they could sit around a campfire singing "Kum-baya." I remember that when I got to the Senate, Senator Sam Nunn harshly criticized me for that comment. And you know what: thanks to some reforms of the program instituted, oddly enough, by my opponent in that 1994 race, Harris Wofford, Sam Nunn turned out to be right.

I still think President Clinton was wrong to call people being paid "volunteers"—and initially, far too many "volunteers" were just padding federal agency payrolls. But I came to realize through my visit to William Penn and other poor communities that these energetic, mostly young people could play an important coordinating role with community and nonprofit service organizations to help build up social capital. So after being one of AmeriCorps' harshest critics, I began working closely with its new director, Harris Wofford, to move the program in a more community-oriented direction.

AmeriCorps is by no means perfect, and I am working on ways to get more volunteers into community-based nonprofits. But this program does encourage young people to reach beyond themselves to serve people and communities in need, to build up social capital where it has been depleted. I am also a supporter of President Bush's USA Freedom Corps, which further reforms and expands service opportunities through the AmeriCorps program by transitioning the service program toward a model with voucher-like awards to individuals desiring to serve low-income individuals or communities. This is the selfless behavior we need to promote in order to build a stronger society. This message of the importance of service to others may just be having a positive impact: an increase in youth volunteerism is about the only indicator of social capital that Putnam reports is going *up* in his book *Bowling Alone*.

VIII

Subsidiarity vs. Central Control

It is fairly easy to see when social capital is eroding. But how is social capital created? If we have inherited an America that has for a generation been spending down its social capital account, we need to know how to make deposits if we are going to fulfill our role as stewards of an inheritance. It seems to me that social capital is created at three levels in society: by and within the family; by and within organizations such as churches, schools, and civic associations that are often referred to as mediating institutions; and by and within society as a whole. Each is important, but they are not equally important. And understanding where each of these sources of social capital ranks points to the heart of the difference between conservatives and liberals—and to the heart of any *serious* effort to renew social capital.

My Democratic colleague in the Senate, Hillary Rodham Clinton, made a splash several years ago with her book *It Takes a Village*. Those are the words at the beginning of an African aphorism that concludes, "to raise a child." And certainly there's a great deal of truth in that aphorism. Short of living in the wilderness, it is impossible to isolate your children from the world around them. Friends, neighbors, schools, the news and entertainment media, government, and churches all are involved in one way or another in raising our children. But here is the key point that cuts through all of the noise of conservatives and liberals debating social policy: *Who is the village?*

Certainly Senator Clinton didn't mean for us to take the aphorism *literally*; her book did not focus on the problem of America having too many cities and suburban developments and not enough authentic villages. Rather, she intended "the village" to be understood *metaphorically*. Liberals like Senator Clinton see "the village" as society as a whole—influenced by, directed by, supported by, the supposed goodness of the Bigs in general and big government in particular. Forty years of liberal social policy have been built on the notion that the national government in conjunction with the other Bigs can improve the lives of individuals from the top down, and the village elders have spent trillions of dollars trying to do just that.

Now, it is true that some liberal concepts concerning the role of government to have come out of the Great Depression, like Social Security and later Medicare, have provided a safety net for seniors. While those programs are going to be a challenge to sustain because of changing demographics, liberals of generations past can be proud of these important social safeguards. And some aspects of the New Deal program were actually extraordinarily family-friendly, as the historian Allan Carlson has observed.

But unfortunately, most liberal government expansions from the 1960s on have failed the very people they intended to help. They have failed by every sociological or economic measure. They have depleted social capital and crippled the institution of the natural family. Here I'll just point out one startling statistic. The percentage of all children living in poverty in 1995 was almost exactly the same as the percentage of all children living in poverty in 1965. There were some variations along the way, but ultimately, over those thirty years, almost nothing changed for America's poor—except that they came to depend on an impersonal and distant government for help instead of on their families and neighbors. That has led to a disconnectedness, which in turn has led to hopelessness. The warm, fuzzy image of Senator Clinton's book is that of a community rich in social capital, but the truth of the matter is that liberal policies which tie individuals to the government break the bonds of true community and deplete social capital.

Conservatives see "the village" as, well, the village: the local community, with the family at the center of it. We believe that only strong families can improve the lives of individuals, especially children, and make for healthy communities. In our view, the *real* village leaders (*not* what I have been calling the "village elders") are the parents, the ministers, the Girl or Boy Scout leaders, the grandmothers who sit on their porch watching the neighborhood kids at play, the youth baseball coaches. It is these village *leaders* who are really generating social capital, first in the family, and then in the community. The liberals have it exactly the wrong way around.

The village elders believe in top-down because they believe in the supposed goodness of the central government and the Bigs—and, I think, because they *distrust* families and local communities. They think the federal government is fairer, more just, more trustworthy, even more moral, than families and local community groups with their "parochial" and "provincial" concerns. I believe in bottom-up, however, because I believe in the power of the natural family and the mediating organizations that support it. I believe in the power of Tocqueville's *associations*, that peculiarly American genius for cooperating locally to get things done. And yes, I believe in the individual who is nurtured by these institutions.

In developing my understanding of social policy, I have learned a lot from the tradition of Catholic social thought. In that tradition, there is an important concept called *subsidiarity*, the principle that all social challenges should be addressed at the level of the smallest social unit possible, preferably the family. Only when a "lower"—i.e., smaller—level of society is manifestly incapable of handling a problem may a "higher" level legitimately intervene. And even then, the "higher" level may only intervene to supplement, not displace, the function of a lower level. When you want the Bigs, led by the federal bureaucracy, to run the village—as liberals do—you have completely inverted the principle of subsidiarity.

You know what it comes down to? Conservatives trust families and the ordinary Americans that are formed by them. Liberals don't. They border on disdain for the common man. There can be very little common good without the common man, nurtured and formed by a strong natural family. But liberals practically despise the common man. They seem to think that if you would choose to go to a NASCAR race instead of *The Vagina Monologues* you are a completely unenlightened soul whose very existence demands government oversight.

Liberal policies have been top-down. The Bigs indoctrinate through the news and entertainment media, academia, and government bureaucracies. Then they give us more government intrusion to fix the mess their policies have created. That "mess" destroys social capital. That's why I put such an emphasis on subsidiarity. When government steps in and imposes a bureaucratic solution based on individualistic presuppositions, it removes expectations and responsibilities from smaller social units—especially the family. In effect, bureau-cracy robs intermediate associations of their purpose. The stronger the tie is to the government, the weaker the ties that bind the members of a local community to one another, the weaker the social capital in a community. That is one reason why I have promoted President Bush's faith-based initiatives. We need to get the money out of the hands of the bureaucrats in Washington and into these healing, faith-based instruments at the local level.

The classic example of the failure of liberal social and economic policy is the Great Society welfare programs. Aid to Families with Dependent Children (AFDC), as welfare was known until 1996, put government in the role of the family breadwinner. With AFDC, families didn't need dad around anymore. In fact, up until 1988, it was optional for states to provide any welfare to two-parent families—some states gave welfare payments only to single-parent (that is, almost always mother-headed) families.

AFDC was simply about giving money to poor women with children. In return, people getting welfare had to do—well, nothing. It was top down. The notion was simply that if you dropped money from the federal government into poor neighborhoods, all would be well—as if money alone were the answer. Such an approach failed, catastrophically. After thirty years and trillions of dollars of the liberal "war on poverty," the poverty rate was unchanged. During those decades, moreover, the family melted down, and the social capital of low-income communities washed away.

In 1996, Republicans in Congress, almost by sheer will, enacted welfare reform into law. In fact, I helped write the very first draft for welfare reform back in 1994 and, as a freshman senator, managed the passage of that bill on three separate occasions in the Senate. Suddenly, people receiving welfare had to work or be involved in work-related activities—they had to *connect* with the economy. And the number of years people could stay on welfare was limited—they had to take responsibility for their lives. Yes, President Clinton signed welfare reform into law, but only after vetoing it *twice* earlier in the year. It was the strong support of the American people combined with President Clinton's rhetorical pledge to "end welfare as we know it" that forced his hand to sign the bill just a couple of months before the 1996 presidential election.

I will discuss the welfare bill and its consequences at greater length in the next section, but suffice it to say that it has been an unqualified success. Since August 1996, national welfare caseloads are down nearly 60 percent. People are working themselves out of poverty and dependency. Still, the village elders just can't let go of the top-down approach to poverty, an approach that saps our nation's social capital. As I write this book, the U.S. Senate is looking to renew the welfare reform law. Liberal Democrats are trying to add so many exceptions to the work requirements that these requirements might as well not exist. If that happens, welfare will return to the destructive top-down, give-money-but-require-nothing-from-the-recipient approach of the past. In other words, welfare will go back to hurting people and destroying families.

Top-down. It's all they know, all liberals believe in. Because the big village, directed by big government, is the only village they trust.

Now, I certainly recognize that there have been times, and there may again be times in the future, when the federal government *has* to act in the face of gross failure at the smaller levels of the state or community. I mentioned Social Security earlier as one time when the federal government needed to act. Another case was the civil rights movement (though any serious student of federal efforts during that period knows that benevolent federal intervention could not take place until the efforts of individual, often religious, crusaders set the public stage, some by giving their lives). President Kennedy eventually took action against the will of recalcitrant states. Then President Johnson used his skill as an old hand at the legislative process to maneuver the Civil Rights Act of 1964 through the U.S. Senate. Of course, what too many of today's black leaders have written out of this story was the Republican role in the passage of the Civil Rights Act: a higher percentage of Republican senators voted for that bill than Democrats.

So there are times when the federal government has to take the lead. But these examples do not belie the principle of subsidiarity, as liberals seem to think: in the early 1960s the smallest social unit that could make racial justice happen *was* the federal government. What the principle of subsidiarity does is warn us to be very careful in such initiatives, because more often than not, we get a welfare mess, not a civil rights success.

Usually, it is best if the government is the silent partner, not the managing partner. The government in the vast majority of cases can be supportive of the work done by families and communities. Only rarely should the government take the role of calling the shots.

LET ME MAKE THE CASE even more specifically for why, when looking to build social capital, our primary focus has to be on the family—why the building block of all the forms of capital I address in this book is the family.

As we have seen, the currency of social capital is trust. Trust is high in the New York Diamond Market. Trust has left Kelly Bourque's neighborhood.

But again, where do we first learn to trust? From government regulators? No. Trust is first created within and then nurtured by healthy families. The seedbed of the social trust that forms healthy societies is the confidence and trust a child has in her parents. A child's experience of trustworthy parents in her formative years not only influences her ability to establish trusting relationships in adulthood, it will also act as a basic glue within her own eventual family. This is one of the reasons for concern about the widespread breakdown of the family in America: for too many children, family disharmony and divorce shatters their self-confidence. When the primary social bonds between parent and child are broken, trust forever after is almost always hard-won.

Thus, family breakdown is not just a tragedy for that particular family; it is something that affects us all. The fewer unhealthy families in a community, the more generalized trust in that community. In other words, a community that is short on fathers is almost always short on generalized trust or social capital. Therefore, transaction costs go up, and the neighborhood and its people suffer. The common good depends on social capital, and social capital depends on healthy mom-and-dad families.

IX

Changing Lives, Building Families

Julie Baumgardner is the executive director of First Things First in Chattanooga, Tennessee. She recently testified at a hearing of the Senate Finance Committee about what Chattanooga did to address a problem that is facing many American cities. She said,

> While Chattanooga has prospered economically, the health and well-being of our families has not kept pace. . . . While 95 percent of Hamilton County residents agree that the family is the main building block of a healthy society, 33 percent of the population have been divorced. The national average is 22 percent. . . . Eighty-four percent of the Hamilton County residents surveyed agreed that sex outside marriage is not a good idea. However, 50.4 percent of all births in 1994 in Chattanooga were to unwed mothers—the fifth highest unwed birth rate of 128 cities in the nation. The basic noneconomic problems in the Chattanooga area orbit around one concern: the family. Chattanooga was looking for leadership and a way to help its citizens live according to what they believe is important.

So Chattanooga community leaders went into action, forming the nonprofit First Things First in the summer of 1997. Its mission was to strengthen marriages and families through education, collaboration, and mobilization. Its goals were to reduce divorce and out-of-wedlock pregnancies by 30 percent and to increase fathers' involvement in the lives of their children by 30 percent.

The committed men and women of First Things First implemented a plan with three major components:

- Training sessions to equip individuals with the skills necessary to forge a long-lasting, healthy marriage.

- Public service announcements with messages stressing that marriage does matter, fathers are important, and waiting to have sex until you are married is best.

- Educating people through speaking engagements, with classes at houses of faith, civic organizations, high schools, and colleges about the effects of divorce, out-of-wedlock births, and fatherlessness on the community.

The results, according to Julie, are that "since 1997 we have seen a 27.2 percent decrease in divorce filings and a 22.6 percent decrease in teen out-of-wedlock pregnancies. We have experienced a slight decrease in out-of-wedlock pregnancies in women ages 20 to 44. We have seen a significant increase in father involvement in the lives of their children."

She concluded her testimony with a jab followed by a nudge. First the jab:

I think the real question is how can government *not* be involved in helping to strengthen marriage when research shows that high rates of family fragmentation generate substantial taxpayer costs. *The Marriage Movement: A Statement of Principles* report, released in 2000, states that divorce and unwed childbearing create substantial public costs paid by taxpayers. Higher rates of crime, drug abuse, education failure, chronic illness, child abuse, domestic violence, and poverty among both adults and children bring with them higher tax-payer costs in diverse forms: more welfare expenditure, increased remedial and special education expenses, higher daycare subsidies, additional child-support collection costs, a range of increased direct court administration costs incurred in regulating post-divorce or unwed families, higher foster care and child protection service costs, increased Medicaid and Medicare costs, increasingly expensive and harsh crime-control measures to compensate for formerly private regulation of adolescent and young-adult behaviors, and many similar costs.

Then there was the nudge:

I continue to be amazed at the number of people who tell us we are making a difference in the community. I believe that a huge part of this is because we are dealing with the root of the problem [marriage] instead of consistently putting band-aids on the symptoms.

Julie Baumgardner is right. For decades, the village elders have talked about the need to address "root causes" of our social problems. For decades, conservative criticism of liberal policy has argued that the focus on "root causes" was merely a cover for a liberal resolution not to enforce basic laws of public order. But there has been something even more out of whack with liberal policy: it has never really understood what the *real* root causes are.

I NOW TURN TO a mix of policy proposals, examples, and direct appeals to personal action to renew America's social capital. But as you read these, don't think that this is the complete agenda for rebuilding social capital. In order to promote the general welfare, the common good, we need to replenish all of the interrelated stores of capital that make for a strong society—economic, moral, cultural, and intellectual.

It takes a family to build social capital. And it takes a marriage to make the family work best for the future of America, our children. So let's start with marriage policy.

President Bush's administration is heading down the right track, planning to spend $300 million of welfare funding per year for five years in order to test different ways that we can help low-income couples who might want to consider marriage to do just that—and to help already married low-income couples who may be struggling to try to stay married. These projects may include a public education campaign, as in Chattanooga, to instruct people about the benefits of marriage to adults and children, and to spread the word that there are places that can help and support couples. Other eligible projects might include premarital counseling, couples counseling, conflict resolution, and parenting classes.

Earlier I cited a study showing that 80 percent of mothers applying for welfare are in a current relationship with the father of their child, and both partners have spoken of marriage. But no one helps these men and women, and within a year, under stress, almost all have parted ways. How about a program that simply asks of those 80 percent who are considering marriage, "Would you like some help in building that relationship?" And if they say yes, then paying for them to receive counseling from a family therapist or counselor, pastor, rabbi, imam, or priest. This shows respect for individuals and their circumstances, but it also acknowledges that life can sometimes be difficult, and we all may need some help to live up to our better selves.

I would also like to add to the president's initiative another idea, because there are too many children growing up in neighborhoods where marriage simply no longer exists. Ray Ellis grew up in one of those neighborhoods. He did not have a father in his life, and neither did most of the other kids in his neighborhood. There was one father, just one really good dad, whom Ray saw taking good care of his own kids. That man changed Ray's life. What did he do for Ray? Nothing—except that by his example he gave Ray something to aspire to. Ray, a former Philadelphia Eagle, now helps another former Eagle, Herb Lusk, pastor a church in North Philadelphia. Ray runs the outreach ministries of that church, which provide after-school programs for youngsters: job training, literacy, and basic skills programs for dropouts. And all of these are right down the street from where I visited that class from William Penn High School. Most importantly Ray is also a great dad to his own children.

Like First Things First, we need to launch an advertising campaign focused across the country on Ray's kind of neighborhood in order to promote the value of marriage. For too many young women in these neighborhoods, marriage is not just a foreign concept: it is a bridge too far. We need to help women and men understand, through the power of advertising, that marriage can dramatically improve their community and the quality of their own and their children's lives.

One other benefit of stable marriages over the years, a benefit that is almost never noticed, is that in such marriages grandparents are more likely to be involved in their grandchildren's lives. Grandparents can provide support for their children both financially and emotionally, and if they live nearby, they can also help with that all-important need of young parents, babysitting. If you are a single mom of a single mom, your kids are not likely to have four grandparents. Instead, these children often end up with their mother's mother as the only grandparent, and she is working full time just to make ends meet.

Too often we overlook the tremendous gifts that grandmothers and grandfathers can be to their children and their
grandchildren. Financial support from mom and dad is vital for
most young adults getting started in life. A sizable percentage of
Americans buy their first home with the help of their parents,
for example. Grandparents provide their grandchildren with a
sense of belonging not just to their immediate family, but to a
whole network of people who love them: relatives. Grandparents can give a sense of family history and tradition that provides children with context, security, and the wisdom of experience. Even if they don't have money or great stories to tell, every grandparent comes equipped to provide the most important
gift to their grandchildren, the gift of unconditional love. It isn't
their job now to be the heavy. They played that role once before; now they can be the sympathetic ear. In the hustle and
bustle of contemporary family life, with both kids and parents
on the go, grandparents are sanctuaries for children.

When an eight-year-old girl sent a letter to former First Lady
Barbara Bush back in February 1995, she delivered a message
more eloquently than I could about the importance of family:

> A grandmother is a lady who has no children of her own. She
> likes other people's little girls. A grandfather is a man grand-
> mother. He goes for walks with the boys and they talk about
> heroes and fighters and traitors and stuff like that. Grand-
> mothers don't have to do anything but be there. They are old
> so they shouldn't play hard or run. It's enough that they drive
> us to the mall where the pretend horse is and have lots of
> dimes ready. Or if they take us for walks, they slow down past
> things, like pretty leaves or caterpillars. They never say hurry
> up. Usually they're fat, but not too fat to tie kid's shoes. They
> wear glasses and funny underwear. They can take their teeth
> out and gums out. They don't have to be smart—only answer
> questions like "Why do dogs hate cats?" and "How come God

isn't married?" When they read to us, they don't skip or mind if it's the same story again and again. Everyone should try to have one, especially if you don't have television, because grandmas are the only grownups who have time.

One of the reasons it takes a family is because children need grandparents, too.

AS I MENTIONED EARLIER, one of the major criticisms I hear from supporters of same-sex marriage is that heterosexuals have themselves done a pretty good job of destroying marriage already through no-fault divorce, and supporters of the Marriage Protection Amendment have done little about it. My answer to that is: *You are right, and that must change.* One of the positive outcomes of this radical push for same-sex marriage is that it has prompted a national conversation about the meaning and importance of marriage, and that's a very healthy thing. We need to *think* about, not just take for granted, what marriage is. We need this debate as an opportunity for renewal.

One pathway to such renewal is the concept of Covenant Marriages. Started in Louisiana and now also available in Arizona and Arkansas, this policy gives couples an option when they go to get a marriage license. They can choose the usual marriage with the no-fault divorce escape hatch. Or they can choose a covenant marriage, which binds them by law to do two things. First, to get premarital counseling before they get married. Such counseling has been shown to help couples wrestle with the big issues that could cause trouble in the marriage—many of which they may not have thought of—*before* they ever cause trouble. The counseling also occasionally convinces couples who really shouldn't get married not to do so. The second thing covenant marriage requires is that the man and woman getting married agree that they will do whatever it takes, including counseling, to keep the marriage together. Here specifically is what couples in Louisiana agree to when they enter into a Covenant Marriage:

> We do solemnly declare that marriage is a covenant between a man and a woman who agree to live together as husband and wife for so long as they both may live. We have chosen each other carefully and disclosed to one another everything which could adversely affect the decision to enter into this marriage. We have received premarital counseling on the nature, purposes, and responsibilities of marriage. We have read the Covenant Marriage Act, and we understand that a Covenant Marriage is for life. If we experience marital difficulties, we commit ourselves to take all reasonable efforts to preserve our marriage, including marital counseling.
>
> With full knowledge of what this commitment means, we do hereby declare that our marriage will be bound by Louisiana law on Covenant Marriages and we promise to love, honor, and care for one another as husband and wife for the rest of our lives.

Making Covenant Marriage much more widely available is one way to shore up the meaning of marriage throughout our society.

The flip side of marriage policy is divorce policy. Divorce is simply far too easy to get in this country, especially when children are involved. States should put in braking mechanisms for couples who have children under the age of 18. This means a mandatory waiting period and mandatory counseling before a divorce is granted. The village elders believe that such braking mechanisms interfere in the personal decisions of free individuals. I believe that our laws have an educational value: the marriage contract should be at least as difficult to break as a contract for chicken feed.

All our social services programs, ranging from Head Start to hospital maternity wards, also need to be retooled so that the professional staff is trained in how to talk to clients about the value of marriage and the services that are available in the community to help couples interested in exploring marriage.

The same approach holds true for fatherhood. Every welfare caseworker or Head Start teacher or public school educator who deals with parents should be trained to understand the barriers that keep fathers, especially low-income fathers, from being involved with their children, and how to overcome those barriers. Senator Evan Bayh—a Democrat from Indiana—and I have sponsored a fatherhood initiative in the welfare reform reauthorization that is working its way through Congress. This consists of $50 million of spending per year for community- and faith-based programs that promote and foster healthy fatherhood. And this is only a small beginning for what should be a much more aggressive program.

One of the largest fatherhood groups is the National Fatherhood Initiative. Its president, Roland Warren, founded the organization in 1994 in response to the explosion of fatherlessness in America. According to Roland:

> The most disturbing social trend of our times is the dramatic increase in fatherlessness in the United States. In 1960, fewer than 8 million children were living in families where the father was absent. Today the number of children living in father-absent homes stands at 24 million. That means that tonight, one out of every three children in America will go to sleep in a home in which their father does not live.

While it is at times easy to throw around statistics such as these to make a point, the plain truth of the matter is that for every one of these frightening statistics, there is a child attached to it, and, on average, the consequences of father absence for each of these youngsters are not good. Children who grow up in father-absent homes are significantly more likely to do poorly on almost any measure of child well-being. For example:

- Almost 75 percent of American children who grow up in single-parent homes will experience poverty before they turn 11 years old, compared to only 20 percent for families where there are two parents.

- Violent criminals are overwhelmingly males who grew up without fathers, including 72 percent of adolescent murderers and 70 percent of long-term prison inmates.

- Children living in father-absent homes are also more likely to be suspended from school or to drop out; be treated for an emotional or behavioral problem; commit suicide as adolescents; and be victims of child abuse or neglect.

The National Fatherhood Initiative encourages and supports family- and father-friendly policies, develops national public education campaigns to highlight the importance of fathers in the lives of their children, provides motivation for national and local coalition-building, and provides resources to men to help them be better dads.

In January 2005 they hosted a forum at the National Press Club to talk about a new book published by Jason DeParle, a reporter from the *New York Times* who covers welfare issues in Washington, D.C. I was invited to the event to speak about my fatherhood proposal. Jason spoke first about his book *American Dream: Three Women, Ten Kids, and a Nation's Drive to End Welfare*. The book reports on the two years Jason spent studying the effect of welfare on three families in Milwaukee. According to Jason, welfare reform had its successes: women found work, and in some cases satisfying and rewarding work. But welfare reform also had its failures. The biggest failure he highlighted was the lack of social capital in the neighborhoods in which these women lived and, in particular, the lack of fathers and positive male role models for these ten children.

While a subsequent speaker was talking about the importance of more daycare funding as the answer to the problems facing these families, Jason leaned over to me on the panel and commented that daycare was a Washington problem for politicians who didn't understand what was really happening in these poor communities. He said that none of the families he studied or interacted with had a problem finding daycare; they had a big problem finding dads. There simply is no substitute for the natural family, no substitute for a real dad, however flawed.

Take Marvin Charles for example. If he can turn around, become a good father, and help build our store of social capital, then every other father can do the same. For the first forty years of his life Marvin, by his own admission, gave nothing to society. He only took. Born and raised in Seattle, Marvin's adoptive mother died when he was ten. His father became an abusive drunk. By the age of 14, Marvin was on the streets.

"I fell victim to the streets," he says today. "It happens to lots of African-American kids who don't have positive role models and father figures."

"I spent the next 25 years pretty much doing everything under the sun, having children, traveling the country, leading a life of crime. By the time I was 40, I had a pretty bad reputation, a drug habit, and five children for whom I wasn't acting like any kind of father. The only thing I had to show for my life was a bad drug habit."

In 1994 he returned to Seattle, where he met a woman. They were both drug addicts. They had one child. Later she got pregnant again. "I remember sitting at a table, she and I, using drugs, crack, and I saw some water running under the table. I asked

her, 'What's that?' She said, 'I don't know.' When in fact it was
that her water had just broke. It's a miracle that social services
didn't take that baby." That was in 1997.

"Seven months later we were in that same apartment. That
baby spent seven months by herself in a back room because our
thinking was that there in the back room she'd be out of the
way of the drugs and the smoke. Then one day, I'm sitting there
on the couch and some guy comes in and just throws me a drug
like I was some sort of a dog. That was it. I knew I had to do
something, but I didn't know what. I grabbed my little baby girl.
My intention was to leave her on the steps of the hospital. But I
sat there on a park bench. I had no clue what to do. I hadn't been
connected to society for more than 20 years."

Marvin says God found him there on that bench that day. I
would say that God was always there—it was that Marvin suddenly recognized him. Marvin ended up with his baby daughter
sitting in front of a caseworker at Child Protective Services. To
make a long story short, he signed a contract that gave him 90
days to turn his life around; if he didn't, he would lose his parental rights to his daughter and the two other children of his who
were in foster care at the time. He went through inpatient drug
treatment and then outpatient treatment.

"My goal was to see what it would be like to be clean for 30
days and then think on my own power. I got out of treatment
and started attending AA and going to parenting classes. 'Lord,
help me put my family back together again,' I prayed."

A month after that, his girlfriend went into treatment too.
That was five years ago. Then they got married.

"I wanted to be married because I wanted to separate myself as far as I could from that lifestyle and I knew that marriage
was one of the key components for doing that. I was willing to
give it all that I had and my girlfriend did the same."

Marvin and his wife then set about regaining custody of Marvin's other children. It took two years. During that time he learned two important things: that there was no agency or organization that helped men like him navigate the judicial process of reconnecting with their children, and that lots of men are in similar situations. Marvin and his wife decided to do something about it.

They founded D.A.D.S.—Divine Alternatives for Dads. "I left a whole bunch of guys on the street in the same situation I was in," Marvin says. "D.A.D.S. makes it possible for us to use what we learned and the experiences we went through to help a whole lot of other men become good fathers." Marvin estimates that over the past three years, D.A.D.S. has helped more than 160 men reconnect with their children.

Marvin Charles would be the first to tell you that he was an awful human being for a quarter of a century. But he changed and made his community a better place to live. He's proof that there isn't a soul among us who can't do something to improve where we live. It doesn't have to be starting a new program like Marvin did, but it has to be something.

One final point on fatherhood: there are many fathers out there who do want to take an active role in their children's lives, but who are sadly barred from doing so by courts and mothers. Many fatherhood groups rightly complain that the village elders on our family courts automatically award custody of children to mothers, irrespective of the circumstances. It is one of the few places left in our culture where sexism is not only condoned but virtually celebrated. This can lead to devastating consequences for the whole family, however. The village elders on the courts have to understand that children want and need both mothers *and* fathers, even when mothers and fathers may not want each other. Our family courts need to be reminded that their first responsibility is to the welfare of the *children* who are the innocent parties in dysfunctional family situations. The courts must not become a tool whereby children pay the price of their parents' problems.

We must begin the process of connecting and reconnecting fathers and their children, particularly in our poor neighborhoods where the problem of fatherlessness is most acute. To do so will not only help mothers and children, it will ground these fathers in a healthy social identity as part of a family, and so help them resist other antisocial temptations: the destructive social belonging of gangs or the reckless life of radical individualism.

PROMOTING FATHERHOOD for young men who get a young woman pregnant is the first aid: marriage is the cure. Another strategy to foster strong families is to help young people delay sexual activity until marriage. And it is not just unintended pregnancy we need to worry about. We are in the middle of an epidemic of sexually transmitted diseases (STDs). There are about 15 million new STD infections per year in the United States, with about a quarter of these contracted by teenagers. STDs can cause infertility, cancer, even death. Liberals scoff at the idea of abstinence education. Surprisingly, thankfully, teens aren't scoffing. Did you know that it's now a *majority* of high school students who do *not* have sex? According to the National Youth Risk Behavior Survey, conducted every year by the Centers for Disease Control and Prevention, in 1991, 54 percent of high school students throughout the United States had ever had sexual intercourse. By 2001, this percentage was down to 46 percent. The majority of today's high school students are virgins. (I must admit it is unsettling that to say a bare majority of high school students are virgins is grounds for boasting.)

The field of abstinence education has not been studied as long or as intensively as has the "regular" sex ed—so-called comprehensive sex ed. (And comprehensive sex ed, by the way, has not been shown to have *any* impact on pregnancy or STD rates. The *only* liberal program ever shown to lower pregnancy rates involved injecting inner-city teenage girls with Depo-Provera, which, while preventing pregnancy, did nothing to protect them from becoming infected with STDs.) But studies are beginning to show that we can help young people make the healthy choice to delay sexual activity—preferably until marriage, but at least until adulthood.

For example, an abstinence-based public education program in Monroe County, New York, proved successful in both lowering sexual activity among 15-year-olds and pregnancy rates among girls ages 15 through 17. An article in the *Journal of the American Medical Association* by Dr. Michael Resnick and others concluded: "Adolescents who reported having taken a pledge to remain a virgin were at significantly lower risk of early age sexual debut." An analysis of the largest data set exploring adolescent behaviors and risk factors ever compiled revealed that adolescent girls who signed a virginity pledge were 40 percent less likely to have a child out of wedlock than girls who did not sign a pledge. And an abstinence program developed by Grady Memorial Hospital in Atlanta, according to a study published in *Family Planning Perspectives*, reduced the rate of initiation of sexual activity during the eighth grade by some 60 percent for boys and over 95 percent for girls.

I have sometimes asked poor young women who have a child out of wedlock, not why they have done so, but what it means to them to have a child at such a young age. The response is too often the same: having a baby means she will have at least one person in this world who loves her unconditionally, who makes her feel worthwhile. Think about that: for these young women, their pregnancy isn't the result of ignorance about the birds and the bees; it isn't a result of a failure in contraceptive devices; it isn't the result of an uncontrollable sex drive. Rather, it is the result of the deep need for human *connection*—the sort of connection we mean when we talk about social capital. What's lacking in communities with high rates of out-of-wedlock birth is not access to a clinic or the pill; what's lacking is a connection to family and community. What is lacking is social capital.

Liberal social welfare policies have, frankly, been grounded in an assumption that poverty is the ultimate disability, one that the poor cannot overcome. Their sex-ed approach assumes that young people, especially low-income youth, are not capable of making healthy moral decisions. The village elders say we can't impose outdated traditional or religious values on these children. To do so would infringe upon their No-Fault Freedom. So their answer is, in their words, a "value neutral" approach to teen sexual activity that focuses on damage control. Their approach offers "value neutral" services like abortion or school-based clinics to treat pregnancies and STDs. But if many of these teens are having babies because they *want* them, these "value neutral" programs will never work.

In other words, teaching "religious" values like self-control, commitment, and marriage is deemed inappropriate, but the distribution of birth control pills, condoms, and referrals for abortion—all without parental knowledge, much less consent—is "neutral." As amazing as the village elders' distorted view of neutrality is, it is compounded by their continued advocacy of programs that make the problems confronted by teens worse. The only way to really make a difference in out-of-wedlock childbearing is by respecting people enough, including low-income teens, to expect healthy and moral decision-making. It works: a study published in the journal *Adolescent and Family Health* cited abstinence as the leading factor in recent drops in the teen pregnancy rate.

More on this point about abstinence. There is only one country in the world that has dramatically lowered HIV/AIDS rates, and it is certainly not the United States. It's Uganda. In 1991, the rate of HIV/AIDS in Uganda was estimated at 21 percent. By 2001, that figure was down to an estimated 6 percent. Uganda accomplished this tremendous turnaround through a program known by the acronym "A.B.C." A stands for abstinence; B is for being faithful to your partner; and C is for using condoms in high-risk populations. Research has documented that it was "primary behavior change"—that is, the A and the B—that was most responsible for the decline in HIV rates.

Mrs. Janet Museveni, the first lady of Uganda who helped lead the fight against AIDS in her country, has said, "ABC means abstinence, being faithful, and condoms, and we talk about it in that order because we think it's very important to talk about abstinence from premarital sex, especially to the young people who are not married, and being faithful [to those that are married]. And then we talk about condoms to those people who already have AIDS who can use condoms so they don't aggravate their situations and also to people who have no way of practicing self-control." The president of Uganda, Yoweri K. Museveni, simply says, when speaking of his country's great success: "It was not due to condoms, it was actually due to behavior change."

When I visited with Mrs. Museveni on one of her trips to Washington she told me that the abstinence programs have reaped benefits beyond reducing the transmission rate of HIV/AIDS. She told me that the programs' teaching of self-control and self-respect translates to other areas of a young person's life. These programs have helped lower substance abuse and reduced crime.

Yet in this country, we continue to pour millions more dollars into comprehensive sex ed, which "protects" against the "effects" of *unhealthy* behavior, rather than promoting virtue, which will lead to *healthy* behavior. In 2002, the federal and state governments spent an estimated $1.73 billion on a wide variety of contraception promotion and pregnancy prevention programs. More than a third of that money—$653 million— was spent specifically to fund contraceptive programs for teens. In contrast, programs teaching teens to abstain from sexual activity received only an estimated $144.1 million in 2002. Overall, the government spent 12 dollars to promote contraception for every dollar spent to encourage abstinence. When I have attempted to increase abstinence funding at the expense of contraceptive funding, I have been scolded for "trying to impose religious values on children." As if telling children to go ahead and have sex all they want as long as they use a condom is not a value statement. It may not be held by many formal religions, but it is certainly held by the materialist philosophy of the left that defends free-sex-and-condoms with religious zeal. If you ever wondered what moral message was being delivered to your children from Uncle Sam—or should I say Uncle Sigmund?— now you know.

Back here in the U.S., the Best Friends Foundation, started by Elayne Bennett, the wife of former Secretary of Education Bill Bennett, is an in-school, abstinence-only program for girls that practices what Mrs. Museveni preaches. Using peer groups and mentor-teachers, their curriculum and after-school activities teach self-respect through the practice of self-control, giving the child the skills, guidance, and support to abstain from sex until marriage and to reject illegal drugs and alcohol. And the program works. The 2003–04 Best Friends students' behavior, as compared to their peers, demonstrates that in Washington, D.C., public schools, alcohol use is 24 percent among Best Friends, as compared to 55 percent among their peers; drug use is 3 percent among Best Friends, as compared to 36 percent among their peers; and sexual activity is 6 percent among Best Friends, as compared to 30 percent among their peers. "Best Friends is an extra shoulder to lean on, a second family. Best Friends makes it easier to say no to drugs and sex, because you know you have someone by your side supporting your decision," says Shervonda Rowry, a seventh grader from Erie, Pennsylvania.

Similar differences have been demonstrated in the Best Men program for boys. After the boys entered this program, the number of fights they were involved in dropped 75 percent. "Discipline, to me, is one of the biggest parts of Best Men. Now . . . I hardly get into any trouble. I owe all my thanks to the Best Men program for helping me achieve this," says Larry Griffin, an eighth grader from Milwaukee, Wisconsin. Academic achievement measured in Milwaukee also showed an increase in grade point averages and standardized test scores in both Best Friends and Best Men. Programs like these send the message to young people that the grown-up world expects of them healthy moral decisions; the message that condom-based programs sends is that the grown-up world expects you to have premarital sex. Neither program is "neutral": which is healthier?

The National Campaign to Prevent Teen Pregnancy survey indicates that teens are responding to the abstinence message. Fifty-eight percent of teens said that sexual activity for high schoolers is not acceptable, even if precautions are taken against pregnancy and sexually transmitted diseases. Ninety-three percent of teens said that it is important for teens to receive a strong message from society that they should abstain from sex at least until they are out of high school. Christina Duncan Evans, a seventh grader from Washington, D.C., states it best: "Best Friends breaks away from the mixed messages and ambiguity by offering a clear message to teens: abstinence from dangerous behavior is the only way to ensure a happy, healthy, productive youth."

X

Parents and Children

Obviously the duty to build social capital within families lies primarily with parents, with a big assist from churches and community groups. There are a few things government can do to support families, but ultimately it is up to each of us to build up our own families. We need to put in the time, effort, and sacrifice to make each of our families work. That will do more to help promote the common good than just about anything else we do. As I said at the beginning, the general welfare, the common good, is ultimately up to us.

I understand that it will be harder for some to succeed because of socioeconomic status, family breakup, addiction, illness, disability, prejudice, or even a lack of God-given abilities. But we can all make a difference in our own families, and thereby make a contribution to the common good. There are times when the government needs to be there to help as a silent partner, but in the end it really is up to you and me.

Time is a good example. Actually, the lack of it. The lack of time is making things very tough for America's families. Seventy percent of America's parents feel they don't spend enough time with their children. Some decades ago, when Americans

first began to worry about this time deficit, progressive thera-
peutic professionals stepped up and said, don't worry, what
matters is not the quantity of time, but "quality time." Well, as
the years have gone by, and the time we've spent with our children has declined even further, many people have begun to realize that simply isn't so. Quantity has a quality all its own.

From a public policy perspective, this is a tough one, but
there are in fact some little things that government can do. For
example, we can promote telecommuting. Congressman Frank
Wolf and I have been working on a variety of different ideas,
from providing money for regional telecommuting planning, to
providing pollution credits to companies that encourage their
employees to telecommute, to giving a tax credit to individuals
and companies. We can also finally pass legislation to amend
the Federal Labor Standards Act—which hasn't changed since
1938—to give hourly workers, at their sole option, the opportunity to get comp or flex time instead of overtime. Salaried
workers already have the right to refuse overtime pay and take
time off instead—to care for a sick child or go to a child's school
play. Hourly workers under federal law don't have that option:
they must take the pay if they work more hours.

But we parents also have to face the truth. Children of two
parents who are working don't need more *things*. They need *us*!
In far too many families with young children, both parents are
working, when, if they really took an honest look at the budget,
they might confess that both of them really don't *need* to, or at
least may not need to work as much as they do. Some are working because they think they must buy their kids and themselves
more *things they "need"*—instead of giving of *themselves* to
their kids. And for some parents, the purported need to provide
things for their children simply provides a convenient rational-
ization for pursuing a gratifying career outside the home. But in

this world, at a time when it is increasingly difficult to raise children well, we should all recognize that our kids really need fewer *things* and more *mom and dad.*

Many women have told me, and surveys have shown, that they find it easier, more "professionally" gratifying, and certainly more socially affirming, to work outside the home than to give up their careers to take care of their children. Think about that for a moment. What happened in America so that mothers and fathers who leave their children in the care of someone else—or worse yet, home alone after school between three and six in the afternoon—find themselves more *affirmed* by society? Here, we can thank the influence of radical feminism, one of the core philosophies of the village elders. It's ironic. Radical feminists have been making the pitch that justice demands that men and women be given an equal opportunity to make it to the top in the workplace. But they refuse to acknowledge, much less value as equal, the essential work women have done in being the primary caregivers of the next generation. It seems to me that justice demands *both* fair workplace rules *and* proper respect for work in the home.

Respect for stay-at-home mothers has been poisoned by a toxic combination of the village elders' war on the traditional family and radical feminism's misogynistic crusade to make working outside the home the only marker of social value and self-respect. Both have been communicating to women that motherhood is not only confining and frustrating—which it sometimes is—but also that it is also completely unnecessary in the modern world. Sadly, the propaganda campaign launched in the 1960s has taken root. The radical feminists succeeded in undermining the traditional family and convincing women that professional accomplishments are the key to happiness. As for children? Well, to paraphrase The *Wizard of Oz,* "Pay no attention to those kids behind the curtain." But like it or not, the children are there—and our society has let them down by not being supportive of mothers, and even fathers, who dedicate their time and often their lives to their children.

Government has been chief among the bad influences on parents, by the way, starting with its tax policy. We need a tax policy that stops discriminating against families and starts favoring them. That means not only making the repeal of the marriage penalty permanent, but instituting other measures to lower the tax burden on the mothers and fathers who are raising this country's future—our children. That includes increasing both the child credit and the deduction for children. Even the $1,000 credit and the dependent child deduction offset only a small portion of the costs associated with raising a child today.

That was not always the case. In 1950, before government exploded, the average tax burden on the American family was 2 percent of its income. And that figure was the Social Security tax due. Today the burden is 25 percent, over half of which are Social Security and Medicare taxes. And the burden is often even heavier for larger families, because of the phasing out of the child credit for families with a total income of $110,000. Now, before you start complaining about tax breaks for the rich, answer me this: Is a family making $110,000 with eight children as well off economically as a family with one child at that same salary? Obviously not, but the tax code phases out the child credit all the same.

There is often a double hit for these same large families due to the Alternative Minimum Tax. That tax rule was put in place to make sure that the super-wealthy were paying their fair share of taxes at a time when tax shelters were commonplace. But an IRS study now reports that "by 2007, nearly 95 percent of AMT revenues will be attributable to personal and dependent exemptions, the standard deduction, state and local taxes, and miscellaneous itemized deductions." In other words, the AMT will kick in, not because of tax shelters and fancy accounting tricks designed to avoid taxes, but simply because a normal family taking normal deductions is deemed by the tax code to be paying "not enough." The government actually provides less help the more children you have. The opposite should be true, and I am working on some amendments to fix this inequity for large families. (Okay, I admit that with six kids of my own at home, I'm biased: but the tax code really has it in for big families.)

But beyond the tax code, we need to reform our culture. We need to reform what it is we *affirm* socially. Too many parents today are equating good parenting with good taxi service. I am not simply saying: spend more time at home. Rather, I am saying that parents need to really *engage*. Spend more time in genuine conversation with your children, or in helping them with homework, or in daily prayer. Even when hustling from one scheduled activity to another, turn off the CD player and mobile phone and *talk*. It may not be easy; it will take extra effort that you may not feel up to that day. But it will be well worth the effort in the long run. And when you get to soccer practice or to the little league game, try not to just sit in the bleachers and work your cell phone. Instead, *engage*. I know what I am talking about, because I have been guilty of everything I've just told you not to do. We all can do better. I know what you are thinking: that the people at work are depending on you. What your kids may never tell you is that they are depending on you too.

It is not the purpose of this book to be a guide to good parenting. I could recommend a whole slew of books that Karen and I (mostly Karen) have read, books written by smart people whose advice makes a lot of sense: *Bringing up Boys* by Dr. Jim

Dobson, *Family First* by Dr. Phil McGraw, *Compass: A Handbook on Parent Leadership* by Jim Stenson, and *Parenthood by Proxy* by Dr. Laura Schlessinger. They have all served to inspire, chastise, and encourage us. What I can tell you here is that new research is proving that family connectedness—social capital—is the best prevention against alcohol, drugs, sex, tobacco, and violence. Youth who feel they are *connected* to their parents are less likely to get involved in all these unhealthy behaviors.

And this doesn't mean being your child's buddy. Having a good relationship is important, but it's the *parenting* part of being a parent that really counts. Parents who set high expectations for their kids, who make those expectations clear, who talk often and about serious as well as casual matters with their children, monitor their children's activities, and set clear rules and limits (with consequences when they are broken) are the parents whose children feel connected.

One way to stay connected is to take time, at least once a day, to get together as a family. It could be for a walk, or for prayer, or for meals. Television shows from the 1950s always showed families sitting together well dressed and well mannered for dinnertime. The reason was that family dinnertime was actually a firmly entrenched tradition in America. With two parents now working and with longer commute times, this tradition has vanished from many American homes. Yet all of the authors I mentioned above talk about the importance of family dinnertime. We need to renew this American tradition. Research shows that family dinnertime keeps children healthy and safe. Young people living in families who have dinner together five or more times a week are less likely to abuse substances or get involved in premarital sexual activity, for example.

Imagine what would happen if we started a family dinnertime revolution in America. Imagine if American families started eating dinner together again, and actually talked about their day, or an issue, or even prayed together. For some, it may not be so easy, but what a difference it would make. It might anger some executives at fast food conglomerates, but think what it would do for America's families, communities, and, yes, for our nation's social capital.

This brings me back to the word selflessness: it may sound difficult, even harsh, as if I have called upon you to deny life's pleasures and live like an ascetic monk. Far from it. I believe true joy and fulfillment come from serving others. I didn't just learn that from my Catholic upbringing or our Judeo-Christian ethic: I experience it every day as a husband, father, and senator. I realize that this idea is genuinely countercultural in the *me-first*, *just-do-it* society in which we live. I accept that it is a bit idealistic, but when it comes to our children, don't we owe them our best efforts? Shouldn't we be aiming high? Wouldn't we all want our children and grandchildren to live in a nurturing, caring world in which people live by the Golden Rule? That will not happen all by itself. In fact, I assure you that unless we each do something about it, the opposite will.

In 2003, I gave a speech to the Midwest Catholic Conference in Wichita, Kansas. After my speech, in which I made many of the points discussed here, a young man rushed up to me and handed me that cloth bracelet we encountered in this book's first chapter that read F.A.M.I.L.Y. I asked him what it meant. He asked, "Have you seen the same kind of bracelet with the acronym W.W.J.D.?" I said, "Yes, I used to wear one, before it broke. It was a good reminder for me: <u>W</u>hat <u>W</u>ould <u>J</u>esus <u>D</u>o?" "Well," he exclaimed, "this is the answer to that question: <u>F</u>orget <u>A</u>bout <u>M</u>e, <u>I</u> <u>L</u>ove <u>Y</u>ou!"

He was right. Family is about *we* and *us*, not *I* and *me*. Family is the place where we begin to enlarge our hearts to include others. And no, in America today your children are not likely to hear that during the hours they spend in front of a television or movie screen. In my original draft of this book I wrote the following line: "They had better hear and see that during the twenty minutes researchers say most school-aged children spend with their parents each day." Then I thought, How absurd is that? Your child is awake for 14 to 16 hours a day, exposed to six or even seven hours of elite-generated media programming or six or seven hours of liberal academic ideology that promotes an anti-traditional worldview. And I was going to tell you that your twenty minutes of lecturing and modeling would carry the day? I don't think so. Oh, it's better than nothing, but not much better. If all you are spending with your children are those twenty minutes, what you say will be offset by what you do for the rest of your day. It is about *time,* and kids know it.

XI

Religion and Social Capital

I began by arguing that social capital is generated at three levels: the family, intermediate institutions, and the larger community. I've been discussing initiatives aimed at generating social capital at the level of the family. Next are mediating institutions. What are the specific steps we can take to strengthen mediating institutions so they help restore social capital?

The most important answer is to build up what the village elders have spent decades trying to tear down and drive underground—religious institutions and faith-based organizations. The Democrats today have become the party espousing European-style secularism. They have gone to great lengths to create government bureaucracies to displace the work that religious groups have done ever since the days of the Pilgrims, and to marginalize and privatize faith and its moral demands altogether. Their approach to government regulation and programming has worked in countless ways to sideline people of faith.

Earlier, I argued that liberals like my colleague Senator Hillary Clinton say "village" but mean big government. In recent years, however, some liberals have picked up on findings like those reported in Robert Putnam's *Bowling Alone* and have started talking about the importance of intermediary institutions. Nevertheless, when the village elders think about community, they tend to think about political clubs, issue-advocacy groups, community activists, homeowner associations—anything and everything *but* churches, synagogues, and mosques. It is almost as if religion frightens them: and perhaps it does. The village elders see churches as serious challengers to their "expert" authority and to their profoundly secularist worldview. For liberals, faith-based organizations are exactly the *wrong* sort of intermediate institution building the *wrong* sort of social capital. Consequently, even when the village elders try to incorporate social capital into their own agendas, the resulting "image" of American society looks like some bizarre parallel universe: America the secular.

But the simple truth is that religious congregations are, by an overwhelming margin, the most important intermediate institution outside the family for the vast majority of Americans. America is the most churched country in the advanced industrial world. More people are in church in any given week in America than are in the stands at all professional sporting events in a year. America's religious commitment is one of the things that makes America exceptional. Our tradition of religious liberty is an essential element of that. We have a competitive marketplace of faith, and that keeps all religions on their toes. If any religion in America loses its broad appeal for one reason or another, there are a whole host of other believers who are at the ready to make their case. More importantly, religious liberty means there are lots of priests, ministers, imams, and rabbis who are there to help form children, counsel parents, and console the elderly. Religious liberty *works*, and it has made American society what it is: imagine where we would be without it. But the village elders usually act like secular fundamentalists, doing everything they can to marginalize faith.

Religious liberty here in the United States and around the world is a passion of mine. So a few years ago I started, and still chair, the Religious Freedom Working Group on Capitol Hill. It brings together religious liberty nongovernmental organizations, religiously oriented public policy groups, and religious leaders from Seventh-day Adventists to Sikhs to Scientologists who are concerned about religious freedom here in the U.S. and around the world. One of the bills I introduced, with Senator John Kerry, is called the Workplace Religious Freedom Act, which would require religious accommodation in the workplace. Communities of faith transmit the values that build strong families and strong communities. Government should be working *with* people of faith, not against them.

Religious groups are virtually unequal in creating huge amounts of social capital. For hundreds of years, people motivated by faith to serve their fellow man provided originally almost all the help there was to the poor and disadvantaged. As Marvin Olasky pointed out in his book *The Tragedy of American Compassion* several years ago, the village elders have replaced these good works with "good" government—usually to the great detriment of the poor, and even more so to their social surroundings, their families, and their neighborhoods. In the mid-1990s, Olasky, Pat Fagan of the Heritage Foundation, and others in the public policy world—together with former Senator Dan Coats from Indiana, former Congressman J. C. Watts from Oklahoma, and me in the political world—put forth a body of legislative proposals and private initiatives to promote civil society in general and faith-based charities in particular. This work coincided with and greatly influenced the Welfare Reform Act of 1996 and the American Community Renewal Act of 2000. Our group fought for and passed legislation like "charitable choice" and Renewal Communities.

Charitable Choice, which Senators John Ashcroft, Dan Coats, Spence Abraham, and I sponsored, was the first counterattack on the village elders' consolidation of power since the Great Society. It permitted federal and state grant-makers to select faith-based charities to deliver welfare-related services to the poor with money the states are given through the Temporary Assistance to Needy Families program—the program that replaced AFDC after 1996. In spite of fierce criticism from the village elders that all this was doing was promoting religion and violating the separation of church and state, the charitable choice concept was expanded to include more social service programs in 1998 (Community Service Block Grant) and 2000 (substance abuse and mental health), with strong bipartisan support.

I must admit that I was at first mystified at the relatively passive attitude the village elders took toward these programs. Granted, many liberal churches supported the concept of charitable choice, and it was about doing good works for the poor with the government still controlling the purse strings, but nevertheless, they were still supporting an idea that *strengthened churches*. It wasn't until 2001, when President Bush launched his faith-based initiative that the mystery was solved. In 2001, the president and House Republicans introduced an expansion of the charitable choice law to include housing and workforce training, so that even more "armies of compassion" would be eligible for social service grants. Now the village elders inside and outside of the Senate ran to the ramparts to fight this radical invasion of religion into the hallowed, secular citadel of the state.

What happened between the late 1990s and 2001? America had elected a president who was actually going to *implement* the 1996, 1998, and 2000 charitable choice laws. Now I understood. The apparent deal struck by the village elders and their village mayor, President Clinton, was that they would not oppose this reasonable appeal to people of faith in our society—but only so long as President Clinton didn't actually implement what he signed into law. From the village elders' perspective it had been perfect: all of the public imagery and none of the "harmful" effect. Now that President Bush was in the White House, however, it was all a different story.

Liberal senators have now effectively blocked any expansion of charitable choice, claiming that it promotes discrimination. I argue that *not* giving money to faith-based organizations to perform social services, services that serve the common good, is the real discrimination. Their newfound argument goes as follows: Under the 1964 Civil Rights Act and subsequent acts, faith-based organization are exempt from provisions that outlaw discrimination in hiring (Congress rightly placed a constitutional right, religious liberty, above an economic right, employment). But that means, for example, that a Muslim drug and alcohol program that uses tenets from the Koran as its treatment methodology would face no penalty if it declined to hire an orthodox Jew. Liberals argue that religious charities should be stripped of these legal protections if the charity is a recipient of any federal funds. Religious charities would then be required to hire people who do not share their mission or moral vision.

By the way, the village elders do not make similar objections with liberal groups that are funded with federal dollars. For example, the World Wildlife Fund—which has received more than $100 million in federal support since 1996—hires, logically enough, employees who support its position on environmental conservation. Planned Parenthood—the recipient of millions of federal dollars each year—hires those who share its views. Only religious groups, it seems, must be forced by law to hire those who do not share their views.

President Bush has taken regulatory actions to ensure that public funds are used for public purposes; that there is no proselytizing undertaken with federal funds; that government-funded social services are available to beneficiaries regardless of their religion; and that receipt of public social services cannot be conditioned on a beneficiary's willingness to participate in worship activities. In addition, after eight years of experience with charitable choice, there has not been a *single* complaint against a charitable entity for employment discrimination. Yet still the liberals protest.

President Bush has aggressively implemented charitable choice throughout the federal government. I plan on pushing for further expansions that will include housing and workforce programs. And these expansions will include hiring protections for these religious organizations. For the success of any organization, those best qualified to advance a unified vision and to accomplish the organization's mission are the ones who are qualified to be hired. That's not discrimination; it's common sense.

One of the legitimate concerns of some conservatives with respect to government/faith-based partnerships is the ability of the government to undermine the religious character of the faith-based partner. While we have not yet seen this in the area of charitable choice, the village elders have launched an offensive on other fronts against faith-based organizations.

Catholic Charities (CC) is the charitable arm of the Catholic Church. Each diocese in the country has a CC that is under the control of the local bishop. The bishop directs CC to carry out one of the core missions of the church—serving the poor. In California, liberals sued CC under a California statute that requires all employers to provide contraceptive coverage in their healthcare plans. The Catholic Church teaches that contraception is intrinsically wrong and a serious sin. A recipient of government funds long before charitable choice, Catholic Charities claimed it was a religious employer exempted under the law. The California Supreme Court, however, ruled that CC is not a religious employer exempt from the law. The court said that while CC offered social services to the general public as part of a religious mission, it was not preaching Catholic values.

Yet, if CC *were* trying to inculcate Catholic values or refused to serve people of other faiths it would violate its government social service contract. This is called a Catch-22. In addition, the judges of the California Supreme Court are telling the Catholic Church that ministering to the poor is *not* a core value of the church. I am sure most Catholics would be shocked to hear that.

The sole dissenting judge was Janice Rodgers Brown, one of President Bush's nominees for an appellate federal judgeship who was filibustered by Senate Democrats in the 108th Congress. She said in her dissent, "This is such a crabbed and constricted view of religion that it would define the ministry of Jesus Christ as a secular activity."

So why would the village elders take up this cause against a do-good organization like Catholic Charities? Before I answer that, let me add to the question. Why did the village elders try, among many other things, to require Catholic hospitals to counsel for and provide abortions, require orthodox religious universities to fund gay and lesbian groups on campus, require religious organizations to provide spousal benefits to all unmarried couples, and bar even the Boy Scouts from public schools and public funds?

Why would such "tolerant" people as the village elders try so intolerantly to force their agenda on religious institutions? The answer is clear. Religious institutions stand between them and the individuals they seek to fashion in their own image.

Religious organizations nurture and support the traditional family against the onslaught from our popular culture, government, and academia. They teach right from wrong and selfless service to others. In other words, they are a threat to the rule of the village elders, and so, like the traditional family, they must be either co-opted or eliminated.

Congress has sat silently by while the courts have slowly strangled religious freedom for faiths that have the audacity to proclaim that there is a truth and we are bound to follow it—religions like evangelical Protestantism, orthodox Catholicism, and orthodox Judaism, in particular. Even as some liberals talk up the importance of intermediate institutions in our society, they do everything in their power to marginalize religious associations, and failing that, to seize control of them so that they can be re-engineered to serve the agendas of the village elders. We must stop them. Not only must we find ways of providing public funds to these vital intermediate groups serving public purposes, we must protect churches and their ministries from persecution. Religious liberty demands it. If the village elders win on this one, the greatest generator of social capital in America after the family will be bound and gagged by state power.

XII

Where Social Capital Is Weakest

I said at the beginning that one of the major reasons I wrote this book is my concern that my party hasn't crafted a comprehensive policy to address the needs of low-income families, especially African-American and Hispanic low-income families. The other party's policy was for government to take care of the poor. It has failed. They know it has failed, too, so they have added a new wrinkle on top of the old policy: damage control. By that I mean a whole new round of government programs to deal with the damage caused by the Great Society programs of the 1960s and the liberal culture that followed. These programs are failing too. It is time for conservatives to make a difference here.

Everything I have been discussing so far will especially help these low-income families. The policies and trends that have so weakened the American family have especially harmed low-income families because they live in communities where social and economic capital are in very short supply. But there is one issue that tears down social capital in African-American communities which is unique: the high percentage of black men involved in the criminal justice system. The statistics are worth repeating. According to the Department of Justice, a black man has a 28.5 percent chance of going to prison at some point in his life. In 2003, an estimated 12 percent of African-American men ages 20 to 34 were in prison on any given day.

Think about what that means: fewer fathers, fewer husbands, and fewer male breadwinners. And when many of them come out of prison—those who were serving time for a felony—it means lots of men who are never allowed to vote. I realize not much more than half of all Americans vote in any given election, but imagine if you were *barred* from voting. What if it were illegal for you to vote for the rest of your life? No matter how much success you achieved, no matter how much you gave back to society, you would always feel like a second-class citizen.

That's the message far too many ex-offenders are getting. I believe strongly in the power of messages. Advertising is built on it. Politics is built on it. We need to change this message. I believe that after five years, if they stay away from criminal activity, convicted felons should get back their right to vote. We punish these men by sending them to prison. We pray that they experience rehabilitation and, if they do, we should grant them forgiveness. Forgiveness is *powerful*—it brings great power to heal. But right now, in many states, we're withholding our forgiveness, because we never fully welcome the ex-felon back into society.

As my friend Chuck Colson has counseled for years, we also must intervene before the prisoner returns to society. Most men in prison have never had a role model for being a good father. They don't know *how* to be a good father and husband. Data show that approximately 40 percent of prison inmates grew up only with their mother and about 14 percent more didn't live with either of their biological parents as children. How can we expect these men to form successful families without help? The good news—and I'm not trying to be funny when I say this—is that this is truly a captive audience. And most of these men really do want to change their lives.

The village elders have focused their efforts at prison reform on improving the quality of life within prison, for example, by providing exercise facilities and weight rooms, or perhaps education (even college degrees) and training. I assume these are the sorts of things that the village elders themselves would want if they found themselves behind bars. But this attempt to help individual prisoners has mostly resulted in stronger, cleverer criminals heading back to the streets. In other words, it has failed. What Chuck Colson has shown works is focusing on teaching *right and wrong*, building character, fixing that brokenness with the healing power of God, and putting meaning and hope back into lives. He also helps reconnect prisoners with their children and families, and his organization, Prison Fellowship Ministries, teaches them responsible fatherhood. Connections to the family and church and support groups—social capital—have proven to help men avoid more criminal activity when they get out of prison.

Charles Stuart is the Executive Director for Incarcerated Fatherhood Programming at the National Fatherhood Initiative. "These men in prison aren't closed to learning," he says. "They don't understand what the norm is. It's not how they were raised for twenty years—committing crime, being abusive or neglectful of your children. The norm is to go to work every day and to be respectful to the mother of your child. These men don't know that the way to discipline a child is not to take them out back and beat them but to use a time out. But when we teach them these things—and we use their own peers in the prison as the best teachers—they get it."

Stuart's program, called Long Distance Dads, currently

works in about 30 states and 130 prisons. When inside prison, the men in this program learn about anger management and how to be consistent with their children, communicate and listen, and relate to their children's mother(s). "We give them the tools and information they need to come out of prison and live the norm and survive in the community," says Charles.

Pat Nolan is another man who works with men in prison. The difference is that Pat was once in prison himself. "I was a member of the state assembly in California. I was the Republican leader of the assembly. We were a hard-core group of guys. Long before Newt Gingrich had the Contract for America we had the Agenda of Opportunity. My office was raided by federal agents, along with several others. Contributions were made to my campaign through a company that was part of a sting. I ended up pleading guilty to one count of racketeering. I spent 25 months in federal prison and four months in a halfway house."

When in prison, Pat was allowed to go into the community one time—accompanied by a guard, of course—to give his testimony at a local event. Chuck Colson heard him speak. Chuck knew that Pat was his guy—the man to head the Justice Fellowship, the criminal justice reform arm of Prison Fellowship Ministries.

"We work with government officials trying to get them to look at crime differently," Pat says.

> It's what we call restorative justice, a different perspective on crime. At its root, crime is a moral problem. The offender has done something to harm somebody else, he has broken the relationship with the community and he has broken God's heart, because that's what sin is. God wants us to respect each other and live in peace. The criminal justice system should address the harms caused by the offender—harm to the victim, the com-

munity, the offender himself and his family, and to God. The offender needs to restore his relationship with God, restore the victim hopefully to health, pay restitution, and help restore peace in the community. That is why we call it restorative justice."

In four states—Texas, Iowa, Kansas, and Minnesota—Prison Fellowship runs the InnerChange Freedom Initiative. The states contract with Prison Fellowship to take over an entire wing of a prison. "The state provides the prison, the guards, the food, and the uniforms. We provide all the programming," says Nolan.

It's a 24-hour-a-day program that runs for the last 12 to 18 months of a prisoner's sentence, and then at least another six months after the prisoner is released. "It's an explicitly Christian program. However, we accept inmates of all faiths," says Pat. "They have to agree to participate fully in the program. There are no special privileges for these guys. In fact, there are fewer privileges for guys in our wing. They have no TV during the week and they aren't allowed to smoke, for example."

Inmates must volunteer for the program. And then the program must also accept them. "Originally, guards viewed this as 'hug-a-thug,'" Pat says. "Now it's the most popular site for guards because the impact is so dramatic. We teach the inmates that no matter how horrible their crime is, if they sincerely repent and turn their lives over to Christ, make amends to their victims, and work at having a different worldview when they are released, they can lead healthy, productive, law-abiding lives. That gives them hope. Most inmates don't have hope. That's why two out of three will end up back in the system."

But that is not the case with inmates in the InnerChange Freedom Initiative (IFI). "Every day," reports Pat,

> the inmates are up at five in the morning. They have a worship service at 5:30, then chow. After that, Bible study for two hours, then a break, and then educational programs. They have lunch,

and then they work. They work in the community if they are eligible; otherwise, they do work around the prison. If we can't find them private-sector jobs, they work for Habitat for Humanity. It's a prisoner-only project. It gives the prisoners a great sense of pride when they complete the project. It also shows the community that inmates can pay back. After they work, they have dinner, and after dinner they meet with their mentors from the outside.

Every prisoner in the program is guaranteed at least one mentor. These are volunteers from local churches. Pat believes that one of the great benefits to prisoners is the bond they build with their mentors. "The mentors walk out of the prison with them. They help the prisoners with important decisions. Almost all of the time, the IFI prisoners have a job when released. If not, the mentor helps develop a plan for getting a job. They help get a home church lined up for the prisoner. The mentor is there if the released prisoner runs into any difficulty."

Pat hopes that each mentor will stay involved with his former inmate forever. The mentor guarantees he will follow the prisoner for at least six months, and the prisoner must agree to that as well. For most, though, the relationship lasts much longer. "It's a loving, moral adult who walks alongside them who makes all the difference in the world."

The results are impressive, to say the least. Dr. Byron Johnson of Baylor University recently completed a study of the Texas InnerChange Freedom Initiative. He found that the two-year post-release reincarceration rate among graduates of the program was 8 percent, compared to 20.3 percent for a matched comparison group.

We need to expand this program into the federal prisons. But let me assure you: the village elders will cry about the separation of church and state. Those are words that never appear in the Constitution, by the way, but are used as if the founders handed them down on stone tablets. We must fight the village elders here, because the church may be the only thing that can save these men's lives. And it is only by saving these men's lives, giving them the tools they need to be good fathers, husbands, employees, and neighbors, that we can have any hope of restoring social capital among those poor neighborhoods and families where it is weakest.

PHILOSOPHERS SAY THAT man is a social animal. Scientists talk about human sociality. Historians observe man's pattern of organizing families and communities. I would say simply that we need each other. As much as the village elders would like to convince you that you can go it alone, you can't—and even if you could, you most likely wouldn't like where you found yourself going. No, we need each other. But since, as I will discuss later, we aren't born virtuous, we have to work on that and be worked upon. We have to open ourselves up to the needs of others in our communities.

Compared to the rest of the world, America remains rich in social capital. Tocqueville would still notice a huge contrast between Europe and America, for example. But some of the liberal ideas that have devastated social capital in Europe over the last century have taken root here among the Bigs, and they will continue to try to drag the rest of America along with them, tearing apart the ties that bind in the name of their abstract freedom—under the supervision of the benevolent government, of course.

Sometimes these days the deck seems stacked against us. But as long as we concentrate on protecting traditional families and the institutions that nurture and support them—community organizations, and most importantly religious ministries and congregations—we can be certain that we have laid the groundwork for the replenishment of social capital. We can be assured that we are being good stewards of the ties that bind, which are the precondition of the common good. As our founders made clear in the Preamble to the Constitution: this task is up to all of us.

Part Three

THE ROOTS OF PROSPERITY

XIII

Abundant Families in the Land of Plenty

Our founding fathers understood that healthy families and a strong economy go hand in hand, each reinforcing the other. When asked to explain why the colonists in America married more often and had more children than their European counterparts, Benjamin Franklin replied that land is so "plentiful and so cheap that a labouring man, that understands husbandry, can in a short time save money enough to purchase a piece of new land . . . whereon he may subsist a family."

In other words, Americans weren't afraid to marry and start families because they were confident they could pass on to their children enough wherewithal that their children could build lives of prosperity on their own. As a result, Franklin noticed, "marriages in America are more general, and more generally early, than in Europe," and they produced an abundance of children. The greatness of this country, Franklin believed, would be found in the economic realities that made possible the "cause of the generation of multitudes, by the encouragement they afford to marriage."

The founder of the modern science of economics, Adam Smith, also linked prosperity to the strength of marriage and fertility of the family. He connected the creation of wealth directly to the creation of families with children. As he wrote in *The Wealth of Nations*:

> The most decisive mark of the prosperity of any country is the increase in its number of inhabitants. . . . The value of children is the greatest of all encouragements to marriage. We cannot, therefore, wonder that the people in America should generally marry very young.

Both Franklin and Smith were making the same point: the health of the family is tied to economic opportunity. The decision to marry and start a family is a sign of hope for and confidence in the future, and one of the foundations for such confidence must be an economy that *works*—for families. After all, what else is wealth for?

The reverse is also true, I believe: strong families are the basis of lasting economic prosperity. I recognize, of course, that both Franklin and Smith were writing at a time when the vast majority of people tilled the soil to earn their living and children were welcome, in part, because they could help work the family farm. But the basic equation Franklin and Smith were talking about really hasn't changed—as the dire demographic problems of Europe make plain. New human beings aren't simply new mouths to feed: they are new hands to work and produce, new minds to invent and discover. Children are assets, not liabilities. And just as there is no better way to raise children than in a healthy family, so there simply is no better mechanism for building, conserving, and distributing economic wealth than the natural family.

Our very word "economics" is derived from the Greek word *oikonomia*, meaning household management—the business side of family life. When we think about our task of stewardship with respect to economic capital, therefore, the question we need to ask is: how well are our economic policies doing in providing a basis for family economic security and prosperity? America does not have its economic house in order if it is not a nation of prosperous families: that's the real bottom line.

Ever since Ronald Reagan entered the White House in 1981, conservatives have been consistent and clear about what economic policies broadly promote a prosperous America and therefore strengthen family life. Whether you call it Reaganomics, supply-side economics, or something else, conservatives believe in lower taxes; common-sense, predictable regulation; free trade; and less litigation. They believe in the power of markets more than they do the power of government: that is, they wish to promote an economy based on freedom and opportunity. Conservatives believe, and for the most part I agree, that the marketplace, while a competitive and often brutal arena, is the fairest way to reward people for their labor and ingenuity. Free markets are also the basis of all real and lasting wealth creation.

So, at the macro-level, government's role is not to pick winners and losers among business sectors; its role is not to micromanage corporate decisions; and its role is not to substitute for the private responsibilities and initiatives of a free people. In the first instance, government's role in the economy is to see to it that private property rights are secured by law—so that private owners can be certain that what is theirs is theirs. Next, it is government's responsibility to ensure that our currency is sound—since legal tender is a public trust, a promise—and to guard against inflation, which robs savers of the hard-won value of their thrift. Government also has a role in maintaining confidence in the economy by policing against fraudulent business practices and encouraging the transparency of accounting procedures. These are the elementary responsibilities of government in a free society, but some of them—such as our safeguards against

fraud—are also the hard-won achievements of previous generations: they are part of our patrimony.

The kinds of responsibilities I've just described rarely are a
subject of family economic concern—though if government
fails in any of them, they immediately become matters of the
first importance. It is a tribute to the economic systems past
generations have built up in our land that these matters are so
rarely an issue for America's families. Imagine how different
things would be if, when deciding on a bank for your family
to use, you had to consider not only convenient branch loca-
tions and attractive interest rates, but whether or not the bank-
ers would abscond with your money. Imagine not being able
to take out a mortgage to buy a home because you didn't have
clear title to the property. And how different would things be
if inflation threatened to wipe out your whole lifetime's savings in a single year or a single month! In America, these macro-
responsibilities are discharged largely by independent agencies
such as the Federal Reserve and the SEC; Congress plays an
oversight role.

But there is a macro-policy area where Congress plays a
direct role in economics: taxes. Nothing Congress does impacts
American families more concretely than our tax policies. I see
taxes for all but the wealthiest Americans as a freedom issue.
The more government taxes someone, the less they are able to
take care of themselves and their families; the less they can invest in their businesses; the less they can give to others in the
community; the less free they are. It should come as no surprise
that I believe in keeping taxes low, and thereby, freedom high.
In my fifteen years in the House and Senate, I have never voted
for a bill that increased taxes. And of course I supported both
of President Bush's tax reductions that successfully stimulated a
faltering economy. I strongly support keeping marginal rates

for individuals and businesses as well as capital gains and dividend taxes at their current levels, or driving them lower.

America will create opportunities for all if we keep taxes on income and savings low, have common sense, predictable regulation, and reduce the cost and inefficiency of a runaway litigation system that rewards a handful of lawyers at the expense of the common good. And all these factors are particularly important for small businesses and entrepreneurs. Big business after all is one of the Bigs—it can absorb all of these costs, exacted by other Bigs, much better than small businesses can. If the ladder of success is going to reach the poor communities of our country, then there have to be rungs at the bottom of the ladder. High taxes on capital, government mandates and regulations that add unnecessary costs, and litigation that deters investment all work together to saw off the first four rungs of the ladder, making things difficult for small businesses everywhere—and nearly impossible for small businesses in poor communities. We have to grow businesses in all our communities if we want all Americans to participate in the American dream. And that means, as I will discuss later, that we may have to do a little extra for businesses in our most downtrodden communities.

Beyond marginal rates, we must also do more to help families, particularly families that are raising children. As I mentioned before, one reason parents are not spending enough time with their children is because of the increased taxes we have imposed on the average American family with children. The second earner in a family makes on average about 25 percent of what the primary earner brings in. If we look at the increase in taxes on the average family since 1950, it amounts to almost 25 percent of total household income. In other words, working spouses allow the average family to bring in as much net income, after taxes, as the average family in the 1950s.

Justice Marshall once wrote, "The power to tax is the power to destroy." Someone also once said, "You get what you pay for." Working families are the driving engines of our whole economy. If we really value strong, healthy families as the foundation of our society, that fact should be reflected in the tax code. First, we should not penalize two people when they get married, as until recently we did: we need to repeal permanently the marriage penalty. We should be supporting the vital work of raising families with higher deductions for children, as well as a further increase in and indexing of the child tax credit, and a slower phase-out of the credit for bigger families. Strong families are the basis of the common good; all Americans have an interest in recognizing the contributions families make by giving them a fair break on their taxes.

LIBERALS ARE USUALLY HOSTILE to pro-family tax and economic policies. To them, families are a sort of "special interest." There is a paradox here. On the one hand, when it comes to giving working families a break in the tax code, the liberals complain and say: "It's your own private affair if you marry and have children; pay for them yourself." On the other hand, when liberals see children in single-parent households on welfare, they say: "Children are a public responsibility; we need to help these people with taxpayer dollars." (After all, "It takes a village," etc.) So, on the one hand, the children of taxpaying families are a "private" interest, while the children of non-taxpaying families are a "public" interest.

The reason for this paradox, as I have argued before, is that for liberals only individuals are "real." To them, the family is nothing but a social construct. Thus, in these two cases, the liberals do not "see" children in two different social settings, intact families and broken homes: they see only children with good incomes and children with little or no income. They don't bother to ask why it is that more often than not the children in the intact home have good incomes and those in the broken home little or no income: they simply take that as a given.

What is more, for the village elders the traditional family stands between the Bigs and individual children. Therefore, liberal economic policy tries as much as possible to reach past the family in order to make sure each individual gets his or her entitlements. Recall, for example, that the entitlements introduced under the auspices of the Great Society programs had the effect of marginalizing the importance of the family and family obligations. Their goal was equality—ultimately, Equal No-Fault Freedom. And that is what they had written into the welfare state. Of course, to fund the welfare state, you needed to levy heavy taxes on other people, particularly the middle- and upper-income earners, which reduced *their* freedom: but what liberals are after is equality of result, not fair compensation or equality of opportunity.

In their obsessive pursuit of Equal No-Fault Freedom, with few exceptions the village elders have not been especially concerned about the effects of their welfare policies on families. When studies show that their welfare policies lead to the breakdown of the nuclear family and the creation of a dependent underclass, the village elders shrug. It's almost as if they think: "What does it matter, when it takes a 'village'—a government bureaucracy—to raise a child anyway?"

Most Americans, however, and conservatives in particular, believe the natural family is something to be respected, protected, and nurtured. We know that any decent village must be composed of strong families, helping each other, and that strong families, as a vital component in the formation of stable communities, are necessary for the maintenance of a strong and prosperous America. Therefore, the family must be the central object of government policy, especially in those impoverished communities throughout the country where the traditional family has disintegrated.

Traditional liberal welfare policy is all about transferring income to individuals in such a way that their dependence on government is increased and their dependence on family decreased. We need to change these safety net programs so that they lead not only to independence from the government but also create incentives for the formation and maintenance of families. The ultimate measure of our country's economic success is not the poverty rate or the Gross Domestic Product; the ultimate measure of our success is the number of thriving families who are getting by and getting ahead on their own wherewithal, their own economic capital.

The first ingredient in the conservative formula to build up economic capital for families, especially among the least of our brothers and sisters, is *work*. That is why the 1996 welfare reform legislation required all able-bodied people to work. Without work there is no hope for success. It is the foundation of conservative policy. Second, the goal of government policy must be changed from income maintenance to wealth creation. Third, we must instill in the disadvantaged an entrepreneurial spirit through economic and financial literacy. Fourth, we must use smart private-sector investing to turn around poor communities. And finally, we must use faith-based and community organizations to provide the support families and communities need to make economic success a real prospect.

XIV

Economic Responsibility

B efore being completely revamped by the Republican Congress in 1996, our welfare system was successful at nothing except maintaining poverty. It really demonstrated the complete failure of relying on a policy of income distribution, of focusing solely on giving people money and expecting nothing in return—as opposed to providing the mix of opportunities and obligations necessary to build a future.

Ron Haskins of the Brookings Institution is one of the nation's leading experts on welfare and welfare reform. Before Brookings, he worked at the White House, and before that, he worked for me on the House Ways and Means Committee, where he taught me more about welfare policy than I thought there was to know, and helped craft the 1994 welfare reform bill that was part of the Contract with America. Without a doubt he was the greatest intellectual force behind the 1996 Welfare Reform Act. Here is what he taught me about the world of American welfare prior to 1996.

First, studies consistently showed that welfare was anti-work. The higher the benefits and the easier it was to get on welfare, the less likely it was that low-income single mothers would work.

This shows up time and time again in the research literature, so consistently that it is beyond debate.

Second, pre-1996 welfare was an unlimited entitlement that demanded nothing, absolutely nothing, of the recipient. It is interesting to reflect back to when welfare first started in the late 1930s. There was debate at the time over whether the program, at the time called to Aid to Dependent Children (it would be quite some time before it was changed to Aid to Families with Dependent Children), should include never-married mothers. Many policy experts argued that the program should only cover children of widowed or deserted women. They feared the unintended social consequences if government began paying never-married mothers. Others argued that children of never-married mothers had to be covered, since every *individual* needed coverage: family norms didn't matter. The liberal individualists won the policy debate. But the folks who feared unintended consequences turned out to be right, as the destruction of traditional sexual mores that began in the 1960s and the resulting decline of the natural family have made alarmingly clear.

The so-called sexual liberation of the late 1960s took hold in society, I believe, because of two principal factors: the legalization of abortion, which started in the late 1960s and culminated with *Roe v. Wade* in 1973, and—for low-income women— the availability of abortion plus the financial safety net provided by government welfare. The data are clear that welfare enabled out-of-wedlock childbirth (because the financial and, over time, social consequences—i.e., shame—were not as devastating) and, conversely, made marriage unnecessary. "About two-thirds of all the studies conducted had at least one correlation between a measure of how tough the welfare system is and illegitimacy," says Haskins. "The more generous the benefits and the easier to get on to the welfare rolls, the greater the impact was shown to

be on decreasing marriage and increasing illegitimate births."
Welfare pre-1996 was all about subtle economic incentives that
not only enabled women not to work and to have children out
of wedlock, but also gradually removed the social stigma attached to such behavior.

The fact that entitlement welfare failed is beyond dispute. In
1968, about three years into the Great Society programs, total social welfare spending in the United States was $226 billion (in in-
flation-adjusted dollars). By 1990, it had risen to $614 billion.

So what did we get for this increase? Poverty maintenance
and family dissolution, that's what. You could only call this effort a success if, when we first started in 1965, President Lyndon
Johnson had stood up and said, "Today, we embark on a program that will guarantee that 30 years from now, the percentage of American children living in poverty will be about exactly
the same as it is today! A program that will guarantee that during the 1970s, 1980s, and until 1995, black child poverty will
be stuck at about 40 percent! Today, we launch an endeavor
that will ensure that the percentage of American adults living in
poverty in 1995 will be almost a full percentage point higher
than the percentage living below the poverty line in 1966! And
the best part is, to achieve this remarkable success will only cost
this country trillions of dollars!"

Of course, President Johnson didn't say that. We didn't start
off to spend an unfathomable amount of money in order to
keep an unfathomable number of people stuck in poverty. But
that's what we did. In 1965, 21 percent of all American children under the age of 18 lived in poverty. Over the years it
fluctuated some, up and down, but in 1995, the percentage was—
20.8 percent.

In 1974, the percentage of black children living in poverty
was 39.8 percent. Between then and 1995, it never again dipped

below 40 percent, and it stood at 41.9 percent in 1995.

Imagine if President Johnson went on to say: "There is more. As a result of this great new approach to poverty, this great income-transfer experiment, out-of-wedlock births will skyrocket and fewer low-income people will marry!" He didn't say that, either. But that too is what happened.

From 1960 to 1995, the percentage of births occurring out of wedlock among the total population rose sharply. In 1960, 5.3 percent of all births in this country were to unmarried mothers. By 1995, the figure was 32.2 percent. For whites, the percentage rose from 2.3 percent to 25.3 percent. Among blacks, it rose from 21.6 percent to 69.9 percent.

Pick a number. Pick a statistic. Pick a social impact. What you get is all the same. Welfare, prior to the enactment of reform in 1996, was a disaster. Based on the condescending belief that poor people could not or would not work, it provided nothing but an income transfer. This was billed as a "humanitarian" project, but there was nothing humanitarian about the intergenerational poverty it maintained, or the destruction of the natural family it brought about, or the way in which it evaporated hope in our poor communities. In terms of the human lives wrecked, human potential wasted, marriages destroyed or discouraged, and children denied a future, it was the greatest social policy debacle in American history.

After the election of 1994, when Republicans took control of the Senate and the House for the first time in 40 years, this dysfunctional welfare system was changed. That change had its roots in a group I chaired when I was a member of the House Ways and Means Committee: the Human Resources Subcommittee, of which I was made ranking minority member in 1993.

How I got to be ranking member of that subcommittee does say a lot, I'm afraid, about how Republicans used to view welfare—and too many still do. Something like five Republican members more senior than I on the committee chose to claim a regular seat on either the Health or Trade subcommittees instead of taking the ranking position (minority chairman) on the Subcommittee on Human Resources. Now, being the chairman or ranking member of a committee or subcommittee is a big deal, coming as it does with additional staff, responsibility, and a title. Yet none of my Republican colleagues saw this subcommittee as particularly important to them or their constituents. So I became the ranking minority member, Ron Haskins took me under his wing, and we sowed the seeds for the fundamental shift in welfare policy that passed in 1996.

I soon hit the road to talk with women on welfare and the people that worked in and around the welfare system in Pennsylvania. The more I learned, the more the whole thing just seemed to make no sense.

You may recall the promise Bill Clinton made when he ran for president in 1992 to "end welfare as we know it." That promise was a central part of his attempt to convince Main Street America that he was not a liberal. But by late 1993 he had introduced a radical health-care proposal, passed tax increases, and tried in various ways to increase welfare spending (remember midnight basketball?). He had all but shelved his plan to reform welfare. Our Minority Whip Newt Gingrich asked me to get together a group of members to draft our own welfare reform bill. The bill we drafted was an integral part of the now famous Contract with America.

When we introduced our bill, the liberals savaged it, calling it cruel, heartless, and mean-spirited. We had actually had the audacity to call for *time limits* on welfare for the *able-bodied*! Not only that, but we wanted to require them to work or else lose their benefits! Despite the criticism, we knew that such measures were necessary if we were to help people get off the tread-mill of government dependency.

The election of 1994 changed the entire landscape of re-form. Our bold proposal became just a starting point for more innovative ideas introduced when that 104th Congress got go-ing—by which time I was in the Senate. Even though I wasn't on the committee of jurisdiction, I began working with the chair-man of the Finance Committee, Bob Packwood, and an infor-mal group he put together to help him craft a new welfare re-form bill. The House had already passed its welfare reform bill when the Senate finally moved a bill out of committee. But the week before the bill was finally scheduled for action on the Sen-ate floor, Chairman Packwood resigned from the Senate. The Republican leader, Bob Dole, needed a new floor manager, and I volunteered to take the helm. Since I was one of the few Re-publican senators who knew anything about welfare, I ended up doing most of the managing of the bill.

That job of welfare reform floor manager remains not just one of my proudest accomplishments in public life, but also one of the most *surreal*. I remember a welfare rights organization that brought busloads of welfare recipients and caseworkers to a church just off Capitol Hill. I was invited to share with them the changes being contemplated in the system. It was like at-tending a dinner party with wolves, and I was the entrée. I walked in the door, down the center aisle, between people shouting and making threatening gestures toward me, up to the pulpit. Capi-tol Police surrounded me, just in case. I wasn't able to finish a single sentence without being interrupted.

This audience of angry people had been stirred up by the village elders. They had been locked in the system for so long that they had become convinced that entitlement welfare was the best they could "hope" for. But beneath the anger there was also fear; these welfare recipients had become frightened of doing something that they had been told all their lives wasn't possible—to become independent, hard-working, productive citizens. In the end, this display of anger was but the ferocious last growl of the victims of the Great Society drug-peddlers, those who had addicted generations of poor Americans to the narcotic of dependency.

So-called welfare rights groups weren't the only ones who raged against our bill. Senator Ted Kennedy opined, "There is a right way and a wrong way to reform welfare. . . . Punishing children is the wrong way. . . . The Senate is on the brink of committing legislative child abuse." And the ranking Democrat on the Ways and Means Committee, Sam Gibbons, spoke for the village elders when he claimed, "This is a cruel piece of legislation. It punishes the children, the innocent children, because of the errors of their parent or parents. It punishes them not just at birth but it punishes some of them for a lifetime, and certainly it punishes others through all of their childhood era. It will deprive them of food, of clothing, of housing, of education, of *love*."

Lets get this straight: the family is the *problem* and the "loving" government is the *answer*? Yes, there are parents who make mistakes, but as we have seen, government dependency is *not* the loving answer.

My chief adversary on the Senate floor, Senator Daniel Patrick Moynihan, was predictably more forthright in defining the situation. He said, "This legislation does not reform Aid to Families with Dependent Children. It simply abolishes it. It terminates the basic federal commitment to support dependent children in hopes of altering the behavior of their mothers."

He was right: that was what we hoped to do. And those hopes were realized, because unlike the village elders, we believe people, including poor people, can change for the better.

Despite the opposition, under the terrific leadership of my successor as chair of the House Human Resources Subcommittee, Clay Shaw of Florida, welfare reform passed. After two vetoes, it was finally signed into law by President Clinton in 1996. It is interesting to note that Wendell Primus, Mary Jo Bane, and Peter Edelman, all liberal senior officials at the Department of Health and Human Resources, resigned in protest when President Clinton signed the bill. And in typical Clinton fashion, immediately after the 1996 elections the president called for the repeal of some of the reforms. These rollbacks were stymied, however, and one of the most important public policy shifts of the past half-century was set in motion.

XV

Work and Human Dignity

It was the power of work that we Republicans insisted on when welfare reform legislation was finally passed in 1996. AFDC was scrapped and replaced with Temporary Assistance for Needy Families (TANF). Recipients were required to work or participate in work-related activities. For the first time, welfare was time limited: no more able-bodied welfare lifers.

Liberals howled. The Urban Institute released a study predicting that the bill would cause 2.6 million persons to fall below the poverty line, and that 1.1 million of those impoverished would be children. There were no jobs for these people, Democrats screamed. But the liberal critics miscalculated a bit.

Yes, welfare reform moved millions off welfare. The rolls have been more than cut in half. But what made this legislation a groundbreaking success was that it moved *parents* off the welfare rolls and into *work*. This reform sparked one of the greatest increases in employment of low-skill workers in United States history. "The Census Bureau shows unequivocally that, in terms of employment, one of the biggest demographic changes and most rapid ever in the history of the United States for any group, is this huge increase in employment by these low-income, poor mothers. And the biggest impact was on never-married mothers," Ron Haskins notes.

There are about one and one-half million mothers who used to be on welfare who are now working. They are working because we required them to work and then thanks to the work incentives we enacted (expansion of the Earned Income Tax Credit, childcare and transportation funding, job training and counseling), low-skill, low-wage mothers were financially better off working than being on welfare. It was almost that simple. And once they got off the dependency treadmill and into the workplace, we made sure the support was there to make work *work* for them.

Research has shown that in every state in the union, a mother working half time at minimum wage is still better off than if she were on welfare. And these women aren't making minimum wage ($5.15 per hour). They are averaging somewhere around $8 per hour.

If you look at the income data for single-mother-headed families starting in about 1993, it looks like a big "X." Income from food stamps, housing assistance, and welfare payments is a diagonal line heading down. Income from wages and earnings, plus the Earned Income Tax Credit (EITC), is a diagonal line heading up. And overall, these families are better off in constant dollars by 20 to 25 percent.

The village elders in Congress, who refuse to accept that they were wrong, always dismiss this success story by crediting the booming economy of the late 1990s: in their minds it was all a historical fluke. Wrong again. If the success of welfare reform was due to the roaring economy of the 1990s, then we should have seen welfare caseloads going down after the recession ended in 1991, before we enacted welfare reform. But the caseload had in fact exploded, increasing every year from 1989 to 1993 (from 3.77 to 4.98 million people), even when the economy rebounded. It began to decline in 1994 mostly because of welfare reform efforts undertaken by the states. We also should have seen caseloads rising again during the recent recession, which began in March 2001. While the caseload did rise slightly during the fall of 2001, by April 2002 the number of families was still lower than the previous April by 34,698.

Furthermore, groundbreaking research by June E. O'Neill (the Democratic former director of the Congressional Budget Office) and M. Anne Hill shows that half or more of the drop in welfare rolls after 1996 was due to the policy changes made by welfare reform. Less than a fifth was due to the overall economy.

But for some liberals that's *still* not enough. They cannot accept that having people get up each day and work is good and changes lives. They claim that all we are doing is putting people in dead-end jobs. Their doctrine of No-Fault Freedom leads them to believe that a person can't truly be free if she is in a job that is "going nowhere." Never mind the traditional view that all work is ennobling if done well, or that an individual can only perform the jobs for which she has the necessary skills. According to liberals, every person deserves a "living wage" regardless of her contribution to a given enterprise.

Prior to 1996, the village elders asked the American people to pay for programs that fed, housed, clothed, and provided free medical care to mothers who were not working. Now these proponents of No-Fault Freedom believe that taxpayers should pay for four years of college for those who cannot get "good" jobs, even as most American working parents struggle to put their kids through college. I am all for providing women on welfare with basic training so that they can take entry-level jobs, but beyond that I believe that they should provide for their education under the same circumstances as everyone else—through a combination of financial aid, loans, savings, hard work, and sacrifice. In other words, they must earn it.

Liberals, on the other hand, want to amend the welfare reform law so that tax dollars can be used to pay for the tuition of welfare recipients who want to go to college for four years. And not only do they want to pay for college for people on welfare, they also want to count going to college as a work-related activity.

But the notion that college education is a cost-effective way to help poor, low-skill, unmarried mothers with high school diplomas or GEDs move up the economic ladder is just wrong: both according to common sense, and according to social science research.

When we pushed the welfare reform law through in 1996 we were purposefully heavy on work and light on education. That's because education and training programs have not been shown to lead to job advancement for mothers on welfare. Data show that welfare recipients who are put in jobs see their earnings increase twice as fast over five years as welfare recipients who are put in education programs before going into work. For low-skill jobs, employers want people who have proven they can show up for work on time, work a full day, handle real-life work experiences, and deal with a boss and fellow employees. Remember when you were looking for that first job, and all your prospective employers wanted someone with experience instead? As a result of TANF, welfare clients are getting the experience and know-how employers want. Job experience is the key to future advancement and opportunity.

Not only did welfare reform improve the economic lot of welfare recipients—which of course helped keep families together, contrary to liberal predictions—it strengthened families in other ways as well.

For example, after a steady decline for many years, since

1996 the number of African-American families headed by a married mother and father has *increased* by about 520,000. In 1994, the year states began reforming welfare, the birth rate of unmarried teenage girls peaked at 45.8 children born per 1,000 girls. The rate has dropped every year since, and in 2001 it stood at 37 per 1,000. For white teenage girls there was a drop from 35.8 in 1994 to 31.3 per 1,000 in 2001.

For black unmarried teenagers the drop was dramatic, from 99.3 per 1,000 in 1994 to 69.9 in 2001. In addition, the percentage of out-of-wedlock births among all blacks dropped between 1995 and 2000 for the first time since the early 1950s. Changing expectations for young girls from poor homes from dependency to hard work and a five-year time-limit on benefits changed behavior for the better.

Statistics are telling, but nothing tells the story like the young mother who spoke to me at a hearing on the progress we had made with welfare reform. She recounted that when she got her first paycheck, her children were unusually excited to go to the store. When she asked them why, they said that they couldn't wait to go to the checkout line and not feel shame as people stared at them for using their food stamps. Self-respect is being restored.

Another young man told me that he had gained renewed admiration for his mother for holding it all together—her job, their house, and her children. He never thought she could do it. Respect for others is being restored.

Finally, there is Billy Jo Morton. When I was sworn into the Senate in 1995, I decided that since I was going to take an active role in reforming welfare I had better see how it works firsthand. So I immediately hired five people on welfare, about 10 percent of my staff, to work in my Pennsylvania offices. Billy Jo worked for me in her first job off welfare in my Harrisburg office. She told me that until she was forced to move off the rolls she thought she was stuck with two kids at home and no chance for a better life. Billy Jo was a great employee. After a while, we provided her a flexible enough schedule that she could go to community college to pick up some college credits part-time. There were some bumps along the way, but after a few years she moved on to something better. She was offered a scholarship to finish her degree, which she did, in education. She is now working as a teacher. Hope is being restored.

This is what happens when you have enough faith in everybody to rise to take responsibility for their lives and to make the right choices. With welfare reform, the government stopped enabling destructive behavior. We changed the paradigm for unmarried women: having children no longer means life-long government support, but rather (as it should) work and sacrifice.

Recall for a minute those poverty figures I mentioned earlier: they changed too, but not in the way the Urban Institute or Rep. Charles Rangel predicted. Congressman Rangel had said our bill "will devastate programs for the poorest among us, especially our children," and that it was "a moral outrage and an affront to the basic tenets of every religion. . . . The bill is the most radical and mean-spirited attack against the poor that I [have] witnessed." Now the percentage of all American children living in poverty was, at the time of his statement (1995), 20.8 percent. By 2001, it had dropped to 16.3 percent. For black children, the figure was 41.9 percent in 1995. In 2002 it stood at 30.2 percent, the lowest figure ever recorded.

It's worth dwelling on this last fact. This conservative approach, which thinks in terms of families instead of mere individuals and puts work and responsibility first—this approach that was and still is condemned by every national liberal organization that purports to represent the interest of blacks—

lowered black poverty among children to its lowest level ever. Is the national leadership of the NAACP paying attention? Many of these national leaders, unlike many of their members, may see but not believe because they are liberals first, Democrats second, and advocates for African-Americans only because it gives them cachet with other liberals and Democrats.

There's only one conclusion to draw from all this. Before 1996 welfare was a mammoth federal income-transfer program that, while it was certainly not designed to do so, acted as a huge barrier between low-income families and the U.S. economy. Our economy had the jobs for unmarried women on welfare. The problem was, the liberal welfare programs neither encouraged nor required poor mothers to get anywhere near those jobs—until we pushed through welfare reform.

I GAVE YOU A FEW anecdotes earlier, but this story will give you a better understanding of what has happened since 1996. It is the story of Michelle Turner.

Michelle came to work for us in 1996 as a staff assistant in Philadelphia. Prior to that, she had been on and off welfare for about five years. She had left home as a teenager, mostly because she never got along with her father. She ended up living with a man who would be the father of her first two children, both girls.

"He never actually hit me," she says today. "But he put his hands on me. He'd grab me, threaten me. There was shoving, name-calling, verbal abuse. He was cheating, doing the whole thing. I remember sitting on the bed one day in the afternoon. I knew he would be home from work in about 15 minutes. And my hand started visibly shaking because the stress was so bad. When I saw that, I packed up my two daughters and left."

Michelle ended up in a Philadelphia shelter for recovering substance abusers—something she wasn't, but it was the only place she could go. "I decided to stay there until I could afford my own place. As a means of getting out of the building and off welfare, I took a class at Drexel University in automated office training, and then fixed up my résumé, which wasn't too hard because I had some college.

"I just had to get off welfare. The people at the welfare office who would give you the check, their attitude was that it was their money. They would talk to you in such a demeaning manner. Plus, it wasn't enough to live on.

"So I ended up getting an internship at the People's Emergency Center, a domestic abuse shelter, as part of their welfare-to-work program."

From there, Michelle took a job as a staff assistant in my office—in her words, she became "a glorified receptionist." Soon, she became a caseworker and eventually she became our Director of Constituent Services. She's been married since the spring of 2000, giving birth to a third daughter. In 2003, after nine years, she left our office to take a job at Drexel, where she is the administrative assistant for a surgeon. She and her husband just bought a new house.

When asked how her life would have been different if she had stayed on welfare instead of getting a job, she quickly answers, "I would probably be married, but I probably would have repeated what I had found myself falling into—an abusive relationship. I never would have ended up working in a Senate office, and never would have had the confidence to get a good husband and buy a house. I would have ended up in some dead end."

The power of work, and people who believed in her, gave Michelle Turner the break she needed. She did the rest herself.

XVI

Wealth and Ownership

Earlier, I discussed an important next step in welfare reform, the building of social capital in poor communities through the renewal of fatherhood and marriage. Along with that step must come another—a transition in government's role from one in which it does little more than help the poor keep their heads above water in a turbulent sea to one in which it helps them to swim to safer shores. In part, that transition requires changing the focus of welfare from income maintenance to wealth creation.

As we have seen, the village elders' welfare policy concentrates on transferring income via government bureaucracy. But such *income* policies produce a culture of dependency; what is needed instead are policies that try to work with the natural desire of families to better themselves, which means policies that focus on the building up of family *assets*, so that every family can have the dignity that comes from standing on its own.

The conservative goal is not bureaucratically administered income transfers, with the dependency that usually fosters; rather, the goal is to "capitalize" families that so far have not had a chance to get a piece of the American dream. It's about prosperity through opportunity for all American families.

The "capitalization" of families refers to the whole range of things that make a family work from an economic perspective: skills and knowledge, savings, retirement and education planning, estate planning, access to capital and lending institutions, and home ownership and private property. Reading this list you can't help but be struck by one thing: this is fine for the middle class and above, but it's irrelevant, a pipe dream, for many of today's low-income families. That's the problem in a nutshell. We have not democratized access to economic capital. In fact, millions of families, including many among the middle class, are effectively frozen out of the American dream.

We can fix that by setting a course designed to create nest eggs for all American families. To be more independent, families must be able to accumulate more assets. Ownership fosters self-reliance and independence while also creating jobs. Wealth makes it possible for Americans to save for a home, improve their earning potential by getting an education, turn a good idea into a family-supporting business, save for retirement, contribute to their communities, and pass real wealth on to their children.

Later, I will discuss some ideas and organizations that are playing a crucial role in this noble effort to democratize access to wealth. But first, I want to turn again to the essential difference between conservative and liberal views of poverty, income, and wealth. For me, the liberal view is best represented by a question asked not long ago by one of my colleagues: "Mr. Chairman, if the roof leaks, who will fix it?"

When I heard that question during a congressional debate, I finally understood how the village elders viewed people living in poverty.

The woman who asked the question about leaking roofs— her voice full not with sarcasm, but rather with sincere curiosity and a dose of anger at what we were proposing—is a leader of the liberal wing of the Democratic Party in the U.S. House of Representatives. What amazed Representative Maxine Waters was that we were proposing a new program to turn dilapidated housing projects into rehabilitated structures in which tenants could own their own units. And she wanted to know, "If the roof leaks, who will fix it?"

I was shocked at the low regard in which she held her own constituents. But the subtext of her question epitomizes how the village elders see the poor. To them, poverty is not a temporary situation that one strives to overcome. It is a permanent condition, so severe that government must step in to tend to every little problem an impoverished person might face—like fixing the roof. No American homeowner likes dealing with a leaky roof, but that is a responsibility that comes with ownership.

America needs more ownership, not less, as well as the responsibility that comes with it. The village elders' opposition to the ownership society, however, makes sense when you remember that they consider a large percentage of our population to be essentially helpless: they're not going to worry about how to empower the poor to build wealth, to access the capital that can make them part of the American dream. Like Jack Nicholson in *A Few Good Men*, you can almost hear the village elders sneering, "You want wealth? You can't handle wealth!" Or rather, "You want to own a home? You can't handle a leaky roof!"

Conservatives, on the other hand, reject the notion that poverty is a disability. In America, poverty really needn't be more than a temporary (albeit difficult) condition. And this is what Maxine Waters just didn't get. *Owning* a home is about more than shelter. It is about changing a life and creating a future. It demands that the homeowner take responsibility for a major

asset, which means managing finances, making mortgage payments, keeping the home in good working order, and yes, occasionally finding a roofer and mustering the resources to get a
leaking roof fixed. Home ownership demands responsibility. But
it also provides the deep, irreplaceable satisfaction of knowing
that you are exercising responsibility for the good of your family. Home ownership also builds stronger communities, because
it is in the financial as well as personal interest of owners to
build "good" neighborhoods for the time when they eventually
sell. Finally, owning a home builds wealth, the basis of both
security and opportunity. A low-income homeowner can take
out a home-equity loan, if necessary, to pay for a new roof, just
like lots of middle-income homeowners do. These tasks aren't
necessarily fun, but they demand a certain degree of mastery
over life, which leads to success in America.

Mastery of his life is something that Scott Syphax didn't
have, but his story is one that shows the power of hard work
and smart ownership.

ONE OF THE BENEFITS of being a senator is that I get to
meet today's crusaders. Scott Syphax is a crusader for wealth.
He's African-American. He dresses like the fast-track corporate
executive he once was. But as he says, "I was a guy who was
basically homeless twelve years ago, living on the streets of East
Oakland. I was sleeping in my car and taking showers at gyms
when I could sneak in. I was stealing food out of happy hours at
bars, stealing food out of grocery stores. I was pretty bad off at
that time.

"I had been in a very bad traffic accident and was disabled
for over a year. I basically lost everything I had at that point, but
I came back. I rehabilitated myself and everything else in my life."

Scott got back into the workforce and eventually rose to the position of managing federal, state, and local government business for Eli Lilly in California. But he walked away from the executive suite and joined a faith-based organization founded by the pastor of a small black church in the state capital Sacramento. This pastor was committed to revolutionizing the way families get a piece of the American dream, and his organization is called the Nehemiah Project. It helps people buy their first homes by helping with the down payment and then leverages millions of dollars to rebuild some of the worst parts of Sacramento.

Scott is often asked, even today, how he could have walked away from the corporate ladder. "I did it," he responds, "because after I rehabilitated myself, I remember never believing I could own a house, that that was beyond me. I thought, How was I ever going to get married? How was I ever going to be able to raise a family? I couldn't even start with the cornerstones of what I thought constituted an adult life."

Before joining the Nehemiah Project as the organization's president and before zooming up the career track at Eli Lilly, Scott had a chance himself to take advantage of Nehemiah's signature program, one that gives people the money needed to make a down payment: but he turned away from the opportunity. A scam, he scoffed at the time. (He did buy a house, however, thanks to the kindness of a number of people who helped him with his down payment.)

Not long afterwards Scott was sitting with a friend who had just started working for the Nehemiah Project. The organization, his friend related, had entered a fight with the federal government, specifically the Department of Housing and Urban Development, or HUD. This was 1999.

The Nehemiah Project's down payment assistance program, still relatively new in 1999 and the first of its kind anywhere in the United States, flew in the face of traditional social policy. Up until that point, if you couldn't come up with the down payment for a house, you couldn't own a home. The Nehemiah Project was changing that, but there were some—especially some folks who worked at HUD—who considered this an unwise, even a dangerous development. They feared it would make it possible for so-called "unworthy" people to buy homes and, as a result, push up default rates.

Upon hearing this, Scott bristled. He realized that he was once one of those so-called unworthy people. Unworthy for what? Unworthy to be part of the American dream? Unworthy to *own* a piece of the pie, as opposed to just renting it?

Scott entered the fray. He volunteered to help the Nehemiah Project. He came to Washington, and the organization hired lobbyists and lawyers. The fight, over regulatory compliance, was eventually put to rest. The Nehemiah Project is thriving today. But every time he comes to Washington, Scott feels as if he's fighting a war.

"I was with professional staff members of a congressional tax committee recently," he says, "the technical people who score everything for budget purposes. And I was explaining our down payment assistance program. They simply couldn't understand why we would ever allow a person making as much as $50,000 a year to get a gift for down payment assistance. Let's assume you came from a poor family, I told them, and you are the first person from your family that has ever been sent to college. Your family basically exhausted their assets, the little bit they had, to send you to college. When this person gets out of college, sure, she may get a job for $50,000 a year, but there's no way the family can afford to help her purchase a house. And this indi- vidual—and we see this all the time—has student loans to pay off and has bills that mean at the end of the year she has two dollars left. But the staff on this congressional committee still asks: 'Why would you be helping this person out?'

"The fact of the matter is that this person is just as deserving of help as the people on welfare. We never want to forget the indigent poor, but ultimately the ladder we build has to help people being taken care of by both government and the community all the way up to the solid middle class. In order to truly move the bar in this country—to move a broad class of people, regardless of ethnicity, race, or gender, into the middle class— we can't just look at income as the final and sole benchmark. But all social policy in this country is driven by income—which is a good indicator, but not necessarily an accurate predictor of where people are. Relying on income as the sole driver behind our economic policies is the reason why for forty years we've basically been in this spin cycle that has gone nowhere."

A SPIN CYCLE. That describes perfectly what our welfare policies have been doing for nearly four decades. "Treadmill economics," is what John Bryant, a unique African-American social entrepreneur who you'll meet in just a bit, calls it. The message from the village elders was: if you're unmarried and poor, government will help, but only so long as you *stay poor*, only so long as you never get married and never get ahead. It wasn't until Ronald Reagan signed the Earned Income Tax Credit, which supplements the income of low-income families, that working poor families were rewarded for their own efforts to get off the treadmill.

What Americans really need are more public policies that free us from "treadmill economics," policies that allow and encourage families, especially low-income families, to build up *economic capital*, a family nest egg. Focusing on income only is, as Scott Syphax says, "insanity." Assets are what help build families, and building families is what our economic policies must do.

I'm certainly not advocating that we simply tell the poor to just pull themselves up by their own bootstraps. But I want social policies that are based on a belief in the ability of *all* people to take responsibility in their lives—policies that instill, instead of deplete, *hope.* Liberals were warned of the need for hope many years ago, not from a conservative, but from President Franklin Delano Roosevelt, who said in his annual message to Congress on January 4, 1935:

> The lessons of history, confirmed by the evidence immediately before me, show conclusively that continued dependence upon relief induces a spiritual and moral disintegration fundamentally destructive to the national fiber. To dole our relief in this way is to administer a narcotic, a subtle destroyer of the human spirit.

Developing mastery over life is a voyage we never finish. But we can successfully navigate that voyage when we are animated by a spirit of hope that is nurtured by the support and love of our family, friends, and neighbors.

Overcoming poverty and strengthening family life among the least well off among us requires expanding opportunities to build wealth. But there is another, related problem: Americans today are not saving. In fact, our savings rate (that is, the percentage of personal income saved) has declined over the past 40 years from an average of 8 percent to 1 percent. Needless to say, it's hard to build wealth if you don't save.

Savings act as a cushion for workers to fall back on when times are tough. They can also act as a ladder to help individuals reach the next level of success. Without that cushion, workers are often one paycheck away from financial ruin. Without that ladder, the next level is sometimes too difficult a climb.

Not only the poor but also the middle class needs to be put in the asset accumulation game. The great financial divide in America is really between those people with assets—and thus the potential for building wealth—and those who either don't have or haven't grasped that they do have that opportunity, who only worry about paying the bills. When the top 20 percent of our population commands 83 percent of the wealth, we have a wealth gap that is unhealthy. It leads to class envy and hopelessness, in addition to political hyperbole. The opportunity to build wealth, and the understanding of how to do that, needs to be democratized.

Senator Joe Lieberman and I have been promoting an idea to do that ever since I arrived in the Senate. Individual Development Accounts, IDAs, act like a 401(k) program for low-income individuals. These programs are set up, many by faith-based organizations, with a mix of federal, state, and private dollars. These organizations help their low-income clients set up accounts at their local banks or credit unions, provide training on how to manage and grow these accounts, and then match individual contributions to these accounts dollar-for-dollar up to $500 a year. These accounts earn tax-free interest and can be used to pay for education, to buy a home, or to start a business. In other words, these accounts launch low-income people into the asset accumulation game.

States can create IDA programs with TANF dollars, and a majority of them are doing so. Our legislation will create approximately $2 billion in tax credits for financial institutions and private investors that create IDAs. The payoff, in terms of economic capital for families and society, will be great. The Corporation for Economic Development analyzed the data for a hypothetical national demonstration program supporting 100,000 IDAs for families earning less than $25,000 per year, assuming a $105 million investment from the federal government matching $186 million in combined family savings, private investments, and state and local expenditures. This total investment of $291 million would produce a net return to the country of $1.63 *billion* as measured by new businesses, new jobs, increased earnings, higher tax receipts, and reduced welfare expenditures. Imagine how many people, especially among our poorest communities, would quickly become convinced that they were truly *empowered* as full participants in the American dream.

Senator Lieberman and I have tried for years to create a federal IDA tax credit as part of a broader initiative called the Charity Aid Recovery Empowerment (CARE) Act, which would help charitable organizations help the poor. It passed both houses in 2004, but was blocked by former Democratic Leader Tom Daschle.

I have also been working with another Northeastern Democratic senator, Jon Corzine, on an idea that I kicked around years ago with former Senator Bob Kerrey. It is titled the America Saving for Personal Investment, Retirement, and Education Act (the "ASPIRE" Act). It creates a savings account called a Kids Investment and Development Savings (KIDS) account for every child born in America. Under this plan, the federal government would endow each account with a one-time $500 contribution. Every child living in households earning below the national median income would be eligible for an additional contribution of up to $500. These accounts would encourage savings and promote financial literacy for all children, and they would give low-income children in particular a sense of ownership, a stake in the American economy, and a source of wealth to help them through life. The money must be invested in privately managed mutual funds set up under the act in a manner similar to a federal employee's Thrift Savings Account. All earnings in the account would be tax-free until withdrawn, which could not take place for any reason until the child reaches age 18. After that, she could withdraw all but $500, which must remain, hopefully added to during her working years, until it is eventually used for postsecondary education, or buying a home, or else rolled over into an IRA and saved for retirement.

Anyone—family, friends, community organizations—could contribute up to $1,000 each into these accounts. To further encourage investment for lower-income children, these children would be eligible to receive a dollar-for-dollar match on the first $500 contributed to their accounts each year. Each child would therefore grow up knowing that she owned a modest pool of resources that could help her get started in life as a young adult. For some, this asset pool could be used to seed profitable and productive investments; for others, it could provide that "cushion" I wrote about earlier. A typical lower-income family making modest but steady contributions could create a KIDS account worth over $20,000 in 18 years. (Upon reaching 18 the child must pay back to the federal government any federal contribution to the fund; the federal contribution is like a no-interest loan for up to 18 years.)

THROUGH PLANS SUCH AS these we can help the poor, not to mention the middle class, become savers. And we can create banks that work for low-income children. But there is something else we need to do, and that is to give them, and indeed all families, a Social Security system that works. And we can do that in a way that makes everybody an investor. I have for a long time advocated reforming Social Security to keep the current system's strong safety net protections in place while at the same time allowing workers to put some of their payroll taxes into real savings—into a personal retirement account (PRA).

Now, the need to create more ways for Americans to create wealth is not in itself a sufficient reason to change the Social Security system. In fact, if the system were not at great risk, I would not be recommending a change at all. But as of 2005 we are facing an $11 trillion unfunded liability in the system. When combined with a liability in the Medicare program of almost $60 trillion, the economic viability of our nation *will be* at stake. I emphasize the words "will be" because the problem is not immediate. The system, admittedly, will be fine for the next decade. But we are looking in the eye of a "perfect demographic storm"—a combination of low birth rates, longer life expectancies, and a huge generation (the baby boomers) that is beginning to retire.

First, let's look at how the system currently works. There is a 12.4 percent payroll tax on the first $90,000 (the 2005 figure that adjusts every year to wage inflation) people earn. The taxes come in and the benefits are paid with those tax revenues. This has worked well in the past, but with an ever-increasing cost to future generations. For example, up until 1950 the maximum contribution to Social Security for a millionaire was only $60. It's a bit more than that now (that's an understatement) because when contributions didn't match the benefits due, Congress and the president have simply raised taxes on workers. That has happened 49 times. Furthermore, within the last 20 years, benefits have been reduced, either by taxing benefits or by raising the retirement age.

Liberals contend that there isn't a problem with Social Security, or else that the problem is so far off—the year 2041—that we can wait to see if it really materializes. The Social Security actuaries say that current benefits will begin to exceed revenues in 2017: that is when Social Security begins to add to the annual deficit. And I agree that nothing needs to be done to Social Security benefits for roughly the next 15 years. In other words, there don't need to be any benefit reductions for current and near-term retirees.

But in about 20 years, our deficits will soar to record heights—somewhere between 6 and 8 percent of the Gross Domestic Product, which is three to four times the post–World War II average. That means general government spending will have to be slashed or taxes will have to be raised. Over the following 20 years, the federal government will have to pay trillions of dollars into the Social Security system as it redeems the bonds in the Social Security Trust Fund. And *that* will mean some big tax increases or else some huge spending cuts. The actuaries tell us that in 2041 we will have to either increase payroll taxes by more than half or cut benefits by a third, or some combination of both.

Why will this happen? The answer is demographics. First, our birth rate is not high enough to replace our population; were it not for immigration, America's population would be declining. Second, we are living longer. In 1937, average life expectancy was 61 and the eligibility age for Social Security was set at 65. Today our life expectancy is 77 and increasing by one month every two years, while the eligibility age is 66, eventually going up to 67. People are not only living longer, many are retiring earlier: over half of beneficiaries begin to take their Social Security benefits at age 62. Finally, the baby boom generation begins to take benefits beginning in 2008. Over the last 40 years roughly 2 million people have turned 65 every year. In

15 years, however, that number will double and remain for many years at 4 million people.

These three demographic factors will dramatically change our pay-as-you-go system by reducing the ratio of workers paying for retirees from 3.3 workers to every 1 retiree to less than 2 workers to every 1 retiree. That is a roughly 50 percent reduction in the ratio, which is why, unless something is done, we will eventually need a 50 percent increase in taxes.

Can we solve this problem? Yes, but depending on the solution, one or two other problems might be created that we must be concerned about. If we solve it simply by increasing taxes gradually over time, we put a huge burden on future workers at a time when global competition will be fierce. This will cause a reduction in the growth of our economy and jeopardize future workers' opportunities to have and hold jobs. If, on the other hand, we solve it by cutting benefits by 30 percent, we obviously jeopardize the retirement security of future retirees. That is where investment comes in.

The village elders have already lined up in opposition to any proposal that involves personal investment with existing payroll taxes. They would go for a tax increase to establish PRAs, but they will not support a "carve out" of the current revenue stream. They say they don't want to jeopardize the Social Security system, and they point out that allowing workers to invest some portion of existing payroll taxes in PRAs could increase the current deficit. When asked about their own proposals to solve the long-term problem, their response is either that there is no need for a proposal, since the system is in fine shape, or else they suggest increasing taxes on the "rich."

But if we do not act now, before the crisis strikes, we will provide no hope to younger workers that they will receive the benefits that the current system promises them, benefits that, pending some sort of action, we will not be able to pay for.

There are really two reasons liberals in and out of Congress are so dead set against PRAs. First, liberals trust government more than markets. Second, liberals see PRAs as a threat to one of their most effective levers of power: dependency. They do not want to sever the umbilical cord that connects them to a very important part of their political base. As long as lower-income older Americans are dependent on the government for a big part of their financial security, then liberals can continue to use political scare tactics to keep those voters in their camp. If seniors relied upon the health of the economy and markets instead of just the benevolence of the powers in Washington, then the village elders' hold on that increasingly important block of voters would be diminished.

So how do PRAs work? First, almost all the plans now being proposed are voluntary, at least for current workers. The plans don't reduce the current value of benefits for any current beneficiary or anyone over the age of 55. They don't increase the payroll tax. And they all permanently fix the system so that benefits match our ability to pay them.

Let me lay out one simple plan by way of example. Every worker currently pays a 12.4 percent payroll tax. About one third of that—four percentage points—would instead go into an account that is owned by the worker. (These accounts would be structured so that lower-income workers have a higher percentage of their Social Security taxes going to their PRAs than higher-income earners, but the average would be 4 percent.) The money would be invested in a way similar to the Federal Thrift Savings Plan. That plan includes five different mutual funds in which to invest one's money—three stock funds, one corporate bond fund, and one government bond fund. There would be no investing outside of the system, no purchase of individual stocks or bonds, and no expensive fees. (The cost of managing the plan would be very low—only about $20 per $10,000 invested per year). Each worker participating in this plan, then, would have an investment that, based on the historic return on stocks, could deliver roughly 7 percent a year, compared to the measly 3 percent that Social Security returns.

Furthermore, each individual would own her PRA, so it could be passed on to a spouse, children, or grandchildren. Under the current system, if your spouse dies when you are age 51—and one in six women will be widowed by age 60—you get a $255 death benefit, but your survivor benefit doesn't start until age 60. A PRA, however, could help a surviving spouse with no savings get through a difficult time in her life.

Upon retirement, each person would get her Social Security benefit based on the taxes she paid into the system, plus an annuity financed by her PRA. Thus, not only would this PRA plan save the system for younger workers, it would at the same time turn millions of Americans into investors and make them part of an ownership society.

Helping people become savers and investors is the first step toward building economically successful families. Then comes the biggest investment we can help more American families make, which may be the biggest key to wealth creation of all: purchasing a first home. That brings me back to where I started: the Nehemiah Project in Sacramento. We're going back there, to a faith-based organization founded by the pastor of a small African-American church, an organization that now occupies an entire floor of a modern office building across from a huge mall and next to a rather new hotel, ten minutes from downtown Sacramento.

Nicole Learned sits in a cubicle with a "Don't Mess with Texas" bumper sticker tacked to the four-and-a-half-foot-tall cloth-covered wall separating her from one of the 17 call specialists she supervises. In front of her is a computer screen displaying a colorful database record with fields for property information, seller information, real estate agent, lender information, income, sale price, closing office, and closing agent.

The office is modern, airy, and bright, with sunshine streaming in through large windows along two sides of the building. It looks like Nicole could be working in any financial institution in the country. She is not. She is working at the Nehemiah Project, where she heads the call center. Her title is DAP Supervisor, Homeownership Services. The DAP stands for Down Payment Assistance Program.

The information on the screen in front of her includes data such as: "income: $45,000; sale price: $150,000; # in house: 2; gift percent: 3; gift: $4,500; fee: $750."

Without ever talking to that person making $45,000 a year buying that $150,000 home, and without ever talking to the lending institution, Nicole reviews the record in front of her, quickly whips her fingers across the keyboard, and makes what was the impossible possible: a new homeowner. In just a matter of moments, those keystrokes helped one American build wealth, wealth that just a few seconds earlier was beyond his reach. As Scott Syphax says, "America is blessed with an ever expanding pie. It's getting people into the kitchen that's the problem.

"Because property ownership is the primary asset development vehicle in this nation going back to its founding, by democratizing access to home ownership you are bringing more people into the civic and economic fabric of the United States," he says. "Home ownership should not be a privilege reserved for those who merely had the good fortune to be born into a family of means who can loan or give them a down payment."

And with that insight was born the down payment assistance program. Those numbers on the screen of Nicole's computer tell the story. The "3" next to "gift percent" means that Nehemiah is giving this homebuyer a gift of 3 percent of the purchase price, or $4,500. This gift goes right to the lending institution to pay all or some of the down payment. The fee of $750 refers to the amount the lender—not the homebuyer—will pay Nehemiah. That's above the contribution the lender or builder will make to the Nehemiah Project for the exact same amount that Nehemiah paid for the down payment.

It is, frankly, just a circle of money, with Nehemiah ending up with a $750 fee and the homebuyer ending up with a home. The entire concept was created by the folks at Nehemiah to break down what they saw as one of the greatest barriers to wealth creation: the requirement that the homebuyer come up with a down payment.

Federal regulations for HUD loan products—and most first-time mortgages in America are FHA loans—do not let the seller or builder pay the down payment. But a charitable organization can make a gift to the buyer for the amount of the down payment. And of course, a builder or lender can make any size contribution it wants to a nonprofit organization like Nehemiah.

The natural question is: Why does the lender or builder not only give the Nehemiah Project a contribution in the amount of the down payment gift, but also pay Nehemiah a fee? The reason is that when the program first started, the real estate market in most places was soft and builders were finding it hard to move their houses. It just made good business sense for the builders to sell their houses and help subsidize the loans. Today, it's a different market, but builders still need to move product, and they, along with lending institutions, view this as a relatively easy way to do some social good.

Nehemiah makes approximately 3,400 gifts per month, working with about 12,000 lenders and 15,000 builders nationwide. The average gift over the past year is about $4,000. They pay anywhere from 1 to 6 percent of the sale price of the home. That gift can cover all or some of the down payment and closing costs as well. The average sale price of a home is just under $150,000.

Consequently, in any given month the Nehemiah Project makes it possible for the real estate industry to do about $500 million in new mortgages. They have helped put more than 150,000 families into single-family homes in less than six years. According to Scott Syphax, that adds up to somewhere in the range of $15 to $20 billion of real estate.

Remember, it is Scott who rails against the notion that people who can't come up with a down payment are somehow unworthy to own their own home. The data seem to support Scott's point of view. In 2001 and 2002, when businesses were downsizing and the economy struggling out of a recession, the default rate among mortgages made possible thanks to Nehemiah's down payment assistance program was 8.61 and 10.39 percent, respectively. For all FHA loans nationally, it was 10.4 and 11.37 percent.

The Nehemiah Project was started with a $5,000 loan from an African-American church. It now generates $200 million in annual revenue from fees alone. Those fees help Nehemiah keep the lights on and the staff paid, and also allows Nehemiah to do even more charitable work.

I asked Scott what the federal government could do to help support this model. "Get out of the way," was the first thing he said. He also said the government needs to find a reasonable way to regulate down payment assistance without squashing innovation, as regulation so often does.

In response to Scott's concerns, I introduced a bill, along with Senator Dianne Feinstein of California, called the Down Payment Assistance Act. This bill clarifies that down payment assistance programs like the Nehemiah Project that are directed toward low- or moderate-priced homes are permitted charitable activities under the IRS Code. This bill will ensure that legitimate nonprofit assistance programs are protected while also providing some congressionally directed oversight to prevent abuses.

But with or without this congressional oversight, the good work being done here is happening *without* the government—and it is helping to stabilize the American family and provide for the common good.

XVII

The Power of Knowledge

T he final section of this book is devoted to a discussion of the state of our educational system, but here I want to focus on one specific, and too often unrecognized, educational deficit: economic illiteracy. Economic illiteracy is a galloping form of American ignorance that knows no racial or ethnic boundaries. It is equal-opportunity ignorance. But in order to swim in America's vast pool of economic opportunity, everyone must first understand the basics of the market: how it all works and how he or she fits in. Economic knowledge *empowers* people.

John Bryant is one of America's leading social entrepreneurs, someone who is using the forces of capitalism to achieve positive social change. I first met him when I went on a tour of poor areas in Los Angeles with then-Congressman J. C. Watts back in 1995. This initial encounter was one of a series of meetings with leaders from various walks of life on the West Coast. It was held in a public housing project—ironically, in Congresswoman "Who Will Fix the Roof" Waters's district—with a group of social entrepreneurs and philanthropists. Among the dozen or so presenters at this meeting was John Bryant, about whom

I immediately thought: "This is a man that sees a missing ingredient to the soufflé of success and has the recipe to make it rise." He was way ahead of me: where I had only been theorizing about economic literacy, he had thought the issue through and was already doing something about it.

In John Bryant's words, Operation HOPE, Inc., founded in Los Angeles more than a decade ago after the Los Angeles riots, is "America's first nonprofit, social investment banking organization, and one of the nation's leading providers of financial literacy and economic empowerment tools and services."

"No matter how much I love you, my son or my daughter, if I don't have wisdom, then I can only give you my ignorance," goes the saying. According to Bryant, there's a whole lot of economic ignorance being passed on from parents to children in this country, and not just among poor families. "The average college senior has debt in excess of $7,000 and four credit cards," he notes. "This is before they ever get out of college and they don't even have a job yet. That's not including student loans. This is just credit card debt. And look, that's mostly white kids. Imagine what happens if you go into the urban core."

He also makes a crucial distinction: "There is a difference between being broke and being poor. Being broke is a temporary economic condition, but being poor is a disabling state of mind and a depressing of your spirit; each of us must make a vow never, ever, to be poor again."

Operation HOPE has a number of programs. One of them is the "nation's only year-round national urban delivery platform for financial literacy." Working with several major financial institutions, including CitiBank and Wells Fargo, the program, called "Banking on Our Future," has over 1,500 trained and certified volunteer banker-teachers working in over 500 urban schools. So far they have taught well over 125,000 kids about financial literacy: about savings and checking accounts, compound interest, mutual funds and stocks, credit and mortgages. Some of those children live in Philadelphia, where I arranged a partnership between Operation HOPE and PNC Bank last year.

"Economic literacy is critically important to wealth creation," Bryant says. "There were 1.5 million bankruptcy filings in 2001. The largest number of bankruptcy filings was by young people between the ages of 18 and 24."

You can't build wealth if you are economically illiterate. If you assume that poor people are, and always will be, economically illiterate, then yes, they will never muster the means to fix the roof. But if you expect all people to become economically literate, and to use that education to better manage and improve their financial conditions, then you can safely expect people not only to fix their roofs, but to get their whole economic house in order.

In other words, economic literacy is one step along the road for people to become "stakeholders" in our economy. "Stakeholders" is Bryant's word for people moving from relying completely on income, concerned only for the dollars that keep them alive today from paycheck to paycheck, to building wealth, their own nest egg.

One of the first things we need to do is to put economic literacy programs like Operation HOPE's into *every* school in America. While the problem is most profound in poor communities, millions of Americans often do not receive any training at home in responsible financial management. Programs like Operation HOPE will at least prevent economic illiteracy from becoming a hereditary disability.

We also need to turn spenders into savers. John Bryant's Operation HOPE is doing just that. Did you know that as many as 20 percent of American adults are "unbanked": they don't have a checking or savings account. Bryant hates check-cashing shops, those small stores that you see in every urban neighborhood with large neon signs announcing that they will cash your paycheck. He hates them because they turn paychecks into immediate cash, into quick spending, into *gone*. So what did Operation HOPE do? It bought itself a 40 percent share in NIX Check Cashing in downtown Los Angeles. "We did it so we could convert check-cashing customers into banking customers," Bryant says. "Three years later, we are now turning 30 percent of the people who come in to cash their checks into people opening bank accounts."

We also need banks that can work effectively in low-income communities. Operation HOPE is itself a bank as well as a nonprofit foundation. In fact, it is the only nonprofit organization in U.S. history to start and build a bank and then sell that banking operation to a traditional, for-profit bank. Its banks are called HOPE Centers, and on the wall of each HOPE Center is a sign. It says: "No Loan Denials." There are three HOPE Centers in Los Angeles. Operation HOPE is building another in Anacostia—a part of Washington, D.C., that still bears the boarded-up scars of the 1968 riots. And as I write this book, I am also working with John Bryant and a local bank to bring a HOPE Center to Philadelphia.

"HOPE Centers are like a cross between a bank branch and, say, a Kinko's for empowerment," says Bryant. "We really mean that sign, 'No Loan Denials.' We approve you day one—subject to the resolution of the primary denial factors. We create a program for you: credit counseling, case planning, dollar-to-dollar planning, credit CPR if need be. It can take between three months and three years, but we get you in financial shape. We help resolve the credit report issues, disputing illegitimate bad credit marks and making sure the legitimate ones get paid off."

The HOPE Centers also help people build credit histories. Since a lot of low-income people have never had the chance to build credit, HOPE Centers help people build what John calls "thick file underwriting." Utility bills, rent payments, and car payments over a period of time represent a legitimate form of credit, a basis for getting on the ladder of the American dream.

HOPE Centers also make mortgage loans and small business loans that have totaled more than $120 million in lending since the first one opened nine years ago. Out of the almost 700 home loans they have made, not a single one has gone bad. That is the kind of amazing result we can hope to see repeated in countless more lives if we make economic literacy a priority.

XVIII

Faith-Based Transformations

I have been focusing on the means to build up economic capital in families. Now I want to turn to the problem of generating economic capital in entire communities. I hope it is evident that I am constructing a sort of inverted pyramid of economic policy: give individuals and families the capacity to build wealth, and then create communities that can be breeding grounds for opportunity and wealth creation. That's the way to build up an economy that works for everyone.

In the past, urban renewal started from the top down and focused on replacing physical structures at government expense. So-called "blight removal" sounded good: it involved pouring hundreds of millions of dollars into poor neighborhoods. It may even have looked good—at first. But in the end, this approach to urban renewal did little more than tear down and then re-build city blocks, all the while dislocating people and shattering communities. It did little if anything to renovate local economies and, therefore, made little real difference for families living in blighted areas. Indeed, the relocation and disruption it caused was, for many families and communities, devastating, creating prime conditions for social predators.

The innovators in community redevelopment today are not focused so much on renovating physical structures as they are on creating projects that work with market forces to change people's lives for the better. They look to transform targeted and selected parts of communities. Doing so, they hope, will direct the self-interest that Tocqueville championed toward actions that both strengthen a community's economic backbone and improve its quality of life. In other words, these innovators are creating projects that will tip the balance of a distressed area toward private economic investment and success.

There is no sure-fire abstract formula for doing this, at least not yet. But what seems to work is a complex interplay of the following factors:

- building on a community's natural institutional anchors,

- investing public funds on infrastructure that will create incentives for private-sector investment,

- orienting the economic self-interest of community residents toward a common good, and

- investing in projects that contribute to a higher quality of life, economically and otherwise.

The examples that follow illustrate these strategies. These projects are helping to create communities that support the economic and moral endeavors of strong families. We have already seen how the policies of the left have helped to degrade individual lives, families, and communities. Here, I will present cases where collapsing villages can be completely turned around so that strong families can thrive. We'll return first to Sacramento and the Nehemiah Project. Then we will come back home, for me, to Pennsylvania.

The Meadowview section of Sacramento didn't have much going for it until two years ago. To use John Bryant's terminology, the residents were poor rather than broke. The Meadowview section is right on Interstate 5. Until recently, you never got off at its exit unless you were unfortunate enough to be stuck living there. Scott Syphax lived there as a boy.

As you turn off I-5 into Meadowview, on your left is a liquor store. It used to be a 7-11. Scott was held up there at gunpoint when he was just eleven years old. On your right is an apartment complex called Whispering Pines. It used to be referred to as Danger Island. Unless you were a crack addict or a dealer, you didn't walk in there at night. Squatter apartments were used for everything you can imagine.

Scott cites the movie *Malcolm X* when describing the community redevelopment strategy that Nehemiah used in this neighborhood. "Sometimes taking a chance on people and giving them something nice, showing that you respect them, they'll make the right choice," he says. "It's like in the movie *Malcolm X*. Elijah Muhammad was talking to Malcolm and he had two glasses of water. He poured ink into one of the glasses. Muhammad said, 'You give the people the choice, they'll always drink the clean water.' We've given people the choice, and they have chosen to drink the clean water."

Here's what happened. Up until about three years ago, right across the street from Whispering Pines, there was a vacant lot that had stood empty for at least thirty years, overgrown. At about that time, Home Depot was looking for a site on which to build. They looked at the vacant lot, but passed it by because there really was no local economy in Meadowview—unless you counted drugs.

Then the Nehemiah Project and God came in. To be precise, God was always there, although the people didn't always realize it. But a Baptist minister had a vision: to build a huge new church back in that neighborhood behind Whispering Pines.

The Nehemiah Project, through its Community Reinvestment Fund—which is supported in part by the fees collected as part of its down payment assistance program—loaned Antioch Baptist Church $12 million to build a 60,000-square-foot church with classrooms, a community multipurpose room, and, of course, an altar.

Soon, Home Depot heard that this was happening. They looked again and decided to build on that vacant lot. A retail oasis grew up around Home Depot. Today, in addition to Home Depot, there is a Staples, an IHOP, a Wendy's, a Starbucks, a gas station, and numerous other smaller stores.

Antioch Baptist became the institutional anchor of the neighborhood, a place that at almost any given time of day is filled with children attending a summer camp, pursuing religious studies, or coming together for tutoring sessions.

But here's where people chose the clean water. Suddenly, self-interest took over—along with pride and hope. Fences that hadn't been painted in years got painted. Dirt patches and weeds became green lawns—and there were even a few new roofs.

Then, on the other side of Antioch Baptist Church, a private developer broke ground for a new community. These aren't low-income housing units, but two-story homes with pastel-colored walls, much in the design of high-end California living. Young, upwardly mobile families are buying these homes.

For the people who used to feel stuck in this community, the world has changed. And they got something else they didn't have any, or not much of, before—*home equity*. Property values have increased rapidly. Families who owned the homes that had been there for years suddenly had more wealth because the value of their homes had increased. All this started when a Baptist minister built a house of God, with the help of Nehemiah.

Before we leave Sacramento, there is another place I want to take you to. It is called Oak Park. This neighborhood used to be the cultural center of Sacramento back in the 1950s and early 1960s. At the heart of the community—the intersection of 35th Street and Broadway—stood the Guild Theatre and the Woodruff Hotel.

Slowly, like countless other urban communities, decline took hold in Oak Park. Jobs began to disappear. Welfare took over. The Guild Theatre stopped showing movies. The Woodruff Hotel closed. Drugs and prostitution moved in. Oak Park became one of Sacramento's worst neighborhoods.

Kevin Johnson, the former Phoenix Suns basketball star, grew up in Oak Park. He has been investing in Sacramento now for a few years through his own nonprofit, St. Hope. Last May, St. Hope finished construction on a new institutional anchor for Oak Park. The Guild Theatre has been completely refurbished so that today it is used to host public speakers, plays, movies, and community meetings. The Woodruff Hotel has been rebuilt into a mix of top-end apartments and three businesses: a bookstore, a coffee shop, and a barbershop. The business spaces are designed to invite community participation: the coffee shop has a stage for bands and other performers, the bookstore has a large corner used for community meetings and dialogues, and the barbershop has lots of chairs and a large flat-screen television for men (and some women) to gather and watch sports.

The Nehemiah Project was the largest private lender for this undertaking. After the new anchor opened its doors, the change in the community was almost immediate. Two new bank branches came to the neighborhood. Small businesses started to appear. The Guild Theatre and the new businesses immediately became the cultural center of a community where the only culture, up until then, had been found on the flickering television screens inside locked houses or apartments—especially after dark.

These neighborhoods in Sacramento are examples of how strategic investing in high-risk areas can sow the seeds of economic and cultural change. And it took local churches, faith-based groups, and business and community leaders to make this work, not the village elders.

BACK TO PENNSYLVANIA, then, my state.

Reverend Luis Cortes is another community crusader. He operates out of North Philadelphia, where he runs Esperanza USA, a nonprofit program dedicated to, in his words, "creating Hispanic-owned and -operated institutions that serve familial, economic, and spiritual growth."

"Historically in America it is through institutions that you actually create change for minority communities. We have to create institutions that let us interpret majority culture back to our minority culture so that we can meld the two. We need to control and operate these institutions—that's empowerment," Luis told me.

One of the things that Luis and Esperanza have done is to create a junior college and a charter high school. According to Luis, "Governor Tom Ridge provided our organization with a grant of $3 million. We leveraged that to get another $5 million to buy a property that today contains a charter high school and a junior college. We've managed to create, in a place that was deserted, an institution with $10 million running through it every year, and 100 jobs that weren't there before."

Esperanza is also dedicated to helping Hispanic families in North Philadelphia buy their own homes. "When we do housing, we do home ownership, not rental. For people who are bringing in $17 to $25 thousand a year, a house will be the only asset they will have. You're going to protect that asset, even though it's in a lower-income community. You're going to make a better neighbor. In poorer communities, home ownership is even more important than in middle-class and upper-class communities, because better neighbors are what we need.

"We can buy homes, turn them around, and sell them for $50,000. We can help low-income families purchase a home, and that will get them out of poverty. Over a 10-to-15-year period, they will build equity. It also helps them understand how to save money, because when you own a house, there's no landlord you can call to get something fixed."

Esperanza has helped more than 1,000 families purchase their first home. The average income for these families is not much more than $20,000 a year.

Reverend Cortes sees his mission as more than helping Hispanic families buy homes, more than creating institutions that empower people, and more than teaching low-income Hispanic children that Hispanics participate in the American dream. He sees his mission as helping to strengthen Hispanic culture, because, in his view, American culture has a lot to learn.

"We are a people of hope because we are a people with a future. If you look at the Latino community, our sense of family is a major focus—more so than in the Anglo community. Our sense of faith is a major focus. And so is our belief that no matter how bad today is, tomorrow will be better. That is part of our culture. We have to be missionaries back to America, because part of America has forgotten that. The majority culture, more and more, is focused only on the here and now."

Reverend Cortes wants us all to be talking about the future, one in which more and more families, especially low-income families, believe in their future because they believe owning property, and making change, is achievable for them and their children. Government partnerships with faith-based groups like Esperanza work not only in building social capital, but in building ownership, creating jobs, and giving families hope for a prosperous future.

XIX

Smart Reinvesting

Conservatives understand that one key to community renewal is smart investing. They also realize that it often takes powerful incentives to overcome the disadvantages of doing business in the most depressed communities. With that in mind, Congressman J. C. Watts and I authored the American Community Renewal Act that was signed into law in 2000 as part of a collaboration between Speaker Hastert and former President Clinton. The act includes a menu of economic incentives for community investing by creating 40 "Renewal Communities" in distressed urban and rural areas around the country. Renewal Communities operate like expanded and improved Empowerment Zones and Enterprise Communities. They provide a variety of tax incentives, including a zero capital-gains rate for investments in these communities, while requiring those local communities and governments that wish to participate to shed unnecessary regulatory burdens. In the end, the American Community Renewal Act has provided over $20 billion in investment incentives to encourage investors to take a second look at our poorest communities.

I am proud of that accomplishment, but I wish I had met up with Jeremy Nowak before the bill passed. I would have done a few things differently, and better. Jeremy is the president and founder of one of the nation's most innovative community investors, the Reinvestment Fund, which is involved in some of the same types of investing that the Nehemiah Project and others are undertaking. But the Reinvestment Fund fulfills its mission more intelligently than any group I have ever seen.

The Reinvestment Fund is smarter because it collects the best, most comprehensive information about a neighborhood before making a decision to invest there. The Fund is doing some of the country's best work in learning how to mine demographic data and apply that information to community redevelopment decisions.

On the wall at the Reinvestment Fund office is a map of the city of Philadelphia. It is color-coded, with sections in green, red, orange, yellow, blue, purple, and black. Each color refers to a classification—such as "reclamation," "distressed," "transitional," "steady," and "high value."

"We get data on home ownership levels, vacancy rates, commercial and residential mixture, existence of publicly subsidized units, dangerous building data, code violations, and real estate value," says Jeremy. "We look at prime versus sub-prime debt. We get poverty data, education and workforce quality data, data on school performance, and credit scores. We look at policing data and drug corner activity data. And we aggregate these data down to the city block group.

"We do this, number one, to try to understand broad trends and patterns in housing and business markets. Number two, so that we can begin to integrate some of the social indicators with the economic and real estate indicators, and we can look at how they interact. Number three, to help public officials make public investments in ways we think can work. Number four, to help make our own investment decisions smarter. And finally, so that we can create a framework for long-term evaluation, so we can see where we are being successful and where we are not."

It's a fluid analysis, Jeremy readily admits, because his organization is continuing to learn. All sorts of information lie behind that color-coded map, and the result is an incredibly powerful tool. Someone can look at a map of the city and recognize that an area marked as "reclamation" is not, at this point, a smart place for major real estate or infrastructure investment. The area is too far gone, frankly, for anyone to come in and make the kind of strategic investment that would start to push that neighborhood toward economic viability.

Can you imagine all the Great Society money we could have saved with this sort of common-sense, data-driven, market-based analysis? The Reinvestment Fund's approach flies in the face of every welfare policy the village elders have promoted for 45 years, policies that continue blindly to pour money into the worst neighborhoods in America. That's like pouring water into a bucket with a big hole in the bottom. As I have witnessed many times in Congress, the village elders like to show they care for the poor among us simply by spending more money. How much more doesn't matter, it just has to be more than the other side is offering.

What Jeremy is doing would make perfect sense to any businessperson: don't spend precious resources on bad investments. To do so doesn't show you care; it actually shows that you couldn't care less, that you are content to continue to do nothing that might actually work for people trapped in those communities; it shows that all you want is credit for good intentions. Jeremy, on the other hand, believes that the point of investment is to make change happen. The smart thing to do in neighborhoods that are too far gone to profit from infrastructure investment is to invest in the *people* with things like workforce development programs and "reverse-commuting" mass transit programs.

(Thus, for example, the Reverse Commuting Program that I authored and added to the 1996 welfare law, along with former Democratic Senator Carol Mosley Braun, ensures that the people who live in these reclamation and distressed areas have the opportunity to get where economic opportunity currently resides. Too many mass-transit commuter routes are designed only to bring people from a metropolitan area into the urban business district. But in many cases, jobs for low-skill workers have migrated to the suburban ring around the city. Unlike suburbanites, most of the urban poor do not have cars. Without some means of transportation, these jobs are literally out of reach. Federal reverse-commuting dollars help subsidize routes from reclamation areas to suburban job centers.)

While you're working on the necessary programs for reclamation areas, says Jeremy, you focus on a "transitional" area (one either getting better, but still not steady, or one getting worse, but still not distressed) or even a "distressed" area adjacent to a reclamation zone where there is some basis for optimism. There you can do the kinds of investing and infrastructure improvement that will start to tip the neighborhood. And slowly, the economic benefits of that neighborhood may begin to seep into that reclamation area next door; if not, then economic incentives, coupled with workforce development for people living in the reclamation area, will result in residents leaving the reclamation area. Then, building on the base of the transitioning-up neighborhood, you begin to gut and rebuild the worse-off area.

In these "reclamation" zones, Jeremy says, "in the near term, it's an environmental disaster. We'll say to the local, state, or federal government, 'Look, don't build another house there.' Nobody wants to hear that. We're not saying to write off the people who live there. Rather, we say: help the people, but not the place. Let's figure out how to get them social services, or work-skills development, or a relocation allowance.

"In the most distressed neighborhoods, you can have 25 percent vacancy rates and high levels of deterioration, but with many very good people holding on. Nobody wants to hear that his or her neighborhood isn't a viable place, but sometimes that's what we need to say."

Overall, Jeremy says, "we can take all this data, analyze and model it, and then try to figure out the best use of public money and the best use of private investment funds—such as our high-risk private investment—to facilitate market recovery."

Armed with this businesslike approach to housing and economic development, the Reinvestment Fund strategically helps finance a mixture of housing in stricken Philadelphia neighborhoods that includes building new affordable rental units and moderately priced homes for purchase. The result is that a neighborhood is completely changed, both in terms of quality of life and in terms of local economics. Residents begin to make decisions (to make the "clean water" choice) to move out of close-to-dilapidated rental units, leaving landlords of these properties the choice of repairing them or selling to a developer, who suddenly sees a good investment opportunity.

Notice again how different this approach is from old-style urban renewal, which just gutted blocks and then rebuilt while dislocating entire communities and paying little attention to the micro-economy of the neighborhood. This new type of redevelopment transforms a community as economic incentives lead people to move and make positive changes—but within their same community.

YOU CAN SEE THE RESULTS inside one of Tommy D's Home Improvement Centers. Here is where you will find one of the most important achievements of community redevelopment work such as that being done by the Reinvestment Fund: *jobs*.

Tommy D's sits on the corner of 57th and Walnut Streets in West Philadelphia. It is an old brick building with a small parking lot adjacent, filled inside with most of what you would find at a Home Depot. The building was left over from a failed business before Tom Delany bought it.

"The Reinvestment Fund—there's a real difference between them and a bank," Tom says. "They got to know our business. Alan Wilson [an executive at the Fund] was a customer of ours. They are more willing to look at inner-city businesses. That's something most banks pay lip service to—but the truth of the matter is, they don't want to be involved with some of the inner-city businesses. I don't think we're a marginal loan for the Reinvestment Fund, but they do take chances. They're trying to create jobs and opportunities in the inner city."

Tom has built a business that competes very well against the Home Depots of the world. "Our Castor Avenue store is four blocks from a Home Depot. The Walnut Street store is twelve blocks from a Home Depot." (Credit should be given to Home Depot for maintaining a presence in the inner city.) "We have a niche that allows us to compete very effectively. We buy manufacturer's close-outs, discontinued models, buy-backs: we can often buy stock from Home Depot itself, for example, at 50 or 60 cents on the dollar, because they have to change over stock. We were in our Castor Avenue location before Home Depot opened, and after they opened, business went up about 20 percent. They literally send us customers. We don't have everything, but if we have it, we're cheaper. In the markets we are in, people are shopping price."

But Tommy D's is selling more than just affordable merchandise. It's also selling jobs. One of Tommy D's best marketing tools in the community is the people who work there. "In our stores, 90 percent of the workforce can walk to work, and probably 60 percent do just that," Tom reports.

With the help of the Reinvestment Fund, Tom has put together an impressive employee benefit program. "Most of the businesses in the inner city strictly serve the needs of the owner. But we have an ESOP in place. We do monthly bonuses. We participate in First Call, a program coordinated by Jefferson Hospital. If any of our employees have counseling needs, or need to speak to an attorney about child-care issues, or if they need help trying to figure out finances, they can dial an 800 number and speak with an expert, 24 hours a day. It's available to employees and their families. Once an employee is here a year, we pay 100 percent of their healthcare."

And Tommy D's believes in *all* the people who live in the community. "We've been through a number of strategies trying to get dedicated people. We ended up hiring a couple of people who had been incarcerated previously—and then some more. For the most part, we get the people that want to go to work. There are some bad ones, of course, but I think maybe only two or three ever turned around and ended up going back to jail. We seem to get the ones who want to straighten their lives out. It's hard to get people with good reading and writing skills around here, because of the schools." Tommy D's has about 40 employees. About half have served time in prison.

Investors like the Reinvestment Fund and the Nehemiah

Project are proving that it is possible to invest strategically to alter the economic incentives so that the entire community changes and becomes a place where families can flourish. What the Reinvestment Fund is giving us with their unique model of data-driven investment is the beginning of a map for how to do it, and how to do it *smart*.

"In order to be successful, you're going to need a certain kind of smart public investment and you are going to have to be very smart about where you can build from strength in communities," Jeremy Nowak says. "There are areas where there are clusters of strong blocks with good transportation access or pretty solid public assets, or where there is reasonable proximity to some kind of major institution. Or perhaps there is an indication of some sort of private investment that has the potential to move the neighborhood in the right direction. And you can begin to build a framework and understand where the public sector needs to make an investment and where private investment can have the biggest impact."

By the way, you do not have to be a graduate of the University of Pennsylvania with a degree in statistics to use data this way. Before founding the Reinvestment Fund, Jeremy was a neighborhood organizer with a background in teaching. He majored in philosophy in college.

Now let me tell you about another community in my state where until recently there has not been much smart investing. It is a town of about 37,000 people, located ten miles from a major city and the same distance from a huge international airport. As you might guess, it has ample access to interstate highways. In fact, one goes right through town. Railroads—including one of the busiest lines, both freight and passenger, in the country—go through town, too. Ships? It abuts a busy commercial river with huge ports on either side of town. Want more? This town also has within its borders a university and a large medical center.

Most American cities would give their eyeteeth for any of these assets. The City of Chester, located just ten miles south on I-95 from the Philadelphia International Airport and along the Delaware River, has them all. But very few communities in America would want to trade places with Chester. Forty years ago Chester had 50 percent more people than it does today. In 1995, the city had 24 murders, 81 rapes, 616 robberies, 1,912 assaults, 1,025 burglaries, 1,606 thefts, 814 vehicle thefts, and 139 arsons. The official unemployment rate was three times higher than the regional rate—but only because a lot of people had simply given up hope and stopped looking for work. And to top it all off, shortly after my election to the Senate the school district was in such dire financial straits that it was taken over by the state.

After I was elected to the Senate I visited Chester. When I read the staff briefing, I was shocked by two things: first, how *bad* it was, and second, that a town that was over 70 percent African-American had an African-American *Republican* mayor.

I met Mayor Aaron Wilson and asked him to partner with me in using conservative principles to turn *our* city around. His response was positive, but he also shared with me the countless failed attempts by the village elders with their latest academic plans and projects. There had been no shortage of master plans, press conferences, and ribbon cuttings over the last fifty years: just a big shortage of genuine progress.

I asked the mayor and a terrific young city councilman, Dominic Pileggi, to help me convene a group of local stakeholders. About 50 people came to talk with me, but before the exchange I set some rules of engagement. First, no press was invited, and that would hold true for all future activities unless *they* wanted the press there. Second, this was their city; I was here to help but not to lead. Third, they would have to do the real heavy lifting, like creating a positive business climate (one marked by lower taxes and reduced regulation) and building social capital.

At our meeting, I learned about Chester's problems, its dreams, and, of course, its programs that needed federal funding. However, I sensed that if you asked any of my interlocutors to be honest, they would tell you that they didn't really believe their dreams for Chester could come true. Real hope—the kind that never lets you give up no matter what the odds—wasn't present in Chester.

I pledged to work with local leaders, but I emphasized that my approach would be very different from the past. I spoke of charter schools, university spin-offs, private sector brown-field re-use, a better business climate, faith-based social services—all with the goal of developing economic markets and strengthening families and communities of faith.

It turned out that Chester is the story of two sets of problems requiring two sets of approaches. One set of problems is the area east of I-95 bordering the river. This used to be the bustling industrial side of town. The city's waterfront once had major employers, including Scott Paper and Ford Motor Company, where Lee Iacocca was once the plant manager. Sun Shipbuilding had once employed as many as 35,000 workers. That's all gone now.

The biggest asset east of I-95 is the Delaware River waterfront. The Commonwealth of Pennsylvania has a program called Keystone Opportunity Zones, or KOZs, which are much like federal Renewal Communities. These are designated sites in which business investment is virtually exempt from all state and local taxes. On the waterfront sits a massive old brick electric generating plant smack in the middle of the KOZ. It was built during the days when industrial might was celebrated with beautiful architecture and broad, imposing structures, but it had been abandoned for twenty years. So the city and I approached Mike O'Neill of Preferred Real Estate Investments with a great building and a story of a community on the way back. He was interested, but he asked, "What about access to the site?"

Route 291 is a single lane in each direction that runs parallel to the Delaware River near this great building. It is cracked and bumpy and marked by stoplight after stoplight. With the help of federal dollars, however, Route 291 is being turned into a modern, four-lane, tree-lined boulevard that will run along the length of the waterfront with a new ramp that will directly connect it with I-95.

Now Mike is investing over $50 million to turn the building into 400,000 square feet of office space. With Preferred's commitment, another half million dollars in federal money was provided to fix up Highland Avenue, the road that runs from I-95 down to 291 and to the old generating building, now called the Wharf at Rivertown. Mike estimates that the entire project will eventually bring 4,500 new jobs to the Chester waterfront.

The Rivertown deal with Preferred was negotiated in large part by Thomas Moore, one of my former staff members who in 1999 was hired by the city to oversee economic development. Thomas made sure that the community would benefit even beyond the jobs this project created. According to him, "The public has been shut off from the water's edge because of all the industrial users. So we negotiated a permanent public easement and now the public will be able to enjoy a park and a riverwalk presently under construction with the help of federal, state, and local dollars."

All of this development will also positively affect Chester's housing market. The families who live on this side of Chester will no longer feel like they are in an economic Siberia. Businesses and jobs, increased property values and equity—all will combine, for the first time in a long time, to give families in Chester the opportunity to build genuine wealth.

Now to the other side of Chester, the west side of the so-called Berlin Wall formed by I-95. Here is a different Chester, with two institutional anchors, neither of which until recently had been very connected to the economic life of the community. One is Widener University; the other is Crozer Chester Medical Center. They sit less than a quarter mile from each other, directly on an I-95 interchange, together forming about a 200-acre opportunity. That opportunity has been turned into University Technology Park.

Sounding much like Jeremy Nowak, Thomas Moore told me, "We decided to build on our anchor institutions. We've had Widener University here for more than a hundred years, but the city didn't take advantage of it and build around it." So, in a city neither known for office buildings nor technology, the idea for University Technology Park was born. Community leaders decided they needed to create some sort of medical, educational, and technological corridor. A nonprofit organization was formed with Widener and Crozer Chester Medical, and the city sold them the ground that stretched between the two institutions. With a combination of private and public funds they constructed a 30,000-square-foot, high-tech, fully wired office building. A second 40,000-square-foot office building was completed last year.

The value-added benefit is that new businesses are deciding to open up in and around University Technology Park. An investor bought an old abandoned storefront, invested over $1 million in it, and opened a medical imaging business. Just around the corner, a new sports medicine clinic has opened.

All of this happened because Chester held up its end of the bargain. It hasn't raised property taxes in ten years and has cut both wage taxes and business taxes. It has also contracted out services to cut costs and improve the regulatory environment. The result is over $1 billion in new investment since 1996. New jobs are being created, the quality of life is improving, and neighborhoods are safer. In fact, crime, including violent crimes like rape, murder, and assault, has dropped 74 percent since 1995.

The people of Chester have accomplished a great deal, but there is still a long way to go. Nevertheless, there is more real economic activity and more hope in Chester than there has been in a long time. I've focused on the economic side of the rebirth of Chester here, but there is so much more going on: the churches, community organizations, and the people of Chester, along with many social entrepreneurs like Foster and Lynn Friess and Dr. Jack Templeton, who have wanted to be a part of this transformation have made all the difference. Hope is being restored.

XX

Wealth and Race

I have a particular concern for our nation's African-American community. Their story has so often been at the center of America's journey over the last 300 years. It is a story of enormous suffering: America's blacks were most assuredly victims in countless ways. Obviously, too, as I know from my personal conversations with African-Americans, racism and discrimination still do exist in this country.

But it is wrong to believe the African-American story is one of victimhood only. To think in those terms is to deny the real accomplishments of the black community in our history. And not the least of these accomplishments has been a tradition of business acumen and entrepreneurship. In his book, *The Triumphs of Joseph*, my friend Robert Woodson, the dynamic African-American social entrepreneur, writes:

> Neither the 1896 *Plessy v. Ferguson* decision (which approved the "separate but equal" segregated facilities) nor the Jim Crow laws (which were passed to eliminate black entrepreneurs and professionals from market competition) could stem the tide of successful black entrepreneurs. Between 1867 and 1917, the number of black enterprises increased from four thousand to fifty thousand.

In other words, even in the worst of times, as far as racial discrimination goes, our African-American community was getting ahead economically, through hard work and know-how. Bob writes about Durham, North Carolina, which used to be known as the black Wall Street. "There were over 100 black-owned businesses there, and not a single one went under during the Depression," he says. He also mentions a black-owned Harlem real estate company that employed over 200 people by 1900.

"A black company was one of the first to sell nylons nationwide," he continues. "It was a black-owned firm based in Durham that hired an all-white sales force to sell nylons across the country." But today, he points out with sadness, "Blacks do not own a single major downtown office building from the Canadian border to North Carolina."

What happened to America's thriving black entrepreneurial class during the twentieth century? Why did it seemingly vanish? It's hard to place the blame on ongoing racism, since racism was at least as much of a problem during the heyday of black enterprise in the early decades of the twentieth century as it is today. No, what really changed the economic terrain for African-Americans was something else: the arrival of liberal welfare policies, the liberal cultural of victimhood, and poorly thought-out liberal urban renewal.

But let's avoid for a moment the tired argument about *what happened*. The fact is that what happened *has* happened: somehow, a legacy of African-American economic achievement was dissipated during the twentieth century. An inheritance was squandered. The really important question is: What do we do about it *now*? How do we build up wealth and economic know-how in parts of American society where economic wherewithal has worn bare?

The Selig Center for Economic Growth at the University of Georgia predicts that the buying power—defined as total after-tax, personal income available to spend on goods and services—of black America will increase 189 percent between 1990 and 2008. This compares to a predicted increase of 128 percent for whites. Economic progress is being made in America's minority community. Still, there remains a very troubling economic disparity between whites and blacks. And this is really the result of a missing economic fundamental: business building and wealth creation.

Surely the most *affirmative* program to build up America's minority families would be one aimed at just this. But the village elders fail to understand this. Instead, as Bob puts it: "Leadership in the black community is defined by who is able to give the worst case of victimization, with a bunch of whining and complaining. Every year, the old civil rights leaders have a big celebration commemorating the Selma to Montgomery marches. They march right through Lowndes County every year, and every year they have walked past about 2,000 homes of African-Americans who don't have indoor plumbing and whose only heat is from a coal or wood-burning stove. They do nothing."

But Bob *is* doing something. His National Center for Neighborhood Enterprise has initiated a project using market-based solutions and public-private partnerships to help Lowndes residents improve sanitary conditions, reduce their living expenses, create economic development programs that will result in jobs, and improve facilities for education and job training. NCNE's assistance was requested by a bipartisan group of local leaders in Lowndes, including mayors, county commissioners, businessmen, and clergy.

NCNE has assembled a national task force of business and

civic leaders, wastewater engineers, and economic development experts to devise practical solutions to remedy the problems in Lowndes. Partnerships have been established with
private-sector entities, nonprofits, and state and federal agencies. As Bob likes to say, the role of all of these players is "to
be on tap for, and not over the top of" the residents of Lowndes.

Bob Woodson has been frustrated by liberals, but he doesn't
let conservatives off, either. "What really frustrates me," he
says, "is that there *can* be a political answer: if Republicans
would choose to compete for the black vote by emphasizing
business creation. But they don't do that, they just cower, play
games, and patronize blacks by assuming they have to walk
through the traditional old civil rights door. As a consequence,
nothing changes."

He's right. Conservatives should stand up for the principles
of free enterprise and help black America understand the importance of participating in the economy, rather than (like the
village elders) being patronizing and pandering to victim-
mongers. Conservatives need to bring the message of economic
opportunity to a community that once excelled at entrepreneurship—and can do so again.

Like John Bryant's HOPE Centers, we need to hang up
"No Denials" signs in urban communities—the opposite of red-
lining. But it won't be government that makes all this happen.
Innovators like Scott Syphax, John Bryant, and Jeremy Nowak
are the ones who are proving how it can be done. They are
proving that investing in riskier enterprises in inner cities, for
example, can deliver real returns. The role for government
here is very much that of a silent partner. Government should
stand beside the social entrepreneurs who are pushing forward
in every city in America; it should not displace them. Remember, government *promotes* the general welfare, but the com-

mon good is *achieved* by the public-spirited actions of citizens coming together in their communities to make a difference.

The results will be profound. The results will be empowered families and a dramatic increase in new businesses, which will build up wealth to be passed along to give future generations a leg up. We will see the rebirth of black enterprise. By working with the market rather than against the market, we can turn victims of all races into entrepreneurs of all races.

"We need dramatic demonstrations that economic development and nonracial social policies based on economic self-sufficiency are the way to go," says Woodson. And there is no reason we can't do that in every city in America. The ideas are out there, and they are working. Those "dramatic demonstrations" are not just possible: they are already happening. Here I've told you about just a few of the "points of light" that are making a difference to the bottom lines of families and communities.

August 2003 marked the fortieth anniversary of the "I Have a Dream" speech by Dr. Martin Luther King, Jr. Somewhere between 10,000 and 20,000 people gathered at the Lincoln Memorial to commemorate that great event. The leaders of the rally proclaimed that Dr. King's dream of equality had not, in their view, been achieved. Their proof was that far too many minorities in America are poor, homeless, and lack health care. The leaders called for a new burst of government activism, a return to the Great Society programs of the 1960s. And sometimes they spoke as if nothing at all had changed in American race relations between the era of segregated buses and water fountains and today, when Condoleezza Rice is Secretary of State, succeeding Colin Powell. No one wins, no one gains, if we simply agree to repeat worn-out slogans that then excuse us from tackling the very real problems facing a part of the

American community. The major roadblock to economic progress in America's black community is the treadmill economics of income transfer, economic policies that have had the unintended consequences of squashing economic initiative and sapping the strength of families.

Standing opposed to that kind of economic policy failure are policies that attempt to build economic capital in poor neighborhoods. That cannot be done without a growing economy, which means we need an economy with low tax rates on income and capital for all taxpayers; balanced, common-sense regulation; reasonable and predictable legal costs; an increasing flow of highly skilled workers who are globally competitive; and a secure homeland. Families who reside in low-income areas will not prosper without an environment that allows businesses to thrive. That will require each community to do all of these things on a local level, together with sound community planning, strong community organizations, and efforts to ensure healthy marriages and families.

With that as the backdrop, the ideas I have put forward here will build economic capital in the poorest neighborhoods and make for more financially stable families all across America. They will help to put an end to treadmill economics, and the result will be poor and low-income families—of every race and ethnicity—having more opportunity to fully join *We the People.*

Part Four
MORAL ECOLOGY

XXI

Liberty and Virtue

Perhaps no other man thought more about what the American nation ought to be, before we were a nation, than John Adams. He predicted our greatness. In a letter to his wife Abigail, he envisioned the annual explosion of fireworks that would ever after mark the Fourth of July. His work as the principal author of the Constitution of Massachusetts helped to define what our federal Constitution would look like. And this farsighted founder of the United States also thought that American freedom could not endure without a firm grounding in religion and virtue. Freedom is not self-sufficient.

Even in those days there were secular Enlightenment philosophers who argued that the institutions of democracy, properly devised, could amount to a machine that would go by itself, regardless of the moral character of the people. But that was not Adams's view. In June 1776 he wrote:

> Statesmen, my dear Sir, may speculate for liberty, but it is Religion and Morality alone, which can establish the Principles upon which Freedom can securely stand.
>
> The only foundation of a free Constitution is pure Virtue, and if this cannot be inspired into our People in a greater Mea-

sure than they have it now, they may change their Rulers and the forms of Government, but they will not obtain a lasting liberty.

In October 1798, during his presidency, he argued the same point in a speech to the armed forces of the United States:

> We have no government armed with power capable of contending with human passions unbridled by morality and religion. Avarice, ambition, revenge, or gallantry, would break the strongest cords of our Constitution as a whale goes through a net. Our Constitution was made only for a moral and religious people. It is wholly inadequate to the government of any other.

Concerning his own sons, he said: "Let them revere nothing but Religion, Morality and Liberty."

These statements by Adams do not reflect the curious private opinions of a stern Massachusetts Puritan; rather, Adams was voicing the nearly unanimous view of the other founders from every section of the new nation. The liberty they had fought for required that free citizens act decently, fairly, *and morally*—in both their public and their private dealings. The greatness of America's Great Experiment in self-government was not the mere mechanism of democracy, majority rule; no, the greatness lay in the kind of people capable of exercising the democratic franchise responsibly. America's greatness lay in a good, a moral, and a *virtuous* people.

George Washington echoed this sentiment when he said, "Let us with caution indulge the supposition that morality can be maintained without religion. Reason and experience both forbid us to expect that national morality can prevail in exclusion of religious principle."

But how do you develop a virtuous people? How exactly is virtue cultivated? Political philosophers through the centuries have debated that question, but on this question our founders were strangely silent. There are no mechanisms designed to directly cultivate virtue in the federal Constitution. This is a stark departure from the ancient republics: for those ancient city-states, cultivating virtue was a constant worry and the direct object of legislation. Why the absence of virtue-talk in our formal constitutional design, even though virtue was much talked about by the founders amongst themselves?

Liberal political theorists often contend that the absence of virtue-talk in early American state papers indicates that our founders shared the secular Enlightenment view holding that, properly devised, constitutional democracy could "work" even, as Immanuel Kant put it, "in a Republic of devils." There is no explicit endorsement for moral cultivation in our founding documents, they say, because our founders were profoundly indifferent, or even hostile, to the demands of virtue. Instead, they say, the Constitution favors individual self-expression and moral emancipation: in other words, many liberals end up arguing that *repealing* traditional morals legislation is the *essence* of America's constitutional tradition. But as we have seen with John Adams, virtue was no matter of indifference to the founders: it was the very foundation of self-government.

The reason for this absence of formal constitutional provisions concerning virtue and morality was the founders' view that moral cultivation is properly carried on by churches and families, not by the government. (At least, not by the *federal* government. Too often we forget that the federal government is not the whole government of the United States: the state and local governments, under the original federal Constitution, retained traditional jurisdiction over morals legislation.) The key to a virtuous public, they believed, would be vibrant churches and stable, traditional families. The First Amendment took care of the churches when it made sure that no religion would be established and that the people would be able to freely exercise their faith in public as well as privately. Constitutionally securing religious freedom was a high priority, given the founders' roots in a country, England, where there was a state religion.

On the other hand, the idea that the traditional family might need any kind of special constitutional protection would have been met by the founders with universal disbelief. It would have been the same as asking for constitutional protection for the sun to shine. In eighteenth-century America, only a lunatic could have imagined the fanciful Brave New Family arrangements that we find ourselves talking about at the dawn of the twenty-first century. In short, the framers of the Constitution believed that the government they had devised would be naturally supportive of the efforts of families and churches in this vital area of moral cultivation: they certainly could not imagine that a democratic American government would be "neutral" or even downright hostile to the efforts of families and churches to raise up a virtuous citizenry.

That America's founding genius was supportive of virtue is revealed in Article 3 of the Northwest Ordinance of 1787 that was passed by the Congress of Confederation. There, Congress proclaimed, "Religion, morality, and knowledge, being necessary to good government and the happiness of mankind, schools and the means of education shall forever be encouraged." Here, in one of the fundamental documents of the founding period, Congress envisioned publicly supported schools aiming not at mere intellectual development, not at moral neutrality and simple tolerance, but instead at a moral and even a religious citizenry. It was because America's founders expected such *public* support for religion and morality—religion and the family, the seedbeds of virtue—to be natural, even inevitable, in a democracy that they did not think it necessary to formally incorporate provisions concerning virtue into the Constitution.

In other words, high moral standards, widely shared and publicly honored and nurtured, are part of the common good, and our founders knew this. But they are a part of the common good that cannot be directly achieved through government action. Promoting this part of the general welfare is up to us, *We the People*. Yet government can frustrate the efforts of families and churches that are undertaking the important work of moral education—and all too often has, in recent years. That is the tale of America's squandered "moral capital," and that is the story I'll try to explain here. But from the first we have to remember that a concern for common morality is very much part of the American tradition, a part that conservatives, quite rightly, work to conserve. The motto of my own state of Pennsylvania is: "Virtue, Liberty, and Independence." Virtue comes first.

VIRTUE COMES FIRST, but that's not the end of the story: after all, there is also *liberty*. The village elders promote the view that conservatives who are concerned about moral matters are intolerant "virtuecrats," hostile to American liberty. The truth, as I have been trying to show, is that it is conservatives who truly embrace American *liberty*—while the liberals' No-Fault Freedom is a recipe for breaking down the moral and social bonds of our nation, which creates, in turn, the need for more government power. And with that comes less freedom.

Several years ago I organized a Senate Republican retreat in Williamsburg, Virginia, in the magnificent Governor's Mansion. We brought in the profound Irish social commentator Os Guinness, who gave a lecture that had a tremendous impact on many of my colleagues and me.

Guinness credited America's founders with a brilliant conception of a free society: a constantly moving triangle made up of religion, virtue, and freedom. The three points on this triangle were envisioned by our founders as three distinct mechanisms that work together like an engine to keep the Great Experiment running. Guinness called this scheme an "enduring triangle of first principles," and he credited it with making the United States the "greatest Republic since the fall of Rome."

Since I cannot improve on Guinness's speech, here is its core:

> [America's founders] realized there were three tasks to establishing a free society. This is so absurdly obvious that it hardly bears repeating, and yet many Americans miss the second and most miss the third.
>
> For the framers the first task was the obvious one: winning freedom, the revolution in 1776. But they saw that was the easiest and the shortest task. The second task was ordering freedom. Thirteen years longer—Philadelphia, the Constitution. [This was] much harder and much more daring, politically and intellectually. The French won their revolution, the Russians won their revolution: but they never *ordered* their revolution. They spiraled down to demonic disorder. The genius of the American Revolution was that they won it *and* they ordered freedom.

(This, by the way, is a lesson we are currently trying to impart to our Iraqi brothers and sisters.)

> But they realized the third task was by far the hardest: winning freedom, ordering freedom, *sustaining* freedom. . . .
>
> Last year in Washington I heard one of your most brilliant pundits say this: "America's destiny is to be the richest, freest, most powerful nation on earth and to remain so forever." Not surprisingly the audience burst into applause. But I heard the British talking like that when I was a boy, and so did the French, and so did the Spanish, and so did the Romans, and so did the Greeks. No success is forever and the framers realized that the

hardest task was not just winning and ordering but *sustaining* freedom, which is surely our challenge today.

Here you see how your framers with tremendous realism sought to use history to defy history. Polybius in particular discussed the reasons why republics rose, prospered, and fell. As that ancient author saw it, there were three [causes for the fall of republics]. Madison and Jefferson in particular wrestled with these because the American experiment was a national attempt to beat the odds and to overcome the cycle.

The first menace was external: a nation suddenly finds itself with greater power outside it. That is something not many can do anything about but be vigilant. Obviously, this was not America's main problem and the framers realized it. . . . [T]hat will never be America's main problem.

The second menace is harder, what Polybius and Madison discuss as the corruption of customs. Polybius argues that what is decisive for any nation is its Constitution. But a Constitution with a capital C, the laws, is only half the story. There is a constitution with a small c. Think of our physical constitution: what makes it up? For Polybius the small-c constitution was the beliefs, the customs, and the traditions of a people. And he argues that if even the best customs slowly become corrupted, even the best Constitution will be subverted. . . .

In other words, morals and manners make a difference: more of a difference even than laws—as Tocqueville knew.

Remarkably, if you ask Americans today, even scholars, what was the framers' answer to that cycle of rising and falling [of republics] most Americans would say, as the polls show: checks and balances, the separation of powers, *Federalist* 51, and so on. And that is clearly half the story, very much so: but *only* half of the story. The other half is what you might call an enduring triangle of first principles, which is so obvious to the framers that many people have missed it or just dismissed it as rhetoric and cant. Put very simply the triangle goes like this: freedom requires virtue, virtue requires faiths, faiths require freedom, which requires virtue, and so on ad infinitum.

I've discussed above freedom's dependence on virtue, as John Adams expressed it. But what about the rest? Guinness continued:

> Virtue requires faiths. With all the differences they had about faith, and their different views of religion in public life, to a person, without any exception, they all believed that virtue had to have an inspiration and content and sanction. And that had to be rooted in faith. . . .
>
> Of course the third leg of the triangle, the most daring of all: faiths require freedom. The disestablishment of the church beginning here in Virginia started something that was new in 1,500 years of European history. Now that enduring triangle of first principles, as I said today, is often dismissed as cant or rhetorical hype, but for the framers it was realistic. The Constitution alone would not hold things back if you lacked this sense of freedom and virtue and faiths [working together]. Law alone would not do it. Virtue is also needed. Virtue alone would not do it. But both of them are needed together.

Guinness is crediting our founders with a brilliant creation capable of resisting the cycle of rise, prosperity, and fall:

> Religion teaches virtue.
>
> Virtue is needed to sustain freedom.
>
> Freedom allows religion to prosper.

And so on, ad infinitum. I mentioned earlier that certain Enlightenment thinkers at the time of our founding believed a liberal political structure could be created that would "go by itself," forever. Well, America's constitutional order is now among the oldest political regimes on earth. But according to Os Guinness, this amazing endurance has *not* been because of atheistic Enlightenment principles. Rather, it has been because of America's peculiarly "un-Enlightened" openness to the role of religion in our common life.

Actually, "un-Enlightened" may be too tendentious. In her recent book *Roads to Modernity*, Gertrude Himmelfarb suggests that there was not a single Enlightenment in the eighteenth century, but three different, concurrent Enlightenments: a French secular Enlightenment, a British liberal Enlightenment, and an American theistic Enlightenment. Each had distinct characteristics, but most importantly, the American and British Enlightenments did not throw out tradition and religion as the secular French did. Both the British and the Americans approached Enlightenment in a way that preserves the moral underpinnings of a free society.

Does that mean we can rest on our laurels, content that this triangle will run effortlessly, forever? No. Guinness contended that the United States is the greatest republic since Rome. That's true: but even Rome fell. There is no substitute for careful, courageous, and intelligent stewardship of our inheritance. In America's case, it was probably predictable that our Achilles' heel would concern *liberty*—and its metamorphosis, over time, into No-Fault Freedom, a freedom that does not work together with virtue and religion but which is frankly hostile to both. With No-Fault Freedom, we come to our own "corruption of customs."

Another way of thinking about this "corruption of customs" is as a depletion of *moral capital*. I think that we can define moral capital using Polybius's terms: as common beliefs, customs, and traditions exhibited both in public and in private, together with a willingness to make ethical judgments in public and to act upon those judgments. Some traditional liberals, descendents of the British Enlightenment in contrast to the secular liberal descendants of the French one, have themselves held to this understanding of moral capital, and appreciated its role in the ordering of society and the pursuit of justice. However, as

Guinness demonstrates, America's particular moral capital is also deeply connected with religious faith. There is a *transcendent* dimension to our morality, an acknowledgment that our morals reflect not mere social convention, but are the gift of our Creator—and just as rights are not created by the state or by the consensus of the majority, but are inalienable owing to our being made in God's image, so too morality is not a human construct. Nevertheless, we can be bad stewards of that gift.

When moral capital is depleted, so is our social capital. Recall that social capital is a connectedness that comes from *trust*, a confidence in our dealings with other people that encourages association and cooperation. But where does such trust come from? The not very mysterious answer to how a society gains greater *trust* is by countless small acts of . . . *trustworthiness*. Social capital depends crucially on widespread practical adherence to certain common beliefs or moral norms. Social capital depends on moral capital. And when moral and social capital decrease, lawlessness increases, because there is little left to govern relations between citizens. In turn, the government's power necessarily increases as political leaders have no choice but to pass more laws and become ever more present in ever more aspects of the lives of citizens. That's what is happening today.

Guinness mentioned three menaces to sustaining freedom. Here is the third: time. "Abraham Lincoln called it 'the silent artillery of time.' By this process the vibrant beliefs and ideals of one generation become 'the antique manners' of another."

How often do we hear acerbic, condescending, sarcastic lampoons by the Hollywood/Harvard crowd about "old-fashioned" manners, customs, and moral duties? It is that kind of sarcasm—which is sometimes called, self-importantly, "irony"—that gnaws away at America's moral capital. The duty of securing America's *liberty* from the external threat of Islamic fascism has fallen to the courageous young servicemen and women on patrol in the Middle East. But the duty of maintaining our American liberty from the threat of depleting moral capital and the artillery of time is up to us all.

AS THE PUNDITS SET TO WORK deciphering the meaning of the 2004 elections, many focused on an unexpected finding that had showed up in exit polling data: the number one reason given for casting a vote either for John Kerry or for George W. Bush was a concern with "moral values." This issue was mentioned ahead of the economy, ahead of the war on terror, ahead of health care or Iraq. And of those who mentioned this as their number one issue, 80 percent voted for President Bush.

The mainstream media were stunned because the president had campaigned largely on the war on terrorism, while the mainstream media in its efforts to support the Kerry campaign had long been trumpeting troubling economic trends and difficulties in Iraq—nothing about moral values in any of that. They were stunned because Senator Kerry had spent a month during the campaign speaking frequently about his own commitment to "values," thus—it was said—neutralizing whatever advantage President Bush may have had in that area. They were stunned, as well, because they believed they had successfully portrayed issues like same-sex marriage as a civil right whose time had come, while all opponents of same-sex marriage were portrayed as irrational, fundamentalist bigots. In eleven states where banning same-sex marriage was on the ballot, it garnered on average almost 70 percent of the vote—at least 10 percent more than preelection polls had indicated. "Moral values" was a nonissue for the media: and it was the most important issue to voters in 2004, the issue that decided the election.

What was missing in the subsequent media coverage was any awareness that concern about the moral health of our country is not some special interest of conservatives: it is a worry shared by the vast majority of the American people. In 1965, 52 percent of the public felt that "people in general do not lead lives as honest and moral as they used to." That figure had risen to 71 percent by 1998. When asked to agree or disagree with the statement that "young people today do not have as strong a sense of right and wrong as they did 50 years ago," 46 percent said yes in 1965. That figure had risen to 70 percent in 1998. "Moral values" may have become a "problem" for the village elders in 2004, but the deep public concern about morals in America has been a long time coming, and it is a *common* concern, a majority concern, by a wide margin.

But this issue of "moral values" enrages the village elders because they believe these are nonissues, since the courts have made it unconstitutional to do anything about them legislatively; because they believe "moral values" are a mere smokescreen used by "the right" to lead working people into voting against their economic self-interest; and because they believe that their values are no less moral than anyone else's. But if you listen to ordinary Americans at backyard barbecues or sitting around kitchen tables across our land you will hear troubled parents worrying about what their children are learning in school, on the Internet, and on television; worrying about whatever happened to the common decencies of yesteryear; and worrying about how to raise children the right way when everything seems set against them.

Most liberals seem really to believe that this widespread worry about values is nothing more than a version of Marxist "false consciousness," a form of mass hysteria created by urban legends and stoked by talk-show hosts like Sean Hannity, Dr.

Laura, and Rush Limbaugh and evangelicals like Dr. James Dobson. Most liberals ignore this worry or make fun of "values" issues and their advocates in an attempt to convince the American people that their concerns are groundless.

More gifted liberal politicians take a different tack. Rather than dismissing moral concerns, they go out of their way to make political gestures shrewdly designed to try to convince the electorate that they *share* a concern for eroding American values. But these political efforts, despite megaphone publicity, touch only on small matters, and often matters over which the liberal politician has no control: remember President Clinton's "campaign" for school uniforms? Then, their "image" properly "managed" so as to appear "moderate," these politicians of the left proceed with their real agenda, an agenda utterly hostile to traditional morals.

School uniforms. They happen to be a good idea, but they're not the responsibility of the president of the United States. Yet as a politician I have to shake my head in wonderment at the sheer political artistry of such a move. It cost Bill Clinton nothing; there was no chance that this "campaign" would go anywhere. Yet by loudly trumpeting his interest in school uniforms, President Clinton was able to portray himself as someone who got it when it came to questions of America's moral health.

The same is true, of course, of Senator Hillary Rodham Clinton. In her book *It Takes a Village*, she writes about many concerns that boil down to moral values: she sounds like she shares the worries of most Americans about the moral health of the country. But when you actually look at the policies she would change, her "politics of meaning" boils down to little more than feel-good rhetoric masking a radical left agenda.

XXII

Moral Capital and the Moral Environment

In the past generation, one of the slogans of liberal feminists (both women and men, by the way) was "the personal is the political." They set about to advance a sexual revolution, from legitimizing free love (changing norms and laws with respect to premarital sex) to escaping the consequences of it (legalizing abortion). Thanks to rogue decisions by liberal judges, liberal feminists and the other village elders have let the horses of No-Fault Freedom run wild and have boarded up the proverbial barn door to ensure that traditional morals are locked out. Now they say: there's nothing "public," and so nothing political, about personal morals. The personal is *not* the political. The courts have spoken; democracy has no role here.

Many Americans sense that we have in the past generation or two thrown away much of our moral inheritance. They can just feel it in their bones that something is *not right* with both our public and our private morality today. In trying to give an account of this, conservative commentators and intellectuals talk about the corrosive changes brought about by the upheavals of "the Sixties." I have heard it said that you could tell whether someone is a conservative or a liberal after only one question:

Do you think the Sixties were good for America? For liberals, that decade was the time of liberation from all the repression of traditional values. The tremendous real achievement of civil rights aside, ever since the 1960s—the "Great Disruption," in the words of Francis Fukuyama—conservatives have been trying to make the case for a more moral and decent America while trying to repair and heal the broken families and lives that that era wrought.

Liberals of my own generation who are now our village elders tend to react angrily to this sort of talk. They paint a very different picture of America's moral history. According to the village elders, America in the 1950s was a society of sexual repression, and therefore sexual hypocrisy. It was a society riddled with racism and intolerance. It was a society of morbid and unfounded fears (of communism, for example). It was a society that imprisoned women on a pedestal of stultifying expectations. From these liberals' point of view, we have not driven off any moral cliff. Rather, equipped with the wings of the 1960s, America has launched itself to soar to greater moral heights. Far from squandering our moral capital, we have broadened and enriched it with greater tolerance, openness, and appreciation and respect for moral diversity.

Now the first thing to be said about this liberal story is that it is partially right. The 1950s were not without moral blemishes. Many conservatives recognize that there was something unsustainable about the roles for women made normative in that period, for example. Allan Carlson has argued that whereas the household had once been a center of productive activity, the advance of industrial technology and suburbanization often left women with few roles beyond those of infant caregiver and consumption specialist, i.e., shopper. Moreover, the 1960s civil rights movement, advanced and led by people of faith, was a great leap of moral growth in America. No one can deny that. In fact, America's racial reconciliation over the past generation is an extraordinary achievement in the moral history of the world. African-Americans rightly celebrate this progress, and so should we all. And there is more work to be done in healing the scars of racism in America. Unfortunately, the political allegiances formed by African-Americans with liberals in the 1960s have not served that community well in the post–civil rights era. I hope that more people in the African-American community will come to recognize that fact: and I hope that more conservative leaders will join me in trying to reach out to African-Americans.

But if the liberal story is partially right, where does it go wrong? Why, even in light of the moral advance of civil rights for blacks, do conservatives, Americans in general, and even many African-Americans, still think our moral values are on the brink?

THE ROOT OF THE DIFFERENCE between the village elders and conservatives lies in their different assessments of human nature itself, which lead to different conceptions of morality. Conservatives follow the traditional Judeo-Christian worldview, which includes the concept of original sin. It is a view of human beings as fallen creatures given to sinfulness. Personal moral growth, therefore, can only mean an effort of *disciplining* our sinful inclinations, so that we can become something other (and better) than what we "naturally" are. Liberals, however, follow one of two tracks that nevertheless lead essentially to the same view of man's role in society. They side either with the philosopher Rousseau, who viewed human beings as naturally good, or with postmodern materialist thinkers like Steven Pinker, who views us all as pre-wired machines with no free will and ultimately as living in a world with no transcendent categories of good or evil. Moral corruption in either case, therefore, does not come from within, but from without, from "society." Morality is not so much a matter of self-discipline as it is a matter of personal "authenticity" and of reforming traditional norms and their purveyors, the traditional family and faith-based communities, so that they don't interfere with such authenticity.

That is where "it takes a village" comes into play. For many liberals, the village elders are there to safeguard the individual from these outside forces—families and churches—that are tyrannically hostile to the individual's authentic or predestined desires. Any external restraint keeps one from fully "self-actualizing," and therefore institutions of traditional morality are actually harmful to the individual and keep society from progressing. That means that the village elders must drive traditional orthodox religion and traditional moral values from the public square—and particularly from influential places like schools and the entertainment media. The village elders do not protect the moral capital of the village: whether they know it or not, they are in an all-out war against it.

Martin Luther King, Jr. famously looked forward to the day when a man would be judged not by the color of his skin but by the content of his character. The difference between liberals and conservatives lies with "character." We view character as our founders did. Character is the fruit of a long process of self-discipline that subdues man's untamed impulses: a man of character is a better man than the man he would naturally be. Thus, his upright character is worthy of respect. That is why King's words were so powerful, so convicting: they resonated with the deepest moral traditions of the American people. And that is also why conservatives today rightly cherish the words and aspirations of

Dr. King: his appeal was a conservative moral appeal. Even many white Southerners recognized the truth of Dr. King's words.

But how do Dr. King's words sound to those who adhere to the liberal understanding of human nature? If man is believed to be naturally good or just a complex machine, then talk of honoring character makes no sense. In fact, habits of self-discipline look hypocritical: to cultivate one's moral character is to depart from one's authentic self. And so, despite the lip service paid to the memory of Dr. Martin Luther King, Jr., the rule the village elders really go by is something like this: we should judge a man not by the color of his skin, *nor* by the content of his character; we should not judge him, his words, or his deeds at all. From the liberal point of view, morality turns inside out. It's not about working on yourself to become a better person than the sinfully disordered person you naturally are; rather, it's about being open to and tolerant of the authentic self-expressions of others, and of yourself, whatever they may be. It's about self-esteem, not self-respect; it's about self-indulgence, not self-control.

Our whole pop culture is so self-centered, focused on maximizing self-esteem. The television talk shows, the infomercials, and our public schools are drenched in such talk. We also see it in our movies and video games and hear it in our pop music. As a result, we see selfishness and the consequent lack of civility and decency toward other people. But Americans know there is something wrong in the left's view of human nature and morality; they know there is something wrong with what we are communicating to our children. Decency and civility do not come from everyone doing what he or she wants to do—from being "authentic." They come, rather, from abiding by a moral code of conduct that is instilled by our loved ones. That is the traditional Judeo-Christian account of human nature, and whether we admit it or not, it is what Main Street America is crying out for in our society today.

A society rich in moral capital must be one in which moral aspirations are shared in common, even if not everyone can always live up to those ideals. The truth is that human beings are not born naturally inclined to do the right thing. A philosopher once said that the only empirically provable philosophical doctrine is that of original sin: I know it and you know it, and as a father of six, I know none of us is born without it. I said it before, and I'll say it again: sometimes I have to wonder if the village elders have ever had children of their own, because if they did, they would know it as well. But as adults we are no longer little children whose selfishness and temper tantrums have few lasting consequences for society at large. As adults, what we do matters; therefore, our goal must be to be something better than what we are by nature. Wouldn't it be easier to meet our goal if others in the community were also trying to live up to the better angels of their natures? And wouldn't it help if the media, the schools, and the government weren't "neutral" or indifferent (at best!) about our efforts to instill moral values in our children by acting as if character development really doesn't count?

I am not advocating a replenishment of our moral capital because I want everybody to be alike. I don't want our government snooping through people's private lives, either. But I do want a government that is supportive of the difficult efforts of families trying to instill character in their children. I don't want a government that is neutral between virtue and vice. I do want a government, and a community, that is willing and able to judge people by . . . the content of their character.

And there's one more thing about the value of virtue for the common good, an implication from Os Guiness's reflections.

Our founding fathers recognized a simple formula, perhaps a scientific law of politics: virtue and legislation are inversely related. At a human level, we all know this. When our teenagers are rebellious and refuse to "get with the program," then as parents we devise an elaborate set of rules so that they know exactly what is expected of them and when they've crossed the line. At the level of private business relations, every businessperson and lawyer knows this lesson by heart. The more difficult and suspicious a business relationship, the longer and more complicated the contract.

At the political level, the same thing is true. I've made the case: the more moral a people, the less need there is for laws; the less moral a people, the greater the need for legislative intrusion, for police and for government to poke into our business. The village elders have it exactly the wrong way around. They think moral norms are somehow tyrannical, but the opposite is true: we are a freer people when we are a more moral people.

This, by the way, was an insight of the eighteenth-century British statesman Edmund Burke, who is usually recognized as the father of modern conservatism. He wrote, "Men are qualified for civil liberty in exact proportion to their disposition to put moral chains upon their appetites. . . . It is ordained in the eternal constitution of things, that men of intemperate minds cannot be free. Their passions forge their fetters." In other words, self-government requires moral self-control. When a people no longer controls its "appetite," the public consequences require an external force, most likely the government, to step in.

THERE IS ANOTHER WAY of thinking about questions of "moral values" in America. Have you ever walked through a major library with a government documents repository? It is an impressive sight. You probably never imagined that your federal government was publishing *so much stuff*. There you will find countless volumes running into many thousands of pages recording what has been said in the U.S. House and Senate. You will find thousands of pages of regulations churned out daily by various federal bureaucracies. You will find informational brochures and research reports from various agencies.

You will also find here and there massive multivolume works called Environmental Impact Statements. These are a sight to behold: reams of scientific data and analysis documenting, or speculating, about the environmental effect of a dam across a small stream or a stretch of highway through a wetland. Every variable is measured, every animal habitat mapped, all in an effort to determine the potentially negative side effects of a construction project.

Liberals love Environmental Impact Statements. And while they are costly, and while they may easily be abused as a mere tool to stop a development project altogether, they do reflect a true insight: namely, that nature is a subtle web of intricate organic connections, and even small changes in an ecosystem can have large and unintended negative effects downstream. Some call it the "butterfly effect": the mere flapping of a butterfly's wings may contribute to causing a hurricane on the other side of the globe. Trying to look ahead to what might be lost is simply prudent.

What has always baffled me is that the village elders who are so sensitive about interventions in the natural ecosystem are almost always the same people who champion the wholesale destruction of our society's *moral* ecosystem. Human societies are also a subtle web of intricate organic connections, of moral bonds, communities of memory and mutual aid, as the legal scholar Mary Ann Glendon puts it. Yet when it comes to the moral ecology of our society, liberals turn into the dirty dozen, thoughtlessly clear-cutting forests of rich, ancient moral norms, paving them over with contempt, and building in their place the moral equivalent of strip malls. Where is the prudence, the foresight, the sound science, and the sensitivity to our moral ecosystem? Shouldn't we spend at least as much time on exhaustive research for a Moral Impact Statement when proposing moral alterations to our environment as we do when building a bridge that *may* adversely affect a box turtle in rural Pennsylvania?

Consider, for example, the divorce revolution of the past generation. Our society once had a settled consensus supporting marital fidelity and marital perseverance: "for better or worse, as long as you both shall live." But in the historical blink of an eye in the early 1970s, we changed our moral norms, and with them our laws. At the time, it was said, no-fault divorce would be nothing but a benefit—freeing unhappy men and women from a yoke that had become oppressive. The children would be better off, too, freed from a household of bitterness and conflict. No one would be harmed.

Well, it didn't turn out that way. The new moral norms made all marriages less secure, and what is more, the children of divorce ended up, all too often, harmed in very deep ways, as I showed earlier with the statistics regarding social capital.

It was supposed to be win-win. But decades of social science studies now demonstrate with absolute certainty how many have suffered on account of this moral revolution. To take but one statistic, the children of divorced parents have a far lower chance themselves of forming stable lifelong commitments. Yet the old wisdom is true: it is in such commitments, in marriage, that the greatest happiness in this life is to be found. Beyond the higher drug use, the higher delinquency rates, the higher suicide rates of children of divorce, there is that less measurable but more profound change in our moral ecology: many of the children of the divorce generation do not have the courage to themselves manage a happy marriage. But how do we put this tradition back together again after it has been broken? How do we restore the delicate beauty of the old-growth forest after it has been clearcut? How do we restore a moral environment once it has been destroyed?

Secular liberals have only one answer to that question: you can't. There is nothing external, transcendent, absolute, or permanent to appeal to. Old morality falls away as society evolves and "progresses" into something new, more tolerant, and more permissive. They tell us to stop being "nostalgic," stop holding on to the repressive past. But for conservatives, that is simply inadequate: we *have* to think about how to restore the moral ecology, because that is the burden of stewardship we face in our time—that is what we owe to our children and their children. We have to replenish our moral capital.

A generation ago, portions of our Great Lakes were dead and rivers caught fire in Ohio, such was the extent of environmental degradation. Thankfully, we did something about it, and today life has returned to lakes, rivers, and streams across America. Nature has a power of restoring itself; so too does human nature. "Traditional morality" is, quite simply, the morality that corresponds to human nature, and human nature has as much power to restore itself as any river or stream. What is needed is leadership and legislation, but more importantly, a renewed commitment from all of us in our daily lives. We owe it to our children to restore the moral environment.

XXIII

The Rule of Judges

Earlier, I asked why Moral Impact Statements are not demanded by liberals. There is at least one reason for that. The requirement of Environmental Impact Statements is a result of congressional action after much deliberation. Congress made sure that the public would have input into the process—some say far too much public input, but the politicians knew they would be held accountable to that very public one November election day. Congress also gave the executive branch authority to consider and decide on the intricate details of this procedure after public hearing and a formal rulemaking procedure, which is subject to further review by Congress and the people. You may or may not like the idea of Environmental Impact Statements, but the idea went through the democratic process and was refined to become what it is today. However, that is not how liberals operate when it comes to changing the moral landscape of our country. They prefer to circumvent the democratic process and legislate by judicial fiat.

The village elders introduce very few bills—almost none that attract more than one or two cosponsors. There are no hearings where Congress and the public can hear arguments about the merits to society of changing its moral fabric. Did Congress pass a law that said it was illegal to display a Christmas crèche on public property, tell us we could not recite the pledge that we are "one nation under God" in schools, or legislate away displays of the Ten Commandments from public buildings? Did we pass a constitutional amendment that gave anyone a right to marry as many people of whatever gender they want? Did we pass an amendment that gave women the right to abort their children at any time, for any reason, during pregnancy? Did we pass a law that minors could undergo the surgical procedure of abortion without parental consent or notification? The answer to all of these questions is: *No!* Not in one state legislature, much less in the U.S. Congress, did the democratic branches of government, the people's branches, pass such amendments or enact such laws. How could the moral fabric of America be so torn apart without so much as a single act of Congress duly signed by the president?

The answer is, of course, the courts—most particularly, the federal courts. A generation ago, liberals figured out something that most conservatives couldn't have dreamed of in their worst nightmare. A few well-positioned autocrats can do what most Americans thought, and the Constitution says, takes two-thirds of the Congress and three-quarters of the state legislatures to do: namely, change the Constitution to mean whatever they want it to mean. The plan was simple. Put justices on the Supreme Court, backed up by lower court judges, to "modernize" our Constitution by fiat, with the claim that Supreme Court decisions, whether based on the words of the Constitution or not, have the same status as the Constitution itself.

How often do we hear that our founding compact needs to be a living, breathing document whose meaning changes with the times? Never mind what the words of our Constitution actually say; never mind the clear intent of the Constitution's writers and signers; never mind two hundred years of judicial interpretation; never mind the centuries-old wisdom of the common law: we are much wiser today than our predecessors. Or so goes the liberal boast. In fact, it is said, we are now able to see just what they were "getting at" even better than they could—as if the U.S. Constitution were only a "nice try" at a plan of government.

Throughout this book I have been referring to the left as the "village elders." Well, when it comes to the Court and its activist decisions, we have come to the high oligarchy of the village elders: accountable to no one, deciding the most important and troubling issues of our time, issues that speak to our very identity as a people and even as human beings. And all of this has been done undemocratically—even anti-democratically.

With Congress, if the people decide its representatives have made a mistake, the people can throw them out and bring in different ones to correct with new laws any errors perpetrated by the old. But the Supreme Court almost never has second thoughts: it certainly has not had second thoughts about its fundamental project of the past generation, the project of moral revolution enshrined in law. In fact, in the infamous *Casey* decision in 1992, which reaffirmed *Roe v. Wade* and the abortion license, the Court's majority opinion actually said that widespread popular opposition to *Roe* was an important reason for the Court to *stick* to its pro-abortion decision: to do otherwise would "subvert" the Court's "legitimacy." In other words, the village elders have spoken, and it is up to the American people to shut up and *obey*.

Alexander Hamilton in the *Federalist* papers called the courts the "least dangerous branch" of the new federal government. Could our founders, who had thrown off monarchic rule in the name of democracy, ever have imagined such judicial arrogance? Actually, some eventually did. Thomas Jefferson said in 1821:

> The germ of destruction of our nation is in the power of the judiciary, an irresponsible body—working like gravity by night and by day, gaining a little today and a little tomorrow, and advancing its noiseless step like a thief over the field of jurisdiction, until all shall render powerless the checks of one branch over the other and will become as venal and oppressive as the government from which we separated.

We now see who was right. Sodomy and abortion are now not only legal; they are constitutional rights. What is more, our courts have been coming closer with every decision to proclaiming that there can be no difference, in law, between marriage and cohabitation. And of course we are also on the verge of court-mandated same-sex marriage.

I have been using the extended metaphor of various kinds of "capital" throughout this book. When it comes to what has happened to our *moral* capital in the past generation or two, I am stymied for a verb to use. It wasn't "squandered" or "spent down"; it didn't "trickle away." The verbs that come to mind are *destroyed* and *replaced*. Traditional morality is being destroyed, and being replaced by something that claims to be morality, but ultimately has little social benefit or ability to sustain the democratic experiment. In China during the so-called Great Leap Forward at the end of the 1950s, Chairman Mao ordered every town and village to participate in smelting iron for steel production. The promise was that through the new techniques of communism, China would quickly surpass Western capitalist nations in steel. Obedient to their orders, peasants melted down pots and pans and farm implements, with the promise that shiny new and better utensils of steel would be quickly returned. What in fact happened was that these villagers were left with large lumps of useless iron—and with no tools left to farm with. One of the world's greatest famines soon followed. What we Americans did with our moral capital over the last generation is like what those Chinese peasants did with their capital tools for farming: on government orders—in our case, on Court orders—we melted it down, for nothing.

How did this all start? Several "strands" of major Supreme Court decisions, bound together, have dismantled older constitutional understandings and enshrined the new morality. On the questions of marriage, family, and sex, that string begins with the 1965 *Griswold* decision. In that case, a Connecticut law that outlawed the use of contraceptives, even by married couples, was ruled unconstitutional. Now, before you jump to conclusions, let me clearly state that this law was badly written, and I would not have supported it or its intent. Nonetheless, it is in this case that the Court "discovered" a "right to privacy" in the U.S. Constitution. Of course, such a right does not appear anywhere in the text of the Constitution. Rather, the Court's majority discovered—or invented—such a right from the "emanations" and "penumbras" of rights found in the First, Fourth, Fifth, Ninth, and Fourteenth Amendments.

It is significant that what seems to have been decisive in the minds of some of the justices in the *Griswold* majority was actually something quite traditional in the common law: the notion that marriage was a privileged institution into which law should not interfere. The case involved Planned Parenthood dispensing contraceptives to a married couple, and throughout the decision, it was *marital* privacy that was discussed. So, an aspect of the traditional moral view was a motivation for the Court's majority decision: but the jurisprudential novelty it established—the right to privacy—would quickly become a constitutional wrecking ball.

Justices Stewart and Black were scathing in dissent, observing that while both disagreed with the law personally (as do I), they could find nothing in the U.S. Constitution that prevented the Connecticut legislature from making such a law (which had been on the books in the state since 1879). The dissenting justices mocked the reasoning of the majority, which in some cases based itself not on the Constitution's text, but rather on the "traditions and [collective] conscience of our people." How, asked the dissenters, could the Court *know* the conscience of the people better than legislators? Did not such reliance lead only to the substitution of judges' "personal and private notions" for the decisions of legislatures? "Use of any such broad, unbounded judicial authority would make of this Court's members a day-to-day constitutional convention," warned Justice Black. And so it has been! Finally, Justice Black observed that "privacy" is a "broad, abstract and ambiguous concept," lacking the specificity of a genuinely *constitutional* rule. However traditional it may appear in the guise of marital privacy, which as a legislator I support, this novel right was bound to do harm in our jurisprudence.

And so it was and so it did. Just seven years later, in *Eisenstadt v. Baird* (1972), the Court struck down a Massachusetts law that made contraception legal only for married persons. The distinction between the married and unmarried was breached, and the "right of privacy" became unhinged, essentially protecting (heterosexual) sex, as such, from any moral regulation.

Again, although I disagree with the Massachusetts law and its intent, the Court's solution to the problem presented by such a law was neither judicious nor prudent: the Court in effect codified the sexual revolution then underway—with the supremely powerful protection of a constitutional right. Marital privacy had now morphed into "the right of the individual, married or single, to be free from unwarranted governmental intrusion into matters so fundamentally affecting a person as the decision whether to bear or beget a child." The arguably traditional marital dimension upon which the Court had discovered the new "privacy right" was simply dropped with respect to having heterosexual intercourse. Rather than encouraging the legislature to repeal an outdated law, the Court expanded further the ungrounded right to privacy.

The next step, of course, was *Roe v. Wade*, the abortion decision of 1973. Today, most honest constitutional experts agree that as constitutional law, this decision is a monstrosity, a pure act of judicial legislating with no warrant in the Constitution's text. Having invented a "right to privacy," a right with a special emphasis on sexual matters, the Court was driven by its new moral logic to extend protection to what was all too often the result of the new sexual ethic: unwanted pregnancies and their "termination."

The *Roe* decision established an elaborate system of "trimesters" of pregnancy and delimited when the states might and might not have a "compelling interest" in protecting the life of the unborn, "balanced" against the "privacy right" of the mother. In immediately subsequent decisions, however, this elaborate system quickly became meaningless, a dead letter. By the Supreme Court's lights, *no* legislative regulation of abortion was permissible, for abortion was, after all, a "fundamental right." What could possibly count as a legitimate weight in the balance against a "fundamental right"? In effect, *Roe* created a private license to kill a certain category of Americans, the unborn, and raised this license to a constitutional principle.

The strands of these Court cases had made the rope thick. The legal reasoning continued to evolve, and the right to (sexual) privacy approached its terminal point. In the 1992 case, *Planned Parenthood of Southeast Pennsylvania v. Casey,* the Court handed down a complex ruling on a Pennsylvania state law that sought to reduce the number of abortions by a whole set of restrictive measures. The *Casey* decision actually stepped back from some of the most extreme Court decisions that followed *Roe*: certain measures to ensure "informed consent" are now ruled constitutional, for example. But finally, the Court would not allow any legislation in America that would actually *prevent* a woman from procuring an abortion she desired. That is the bottom line. And the reason for this is found in the so-called "mystery passage" I cited earlier. It formed the basis of the ruling: "At the heart of liberty," Justice Kennedy wrote for the majority, "is the right to define one's own concept of existence, of meaning, of the universe, and of the mystery of human life." The privacy right had now been expanded to its philosophical extreme.

I have been arguing that moral capital involves shared moral aspirations and norms, which for most of our founders was our human, legislative effort to approximate a transcendent moral order. I have been arguing that such moral capital is part of the common good. Here, however, the court tells us that liberty must mean that there *is* no common good: each of us is locked in the prison of our own self-created moral universe. We are, each of us, lords of the world, divine legislators. There is no transcendent truth, no common truth, just myriad individual truths.

Where does the right to privacy go from here? As our culture continues to "progress" and old inhibitions are cast off, what boundaries—what guardrails—will be left? In his 1995 book *Rethinking Life and Death,* Princeton professor Peter Singer liberates moral theory and practice from any truths that pose an obstacle to our will to power and control. In that book he champions "neonaticide"—that is, the legal destruction of newborn human beings with physical handicaps up through the 28th day *after* birth. Singer has been dubbed by his critics "Professor Death"—but he professes his views from a tenured chair at Princeton.

Is Singer alone in promoting such a radical "concept of existence, of meaning, of the universe, and of the mystery of human life"? Unfortunately, he is not. Steven Pinker, a professor of psychology at Harvard, suggests that

> we need a clear boundary to confer personhood on a human being and grant it a right to life. . . . [T]he right to life must come . . . from morally significant traits that we humans happen to possess. One such trait is having a sequence of experiences that defines us as individuals and connects us to other people. Other traits include an ability to reflect on ourselves as a continuous locus of consciousness, to form and savor plans for the future, to dread death and to express the choice not to die.

Under his definition a newborn is not human, and therefore the reality Pinker constructs would allow for neonaticide as well. Pinker points to that conclusion himself: "several moral philosophers have concluded that neonates are not persons . . . and thus neonaticide should not be classified as murder."

How long will it be before the Supreme Court "discovers" that voices like Singer's and Pinker's, coming as they do from some of our most elite educational institutions, represent the evolving "[collective] conscience of our people" and bring us yet another expansion of the right to privacy?

THERE IS ANOTHER STRING of cases that brought forth a second pernicious Court doctrine that has transformed America's moral ecosystem. These cases concern religion in the public square. The "first freedom" of the First Amendment concerns religious liberty: "Congress shall make no law respecting an establishment of religion, or prohibiting the free exercise thereof. . . ." The first thing to notice is that the phrase "wall of separation," cited so frequently as an almost sacred text in most of these Supreme Court decisions, is *not* a phrase used in the U.S. Constitution. It was lifted from a passage in a letter from President Jefferson to the Baptists of Danbury, Connecticut, more than a decade after the First Amendment was added to the Constitution.

The rather odd wording of the First Amendment also is worth noticing: ". . . respecting an establishment of religion. . . ." Here, "respecting" is a preposition that means "regarding" or "about." Congress shall make no law *about* the establishment of religion. We now know that this curious phrasing was a revision of the draft text of the amendment. An earlier draft said only that Congress could not establish a religion: but at that time, there were established churches in several of the states, notably in Massachusetts. Delegates from these states worried that simply preventing Congress from establishing a religion would *not* rule out the federal government *dis*establishing the state churches. The language of the First Amendment, therefore, is the way it is in no small part to *protect* the established churches of states. The Massachusetts Puritan church remained established in that state until 1833.

Of course, that does not mean we should today get into the business of establishing state churches: for one thing, the withering of faith in Europe in the presence of church establishments demonstrates that establishments have negative consequences— *for religion*. But a correct historical understanding of the First

Amendment does show how far the Court has strayed from our constitutional tradition.

Throughout our history up until the middle years of the twentieth century, the "American way" on church-state questions is best described as an accommodating separationism. Earlier I quoted the Northwest Ordinance, with its positive legislation regarding religion and morality. James Wilson, one of only six founders to have signed both the Declaration of Independence and the Constitution, pronounced in his law lectures at the University of Pennsylvania that "Far from being rivals or enemies, religion and law are twin sisters, friends, and mutual assistants." Unsurprisingly, for most of American history, government has looked positively on both religion and morality. Various states worked out particular arrangements reflecting their particular circumstances, but in each case, religious freedom was respected while religion was looked upon as part of the common good, a "seedbed of virtue" contributing to American society.

Things changed with the decision in *Everson v. Board* in 1947. While upholding the constitutionality of a New Jersey law that publicly funded transportation to and from school for both public and parochial students, the Court's majority declared that the First Amendment mandated that neither federal nor state governments could "pass laws which aid one religion, aid all religions, or prefer one religion over another." "No tax in any amount, large or small," the decision continued, "can be levied to support any religious activities. . . ." The "wall between Church and State . . . must be kept high and impregnable." All this, because in the Court's eyes, the Constitution's position on religion is one of "a strict and lofty neutrality."

Never before had our country been "neutral" on religion: now, this newly discovered constitutional principle spread everywhere. *Abington v. Schempp* (1963) held that "in the relationship between man and religion, the State is firmly committed to a position of neutrality." In *Epperson v. Arkansas* (1968), the Court held that "Government in our democracy, state and nation, must be neutral in matters of religious theory, doctrine, and practice. . . . The First Amendment mandates government neutrality between religion and religion, and between religion and no religion."

In most of these cases, the question before the Court concerned either prayer in public schools on the one hand, or public assistance for sectarian (usually Catholic) schools on the other. More recently, the Court has extended itself even to rendering unconstitutional such settled and popular American practices as prayer at public high school graduations or at public high school football games. Just last year, the Supreme Court dodged on a technicality a case that would have removed "under God" from the Pledge of Allegiance: ruling "under God" unconstitutional would have been deeply unpopular, but by the Court's own logic, there is no way to escape the conclusion that it must go. The overarching impulse of the Court's position has been to drive religion from the public square, to secularize our society from the roots up, all in the name of the constitutional principle of "neutrality"—both among religions and between religion and irreligion.

Of course, the term "neutrality" does not appear in the U.S. Constitution. This doctrine is a pure invention of the Court. In her 1985 dissent in *Wallace v. Jaffree*, for example, Justice O'Connor pointed out that the free exercise clause itself sometimes mandates exemptions for religious observers from otherwise generally applicable legal obligations. She concluded that "a government that confers a benefit on an explicitly religious basis is not neutral toward religion," nor was it ever intended to be. While neutrality between religion and irreligion may be required by liberal political theory, something very different is required by the text of the U.S. Constitution.

And what is more, I believe a convincing argument may be made that "liberal neutrality" is never really neutral. The practical effects of such a rule always have a disparate impact. We can see this in the Court's school prayer decisions. The Court's majority rulings have delved into the psychological effects of public prayer in schools for those youngsters who are not themselves religious: would they not be subject to a kind of peer pressure that would violate their conscience? But the Court does not examine the flip side of their psychological investigation: what about religious youngsters who find themselves in a public school hermetically sealed off from all religious influences? Would not the school, and therefore the government, tacitly be communicating to religious youngsters that prayer, religion, and faith are not really welcome in America's public square? That is where we have ended up: Court-sanctioned *hostility* to religious influence in American society, all in the name of neutrality.

I COULD GO FURTHER and discuss the cases that touch on pornography and obscenity, also part of our moral ecology. In fact, I will have more to say about this in the next chapter. But briefly, for decades, communities in America have tried to shore up common decency, have tried to guard their collective moral capital, by regulating *smut*. Congress has likewise responded to Americans' moral sensibilities by attempting to regulate broadcast media and the Internet. But time and again over the past generation America's communities and Congress have run up against a Supreme Court intent to side *against* the American people and *with* the pornographers. The Court's doctrine has been that virtually all efforts to regulate smut run afoul of the First Amendment, which the Court says protects all individuals' "freedom of expression."

But let's look for a minute at what that First Amendment actually says about our freedoms: "Congress shall make no law . . . abridging freedom of speech. . . ." Since this amendment goes on to discuss the people's right to assemble and to petition the government, as well as freedom of the press, it is clear that the "speech" in question concerns, in the first instance, *political* speech—arguments about the public good. At the time this amendment was passed, the English Crown could and did regulate what could be published and said about sensitive political questions; in America, things would be different.

But you may have noticed that in pornography the words aren't really the point, are they? "Speech" implies words, rationally intelligible discussion and argument, *communication*. Pictures also can be "worth a thousand words," of course: sometimes images are central to a political or social cause. But America's huge porn industry is not about political debate; it is not about the communication of ideas. It's about the commercial production of objects of titillation for profit. Based on the text of the Constitution, the courts should have recognized a hierarchy of protected "speech," with political speech and writing receiving the greatest constitutional protection, commercial speech less protection, and mere titillation the least of all. Yet in the topsy-turvy world of the new court-approved morality, limits on political speech like the recently passed McCain-Feingold campaign finance bill are just fine, but congressional restrictions on Internet pornographers are seen as violating the First Amendment and are therefore struck down.

Privacy. Neutrality. Free Expression. None of these terms is in the Constitution. They "look like" terms that actually are there. Freedom from "unreasonable searches and seizures": that's in the Fifth Amendment. "Equal protection of the laws": that's in the Fourteenth Amendment. "Freedom of speech": That's in the First Amendment. That is why liberals believe what they are doing is merely refining the intentions of our founders, making explicit the underlying philosophical tenets of our Constitution. The problem is that these "philosophical" tenets are pure abstractions, fit only for those great abstractions, "liberal individuals." But the U.S. Constitution was the fruit of long experience in the great complexity and wisdom of English common law.

As Harvard's Mary Ann Glendon has written,

> [T]he peculiar excellence of the Anglo-American common-law tradition over centuries, that which distinguished it from continental "legal science," was its rejection of simplifying abstractions, its close attention to facts and patterns of facts. . . . It was this unique combination of common sense and modest . . . theory that enabled England and the United States to develop and maintain a legal order possessing the toughness to weather political and social upheavals. . . . When legal scholars distance themselves from those ways of thinking, they repudiate much of what is best in their professional tradition.

The Supreme Court of the United States in the past half-century has been a bad steward of its own jurisprudential traditions, preferring instead the neat abstractions of the latest "theories."

Privacy. Neutrality. Free Expression. These three abstractions together make for a perfect storm, a jurisprudential hurricane for wreaking havoc on a moral ecosystem. Together they make of our Constitution not a document for democratic self-governance, but instead describe a pure liberal society of isolated individuals each doing their own thing within the politically correct boundaries carefully crafted and enforced by the village elders.

The irony is that the tradition of common law had made marriage and family exactly a *privileged* institution; Supreme Court decisions originally based on this traditional conception (*Griswold*) eventually undermined that privileged status in the name of abstract privacy. Similarly, as Justice O'Connor observed, on its face the U.S. Constitution is not neutral between religion and irreligion. Religion is a specially protected category in the actual text of the Constitution: it gets a special mention as the "first freedom" of the First Amendment. Religion and the family, I said at the beginning, were the two main agents for *moralizing* society, for generating new moral capital. The Court's decisions have undermined these institutions, creating in their place a society of atomized and de-moralized individuals, shielded by the village elders from the natural moral influences of faith and family.

Now that we know where it started, where are we now? You may recall my comments, widely reported in the press, about the *Lawrence v. Texas* case, in which the petitioner was seeking to strike down the Texas sodomy statute as unconstitutional. Before that decision, I made the comment to a reporter that this decision had the potential to further expand the right to "privacy" with devastating consequences. This is how she reported this often-repeated quote of mine:

> And if the Supreme Court says that you have the right to consensual (gay) sex within your home, then you have the right to bigamy, you have the right to polygamy, you have the right to incest, you have the right to adultery. You have the right to anything.

The reporter inserted the word "gay" into the first sentence. This led to claims that I was comparing homosexuality with incest and polygamy, which I was not. What I was saying takes more than a sound bite to explain and that makes it tough for some reporters, and the media in general, to grasp.

First, we have to look at the state of the law before *Lawrence* was decided. I discussed the *Griswold* case above and the right of privacy that it eventually created. With respect to sexual conduct, not abortion, the Court had recognized a zone of privacy around marriage. In other words, married people were treated differently under the law with respect to their sexual activity with one another than unmarried people. In its left-handed way, the Court in *Griswold* gave deference to marriage between one man and one woman as the building block for society and the legitimate purpose for sexual activity and thereby protected it from state regulation. *Eisenstadt* began to change all that, however, and this transformation of our constitutional traditions continued with *Roe* and *Casey*.

What I feared the Court would do in *Lawrence* in striking down the Texas sodomy statute is finally and completely eliminate marriage as a privileged institution in our laws and simply expand the zone of privacy in sexual conduct to all consenting adults. That is exactly what they did: marriage has now completely lost its special place in the law. The Court said in effect that marriage has not only outlived its legal usefulness, it said it is discriminatory to treat people differently based on such an outdated social construct. Therefore, over the past generation, it has decided to change the zone of sexual "privacy" from one man and one woman in marriage to consenting adults, period. So, to paraphrase my own quote above: if consent is now the *only* standard to have your sexual behavior protected by the Constitution, then how can the Court prohibit *any* consensual sexual behavior among two, three, or more people? The answer is logically, judicially, that you cannot—for other than arbitrary reasons. That is why there have already been several cases filed by polygamists seeking similar constitutional protection on the basis of *Lawrence*.

It is also no coincidence that within a few months of the *Lawrence* decision, the Massachusetts state supreme court handed down the *Goodrich* decision, which established in that state a constitutional right to same-sex marriage. And what was the first and most often cited case it used in coming to its decision? You guessed it: *Lawrence v. Texas*. The village elders on the Massachusetts court reasoned that the Commonwealth of Massachusetts could not discriminate against people simply because they were exercising their constitutional rights. They went so far as to say that there is no "rational basis" for treating heterosexual unions differently from same-sex relationships: the only conceivable reason for barring same-sex couples from state-sanctioned marriage had to be "animus"—hatred. That's right, the Massachusetts court said the only reason you could possibly want to protect the sacred institution at the core of every civilization in history is because you are a bigot. Welcome to village legal scholarship.

As for a Moral Impact Statement to determine the extent of damage such a fundamental change would cause: none. The court in Massachusetts ordered no studies or hearings. It simply, by undemocratic, authoritarian brute force, told the people of Massachusetts that marriage as we all know it is over. In fact, it declared that anyone who holds to the traditional definition of marriage is "irrational," since there is no "rational basis" for the traditional view.

And what do the village elders in Congress today say to all of this? What do the liberals who have never met an issue that didn't need "solving" by legislation say about the role of Congress? They say, "It's a state issue: they can handle it." Or they say, "It's a judicial issue: they can handle it." Let me translate: "We can't come out in favor of same-sex marriage since it is too unpopular. So let's let the unelected judges on the state and eventually federal courts do the dirty work for us." The fact is, I could substitute the words "in the 1960s" for the word "today" in the first sentence, and the word "abortion" for the words "same-sex marriage" in the previous sentence, and you now see the strategy laid bare. This calculated plan is undemocratic, it's an abuse of power, it savages the moral ecosystem in this country—and it worked once and is working again.

The good news is that while it is rare, Supreme Court decisions *are* sometimes overturned. We are now only a little more than thirty years on from *Roe v. Wade*. But it took more than sixty years for the "separate but equal" ruling of *Plessy v. Ferguson* to be overturned by *Brown v. Board of Education*. It took thirty years for the ruling in *Lochner v. New York* to be overturned. It *can* be done. Just like the health of the Great Lakes and the rivers of Ohio returned, so too, I believe, can our moral ecosystem right itself. All we need is leadership that understands the gravity of the problem and is determined to do something about it. And that is why disputes over nominations for federal judgeships will continue to be among the most bitterly contested matters in the U.S. Senate.

XXIV

Abortion: A Personal Aside

No discussion of moral capital and its effect on our moral ecology and the family is complete without addressing directly the great moral issue of our time. Abortion is a toxin methodically polluting our fragile moral ecosystem. It poisons everyone it touches, from the mother and her ill-fated child, to the mother and father's families, to the abortion provider, to each of us who stands as a silent witness to this destruction and debasement of human life. As a result of abortion, for more than thirty years over a quarter of all children conceived in America never took their first breath. Before I discuss how abortion specifically affects our country, I believe you may gain some insights by understanding how the issue of abortion affected me personally.

I was very much like most Americans and most nominal Catholics before I decided to enter public life. I didn't like the idea of abortion—I knew it was wrong, but I wasn't sure if it was the government's business to do anything about it. When I decided to run for public office in 1989, I was told that I had to "make up my mind on abortion." I looked at the scientific research about the beginning of life in the womb as well as some moral and ethical literature on both sides of the issue. Through both scientific reasoning and moral reasoning the answer was clear to me. Abortion was the taking of an innocent human life. Scientifically, the embryo is human from the moment of conception (it has a complete, unique human genetic code) and it is alive: therefore, it is literally a human life.

The question boils down to this: Should we allow one human being to take the life of another, no matter how difficult the circumstances are for the mother? If the child is innocent of any action that would permit someone to deprive him of his life, such as a threat to the mother's life, the answer under common law and our common Judeo-Christian code is: No.

I looked at it one other way. Did I see the child in the womb as a person entitled to protection under the law, or as property owned by the mother, with no rights until the moment she was physically separated from her mother? I thought of it as a lawyer still somewhat fresh out of law school. Was the child in *Roe v. Wade* any different than the slave in the *Dred Scott* decision? Since the founding of our republic we have suffered from the moral scars of treating our brothers as chattel. How could another episode in dehumanization, in this case of our littlest brothers and sisters, benefit this country? No, I couldn't see myself on the "mere property" side of this argument.

Finally, I looked at one of our founding documents, the Declaration of Independence. Perhaps the most famous line from the Declaration is, "We hold these truths to be self-evident, that all men are created equal, that they are endowed by their Creator with certain unalienable Rights, that among these are Life, Liberty, and the pursuit of Happiness." It is obvious from that sentence that our founders believed both in truth and in a Creator. They also believed that the Creator gave to each human being rights that attach to them simply because they are human beings. The three rights listed are listed in a particular order for a reason. They flow logically: the first is foundational, the second depends on the first, and the third depends on the second and first. In other words, what good is liberty and happiness if you are dead? You must first be alive to enjoy liberty. And the founders understood that man could not truly be happy unless he was both alive and free to pursue his dreams.

So what does this have to do with abortion? Abortion takes these ordered rights and disorders them. Abortion puts the liberty and happiness rights of the mother before the life rights of her child. Liberty or choice and happiness are highly valued rights, and I know that unplanned pregnancies can be life altering and traumatic, but they do not trump the foundational right to life given us by our Creator and made evident to us by reason. This was tried once before in America, when the liberty and happiness rights of the slaveholder were put over the life and liberty rights of the slave. But unlike abortion today, in most states even the slaveholder did not have the unlimited right to kill his slave.

The answer was clear: I was pro-life.

With that decided, I ran against a seven-term incumbent who had always been easily reelected. I did a poll six months before the election and 6 percent of the people in my district had heard of me. I spent less than $250,000 and was outspent three-to-one in a Democratic district. But with the help of a great campaign manager, Mark Rodgers, many devoted and hardworking volunteers, including my chief volunteer—my bride, Karen—we did the impossible. The year was 1990. It was a bad year for Republicans both in Pennsylvania and nationally and a rather unremarkable year in American history, but it was a big one for me. I was married to Karen in June; in August we found out we were to be parents; and in November I was elected a congressman.

Abortion was not a public issue in the campaign. As in most campaigns, it motivates legions of terrific volunteers, but the issue is relegated to the trenches—direct mail and phone calls to sympathetic pro-life voters. It was also not a big issue for me when I arrived in Congress. During my four years in the House of Representatives (I was reelected in 1992 after the state redistricting map put me in a district designed to defeat me; it was 60 percent new territory with a two-to-one Democratic registration advantage) I never uttered the word "abortion" or took part in any abortion-related debate. I was in the pro-life caucus, but I was a comfortable backbencher.

When I took on Senator Harris Wofford for the U.S. Senate seat in Pennsylvania, abortion remained in the trenches for both campaigns. Pro-life activists were very helpful in our grassroots operation all over the state. Just like in my first congressional race, I was the underdog, but again I won by one percentage point over the incumbent.

When I came to the Senate I had little expectation that things would change with respect to my approach to the issue of abortion. I was now representing a very diverse state in which large segments of my Republican base were not pro-life. In my House seat in suburban Pittsburgh, the seat was heavily Democratic, but also fairly pro-life; not so now.

Even though moral and social issues were becoming more personally important to me and to Karen (never underestimate the influence of a spouse in politics), I would not have raised my head out of the foxhole had it not been for Senator Bob Smith. I was sitting in my office one November day in 1995 with the Senate floor debate on the television. There was Bob Smith describing a procedure, partial birth abortion, that he said was used late in pregnancy. It was as grotesque as it was unbelievable. Abortion is bad enough, but this was, as Senator

Arlen Specter would later say, more like infanticide. I was so outraged that I got up to go down to the floor and enter into the debate. I put on my coat as I continued to watch and think. The more I thought, the more I became convinced that one of two things was true. Either Senator Smith was off his rocker, or he wasn't, and thus the Senate without much debate would ban this horrific procedure. So I took off my coat and sat back down—no need for me to open myself up to the onslaught that would follow in the press if I actually talked about an abortion issue on the floor of the Senate.

You see, all politicians know that when you engage in any traditional values issue, especially abortion, the news media immediately labels you. You become the "ultraconservative senator from . . . ." Adjectives like intolerant, rigid, far-right, mean-spirited, extreme, hard-line, and zealous will routinely be used to describe you and your positions, and not just on social issues. That is probably why most members remain so silent in defending traditional values. Let me quote my friend and former colleague Senator Zell Miller in one of his last speeches on the Senate floor. Commenting about his colleagues' unwillingness to speak out on controversial moral issues, he said, "At times like this, silence is not golden. It is yellow!"

I didn't feel yellow right away, but when the bill was sent back to committee for hearings I got a bit jaundiced. A month later the bill came back to the floor. Hoping against hope that the issue would sail through, I continued to stay on the sidelines. After listening to the opponents of the ban defend this inhumanity, I relented and took the floor. Later that day the bill passed, but not by a margin sufficient to override President Clinton's certain veto.

The amazing part of what happened was not my rather inarticulate couple of sentences in defense of this bill, but that within ten months, when the Senate moved to override the president's veto, I was managing the effort. The eighteenth-century antislavery poet, and author of the hymn *Amazing Grace,* William Cowper wrote: "God moves in a mysterious way, His wonders to perform." And so he did with this rather pale "yellow" wretch. During those first few months of 1996 Karen and I changed quite a bit. Having a few moments to breathe after having been on a high-speed treadmill since 1990 allowed us to focus on our family and our personal lives, in particular the spiritual side. My journey started with my colleagues in the Senate, specifically in the weekly Senate Bible study led by the chaplain, Lloyd Ogilvie. His inspiration led to prayer meetings with a small group of my colleagues in the Capitol chapel. (Yes, the Capitol does have a small chapel, directly behind the Rotunda.)

That turned out to be just preparation. The real reason I managed the effort to override the president's veto that fall was because Bob Smith didn't want the job. As it turns out, he was in a tough election battle and decided not to take the time or the risk of being out front on this issue a few weeks before his election. With the encouragement of our new majority leader, Trent Lott, I leapt into the breach with both feet.

Managing the bill those days in September was one of the most memorable and transforming moments of my life. Many stories have been written about that debate, but two things that happened will forever be etched in my mind. One of the key points made by the other side was the need for this procedure late in pregnancy when things went "wrong." The "wrong" was always a problem with the health of the baby. In other words, this particular baby was no longer the baby the parents were expecting. Senator Dianne Feinstein was one of many who focused on this point: "Some women carry fetuses with severe birth defects late into pregnancy without knowing it. For example, fetal deformities that are not easy to spot early on in the pregnancy include: cases where the brain forms outside the skull, or the stomach and intestines form outside the body, or do not form at all; or fetuses with no eyes, ears, mouths, legs, or kidneys."

Hearing this not-so-veiled advocacy for culling the disabled from our population, I responded: "Think about that message that we are sending to the less-than-perfect children of America and the mothers who are, right now, dealing with the possibility of delivering an abnormal baby. My wife is due in March. We haven't had a sonogram done. We are hopeful that everything is fine. What message would it send to me, in looking at that sonogram in a week or two, if they say that child just isn't what you want?"

A week later, we had that sonogram. The doctor kept looking at this one dark area and finally said, "Your baby has a fatal birth defect and is going to die." (He had obviously flunked bedside manners in medical school.) That wasn't the news we wanted or expected, but I must tell you that our reaction, after the shock and grief, was not to avoid the pain, the cost, or the struggle; it was not to get rid of the "problem," and it was not to put the baby out of his misery like something that was less than human. Karen and I couldn't rationalize how we could treat this little human life at twenty weeks' gestation in the womb any different than one twenty weeks old after birth. At either age, he is helpless, unaware, and thoroughly dependent on us, his parents, to protect him, care for him, and love him unconditionally. So instead of giving our child a death sentence we gave him a name: Gabriel Michael, after the two great archangels.

No, we had no choice but to fight to save our son's life. We did all we could, including intrauterine surgery, but our son was born prematurely, and after two hours in our arms, he died. Gabriel died as a cherished member of our family—forever—

having known only love in his brief time on earth. Life changes us all, but often nothing like death. At that moment, eternity became reality. After Gabriel, being a husband and father was different, being a legislator was different. I was different.

Karen reacted to our loss by throwing herself even more into her faith, family, and something new: writing. She poured out her feelings in the form of a diary, which she began to keep for Gabriel when she first found out she was pregnant. After he died it was her outlet for the pain. Through the encouragement of her parents and the help of a friend, David Kuo, these personal letters from a mother to her unborn son became a book to help others deal with the loss of their baby. The book, *Letters to Gabriel,* was published in 1998.

The concluding paragraph of Karen's last letter to our son recalled the second unforgettable memory of the 1996 debate:

> During the partial birth abortion debate, a Senator was thanking the women who had had partial birth abortions for coming forward with their stories. She said, ". . . they are crying. They are crying because they do not understand how Senators could take away an option . . . they are crying because they do not believe that those Senators truly understand what this meant for their families. . . ."
>
> Daddy said in response, "The Senator . . . said she hears the cries of the women outside this Chamber. We would be deafened by the cries of the children who are not here to cry because of this procedure."
>
> *The Washington Post* described what happened next. "Republican Sen. Rick Santorum turned to face the opposition and in a high pleading voice cried out, 'Where do we draw the line? Some people have likened this procedure to an appendectomy. That's not an appendix,' he shouted, pointing to a drawing of a fetus. 'That is not a blob of tissue. It is a baby. It's a baby.'"
>
> "And then, impossibly, in an already hushed gallery, in one of those moments when the floor of the Senate looks like a stage set, with its small wooden desks somehow too small

for the matters at hand, the cry of a baby pierced the room, echoing across the chamber from an outside hallway. No one mentioned the cry, but for a few seconds, no one spoke at all."

A coincidence? Perhaps . . . a visitor's baby was crying just as the door to the floor of the Senate was opened, then closed. Or maybe . . . it was the cry from the son whose voice we never heard, but whose life has forever changed ours.

Sometimes you hear a faint voice inside whispering what you should do. With respect to this issue, I heard the message over a loudspeaker.

XXV

The Impact of Partial Birth Abortion

Over the past ten years we have passed and failed to pass many other pieces of abortion-related legislation, but none have had the impact on our society like the bill to ban partial birth abortion. It has been the focal point of the abortion controversy, in the state legislatures, the Congress, and the courts. Even the U.S. Supreme Court has debated this issue, and so too has America. The effort to ban this horrendous procedure has failed, succeeded, and failed again. But one thing that hasn't failed is the collective conscience of average Americans. Over the past ten years Americans have become increasingly pro-life.

In the 1980s, for example, 56 percent of people told the Gallup organization that they were "pro-choice," while only 33 percent said they were "pro-life." That gap began to narrow in the 1990s when partial birth abortion was debated. In 2004 Zogby International reported that more Americans call themselves pro-life than pro-choice. A recent CBS News/New York Times poll found that 21 percent of Americans believe that abortion should not be permitted at all, and another 44 percent believe in stricter limits on abortion. Only 34 percent said abortion should be generally available. Another poll conducted by a pro-abortion group in 2003 reported that 51 percent of *women* would either ban all abortions or allow them only in cases of rape, incest, and where the life of the mother is threatened.

Imagine how remarkable that is in the face of what Americans have been force-fed from the Bigs for more than thirty years. The popular culture promotes sexual promiscuity with no consequences. The big media speaks only in supportive tones of abortion as a fundamental right in American life. Big business and big cities pay for abortions in their health care plans, and big labor negotiates for abortion coverage in their contracts as well. The big education bureaucracy in colleges and even in some high schools teaches abortion as liberation for women, and some colleges go so far as to pressure young women to have abortions. In fact, it is not unusual for university health plans to provide full coverage for abortions, but no assistance for maternal health or birth. Yale is one such university. The Democrats, the proudly pro-choice party, permit no dissent because this procedure is sacred to their essence. The Supreme Court ruled that abortion is not only a right, but is *right*. And then there is the people's body, the Congress, that stands quietly by and lets the courts push us around while more than a million American lives are extinguished every year.

After thirty years of legal abortion, a recalcitrant, quiet majority of Americans, including youngsters who know of nothing but legal abortion, still oppose it. That is in the face of every institution in America, save one, saying it is right, just, and legal. The one entity that remains as a fortress against this assault is orthodox religion. Why do you think the village elders are so intent on driving religion, especially religions that proclaim orthodox truth, from the public square? Because liberals hate competition. Despite being marginalized by this liberal onslaught, churches still play a huge role in forming people's values and worldviews.

Why has the partial birth abortion debate made such an impact? Because for years the village elders have been trying to convince us that abortion is about freedom: "choice." They have dropped all of the other arguments they used prior to *Roe* to convince the public that legal abortion would benefit society. Back before 1973, there were all sorts of claims in favor of legal abortion. Legal abortion would lead to less domestic violence, since young women would not be forced into unhealthy and inappropriate marriages. Fewer desperate women would commit suicide. There would be fewer out-of-wedlock births. There would be fewer divorces. There would be fewer children in poverty, less crime, and less child abuse, since all children would be wanted and grow up in stable families. None of this happened. Not a single social ill improved as a result of legal abortion: in fact, they all got worse, much worse.

Oh, there was one "improvement": we now have fewer children born with disabilities than we did in 1973. Prenatal testing in combination with abortion as a form of negative eugenics has worked quite well.

Not surprisingly, the pro-choice advocates have stopped talking about the sociological and human consequences of abortion on demand. When you don't have the facts on your side, you change the subject and appeal to emotions by telling stories. Instead of talking about these chilling statistics, you hear truly heartbreaking stories of the difficult circumstances that some women confront: about the high school valedictorian who made a mistake that could ruin her life; or about a pregnant rape victim; or about the pregnancy that was a threat to a woman's health. Americans are a compassionate people. We sympathize with the pain and desperation many women are experiencing. But it is misguided to take this legitimate sympathy and turn it into support for the taking of innocent human life.

According to liberals, only zealots who want to impose their values and their will on someone else would deny these women a chance to get their lives back. Here, the village elders frame their opponents—orthodox religions—as one of the Bigs. They argue against having these uncaring, intolerant, judgmental (and male-dominated) Bigs decide for you. How convenient. (As an aside, I always found it odd that liberals who say they are so much for choice resist any effort to mandate *informed* choice—that is, to require that women seeking abortions receive materials describing fetal development and outlining the medical implications of abortion, or to require that they see a sonogram of their baby prior to undergoing an abortion.)

What the village elders also don't want you and the women in crisis pregnancies to hear are the *other* stories of women who were faced with the same crisis and had abortions:

> I am tormented. . . . I've lost self-esteem, inner peace, find it very difficult to find joy anywhere in life, am always depressed. . . . He or she would have started school next week. (Julie)

> I often wonder what happened with my baby. Where did they put her. . . ? Was she buried or just thrown away like some piece of rubbish? (Carrie)

> I had a deep sense of betraying the baby who clung within me, it trusted me and I was its only love. . . . (Renaee)

> I can't believe I did it, I wish I could change everything and go back. . . . I will never be forgiven for what I did. (mother of four who gave no name)

It is obvious that for these women, abortion was not a liberating choice. These women and many others say abortion was a last resort, or that they felt they had no other choice. It is a decision, often born out of loneliness and desperation, that can cause a lifetime of suffering.

Alice Paul, the feminist author of the Equal Rights Amendment, was right when she said, "Abortion is the ultimate exploitation of women."

Dorinda Bordlee of Americans United for Life wrote recently, "*Roe* has ruined romance. Every woman's deepest desire to love and be loved has been distorted into a license to use and be used. Women have paid with their bodies and their souls. Abandoned emotionally and financially by the men they loved, and moved by profound grief at the loss of their children, they stand in front of crowds with signs that say 'I regret my abortion.'"

Serrin Foster of Feminists for Life sums it up well: "Women deserve better than abortion."

As I DISCUSSED EARLIER in this book, if you were to ask one of the village elders their view of liberty they would say, "the freedom to do whatever you desire, as long as nobody gets hurt." How does that square with abortion? Doesn't their support for abortion undermine the basic tenet of liberal orthodoxy? Can you honestly say that in an abortion "no one gets hurt?" What about the 327 women who died and countless others who became sterile from *legal* abortions between 1973 and 1999, according to the Centers for Disease Control? What about the four women you just heard from: didn't they get hurt? What about the exploitation and misogyny? And, yes, what about the babies? Is this caveat to No-Fault Freedom just an obligatory yet disingenuous smokescreen? The village elders' response provides great insight into the liberal mind.

The village elders choose to ignore or deny the humanity of the child in the womb and the emotional trauma of the mother and choose to focus solely on freedom or "choice." Think about it. When you hear an abortion supporter argue his or her position, nowhere do you hear that a baby's heart can be seen beating at three weeks; that new 4D sonograms show that from twelve weeks, unborn babies can stretch, kick, and leap around the womb—well before the mother can feel movement; from eighteen weeks, they can open their eyes, although most doctors thought eyelids were fused until 26 weeks; from 26 weeks, when partial birth abortions are still performed, they appear to exhibit a whole range of typical baby behavior and moods, including scratching, smiling, crying, hiccupping, and sucking.

Almost never do you hear about what is being chosen, other than the sterile words "terminating a pregnancy." Nowhere do you hear that over 93 percent of abortions are performed on healthy mothers with healthy babies who were not the victim of rape or incest, which means that in the vast majority of cases abortion is actually postconception birth control. Nowhere do you hear that 48 percent of women obtaining abortions in any given year already had at least one abortion. Nowhere will you see the words infant, baby, or child.

The advocates of abortion, like Planned Parenthood and the National Abortion Rights Action League, teach that if you have to say anything about what is in the womb you should use dehumanizing terms like "product of conception," "embryo," and "fetal tissue." Or, if you must, fetus. Thanks to a lot of help from their allies in the news and entertainment media, they have turned the child in the womb into a *nobody*, and therefore "*nobody* gets hurt."

Recently there was the chilling case of a Missouri woman who murdered another woman who was eight months pregnant and then cut open her womb and kidnapped her unborn child. The mainstream media's handling of this case offers a study in how they value our little brothers and sisters. According to columnist Rich Lowry, here is how AOL News covered the progressing story in their headlines:

"Woman Slain, *Fetus* Stolen";

"Woman Arrested, *Baby* Returned in Bizarre Murder";

"*Infant* in Good Health." (emphases added)

The AP story also kept to Planned Parenthood's instructions: "Authorities said Montgomery, 36, confessed to strangling Bobbie Jo Stinnett of Skidmore, Mo., on Thursday, cutting out the *fetus* and taking the *baby* back to Kansas" (emphases added). It is as subtle as it is dehumanizing.

This is where partial birth abortion has made a difference. In a partial birth abortion procedure, a twenty-plus-week-old, fully formed baby that would otherwise be born alive is delivered outside of the mother, all but the head, and then killed by an abortionist thrusting scissors into the base of the baby's skull and suctioning out the baby's brain. Here, you can't miss the baby. Americans have come face-to-face with the other face of abortion—a *somebody*, a baby. And in an abortion the baby always gets hurt.

If forced, the village elders will say, "Everyone knows that abortion is about . . . well . . . that." Sure, most Americans know that abortion takes the life of an unborn child. But it's one thing to know it; it is another for Americans to see it and then give their consent. The impersonal "it" here is the brutal destruction of a fully formed little human being that would otherwise be born alive with the hands of a doctor trained to heal.

With the partial birth abortion ban, Congress intended to draw a line: a baby that is outside of the mother all but for the head cannot be killed. The curious reader might wonder: Why? What makes a child three-fourths born any different from one who is one-fourth born or completely born? Or for that matter, one that is an hour or day or month before it is born? It is simply about drawing some artificial line, isn't it?

Where do we draw the line and why do we draw it there are questions the village elders must answer. Therefore, it has been a consistent line of questioning that I have employed on the floor of the Senate to my colleagues who defend the legitimacy of partial birth abortion. On October 20, 1999, I had a colloquy with Senator Barbara Boxer of California about where to draw the line:

> Mr. SANTORUM. Because we are talking about a situation here where the baby is almost born. So I ask the question of the Senator from California, if the baby was born except for the baby's foot, if the baby's foot was inside the mother but the rest of the baby was outside, could that baby be killed?

> Mrs. BOXER. The baby is born when the baby is born. That is the answer to the question.

> Mr. SANTORUM. I am asking for you to define for me what that is.

> Mrs. BOXER. I can't believe the Senator from Pennsylvania has a question with it. I have never been troubled by this question. You give birth to a baby. The baby is there, and it is born, and that is my answer to the question.

> Mr. SANTORUM. What we are talking about here with partial birth, as the Senator from California knows, is the baby is in the process of being born—

> Mrs. BOXER. In the process of being born. This is why this conversation makes no sense, because to me it is obvious when a baby is born; to you it isn't obvious.

Mr. SANTORUM. Maybe you can make it obvious to me. What you are suggesting is if the baby's foot is still inside of the mother, that baby can then still be killed.

Mrs. BOXER. I am not suggesting that.

Mr. SANTORUM. I am asking.

Mrs. BOXER. I am absolutely not suggesting that. You asked me a question, in essence, when the baby is born.

Mr. SANTORUM. I am asking you again. Can you answer that?

Mrs. BOXER. I will answer the question when the baby is born. The baby is born when the baby is outside the mother's body. The baby is born.

Mr. SANTORUM. I am not going to put words in your mouth—

Mrs. BOXER. I hope not.

Mr. SANTORUM. But, again, what you are suggesting is if the baby's toe is inside the mother, you can, in fact, kill that baby.

Mrs. BOXER. Absolutely not.

Mr. SANTORUM. OK. So if the baby's toe is in, you can't kill the baby. How about if the baby's foot is in?

Mrs. BOXER. You are the one who is making these statements.

Mr. SANTORUM. We are trying to draw a line here.

Mrs. BOXER. I am not answering these questions.

As I said above, I would not draw a line. A human being is a person when he or she becomes a human being: at the moment of conception. As that conversation on the floor of the Senate shows, it is hard for someone who believes you can take the life of a human being to draw a line, and even harder to explain why he or she drew it there.

You have heard the slippery slope argument from many who argue against abortion. If you don't draw a bright clear line to give constitutional protection—i.e., personhood—to all human life at the moment when human life begins—at conception—then everything becomes just a power game. That is, those in power get to draw the line wherever they choose, since there is no defensible logical, philosophical, or scientific reason for the line in the first place. That is the slippery slope argument, and in a debate in the Senate on September 26, 1996, one senator, Russ Feingold of Wisconsin, slid down that slope:

> Sen. SANTORUM: If that baby were delivered breech style and everything was delivered except for the head, and for some reason that baby's head would slip out—that the baby was completely delivered—would it then still be up to the doctor and the mother to decide?

> Sen. FEINGOLD: The standard of saying it has to be a determination, by a doctor, of health of the mother, is a sufficient standard that would apply to that situation.

> Sen. SANTORUM: That doesn't answer the question. Let's assume the head is accidentally delivered. Would you allow the doctor to kill the baby?

> Sen. FEINGOLD: That is a question that should be answered by a doctor, and by the woman who received the advice from the doctor.

XXVI

How Abortion Affects Our Moral Ecology

Abortion has added to the dulling of our moral senses for so many years that it takes a heinous procedure like partial birth abortion to act as a pair of defibrillator pads to the conscience. As you can see, it didn't work for everyone, but it has for many others. I remember what former Senator Ben Nighthorse Campbell, who is pro-choice, told me when he decided to vote to end this procedure. He was sitting in a hospital bed after a motorcycle accident listening to the 1996 debate on the floor about little children who were being treated viciously because they had medical problems. At the same time he was visiting little babies with birth defects in the hospital where everything was being done to save them. This made no sense to him. A house divided against itself cannot stand. The moral ecology deteriorates.

It bothered Senator Campbell that this procedure was deemed necessary to end pregnancies that had gone awry. "Awry" meaning that the child was no longer the perfectly healthy child that parents were expecting. On March 12, 2003, Senator Hillary Clinton and I engaged on this topic on the floor of the U.S. Senate after she made the following statement about the anatomically correct drawings I was using to demonstrate the partial birth abortion procedure. She said:

> I am also concerned about some of the visual aids that have been used by some of my colleagues. They are as deceptive as they are heartbreaking. Because what do they show? They show a perfectly formed fetus, and that is misleading. Because if we are really going to have this debate, then we should have a chart that demonstrates the tragic abnormalities that confront women forced with this excruciatingly difficult decision. Where are the swollen heads? Where are the charts with fetuses with vital organs such as the heart and the lungs growing outside the body?

After she concluded I asked her about the statement in the following exchange:

> Sen. SANTORUM: You used the term—where is the brainless head? Where are the lungs outside the body? I will just say I will be happy to put a child with a disability up there. But, frankly, I don't see the difference . . . with respect to that being any less of a child. . . . Do we consider a child that may not live long, or may have an abnormality, to be less of a child? Is this less of a human because it is not perfect? Have we reached the point in our society where because perfection is so required of us, that those who are not perfect don't even deserve the opportunity to live? . . . If that is the argument, I am willing to stand here and have that debate. If that is what you want us to show, I am willing to stand and show that. I suggest this (the drawings depicting a partial birth abortion procedure) is the typical abortion that goes with partial birth. That is exactly what the industry says is the case. If the Senator would like me to find a child that has a cleft palate, I can do that. That doctor from Ohio performs a lot of abortions. He says he did nine in one year because of that. If she would like me to show a case of spina bifida, I can do that. I would be happy to show those, but those are the exception rather than the rule. . . .

Mrs. CLINTON. Does the Senator's legislation make exceptions for serious life-threatening abnormalities or babies who are in such serious physical condition that they will not live outside the womb?

Mr. SANTORUM. No, if—

Mrs. CLINTON. That is the point.

Mr. SANTORUM. I understand the Senator's point. I guess my point in rebuttal is that if you want to create a separation in the law between those children who are perfect and those children who are not—

Mrs. CLINTON. No—

Mr. SANTORUM. If a child is not perfect, then that child can be aborted under any circumstances. But if that child is perfect, we are going to protect that child more. I do not think the Americans with Disabilities Act would fit very well into that definition. The Americans with Disabilities Act says we treat all of God's children the same. We look at all—perfect and imperfect—as creatures of God created in his image. . . . No, I do not have an exception in this legislation that says if you are perfect, this cannot happen to you; but if you are not perfect, yes, this can occur. The Senator is right. I do not.

Mrs. CLINTON. To respond, if I could, to the Senator from Pennsylvania, my great hope is that abortion becomes rarer and rarer. I would only add that during the 1990s, it did. . . . The very fact the Senator from Pennsylvania does not have such a distinction under any circumstances, I think, demonstrates clearly the fallacy in this approach to have a government making such tremendously painful and personal and intimate decisions.

Mr. SANTORUM. I, frankly, do not agree there should be a difference between children who are "normal," in society's eyes . . . and those who happen to have birth defects, severe or not. I do not believe we should draw distinctions.

Mrs. CLINTON. If the Senator will yield for one final point, I want the RECORD to be very clear that I value every single life and every single person. . . .

Mr. SANTORUM. (I will) let the record speak for itself.

The African proverb says, "It takes a village to raise a child." The American version is "It takes a village to raise a child—if the village wants that child." In the end, I believe abortion comes down to how welcoming our society is, or better yet, who are we willing to love? Has America really chosen to welcome and love only children who are wanted or who are "perfect"? The answer to that question seems to be, Yes. At a time when the number of Down syndrome children being born should be increasing (since a higher proportion of older women are having babies), the number of children being born with Down syndrome is declining. Why? Because growing numbers of these special children are being aborted. According to hospital studies, 86 percent of couples whose babies were diagnosed with Down syndrome kill the baby after the problem is detected. The moral ecology takes another hit.

And we must never forget the history of eugenics in the twentieth century. My father-in-law, Dr. Ken Garver, a geneticist, once observed,

> It is painful to realize how some of our accepted practices (e.g., prenatal diagnosis . . .) can be considered as negative eugenics. . . . One of the first phases of the (Nazi) German negative eugenics movement was active euthanasia of newborns and young children with congenital malformations and mental retardation. Prenatal diagnosis and selective abortion of fetuses with malformations or genetic disease can be considered an earlier phase of the same philosophy—namely, the elimination of lives not worth living.

I CAN'T RESIST COMMENTING on a phrase used by Senator Clinton. She reiterated part of an oft-repeated line used by the village elders as they justify the right to unlimited abortion. They say they want abortion to be "safe, legal, and rare." As you can see from Senator Clinton's comments, she boasted that during her husband's term abortion became "rarer." I would not use the word "rare" to describe 1,312,990 abortions, or 31 abortions for every 100 live births in 2000. In our nation's capital and our biggest city, New York, there were more than 70 abortions for every 100 live births. Rare means infrequent or atypical—these figures do not add up to "rare," and the reduction from 1,528,900 abortions in 1992, while a welcome improvement, is not "rarer."

But the question I have is: Why the boast? If Senator Clinton and other pro-choice advocates believe abortion should be not just legal but an unlimited right throughout pregnancy and available at all health care institutions, with federal funding, then abortion must be *desirable* and *beneficial* to women, families, and society. Like any other law, it also must be just, right, and moral. So why should it be rare? I'll let the reader answer that one, because I can't.

The only way the number of abortions will ever actually become rare is for the law to change. The only way the law will change is for the hearts and minds of Americans to change. And that will take a family, a lot of families. I know that for so many women this is the most painful decision in their lives: but the family, the churches, community organizations, and even the government have to be there to help. Not just during the pregnancy and after the baby is born, but before. I have introduced a bill to provide government grants for organizations that provide everything from prenatal care to diapers and baby clothes. If abortion proponents are interested in "choice," they should join us in helping poor women afford the choice to have a baby.

Both the big and the little institutions of society have to band together: to replenish our moral capital; to communicate high expectations; and to help form young men and women with self-respect and self-control so that unwanted pregnancies don't happen in the first place.

Remember that wristband I wear: F.A.M.I.L.Y—Forget About Me, I Love You? Family is about selflessness, putting others above yourself. If you are a scared unwed mother with no financial resources and without a family to support you, it is painful and harder, much harder, to be selfless. But it is no less required of you. Doing the wrong thing is never right simply because doing the right thing happens to be hard. Doing the right thing is almost always hard; that is why the rewards are often so much greater. And as you heard from the anguished women who now regret their abortions, the pain doesn't just go away after the abortion.

If we are to succeed as a society we all must adopt our founders' moral vision based on the Golden Rule and selfless acts on behalf of the common good. Abortion is anything but selfless and certainly has not contributed to the common good. The village elders are trying to instill a different moral vision— one that elevates the self, the arbitrary *individual good,* above all else. And frankly, this moral vision amounts to nothing less than a new religion, a polytheistic one in which each individual is his own god to be worshiped. The central cathedral erected by this new religion was dedicated to abortion. That is why those who practice this religion are so extreme in defense of the abortion "right." It is a foundational part of their whole belief system.

The sad part is that many of the women who have had abortions do not accept this belief system, particularly minorities and the poor. But they are surrounded by a society that has been poisoned by it and they don't have the personal resources to escape from the remorseless logic of the new morality. That is one of the reasons why black women have an abortion rate *three times* the rate for white women. Those in need always suffer the most from No-Fault Freedom.

I RECALL BEING AMAZED in 2003 when the Senate Democratic leaders decided to do something that had not been done in the 214-year history of our republic: filibuster judicial nominations. What would cause them to take such a radical step, truly risking the future of an independent judiciary and the balance of powers laid out in our Constitution—not to mention changing Senate precedent? It's not like there haven't been intensely partisan periods in American history. It's not like there haven't been great divides in our country that the courts were in the midst of—slavery, segregation, and the death penalty, to name a few. The reason for this radical step is abortion: that is, the "right to privacy," or better put, the "right to do whatever I want." Abortion is now not only corrupting our people, our culture, and our personal lives, but also the institutions that govern us. The moral ecology is further debased.

Through abortion litigation the village elders have even changed the way the Supreme Court defines the most basic political tenet of our society—liberty. Again, I reiterate what the Court said in the case of *Planned Parenthood v. Casey*: "At the heart of liberty is the right to define one's own concept of existence, of meaning, of the universe, and of the mystery of human life." Let me put that in plain English: you make your own laws; you are a god. The world liberals see is one in which each of us is an island entire unto ourselves, supported by the village elders, doing what pleases us, as the U2 song says, "as long as nobody gets hurt." Except that everybody gets hurt. This is the new moral environment that the village elders seek to leave as their gift to the next generation. Is that the gift that *you* want to leave to your children?

The social critic Christopher Lasch was right when he said, "Every day we tell ourselves lies so that we can live." Americans get up every day in a country that permits, fosters, and on some levels even encourages the killing of the same number of children every year as there are people in Maine. And yet the vast majority of us do nothing. We tell ourselves that there is nothing we can do; or that it is sad, but necessary; or that the country is better off without these unwanted children; or that having an abortion is wrong, but you can't impose your values on someone else. Many Americans simply don't think about it at all, because *they* aren't getting hurt. As another saying goes: All that is necessary for the triumph of evil is that good men do nothing.

The dream of our founders and patriots—of one nation under God, built on virtue, justice, and truth—will be lost, possibly forever, unless this generation begins to fight back: one person, one patriot at a time. Like so many defenders of America, you may not see success in your effort, but your faithfulness to the cause will inspire others. That is what our moral ecosystem needs: more people faithful to the traditional Judeo-Christian ethos upon which our civilization is based.

I WANT TO CLOSE this chapter with a story that is a witness to the role of Divine Providence, again from the debate on partial birth abortion. This took place when the Senate was attempting to override the president's second veto of the bill.

It was September 17, 1998, the night before the vote, and we were three votes short of an override. We had been debating the issue all day and it was now eight o'clock at night. The Senate was closing down for the day, but something inside was telling me that I had to keep fighting. No one was in the gallery or in the chamber except the pages, the stenographer, and the poor senator who had to preside over the Senate. But I felt I needed to say more: maybe some senator who couldn't sleep would tune in on C-SPAN and change his vote! So I called my wife. Karen picked up the phone. I heard our four children screaming in the background as I said, "Honey, I know it's late, but I really feel like I have to say more." She said, as she always says, "If that's what you feel called to do, I will support you— take whatever time you need." Armed with her selfless support, I went back to the floor and I told the presiding officer I would only be there a few more minutes.

I talked about a hundred minutes. I told the stories of the complicated births and inspiring lives of "imperfect" people: like Donna Joy Watts, whose parents were turned away by hospitals who refused to deliver her because she was diagnosed in utero with hydrocephalus (years later she came to the Senate gallery to watch the bill pass in 2003); like Andrew Goin, whose mother was offered a partial birth abortion because he had what Senator Clinton mentioned, his abdominal organs outside his body—omphalocele (he survived excruciating pain and many operations, but I saw his mother recently and he is alive and well); and like the singer and guitarist Tony Melendez, who was born without arms (he plays with his feet). Then I finished. The next day we lost by three votes. I didn't change a single vote in the Senate.

In my eyes and in the eyes of the world, I had failed. I had wasted everyone's time and I didn't get the chance to tuck my kids in bed and say goodnight. I felt I was not only a poor senator, but a poor father.

The following week I received an e-mail. It was from a young man at Michigan State University. The e-mail read as follows:

> Recently while my girlfriend and I were flipping through the channels, we came across C-SPAN, and were fortunate enough to hear your speech regarding the evils of partial birth abortion. We saw the picture of the little boy with the headphones on, who was lucky enough to have parents who loved him and brought him into this world, instead of ending his life. Both of us were moved to tears by your speech. And my girlfriend confessed to me that she had scheduled an appointment for an abortion the following week. She never told me about her pregnancy because she knew that I would object to any decision to kill our child. But after watching your emotional speech, she looked at me as tears rolled down her cheeks, and told me that she couldn't go through with it.
>
> We're not ready to be parents . . . but I am grateful that our child will live. It is a true tragedy that the partial birth abortion ban failed to override Clinton's veto. But please take some comfort in knowing that at least one life was saved because of your speech. You have saved the life of our child.

In May, a beautiful little girl was born. It was not an easy road for this little girl's mother. There were objections and pressure from her family and friends to look out for herself, but she persevered through the social stigma and the emotional and physical pain. Hers was a courageous, beautiful act of selflessness. It was followed by another selfless act after the little girl was born—her parents gave her in adoption to a married couple who couldn't conceive children of their own. Today, somewhere, there is an adopted little six-year-old witness to the selfless acts that make America the last best hope for humanity.

Yes, to the world I had failed. We didn't win the vote. But armed with faith and hope I fought to stop an injustice to all children and was rewarded with the life of one precious child. It wasn't what I was looking for; it was more than I could have hoped.

I have been blessed to speak to so many who answer the phones at crisis pregnancy centers when a desperate woman calls for help. Sadly, she often doesn't get the help she needs from the father, her family, or her friends, so she calls a stranger hoping she can find *someone* who will affirm her love for the child within her. This is the side of the effort to end abortion that the media doesn't talk about. I may have helped in some small way to save one life; crisis pregnancy center volunteers have given thousands of little children a chance at life by giving support that mothers need during and after pregnancy.

Being there to love and support someone in crisis, someone whom many would look down upon as among the least of us, is doing what Mother Teresa of Calcutta always encouraged. She said, "God does not call on you to do great things, He calls on you to do little things with great love." Selflessly loving the least of our fellow Americans and the babies in their wombs is about keeping America that beacon of hope for the world. It is living the Golden Rule and serving the common good. It all begins with a society that welcomes and then nurtures all of its children, including each of the "undesirable, imperfect" ones, in and *out* of the womb, into the American family. It is a society that says to every child: "You are a brother, you are one of us, you are loved." Love is never easy—it requires so much personal sacrifice. But without it we wither and die. Let's not let the legacy of this generation be that it was unwilling to make that selfless sacrifice—that we were unwilling to love.

Part Five
CULTURE MATTERS

XXVII

The Good, the True,
and the Beautiful

As Americans living in the first years of the twenty-first century, it is difficult for us to imagine ourselves back into the minds of the men and women of our nation's founding period. We too often take for granted our country's unparalleled power and prosperity, for example, and unless we consciously check ourselves, we are apt to read assumptions about American preeminence back into our images of 1776 and 1787. Knowing what America would turn out to be, we already see the greatness in George Washington and in the extraordinary collection of men who came together to declare our nation's independence and later to craft our plan of government.

In recognizing the greatness of America's founding moment, we are, of course, seeing something true, but there is also something unhistorical in our unreflective imagination. In 1776, after all, Britain's American colonies were the frontier, the outermost edge of European civilization, hard up against the wilderness. Americans were "colonials," a term that carried the deprecating overtones of "provincials," only more so. Even the grandest of American grandees cut but a small figure in London, and while Ben Franklin might dazzle the salons of Paris, he did so, in no small part, by playing up his own rustic "simplicity" for paradoxical effect.

Of course, we mustn't go too far in talking down the sophistication of early America. For literacy was already more widespread in colonial America than in the mother country. And colonial Americans had an insatiable appetite for reading literature of the highest quality. Blackstone's *Commentaries on the Laws of England* (1765), for example, sold more copies in America than in Britain—at a time when Britain was many times more populous than America, and far wealthier as well. Nevertheless, many in the founding generation did recognize the relative cultural backwardness of their country—and one of their hopes was for the emergence on these shores of a high culture to rival or surpass that of the Old World. In a letter to his remarkable wife Abigail in 1780, John Adams wrote,

> I must study politics and war that my sons may have liberty to study mathematics and philosophy. My sons ought to study mathematics and philosophy, geography, natural history and naval architecture, navigation, commerce and agriculture, in order to give their children a right to study painting, poetry, music, architecture, statuary, tapestry, and porcelain.

Adams's three-generation plan represents a hierarchy of civilizational ends. First comes the securing of a well-ordered political liberty, the foundation for every human good. Second comes acquiring the technical means for prosperity, a no less necessary foundation. Last come the pursuits made possible by leisure, which is the fruit of political liberty and economic prosperity: pursuits that involve the fine things in life, everything we associate with a "cultured" life. As the philosopher Joseph Pieper argued, leisure is the basis of culture. Painting, poetry, even porcelain: Adams wanted to make all those "highbrow" cultural tastes available for his grandchildren, and for all Americans.

And once again, this hope for an American high culture was not some special interest of the fastidious Adams. Thomas Jefferson, John Adams's longtime political opponent and the representative of some of the most thoroughly democratic tendencies in the American Revolution, similarly put enormous effort into "cultivating" an American culture to rival Europe's. This involved, for example, his ultimately failed attempts to cultivate grapes in Virginia in hopes of establishing a tradition of fine winemaking in the New World. It involved architectural work of high quality in the classical style that became an American vernacular. It involved the founding of the University of Virginia. And it involved spending a lifetime (often beyond his means) acquiring the finest cultural artifacts that Europe could produce, especially books: Jefferson's personal library became the nucleus of the Library of Congress.

The common good, as our founders understood it, does not mean that we value only goods that are "common"—in the sense of "low" or "vulgar." Rather, our founding hope was that American democracy might be elevated and elevating, ennobling— every man an aristocrat, rather than every aristocrat brought low. Has America fulfilled its cultural promise?

I AM A LEGISLATOR, and I am a father. And one thing that I have come to appreciate is that I don't perform either role in a vacuum but within a context—a cultural context. By the time an issue works itself to my desk, and eventually to the floor of the U.S. Senate, public attitudes, individual hearts and minds, have long been shaped: by journalists, academics, parents, churches, and, more dominantly than ever, by artists and entertainers. The same is true for my children. Often, when an issue arises that Karen and I have to deal with, our kids' hearts and minds have already been molded, set into a pattern of expectations, by the culture within which they live. Today, too often it is a hostile culture that is doing that shaping. Perhaps the most frustrating part for parents is that somehow "the culture" manages to sneak into our children's lives regardless of how vigilant we are. From Victoria's Secret soft-porn commercials during the 2002 Winter Olympics and the magazines in the grocery store checkout lane to graphic violence on the evening news: it seems there is no way to insulate our families—and ourselves—from these harmful influences.

Parents experience this challenge most intensely as they try to raise their kids to be healthy and happy adults. The clothes your daughter wants to wear are modeled by anorexic preteens made up to look like they are twenty—and ready for anything. That shouldn't be a surprise, though, since the magazine too many young girls are reading tells its readers how they can "satisfy [their] boyfriend's wildest dreams." The video game your son wants is M-rated, but all his friends play it: why shouldn't he? The PG-13 movie his best friend wants him to watch at a sleepover is full of sexual innuendo and violence. And then, charges are brought against his sports hero, a married one at that, for raping a fan. The incoming pop goddess French kisses the outgoing one, while another one, trying to maintain her celebrity status, exposes herself to the world, and your sons, during the Super Bowl. The "F"-word is no longer off limits on broadcast television (depending on the context), so don't be surprised when the four teens at the table next to you at Chili's use it a lot.

It is a hostile cultural climate out there for raising our kids, and virtually every parent I know feels frustrated and angry—also, unfortunately, helpless and hopeless.

Culture has been a powerful force in shaping human lives for as long as civilization has existed. Perhaps this is because culture is wired in our very nature. Edmund Burke noticed this when he said, quite simply, "Art is man's nature." We are made in the image of a Creator, and so we "subcreate." The words of our poems and novels reflect the Word; the images we craft on canvas or in stone are in some sense icons. The great Artist expresses in His handiwork what is true and good, and human artists in turn strive to do the same. An ancient rabbinic saying is that "God made people because He loves stories." I say, "Man makes stories because God made us to love."

As a legislator I know the power of the arts, the power of culture. A movie can touch people at multiple levels, and so is more more powerful than any floor speech could be in exploring an issue like human cloning. And the most effective floor speeches are the ones that tell human stories. The greatest teacher the world has known, Jesus, knew this was true. His teaching is expressed in parables: stories. And the storytellers of our nation today are our artists, singers, and screenwriters whose work is amplified through the media. How many political speeches can you remember from your youth? But what person in his forties or fifties in America today can't sing a verse from "American Pie" or never said "Where's the beef?"

While culture has been important since the dawn of history, there *is* something new under the sun: the technology and means of delivery of arts and entertainment is new—from the iPod and Gameboy to the television or radio in every room and car. What's new is the prevalence, the dominance, the omnipresence of popular culture in the lives of us all, and particularly in our children's lives. Whether through television, the Internet, music, or gaming, there is hardly a minute in the course of a day that entertainment is not being fed to our kids, shaping their hearts and minds. For example:

- The average teen spends three to four hours a day watching television—due in part to the remarkable percentage of households that have more than one television and the even more remarkable percentage that have televisions in their kids' bedrooms.

- Kids listen to radio for nearly 40 hours a week, and CDs for 20 hours.

- On average, children will see 20,000 ads a year; by the time they are 19 they will have seen 300,000.

- 70 percent of households have a video game system.

- Kids between the ages of 9 and 17 use the Internet four days a week, and average two hours online for each session.

- Each of us is hit with over 1,500 advertising images per day, from the Dell symbol on the computer monitor to the Kleenex name on a box of tissues.

In George Orwell's novel *Nineteen Eighty-Four*, the oppressed subjects of a totalitarian state are literally "subjected"—to omnipresent images of "Big Brother" and omnipresent "news and information" brought into homes by radios and televisions. Part of the horror of Orwell's vision, of course, is that all these media are controlled by a tyrannical state—and the televisions can look both ways!—but part of the horror is also the sheer fact that he presents a world in which no one may be merely alone with his own thoughts, no one may pause in quiet reflection. In Orwell's depiction, we can recognize that a life filled with media-born distraction represents a kind of spiritual disease: it is soul-killing rather than soul-nurturing. Yet in our own world, it sometimes seems we have embraced such a disease entirely voluntarily.

There is no question that popular media influences our kids, and us. After all, if it didn't, companies wouldn't spend money advertising their products in the media. An Ad Council study in 2004 showed that television was by far the most popular source of information for teens, and the one that influenced them the most. Of those asked, 56 percent said they relied on television for their news; 11.5 percent said newspapers. Surprisingly, only 9 percent said the Internet. But you know that this isn't just a matter of statistics; this is our reality. The pop culture is everywhere. It shapes what our children "know" about the world; it shapes what they love and what they hate.

The question is: what do we do about this cultural reality in modern America? The answer has mostly to do with how much we are willing to fight for what is good for our families and our society. But before I get to *us*, the consumers of culture, let me first talk a bit about *them*—the storytellers.

XXVIII

The Good, the Bad, and the Ugly

So far in this book, I have been discussing American liberty versus No-Fault Freedom and the importance of virtue, faith, and family. I've talked about the pursuit of truth, of right and wrong, and how this is, ultimately, what our founders believed must drive us as we work to sustain this great republic and achieve the common good. I have argued that for our experiment in self-government to be sustained, the people must be virtuous. For the people to be virtuous, they must be grounded in faith. And the family is the irreplaceable unit that supports these pillars of society.

But I also want to point out that for many, if not all, Americans, what we love and what we hate, and what "everybody knows," is not born only from religious instruction and family precept, but also from the cultural "signals" embedded in what we see and hear that tell us what is acceptable and what is not; what is true, and what is not; what may be said, and what may not. And, as I have argued, in our twenty-first century cultural context, the village elders through the media of popular culture—arts and entertainment—loudly send and exploit these cultural signals, too often to devastating effect.

Indeed, both in our high culture and in our popular culture, it often seems that artists are no longer able to distinguish between art and propaganda. We saw this confusion on display repeatedly in the disputes in the 1980s and 1990s about artwork funded by the National Endowment for the Arts, the government agency that touches most directly on culture. I'll describe some of what your government was funding a bit later. But for now it is important to understand that the radical artists who were crying "intolerance," "artistic freedom," and "freedom of speech" because of oversight of the NEA's grants by Congress apparently believed that it is the government's duty to subsidize, with taxpayer dollars, their idiosyncratic and even subversive messages—no questions asked. Talk about No-Fault Freedom!

That's why culture matters. The village elders long ago understood that culture is one of the key means of producing a consensus about what we as a society believe to be true and good—and therefore what we encourage more of—as well as what is false and harmful—and therefore what we discourage or stigmatize. Through the culture even more effectively than (yet also in concert with) the courts, the creative and artistic cohort of the village elders has attempted to redefine our fundamental moral precepts.

As parents we know this is true through the experiences of our children. The crowd our kids spend time with can have a positive influence or a negative one. Their friends can encourage academic achievement and competition for better grades, or they can belittle it and compete for more dubious achievements, such as who has the most body piercings or how many different people you can have sex with in a week. Similarly, the cultural context within which our children live can encourage good behavior and discourage bad behavior, or the reverse. When you consider that the crowd our kids are spending time with includes dozens and dozens of hours spent each week "with" the characters on television, you get the picture.

Take love for example. We now have a generation that has grown up with a belief, inspired by the Sixties' free-love assault on sexual mores, that true love is a *feeling*, and that it should not be resisted or constrained—rather, its ultimate validation is through sexual relations, without regard to the outdated social convention of marriage. To resist sexual attraction would be inauthentic, a form of hypocrisy. Where exactly would we get this notion? From the family? From religion? From legitimate social science? No, our children receive that consistent message from the popular culture, and particularly from advertising, music, and films. As a character in Whit Stillman's film *Barcelona* puts it in a moment of insight, "The words to pop songs are about the only literature of advice we have on romantic matters. Most of the advice is very bad." In a culture saturated with the Sixties message of sexual freedom, however, such an epiphany is a rare occurrence. In fact, Stillman's very few films are almost unique in their critical engagement with the cultural legacy of the Sixties.

Inauthenticity. Hypocrisy. We've encountered these epithets from the village elders in our discussion of moral capital. They are damning words indeed—*if* the only public moral imperative in our lives is, as the commercial recommends, "Just do it!" In real life, like it or not, we are confronted with many other moral demands. Yet in a culture intent on celebrating the self, we almost never encounter images and stories that illustrate that fact. One of my political heroes, the eighteenth-century British statesman William Wilberforce, argued that hypocrisy can often be a social good. He would much rather have hypocrites encouraging bad people to behave well than to have authentically good village elders encouraging good people to behave badly.

The consequences of the popular culture's promotion of sexual No-Fault Freedom is, just as with all of the well-meaning plans of the village elders, that people get hurt and society suffers. Teen pregnancy, abortion, sexually transmitted diseases, addictions to pornography and its debasing message about women and sex, high school dropouts, depression and suicide: all come in whole or in part from increased teen sexual activity, which has skyrocketed since the popular culture has picked up the village elders' banner of free love. All of this harm done to our children has social consequences, and ultimately public policy consequences.

I don't want to get too hung up on the simply or obviously moral (or immoral) messages of popular culture, however. Because, for one thing, this is only one aspect of the question of culture, and for another, when conservatives do focus on the moral dimension of popular culture, they are usually met with disdainful remarks from the village elders about "moralism." The cultural elite claims that what conservatives really want is a fantasy culture where "the wrong shall fail, the right prevail," a culture of sentimental moral uplift: from the perspective of the cultural elite, such a culture would be false, a lie. Moreover, they say, it is often difficult to see the moral dimension of some forms of art: what is the "moral message," after all, of Beethoven's Fifth Symphony? And there is a partial truth in what liberals have to say here.

Let me take a risk, therefore, and try to do something I am not really qualified to do. Let me try to say what a good or a healthy culture is. It's probably a fair criticism of us conservatives that we know what we *don't* like in the arts—and we are quick to tell you about that—but we don't know or at any rate

we don't say what we *do* like. My family will be quick to tell
you that I do not frequent art museums or know much about
the hottest new bands, but I do appreciate the influence that the
arts have on us both directly and indirectly as a family and as a
society.

I am not going to tell you that good culture is made up only
of paintings of pastoral scenes or finely crafted, life-like por-
traits, G-rated movies, and books without any sex or violence. I
myself am not interested in seeing only pretty pictures, or read-
ings only books that make me comfortable and that confirm all
my preconceptions. So good culture is not just the absence of
ugly words and images. A healthy culture is not one of
unchallenging conformity. What is it, then?

I remember something that the great Southern novelist
Walker Percy once said: "Bad books always lie. They lie most
of all about the human condition." Percy went further, pushing
his challenge to the village elders: "Have you read any good
Marxist novels lately? Any good behaviorist novels lately? Any
good Freudian novels lately?" And to complete his politically
incorrect trifecta, Percy finished by asserting that good
storytelling can *only* arise out of a Jewish and Christian understanding of the human condition: "Judeo-Christianity is about
pilgrims who have something wrong with them and embark on a
search to find a way out. This is also what novels are about." All
of these are controversial claims, but they get to the heart of what
I believe is the real difference between good and bad culture: it is
the difference between the truth and the lie.

GOOD CULTURE, THEN, tells us about life as it really
is—it tells the truth. To uses the title of a great Clint Eastwood
film, it tells us about "the good, the bad, and the ugly." It illu-

minates the truth about the human predicament and our human destiny. And that is not always very pretty. A couple of years ago a good friend of ours recommended that Karen and I watch the film *The Ice Storm*, directed by Ang Lee. It is an exploration of the Sexual Revolution arriving in suburbia. Frankly, it is an ugly film. Many times we were tempted to turn off the video: it was truly painful to watch. But what it has to say is also *true*. It showed the real consequences of free love on a family, both children and the selfish parents, who put into practice No-Fault Freedom. It is "good" culture. Contrast that with almost all of the *Friends* episodes—or worse yet, *Sex in the City*—which tended to present sex as entertainment, mere recreation that was virtually without consequence.

I'm a great fan of *The Lord of the Rings*. My family and I have read all the books and watched the entire film trilogy. Both the books and the movies celebrate that which is best in man— a willingness to sacrifice one's own life for a greater good, to persevere despite seemingly insurmountable odds. It is inspiring, and it is true: human beings really can achieve heroism. Human greatness is possible. And who can forget the last scene in the violent film *Braveheart*, in which an honorable patriot, William Wallace (Mel Gibson), is tortured, but rallies the strength to cry out "Freedom!"? This is both true and ennobling. *Braveheart* is a healthy addition to our culture. But for every *Braveheart* or *The Return of the King*, Hollywood seems intent on turning out a dozen films featuring an antihero, a tortured soul fighting his own demons and doing hardly anyone any good at all.

Good culture won't always be aesthetically pleasing. That is surely evident from another Mel Gibson cultural artifact, *The Passion of the Christ*. I had the opportunity to see a rough cut of this movie well before it hit the theaters. There was *nothing* aesthetically pleasing about it. The crucifixion scene was graphic, yet moving. It overwhelmed my senses. It was also life-changing. I spent the next eight months doing all I could to make sure this exceedingly violent film was as widely distributed as possible. This movie presents the truth, no matter how discomforting. And the truth always has a positive impact on the culture—on us. For example, there have been verified accounts of individuals turning themselves in to the police after seeing this film for crimes they had committed. Now that's great culture.

Then there was Johnny Cash. Just before his death, Cash released the video "Hurt." It hurt to watch. It was about a man coming to his end, singing about how hard, yet at times how good, life had been. It was painful to listen to the lyrics: "Everyone I know goes away in the end and you could have it all, my empire of dirt. I will let you down. I will make you hurt." At that point in the video you see Johnny Cash's wife, June Carter Cash, watching her husband sing this painful admission: and it is still more painful to watch, knowing that she died just ten days before the video's release. That video helped a whole new generation of young people discover Johnny Cash, but more importantly, it reminded them that the most important thing in life is not the empire of dirt you accumulate here on earth, but the treasure you store up in Heaven. The video, a painful plea for something more than mere self, something better than the self—from a dying icon of the generation that brought us No-Fault Freedom—was nominated for an MTV award. It, too, was "good" culture.

Now, the argument I have been making that good culture is a culture richly depicting the truth about the human situation will sound very strange to liberal ears. After all, that's the claim that liberals make for their own cultural artifacts. As the screenwriter character in Robert Altman's 1992 film *The Player* keeps saying to various producers at the culmination of his pitch for his rather depressing story: "That's the reality." So what's going on here? It seems we have come to the point of dueling truths.

I think there is a clue to the answer in Walker Percy's questions: "Have you read any good Marxist novels lately? Any good behaviorist novels lately? Any good Freudian novels lately?" Marxism, behaviorism, Freudianism: those are just a few of the isms that have dominated the intellectual world of the twentieth century. They are ideologies that, like liberalism, are based on abstraction—and on reduction. They reduce the whole truth about human beings to a pat, closed system and then say, "That's the reality." Such reductionist ideologies always have a kernel of truth to them—but they mistake that kernel for the whole of the truth. Consequently they lie, despite themselves.

Most of what passes for high culture, like art films, tends to be depressing because "that's the reality" of the human condition amidst the reductionist isms of modern thought. After all, a materialist view of the human condition, utterly without transcendent hope, is a pretty depressing prospect. The popular culture, on the other hand, is not depressing but ecstatic—because it reflects a different kind of ideology: a liberationist fantasy of human fulfillment in sex without consequences. But this is no less a lie: for the deepest and most lasting human fulfillment is almost always to be found precisely in the true consequence of sex, in the family.

Taking all this together, then, is there a way to extend my metaphor of stewardship of an inheritance applied to various kinds of capital? Is there such a thing as *cultural capital*? I think there is. Cultural capital consists of the stories, images, music, and practices—all the "artifacts" and the activities that are the fruit of leisure—that explain ourselves to ourselves, the *whole* of ourselves, and which do so truthfully, honestly. A society rich in cultural capital has at hand, and widely known, a great range of such artifacts that reach for the heights and plumb the depths of what it means to be a human being. A society low in cultural capital is one in which such rich fare is either lacking or is displaced by one-sided artifacts that constitute a kind of lie.

The moment of liberation from communism in Eastern Europe arrived in the 1980s when, spurred by the call of Pope John Paul II to "be not afraid," millions of people chose to "live in the truth," to courageously name the lies of the Communist regime as the lies they were. Of course, America does not have a culture imposed by a totalitarian regime: but countless Americans have begun to recognize that there is a falseness about the images and stories that the popular culture has been presenting to us. Americans are experiencing a kind of oppression at the hands of our culture-mongers. And just as in Eastern Europe, part of the solution to our cultural problems will be the personal resolution of millions to "live in the truth"—to retrieve the neglected and sometimes denigrated elements of our cultural heritage and make them our own once more.

Before the Information Age, our "values" were often localized and almost exclusively formed by the family, religion, or at times even local government. Now, however, what we love, what we hate, and "what everybody knows" is shaped much more powerfully by the media of popular culture. The purveyors of pop culture, in turn, are often influenced by the ideological enthusiasms of the high culture, which is no less hostile to the whole truth about our humanity. That means the village elders who dominate the leadership and control the content of these institutions are hammering away at your children, your family, and the values of our society. They are doing it through media that are not only becoming more prevalent, but also more niche-oriented, targeting our children with a sophistication of which most of us are totally unaware. What I would like to explore now are some of the particular challenges families face in navigating our popular culture safely with their kids.

XXIX

Culture: Ally or Adversary?

Conservatives often appear to be mere curmudgeons, denouncing everything new and wistfully remembering how much better things were in "the good old days" of their own youth. Allan Bloom in *The Closing of the American Mind* (1987) detailed with great philosophical rigor the baneful effects of rock music on the young, intimating that an earlier form of popular music was morally healthier; Richard M. Weaver in his oft-cited book *Ideas Have Consequences* (1948), however, denounced jazz music in much the same way that Bloom would later denounce rock; and when the waltz was introduced in the nineteenth century it was considered scandalous—decent people danced the minuet.

So we conservatives have to be on our guard against falling into mere nostalgia. One of the challenges we face, especially those of us with a traditionalist inclination, is to appreciate culture, even pop culture, as a possible good and not simply a real harm. Nonetheless, what are we to do when it seems that at every turn the culture, whether expressed through film, television, music, fashion, or even sports, is hostile to the values we are trying to inculcate in our children, such as decency and modesty, respect for parents and others, love of God and country?

I earlier mentioned William Wilberforce, the eighteenth-century British statesman who led the effort to abolish the slave trade. That moral crusade wasn't the only "great object" God had placed before him, however. He wrote in his diary that he believed himself called to bring about a "reformation of manners" in England, which in his time was in thrall to moral corruption and social collapse of a kind we can all too easily recognize. High out-of-wedlock birth rates, child labor abuses, and public drunkenness (even on the floor of Parliament) were all indicators of a systemic moral sickness ailing English society at large. The same condition existed in much of the rest of Europe, leading to the bloody revolution in France.

Wilberforce understood that democratic legislation for the common good would accomplish nothing without a deeper cultural renewal. How could England ever give up something as vitally important to its economy as the slave trade without being motivated by a deeper cultural renewal and respect for every human life? One of the early disciples of Wilberforce's efforts was a princess named Victoria, who would eventually usher in a historical age named after her, an age that would last more than half a century and be defined by a burgeoning of private charity and public decency. The cultural and legislative efforts both succeeded, perhaps because they were undertaken together.

The culture, even popular culture, *can* be a force for good, if it is strategically engaged. Despite the seeming hostility that conservatives encounter when we engage with the arts and entertainment community, we actually have more in common than we realize. Even most of the village elders who produce and purvey the grosser forms of music and movies don't want their own children to have casual premarital sex, experiment with drugs, be exposed to pornography on the Internet, drop out of school, and resolve their personal conflicts through violence.

When it comes to children and the family, there are opportunities to find common ground—as long as we can find a way to avoid the polarization that we too often find ourselves stumbling into. I will explore for a few pages some specific areas of culture that I believe undermine the family, and thereby weaken the very foundation of society that creates the opportunity for the culture to freely express itself. A healthy society and healthy families are very much in the self-interest of the artistic community.

The village elders in the entertainment industry are just beginning to understand this. Indeed, liberals in the arts and entertainment community find themselves in a real quandary. The more they exercise their freedoms without restraint, the more they promote decadence and undermine the family; the more that virtue and basic values are weakened, the more cultural decay produces social pathologies; the greater the social breakdown, the more government is invited to intervene; and the more the government intervenes, the more it eventually restricts and curtails the very freedoms that the arts community enjoys—and should enjoy—in America.

It was the self-interest of the British nobility in William Wilberforce's day that motivated them to join him to "reform manners" and avoid the fate the guillotine brought to their peers in France. I believe it is in our common interest to work with our entertainment "nobility"—we must engage with entertainers and artists to help them curtail the negative influence of popular culture and transform their work into a force for cultural renewal and the common good.

I have spent quite a few pages railing against the recalcitrant village elders: am I now suggesting appeasement, rapprochement, or perhaps even partial surrender? Am I just as starstruck as most Americans? Do I yearn for the opportunity to hang out with Jack Nicholson at a Lakers game? No, the reason I want to try to engage with the arts community is that I believe most artists and entertainers are different from the village elders they work for, different as well from the village elders in academia, government, and business. Most of these entertainers are artists first and liberals, at least in part, only because that's the cultural norm created by the Bigs in their industry—in other words, it is easier for them not to rock the boat and just fit in with the crowd. Of course, there are some in Hollywood who really are committed liberals: you have Babs and Whoopi and Martin and Alec, for example. But they are the exception rather than the rule. I believe most of the artists on and off the screen want more of a Jimmy Stewart America than an Eminem America. We conservatives need to help our cultural community rediscover the better angels of their natures.

TAKE RESPECT, FOR EXAMPLE—and sincerity. More than ten years ago, David Puttnam, producer of such movies as *Chariots of Fire* and *Memphis Belle,* said, "Movies now have an underlying nastiness in them. The thing I loathe more than anything has become fashionable: cynicism."

Merriam-Webster defines cynical as being "contemptuously distrustful of human nature and motives" and cynicism as "having a sneering disbelief in sincerity or integrity." What we are experiencing in today's culture is the trickling down of cynicism. Over and over, in a million different ways, in millions of different film frames and computer pixels, we are being told to distrust what we know to be true—and equally importantly, to distrust the institutions that we as a society have established to further truth. Cynicism toward the family, religious institutions, the military, the government, and established authority in general is an acid slowly eating away these societal foundations. It sometimes seems Hollywood is incapable of portraying a politician, policeman, military officer, or father who is not in some way corrupt: that's what they call drama. And in comedy it's the same story: cynicism with mocking laughter is called sarcasm, but the culturati like to call it something grander, "irony."

I have tried to focus in this book on the effect of the diminishment of various kinds of capital not just on the family, but especially on the low-income family. Cynicism toward traditional institutions such as the family, schools, and religious institutions hits the disadvantaged the hardest. When a role model for an underprivileged child encourages him to "dis the man" rather than to conform to the expectations of society—and even worse, to view academic achievement as a social stigma—hope is drained away for the parents who are trying to encourage a child to rise above his circumstances. How can you keep your eyes on the prize when almost every film you see and virtually all the music you hear tells you that taking "the prize" is a kind of selling out?

If cynicism flourished only among the intellectual elite in their ivory towers, then I couldn't care less. They deserve each other. But it doesn't. Cynicism rains down on us all. The intellectual elite may call it "sophisticated," but I call it poisonous. The real irony is that the liberal elite who espouse their anti-establishment rhetoric, whether in a song or in the classroom, don't have to live with the consequences—at least not yet. In *Destructive Generation*, David Horowitz and Peter Collier pointed out that the generally white, upper-middle-class baby boomer generation that ushered in the Great Disruption of culture in the 1960s had the means, primarily through their parents, to escape the consequences of their ideology. For example, they could militate for legalized marijuana and other mind-altering drugs: and could then just check in to rehab. They could engage in anti-establishment guerilla theater: while finishing up at Harvard or Berkeley. Well-positioned young men could embrace casual sex: and use peer pressure and family money to encourage the abortion that would eliminate any career impediments. The poor have none of these advantages; they are the ones paying the price for the culture of No-Fault Freedom. Nothing makes me angrier than to think of the rich folks living in gated communities making money from commercially successful entertainment that ultimately destroys the lives of the most vulnerable children in our nation.

You may be aware of the comments made by Bill Cosby at a Constitution Hall gala in 2004 marking the fiftieth anniversary of the *Brown v. Board of Education* Supreme Court decision. He lamented that young African-Americans are "standing on the corner and they can't speak English." His voice impassioned, he said, "I can't even talk the way these people talk: 'Why you ain't,' 'Where you is' . . . And I blamed the kid until I heard the mother talk. And then I heard the father talk." At a subsequent event, he bemoaned the fact that the racial slurs once used by those who lynched blacks are now a favorite expression of black children. And he blamed parents. "When you put on a record and that record is yelling 'n—— this and n—— that' and you've got your little six-year-old, seven-year-old sitting in the back seat of the car, those children hear that."

The thrust of his argument is obvious: black parents need to do better for their children. But to me, there is an equal indictment of an elite culture that markets anti-establishment and antisocial fare to our kids for profit, not caring what the consequences are.

In addition to cynicism toward institutions and authority in general, the entertainment media's assault on two institutions—religious bodies and the traditional family—seems to revolve entirely around discrediting these in the eyes of our children. Destroying respect for the authority of parents and churches makes it easier for the village elders to have more influence in shaping the moral lives of our children and society. Remember what I said earlier: liberals hate competition.

Sometimes this is quite subtle. Have you noticed how many television shows aimed at the teen market involve out-of-touch and slightly comical parents who are "enlightened" by their thoughtful and morally "deep" teenage children? Or how many shows aimed at the same market involve teenagers with scarcely an adult anywhere in the picture? Sometimes, teens are depicted more truthfully as full of faults, but nonetheless more "authentic" than adults, and the teens' faults are shown to be funny or cool. The screenwriters may say that a good story has to have a hook; they will say that creativity means doing something new and different; they will say that stories of wise parents conveying wisdom to immature youngsters is mere "conventional wisdom," and the power of a good story comes from "transgressing" conventionality. The problem is that this transgression, this subversion, has itself become part of the conventional wisdom of our post-1960s culture. And it is a lie.

That is not to say there are no positive artifacts in our popular culture. I recently saw the Adam Sandler film *Spanglish*, which depicted a relationship between a wealthy, married white father and his maid, a Hispanic single mother. At the critical moment in the film, you are convinced and even enticed into wanting these two to have a romantic relationship. But the maid calls a halt, saying that "there are mistakes you just don't risk when you have children." That scene, and in fact a lot of that movie, communicated a message for a generation plagued by divorce and adults "finding themselves" outside of their marriage vows that simply could not be accomplished with any political speech or act of legislation. It is the power of art used for the common good. Contrast that film with the weekly onslaught of "follow your groin" programming, from *Desperate Housewives* to MTV, and you can see that in today's media we must sift through tons of lies to find a gem of truth.

I am not suggesting that there is a grand design or plan on the part of the Bigs in the entertainment industry to de-moralize America. In fact, I believe that the current plight of our popular culture is the result in large part of having so *many* media outlets and so *much* content to produce, that it is just easier and cheaper to push the envelope, to increase the shock value, to get ratings. You don't need much talent to produce reality television or gangster rap. We all know that it is a lot easier to shock someone with a lie than to inspire someone with a carefully crafted truth.

In addition to the family, popular culture often demeans the role and contribution of organized religion, both in the lives of individuals and in the life of society as a whole. For a nation in which 90 percent believe in God, and with a large percentage actively engaged in a religious congregation, our media seems completely unable to present the truth experienced by most people in their daily lives. A study conducted in 2004 by the Parents Television Music Council noted that positive and negative mentions of God and religion were only evenly split. Worse yet, mentions of religious institutions or the clergy were at least twice as likely to be negative as positive.

Among religions, the village elders seem to have one primary target: conservative Christianity, either of the Catholic or

evangelical Protestant strain. (They don't like orthodox Judaism either, but they are such a minority that to date they have
avoided much media criticism.) Remember Andres Serrano's infamous *Piss Christ*—a piece of "artwork," funded by the National Endowment for the Arts, that consisted of a crucifix suspended in a jar of the artist's own urine? Serrano's body of work
holds an honored place in today's arts establishment. It has even
been exhibited in the Episcopal Cathedral Church of St. John
the Divine in Manhattan—and nobody batted an eye, much
less complained! As the columnist John Leo wrote, "In painting
and sculpture, the bashing of Christian symbols is so mainstream
that it's barely noticed."

The reality is that religion is a human good—even a public
health good. Studies have shown that people who go to church
live longer, people who pray get well quicker, and people who
believe in God have a greater sense of peace and overall positive mental health. Good culture tells the truth, bad culture
lies.

AFTER A CENTURY OF INDULGING in isms like those mentioned by Walker Percy, the dominant worldview expressed
through much of our culture today is postmodernism. That very
name means a lot. Postmodernism is "post," "after," the modern. But that is all it can say for itself. It has no substance of its
own, no explanation of the world and of the mystery of the
human person; it is only aware of the *failure* of all the modern
isms. But having experienced the falsity of ideological "truths,"
it cannot bring itself to embrace the truth in religion or in moral
tradition. Instead, it holds that there is no truth, and its moral
counsel is not to trust anyone who claims to believe that they
know the truth. The advance of a postmodern worldview and

the disparagement of religion and religious institutions in our cultural artifacts is ultimately an assault on truth itself.

Popular culture no longer supports parents' efforts to teach their children the truth about right and wrong, for example. It used to be, certainly in the 1960s and 1970s and still to a great extent just fifteen years ago, that right and wrong, good versus evil, were common themes for entertainment and art. Thankfully, there are still some good messages, but entertainment targeted to children in particular has lost its moral clarity and now celebrates moral ambiguity and uncertainty instead.

Comic books of a generation or two ago celebrated the struggle of the superhero over the power of evil. It was never a question during the Silver Age of comics who was the good guy and who was the bad guy. Goodness, truth, and the American way were the pursuits of the superhero, vanquishing the diabolical efforts of the supervillains. Although the comic writers' efforts in the 1970s and early 1980s to humanize their superheroes abandoned some of this earlier innocence, they still largely stuck to the old storyline, good versus evil. But the late 1980s and 1990s ushered in something new—the dark hero, tormented, conflicted about his own motivations, unwilling to say good is good and evil is evil. Violence and sexual images began to dominate. Attitudes and language coarsened. Today, comics are largely the domain of the "graphic novel" for late teens and college kids, with "heroes" like Spawn and Hellboy.

Professional wrestling matches, as bizarre as they were and are, at least began as morality plays. Good guys, literally wearing white, fought bad guys, literally wearing black. I freely admit, as a boy in Pittsburgh, I watched the "Living Legend" Bruno Sammartino and George "The Animal" Steel on Saturday morning wrestling. After I became a lawyer, I was retained by the

WWF (predecessor to the WWE) to convince the Pennsylvania General Assembly that although professional wrestling was physically demanding and potentially dangerous, it should not continue to be regulated like professional boxing. We succeeded because we showed that wrestling had changed over time to become entertainment. And like all other entertainment, it has decided in recent years to compete for young viewers by ratcheting up the violence and sex. Today, professional wrestling is more about titillation than ever. The violence has been sexualized.

I had the pleasure to talk with the "Living Legend" several years ago. He is angry and frustrated about how wrestling has changed with the times, how it confuses good and evil: not that the bad guys didn't sometimes win in his day, but you always at least knew that they were bad, and were invited to boo. He also lamented that wrestling skills have been replaced by acting skills, all in a sexually charged theatrical atmosphere.

Why do I spend time writing about professional wrestling? Because it has been the highest rated syndicated program on television and pay-for-view and still packs in crowds of young men and boys around the country. It is a non-elite artifact of our culture that has survived by trying to keep up with the envelope-pushers in Hollywood and New York. It has been sucked into telling some of the same lies. Bad culture lies, good culture doesn't.

IN A 1992 POLL conducted by the Barna Research Group, only 6 percent of all teens indicated that they believed there were moral absolutes. Even more unsettling, only 9 percent of self-described born-again teens indicated that they believed in absolutes. Pope John Paul II warned us that a "soulless vision of life" is beginning to dominate in Western societies, and that we must "confront directly the widespread spirit of agnosticism and relativism which has cast doubt on reason's ability to know the truth."

In popular culture, good versus evil, right versus wrong, are considered passé, boring, irrelevant, and worse—traditional. The goals that artists set for themselves have changed. Richard Grenier writes,

> Any art historian should know that none of the titans of the past centuries—neither Michelangelo nor Rembrandt nor El Greco nor Shakespeare—was ever free to insult and/or belittle the fundamental beliefs of his church and people. Nor until modern times did many of them want to. . . . [Y]et despite these political inhibitions Shakespeare and Chaucer managed to produce works generally thought to have artistic merit.

Things have changed. Martha Bayles, another respected art critic, observes, "To the familiar vices of popular culture— notably vulgarity and kitsch—perverse modernism has added a twist: a radically adversarial stance toward society, morality, and art itself. That stance has gone from being the property of a tiny avant-garde a century ago to being part of the cultural mainstream today."

I may not be a fine art critic, but I acknowledge that art is upstream of pop culture, just as pop culture is upstream of politics. So although my examples are comic books, movies, and wrestling, I appreciate fine art and try to understand culture. I understand this much: that the goals of today's artistic representations have changed dramatically and, for the most part, for the worse. That makes it harder for parents trying to teach their kids virtue. It's especially true for parents working hard to give their children a religious and spiritual foundation.

Yes, the goals of art have changed. Here is a passage from the 1971 autobiography of film director Frank Capra, who gave us, among other films, *It's a Wonderful Life* and *Mr. Smith Goes to Washington*:

> The winds of change blew through the dream factories of make-believe, tore at its crinoline tatters. . . . [T]he God-haters, the quick-buck artists who substituted shock for talent, all cried: "Shake 'em! Rattle 'em! God is dead. Long live pleasure! Nudity? Yea! Wife-swapping? Yea! Liberate the world from prudery. Emancipate our films from morality!" There was dancing in the streets among the disciples of lewdness and violence. Sentiment was dead, they cried. And so was Capra, its aging missionary. . . . To hell with the good in man. Dredge up his evil—shock! Shock!

It's hard for parents today to remember, but popular culture once was a helpful tool for parents trying to moralize and teach virtue to their children. Can you imagine a television series on the WB network today with the title *Father Knows Best*? That was once America's popular culture: now we have *Joe Millionaire* and *The Bachelorette*. The social thinker Irving Kristol writes, "The consequence of such moral disarray is confusion about the single most important question that adults face. 'How shall we raise our children? What kind of moral example should we set? What moral instruction should we convey?' A society that is impotent before such questions will breed restless, turbulent generations. . . ."

Michael Medved is a noted author and media critic. He's on radio, TV, and often in the pages of *USA Today*. I once heard him tell a wonderful story. Michael is an observant orthodox Jew and, as such, honors the Sabbath from sundown Friday to sundown Saturday. He lives in Seattle, and one Friday he was flying home. Unfortunately, his plane was late and by the time he got out of the airport the sun had set. Honoring the Sabbath means no driving, only walking. So he left his car at the airport and walked home—more than 10 miles away. This is a man who knows truth when he sees it and cynicism when he smells it. In his influential book, *Hollywood vs. America*, he writes:

> The changes in high culture cast significant light on recent changes in the entertainment industry. Until the revolution of the 1960s, the leaders of the popular culture served the artist's old purpose as a "celebrant of his society and all its values," but since that time Hollywood has cast itself in an increasingly alienated role.
>
> No single piece of entertainment represents a serious threat to our civilization, but the cumulative impact of this material (which assaults the average American more than thirty hours each week) plays an obvious and inevitable role in shaping the perceptions and values of this society.

Put simply, Medved concludes that Hollywood is "redefining normal."

Am I as pessimistic as Kristol, Medved, and others that all of the artifacts coming from our entertainment industry are destructive and harmful to our culture? No, I'm not—in part because there seem to be the beginnings of a move afoot in America to stop buying the bad culture, the lies.

First of all, as I said earlier, entertainment does not have to be G-rated to be morally and culturally redemptive. The PG-13 and R-rated box office hits in 2004 were *Spiderman 2*, *The Lord of the Rings*, and *The Passion of the Christ*. Each of these had remarkably redemptive storylines. But the real story was the dominance of G- and PG-rated films, such as *Finding Nemo*. I don't want to imply that all G-rated movies have culturally positive messages, but most do. The same can be said for music by newly popular bands such as Switchfoot and Evanescence. With new music and new films that tell the truth, there is new hope.

Second, I have met with enough people in the industry to know that there is growing dissatisfaction with the status quo. This may be partly due to the real-life experiences of the children of the baby boomers—a generation raised amidst divorce and materialism and just now coming of age. They are our next storytellers, and they are under no illusions, for they themselves have suffered the consequences of the post-1960s destructive generation. They *know* that the theme of liberation without restraint is a lie. I think that there is more good to come. The recent film about Ray Charles, for example, shows sin—but shows its consequences too. It tells the truth. I think we will see more truthful stories and hear more truthful songs in the future.

Finally, it seems that we may be at a tipping point. Whether it was Janet Jackson's Super Bowl self-exposure or the constant drip-drip of corrosive culture, parents all around us seem to be saying the same thing: "Enough!" And the entertainment industry seems to be saying: "We hear you!" The only problem is that the industry isn't quite sure what to make of what they hear. David Milch, the creator of *NYPD Blue* and the HBO series *Deadwood,* said recently that television writers should be interested in religion because it is "a part of the rhythm and texture of most people's lives, as something that is embraced or rejected." Yet his approach appears ultimately to be a utilitarian one. "I think religion is becoming prevalent as a part of commerce," he said. "To the extent that you can sell religion, it's just like sex."

I'll explore later some specific ways parents and companies can encourage the good and protect kids from the bad, but the good news is that we are at the threshold of increased parental involvement, aided by better tools provided by the entertainment industry. We may even be at the threshold of a "reformation of manners" of the sort William Wilberforce set in motion.

But there are two additional areas that must be "reformed" before we can say we have crossed over the threshold to a truly new day for our culture.

XXX

Violence and a Coarsened Society

I am an avid sports fan. I know the difference between a ground-rule double and a book-rule double. But I also know that what is really important about sports is what it teaches us: team play (selflessness), good sportsmanship, perseverance, honesty, sacrifice. Sports are genuinely a part of culture. Remember what Joseph Pieper argued, that leisure is the basis of culture? Culture is the whole realm of what human beings make and do when they are most "free" from the necessities of life, most at leisure. And *play* is one of those things—hence, sports.

It was because I love sports so much that my heart grieved when I saw highly paid professional basketball players go into the stands to fight fans in Detroit during the Pacers–Pistons game last year. Players used to be role models for our children. I don't want to sound maudlin here, but in the good old days of professional sports you at least got the impression that people were playing, as the title of the Kevin Costner movie patterned after my colleague and Hall of Famer Jim Bunning said, *For the Love of the Game*. Now, however, sports is best exemplified by a movie about a sports agent, *Jerry McGuire*, and by Cuba Gooding Jr.'s famous line: "Show me the money."

I have come to terms with players' exorbitant salaries, but not with the behavior that has come with their super-celebrity status. I know there were characters and bad apples as far back as Ty Cobb and the Chicago Black Sox, but the bad apple was the exception, not the norm. Today, far too many of these gifted, privileged millionaires are fighting with fans and with each other on a more or less regular basis, or else are being arrested for everything from assault and drunk driving to rape and murder. That is on top of the trash-talking, the showboating, and the lewd gestures on and off the field—not to mention the use of mind-altering and muscle-enhancing illegal drugs. What makes this all worse is that this behavior is tolerated and even excused by their leagues—because these guys generate enormous cash for the industry. The leagues are now trying to address some of these problems, as well they should. But professional sports are not only a contributor to the culture, they also have to deal with the young men who are victimized by it, the players. Many of these problem players come from rough neighborhoods where moral and social capital is low, but like it or not, our kids look up to them. Unlike the sports heroes of the past, kids today don't look up very far.

You get a sense for how negative these cultural developments in sports are, what an enormous opportunity is lost, when you consider some of the sports heroes of yesteryear who are so great that looking up to them can hurt your neck. Two friends of mine come to mind. They are my sports heroes: Mario Lemieux and Darrell Green.

Mario Lemieux, aside from being the greatest hockey player I have ever seen and a member of the Hockey Hall of Fame, is a man whose example can inspire and teach virtue to children and adults alike. He battled cancer, receiving debilitating radiation treatment during the season, yet with his hair falling out he courageously took the ice and helped his team in the playoffs. He persevered through injury, quit the game in protest of the deterioration of its quality, and used his own money and possible return to the game to keep the franchise in his adopted hometown of Pittsburgh (he did return). He and his wife Nathalie have also used the gifts they have been given to do countless works of charity in the community.

Darrell Green played twenty years for one team, and not for as much money as he could have made elsewhere, during a time when loyalty was a forgotten virtue. He stayed with his team in spite of the fact that the Washington Redskins were not of playoff caliber toward the end of his career. His peers all signed with contenders. Darrell was content to remain part of his adopted hometown. To spend twenty years, seven as an all-star, at a position like cornerback where speed and agility are required, is a testament to his stamina, determination, preparation, and skill. He will most certainly be enshrined in Canton when he is eligible for the Hall of Fame—but he has already achieved hall-of-fame stature in Washington for his work with young people in the minority community there. He is the founder of the Youth Life Foundation, where he has helped disadvantaged children through learning centers and after-school programs. He travels the country as the chairman of the President's Council on Service and Civic Participation, talking about the importance of being a good citizen in your community.

So there are still sports heroes out there. But imagine the contribution to our cultural capital if professional sports spent more time celebrating men and women like Mario Lemieux and Darrell Green, and less time trumpeting the trash-talkers who break the rules.

SPORTS ARE NOT THE ONLY KIND of "play" that emerges from American leisure. As you know by now, Karen and I have six children. While we play computer games, we place limits on the software and the amount of time our children can spend with them. Karen is especially vigilant with limiting "screen time" (computers, video games, and television—all three). Our challenge, however, is not what is played at home; it's what some of our kids' friends play. Despite the sincere efforts of the software gaming industry to label games that are not suitable for younger children, too few parents seem to care what their kids are playing on their computers. Our adolescent boys are not allowed to play games with M-ratings, nor are they allowed to play the vast majority of T-rated games. Before any software comes into the house we read the online reviews. Parents, I know this takes time and can be a hassle for you and a point of argument with your children, but please consider what Dr. Michael Rich has to tell us about the consequences of *not* doing this.

Dr. Rich is the director of the Center on Media and Child Health, based at the Children's Hospital of Boston, part of the Harvard Medical School. He is one of the nation's leading researchers into how media impacts children, and I have discussed these issues with him on several occasions. He began his research as a dispassionate observer, but the data have led him to become a passionate advocate for finding ways to help parents protect their children from the worst effects of the media.

"Our ultimate objective is to obtain a scientific understanding of exactly what exposure to various types of media does to us in terms of our physical and mental health," Dr. Rich says. "We're trying to understand what media does to us, just like we understand what taking a certain drug or eating a certain number of calories does to us."

We know quite a bit about violence on television. It's our most researched area. We don't yet know, for example, the biological basis for behavior change, but we do know—and there is lots of good evidence for this—that exposure to lots of violent media changes people's attitudes and behaviors in a number of ways. First of all, it desensitizes us to violence. Humans are adaptive organisms. When we are first exposed to violent images it is frightening and upsetting in various ways.

What happens, he says, is that the more violence we see on television or at the movies or in computer games, the less upset we get by it. Eventually, we become almost numb to feeling anything as a result of violence. And there is more bad news:

The second way we are affected by the amount of violence in the media is what I call the "mean world syndrome." Media inflates the presence of violence in our world. Particularly children, as a result, perceive of the world as a meaner and more violent place than it actually is. On one hand, this creates fears in children that often come out in the form of anxiety, sleep disturbance, and nightmares. In some cases, it can even result in post-traumatic stress disorder. Some children feel they have to approach the world with a "get them before they get me" attitude. It's been shown to lead to increased incidence of weapon-carrying and using weapons.

While I don't have any concerns that my children will carry weapons to protect themselves, what Dr. Rich describes is one of the important reasons my wife and I are serious about limiting how much television our children see and what video games they may play. Karen always reminds me that not only do we have a responsibility to help our children grow into independent adults: we also have the moral responsibility to protect our children from the dangers and evils around us.

Dr. Rich has still more to say:

The third way media images of violence affect children is increased aggression. This holds for laboratory experiments and in so-called natural laboratories, such as areas where television had never been introduced. Two years after television has been introduced in these areas, when we look at aggressive behavior, we find that it actually increases. That doesn't mean we've proven that watching violence increases an individual's violent behavior. It means when you look at populations, the level and prevalence of violence increases in that population. It's not a one-to-one relationship, any more than smoking and cancer is a one-to-one relationship. It is that on a broad basis the risk of violence is greater for those exposed to media images of violence.

Dr. Rich acknowledges that we don't know if watching violent images in the media actually *causes* violent behavior, but it is clear the two are related. "You don't know what comes first: the chicken or the egg. More likely it's a bidirectional relationship." In other words, children who may have aggressive tendencies, even if they have not materialized yet, are more likely to exhibit violent behavior after watching violence on television. "The data do show, though, that over time, even kids with low aggressiveness who watch a lot of television tend to be more violent than children who tend to be highly aggressive but who don't watch that much television."

Some of Dr. Rich's research is starting to show that children's brains process the violent images they see on television very differently from nonviolent images. He and his colleagues have recently launched a project using functional MRI imaging. It's a way of imaging brain activity in real time. The researchers are doing that imaging as children watch various things on television. "Our pilot data seems to indicate that violent media are processed very differently," he says.

There appears to be a biological basis to how we are changed by these images. It's an immediate response when we portray interpersonal violence. It's the same brain circuits that probably lit up when a saber-toothed tiger snuck up on early man and he survived by instantly deciding to either run or beat the heck out of the saber-toothed tiger. These are not higher-level brain processes. The brain doesn't have time to process these stimuli and respond. It's virtually a reflexive response. The problem is, or the question is, what are we doing to our brains when we choose to entertain ourselves with material that gives points for killing a humanoid on the screen or extra points for killing women? From what we've seen, we are deluding ourselves if we think kids can see this is just entertainment and compartmentalize it.

Children and young people clearly lose the ability to understand the meaning of violence. Dr. Rich tells a story of going to a high school and showing the movie *Gettysburg*, which includes very realistic depictions of Civil War battles. Almost instantly, he says, the students started to laugh or cheer and howl when a soldier got killed on screen. Dr. Rich stopped the projector. He told the students about the real horrors of war, about his own experiences in Vietnam seeing real people die. Then he put the movie back on. The students watched silently, many in tears. The point of this story should be obvious. A society unmoved by violence is a society desensitized to humanity.

I started this section talking about how good culture tells the truth and bad culture lies. How badly are we lying to our children if they feel the appropriate response to a graphic depiction of the horrors of war is *laughter*? What does that mean for the health of these young people and for the health of our families and communities?

Sociologist James Wilson and criminologist George Kelling's "broken windows" theory of criminal behavior suggested that when the small things are left unattended to, such as broken windows in a poor neighborhood, it signals a general break-

down in the basic social order, which in turn invites more serious pathological behavior. "If a window is broken and left
unrepaired, people walking by will conclude that no one cares
and no one is in charge," they wrote in a March 1982 cover
story in the *Atlantic*.

What follows unrepaired broken windows is a greater and
greater breakdown of order, so that soon drug-dealers have
moved in and violence has escalated. Wilson and Kelling's solution to violent crime was to fight the disorder that precedes it:
deal with the broken windows, graffiti, panhandling, uncollected
trash, and unrepaired buildings. Their theory was so successfully implemented in Boston in the 1980s that New York mayor
Rudy Giuliani recruited Boston's chief of police to do the same
in the Big Apple. Graffiti was washed nightly from subway cars,
$1.25 subway turnstile-jumpers were arrested, trash was picked
up. Minor, seemingly insignificant quality-of-life crimes were
found to be the tipping point for violent crime. When New York's
"windows" were repaired, crime dropped and the rest of the
story was, as they say, history. New York City flourished might-
ily in the 1990s.

Bill Cosby, again, was on to this when he suggested that the
breakdown of basic order in our society is leading to more and
more violence in our inner cities. "These are not political criminals. These are people going around stealing Coca-Cola," he
said about young African-Americans incarcerated for crime.
"People getting shot in the back of the head over a piece of
pound cake and then we run out and we are outraged, [saying]
'The cops shouldn't have shot him.' What the hell was he doing
with the pound cake in his hand?"

I raise these points about the "broken windows" thesis to
suggest that although many of us focus our concern on the most
violent aspects of entertainment, perhaps as parents we should

be just as careful about the more "modest" incivility that our children encounter as they navigate the cultural waters. It was this, after all, that lay behind the success of William Wilberforce's "reformation of manners" effort. If you fix the small stuff, you end up fixing the big. Yes, we need to beware of our kids' consumption of violent entertainment—but we also need to be aware that their diet of incivility, disrespect for authority, and disregard for others may be even more harmful in the long run to themselves, their families, and society as a whole. We have to fix our culture's broken windows, too.

XXXI

Sex, Drugs, and Rock 'n' Roll: Mostly Sex

Some people ask me, "Why are conservatives so obsessed with sex?" That's a good question—and there is a good answer: because the sexual revolution has had huge public, as well as private, consequences. I am often astonished at the amount of public debate, public policy, and public funds we expend to deal with the consequences of the sexual revolution. Sex outside a monogamous, life-long relationship has consequences: teen pregnancy; out-of-wedlock births and the resulting consequences of teen parenting such as high school dropouts and welfare dependency; abortion and related issues of depression; sexually transmitted diseases, most notably AIDS; rape and sexual abuse; sexual addiction, especially to pornography, lack of self-respect and self-control; and divorce. As I have repeated often in this book, the impact of the sexual revolution is staggering.

Here is a list of the estimated lifetime cost per case, number of new cases among persons aged 15 to 24, and total direct medical costs *per year* of several widespread sexually transmitted diseases:

- HIV: *Average lifetime cost per case:* $199,800; *number of new cases in 2000:* 15,000; *total direct medical cost per year:* $3 billion

- HPV (Human Papilloma Virus): *Average lifetime cost per case:* $1,228 (women), $27 (men); *number of new cases in 2000:* 4.6 million; *total direct medical cost per year:* $2.9 billion

- Genital herpes: *Average lifetime cost per case:* $417 (women), $511 (men); *number of new cases in 2000:* 640,000; *total direct medical cost per year:* $292.7 million

- Chlamydia: *Average lifetime cost per case:* $244 (women), $20 (men); *number of new cases in 2000:* 1.5 million; *total direct medical cost per year:* $284.4 million

- Gonorrhea: *Average lifetime cost per case:* $266 (women), $53 (men); *number of new cases in 2000:* 431,000; *total direct medical cost per year:* $77 million

All are the result of a large segment of society that sees sex as recreational—a point of view aggressively advanced by our entertainment culture.

I don't need to convince you that our media have become more and more sexualized. *Sex in the City*, MTV, and recent video games have done all the convincing anyone could need. And if you have kids who use the Internet, you know how difficult it is to protect them from the onslaught of sexual images and pornography. For every hour of television watched by teens, there are, on average, 6.7 scenes with sexual topics, and about 10 percent of these scenes show couples engaged in sexual intercourse.

Twenty-two percent of teen-oriented radio segments contain sexual content, and studies have shown that 20 percent of these range from rather explicit to very explicit. An analysis of the top-selling CDs in 1999 found that 42 percent had sexual content, 41 percent of which was either rather explicit or very explicit. Sixty-one percent of teens using computers "surf the net," and 14 percent report seeing something they wouldn't want their parents to know about.

And even when we as parents are doing our best to be responsible, we are often caught unprepared. Who was prepared for the ad during the Eagles–Cowboys pregame show pitching ABC's *Desperate Housewives* with a sexually suggestive locker scene?

Kids are inundated with this stuff, and just as with violence, kids are desensitized to the reality of sex—both its goodness and its meaning within marriage as well as the harm it can cause outside of marriage. Kids aren't told the truth; they are lied to. Good culture tells the truth, bad culture lies.

Cara Tripodi is a licensed social worker. She runs the Star Sexual Trauma and Recovery program just outside of Philadelphia. It's a program that is "geared toward people who are sexually compulsive or sexually addicted, and their partners," she explains.

What she's talking about are people who engage in a pattern of out-of-control sexual behavior that ranges from having affairs, to visiting strip clubs, to online encounters. A sexual compulsion occurs when someone's sexual impulses involve behaviors that they can't stop, and which have personal and social consequences.

"The Internet has been kind of like crack cocaine for people with this problem," Tripodi says. "The Internet is like another form of acting out, of getting a high, so to speak. It's what we call the triple-engine theory. The Internet is easily accessible, affordable, and anonymous. It has put more people at risk for developing these types of patterns. People who are at risk may find they start spending hours and hours looking at images on the Internet. They may go to personal chat rooms and place personal ads that are sexually oriented."

The Internet contains everything, and it is so anonymous that Tripodi says she sees lots of people who have indeed become addicted to it. "There are zero parameters, because pornography continues to be the primary income generator on the Internet. I'm seeing the effects—people and their families are being destroyed by it. Spouses see the Internet like having an affair—their partner is more interested in being on the Internet than talking to or having sex with them." When I asked Tripodi if we know much about the effects of Internet pornography on children, she told me that there hasn't been much research to date. "But we know it's very bad," she says.

In fact, very little research has been done on the impact of all this sex in the media on the attitudes and behaviors of youth. Will future studies demonstrate that this vast amount of sex on television is just as harmful as the violence children see? Well, a few years ago when the Institute for Youth Development conducted focus groups with young teenagers, mostly ages 12 to 14, the teens themselves said that they believe that adults *expect* them to have sex at a young age—after all, that's what the media communicates. Indeed, one of the principal complaints these young people had was the pressure they feel to grow up too fast—pressure, they said, that comes primarily from the popular culture. (An interesting and important note from this focus group study and others: the teens also said they need and want *more* guidance from their parents, not less.)

A rare, recent study undertaken by researchers from RAND and the University of California, and published in the medical journal *Pediatrics*, concludes, "Watching sex on TV predicts and may hasten adolescent sexual initiation." It goes on to say that "reducing the amount of sexual content in entertainment programming, reducing adolescent exposure to this content, or increasing references to and depictions of possible negative consequences of sexual activity could appreciably delay" sexual activity.

Unfortunately, television rarely shows the consequences of sexual activity outside of marriage. Rarely do characters end up pregnant or get a sexually transmitted disease. There are 15 million new sexually transmitted infections every year in this country, but television characters rarely, if ever, get one. America's teenagers and young adults don't live inside a television sitcom. That's the point, of course: young people hardly ever see the real-life results of extramarital sexual activity.

On the most popular show on television for years, *Friends*, one character, Rachel, had a baby out of wedlock. The Parents Television Council notes that "Baby Emma was conceived as a ratings gimmick . . . the product of a one-night stand with ex-boyfriend Ross. Over the next few months we watched as Rachel battled baby blues because her pregnancy and growing belly got in the way of her social life."

After the birth, what happened to baby Emma? Rachel was still enjoying a great social life, dating, and hanging out at the coffee shop. *Friends* painted a picture in which having a baby as a single woman is easy, something that changes nothing. Of course, as any parent can tell you, having a baby changes everything. Where was that truth on *Friends*? What happened to the baby? Where were the hours and hours of Rachel's interaction with little Emma, the minute-by-minute loving care, the absolute dependence and the absolute responsibility? *That's* the reality, but it is not what we see on TV. Bad culture lies.

I'm not saying sex has no place on television—though it could certainly use less in the programming, not to mention ads. I'm saying it needs to be honest. It needs to reflect the truth.

Kids conclude from what they see on TV that true love is validated through sexual engagement, that sex is the natural and normal result when two people like each other. And what follows from sex is, of course, true happiness. With all this sex going on outside of marriage, you'd think we should be a pretty sexually satisfied society. Of course, we are not. In a groundbreaking essay on the impact of pornography, Naomi Wolfe asked, "Does all this sexual imagery in the air mean that sex has been liberated—or is it the case that the relationship between the multi-billion-dollar porn industry, compulsiveness, and sexual appetite has become like the relationship between agribusiness, processed foods, supersize portions, and obesity? If your appetite is stimulated and fed by poor-quality material, it takes more junk to fill you up. People are not closer because of porn but further apart; people are not more turned on in their daily lives but less so." The sexual saturation of our culture has had the unexpected effect of depleting real intimacy in our lives. One irony of our times is that surveys show the most sexually satisfied women in America are: married and religious! Hardly what the media would have you believe.

When it does reflect the truth, and the storytelling is well crafted, television and film are *powerful*. On an episode of *American Dreams* one of the principal characters, Roxanne, a high school student, lost her virginity. The sex wasn't depicted, just talked about in a conversation with a friend. And the message that Roxanne communicated to her friend was that it was a mistake: she should have waited. How true—and how rare.

Sexual intimacy is an important part of being human. As parents, sex is one of the most challenging topics to discuss frankly with our children, so we too often leave that job to the neighborhood kids and the popular culture. That may have been all right for your parents to do, but in today's culture it is not.

Sometimes I wonder why we so often fail in this task. Is it because we are uncomfortable talking about our own bodies? Or is it because we have never learned to express the depth of sex's meaning and significance in our lives? Or is it because, sadly, we can't describe spousal intimacy since our lives too are devoid of that intimacy? The vast majority of us want our kids to wait until marriage, but we have trouble explaining why.

This common difficulty of so many American parents points to the "presence of an absence" in American culture. As I said, culture enables us to explain ourselves to ourselves. We understand ourselves through the stories and images that we create and ponder. The stories give us words when we have none of our own. The fact that we have no words to express our deepest feelings and intuitions about sexual intimacy is therefore an incredible indictment of the poverty of our culture, our loss of cultural capital. We are awash in words and images of sexuality, and yet none of this has provided us with a vocabulary adequate to what we really feel and know in the deepest places in our hearts. In a culture of lies, we have no words to speak the truth about sexual intimacy.

XXXII

Not Withdraw, but Engage

If most parents took a tour of a typical Saturday with their children, they would probably be shocked. Starting with morning cartoons and on through the "family hour" on prime-time television, violence and sex are constant. Make a stop at the wrong cable channel at the wrong time of day, and your child may also be exposed to raunchy pornography. Stop by the mall or the movie theater's arcade, and violence is everywhere in screaming pixels and stereo sound. Take in a movie. If it's rated PG-13, be prepared to be shocked and saddened. Profanity, violence, and sex are commonplace in most PG-13 movies. Indeed, PG-13 has become meaningless. Then go home and sit over your child's shoulder as he goes online to check his e-mail and instant messages with a friend. The odds are pretty good a pop-up ad will appear that is at best sexually suggestive, at worst downright pornographic.

All of this is not accidental. It's not just "the way it is." Things are the way they are in our culture because of the conscious decisions of hundreds of well-paid executives in the entertainment industries. They are the ones who are deciding every day what our own "choices" will be. Corporate America understands fully what it is doing when it harnesses pop culture to increase the bottom line. And it is shocking to see how MTV sets the tone, corporate America sings the tune, and we all pay the price—particularly the poor. It's all just another example of the Bigs separating your children from faith and family in order to teach No-Fault Freedom.

It may be impossible to keep all of the evils of the world from our children. But as parents, we have to try to shield our children as much as possible. Not only will that be healthy for our kids, but over time, our choices about what to see, and what not to see, will make an impact on the corporate bottom line. And that in turn will begin to change the culture.

Obviously our children are not growing up in the same culture with the same number of media outlets as we did. When I was a kid we had network television, movies, vinyl records, and the print media. With the advent of the Internet, new broadband capability, and computer software, parents are faced with images flung at their children from every direction. Parents can't afford to look the other way and ignore this responsibility. What I hear from so many parents is that they feel there is nothing they can do. I admit that the challenge is daunting, and it certainly won't make you popular with your kids (that is, until, like so many "restrictions" we place on our children, they are old enough to look back and thank you). Nor will you be popular with some of the neighbors. But parents have to know what their children are watching, where they are surfing, what they are playing, what they are listening to, and what movies they are going to. Like it or not, *you* are in a battle for your children's hearts and minds and souls: and you are up against an entertainment industry that only cares about your pocketbook. Why would you trust someone who only cares about your money with the souls of your children? Yet every time we don't make that effort to screen the cultural artifacts that corrupt our children, we are doing just that. It's time to let your pocketbook communicate to that industry what values you want displayed and modeled for your children.

Take TV, for example. Television can be okay for kids—but not nearly 30 hours a week of television. Too many parents use the television or PlayStation as a cheap babysitter. Giving our children too much television or screen time is one of the worst things we can do for their mental and physical health. Before his untimely death, I had the privilege of getting to know Fred Rogers, the longtime host of *Mr. Rogers' Neighborhood*. He had a genuine love for kids—and yes, he was the same in person as he was on TV. He understood the power of television, both for good and ill. His own format was educational, the segments were sustained, and his demeanor was calm. He was a contrarian in his industry, because he firmly believed that *how much* TV was being watched was just as important as *what* was being watched. Mr. Rogers knew the risks of too much passive entertainment and too little physical activity. Yet we have been raising up a generation of pudgy couch potatoes.

Fred told me once that he was "radical" in his programming. Radical? That's the last thing one would think to call Mr. Rogers. Why that designation? Because he believed that kids could have adult-sized attention spans, and so the segments of his program were much longer than those of other kids' shows, such as *Sesame Street*. Some scholars have even suggested that there may be a correlation between attention deficit disorder, which has exploded in recent years, and the rapid pace of our pop culture's images constantly flickering in front of our children. Between too little exercise and the jerky razzamatazz of "children's programming" on TV, is it any wonder there are so many kids on Ritalin today?

Too many parents are letting popular culture and the messages of the village elders pollute their children's minds and turn their bodies into mush. For change to happen in our culture, it has to start at home. We have to get our kids off the couch and outside. We have to put a limit on how much television our children watch. We have to decide what games they play. We have to monitor what CDs they listen to. As I have been emphasizing, the common good is up to us, *We the People*.

I am sure if he were joining this dialogue, Mr. Rogers would remind you that "you are special." And as a parent, your role as the gatekeeper of your home *is* special. No one else can do that job. Too many parents get so overwhelmed with the deluge of pop culture that they throw up their hands and give up. A few others take the opposite tack and retreat completely. Shut it all down. Pull the plug.

While this response is understandable—Karen and I went through that phase—it is also impractical. It is impossible to keep *all* of it away; other kids who are influenced by the pop culture will end up influencing your kids, exposing them to the culture you are trying to keep at bay. You can't run and you can't hide—but you can *engage*. Teaching your children right from wrong, and setting very clear expectations for what they can and cannot do, is foundational in equipping them to navigate the culture on their own. You'll find that kids—even teenagers—can make the right choices if you communicate high expectations. Remember what those focus groups run by the Institute for Youth Development revealed: teens wanted more guidance from their parents, not less, and they themselves complained about the messages they got from the media.

One example of the kind of guidance kids want and need relates to fashion. (Is fashion a part of culture? Yes, because with the clothes we wear, we fashion ourselves into an "image" of ourselves, we make of ourselves something of a work of art.) Karen and I have promoted the concept of modesty with all of our children, both boys and girls, but the pressure is really on the girls in our society. What are parents thinking who let their 10- or 12- or 14-year-old daughters go out with provocative words or slogans printed on their shorts or sweatpants—or with bare midriffs or other not-to-be-exposed areas of the body? Remarkably, mainstream stores even sell sexy underwear to *pre-teens*. Here, I'm not going to blame the people who make this junk, even though they seem to be targeting younger and younger girls. I blame parents who allow their girls to wear this junk. I know that it is difficult. The cultural and peer pressure on our daughters is intense. Setting fashion rules and sticking with them will most certainly make for louder arguments in your home. But I believe strongly that making rules about modesty and sticking with them will reduce the stress and problems your daughter will definitely experience if she appears too promiscuous among her peers.

All this is to say again that, like clothes, culture is something our kids have to wear. It is not a matter of *whether* culture is a factor in their lives, but *to what extent* and *which aspects* of culture ultimately have an impact.

Because we cannot escape the culture we must work for an improvement in our entertainment media. We must replenish our cultural capital so that it reflects the dignity of the human person. But while that is our long-term goal, parents need answers *now*. I believe the practical strategy for parents today is to equip themselves, and their children, with the critical tools needed for navigating the culture. We must learn how to be discerning. We must search for what is good, and fill up our leisure with that, rather than merely saying "No" to what is bad. We must become culturally literate, familiar with the best in our cultural tradition, and be able to pass that on to our children in a compelling way. In other words, we have to learn how to live "in the world" and yet not be "of the world."

XXXIII

Culture-Makers, Culture-Mongers, Culture-Consumers

There are at least three players in the business of culture—the artifact makers, the artifact sellers, and the artifact buyers. Someone designs a piece of clothing, writes a book, develops a screenplay, or records a song. These are our artists, and they create the cultural artifacts. Then someone packages, markets, advertises, and sells these artifacts. They sell them to the buyer, the consumer: to you, to me, and to our children. The artist celebrates freedom of expression above all else, the merchant celebrates the sale and the profit, and the consumer pursues happiness, albeit often of a fleeting sort without any reflection on what true happiness might be. We are a free society, and free people will make, sell, and buy cultural content that many of us don't approve of. I am not a libertarian, but I do believe that the government should have a very limited role in regulating commerce among adults. However, when it comes to protecting children, I believe that we have a public obligation to work together for their health and well-being. I now want to take a look at the three players in the culture business, each in turn.

I CANNOT PRETEND to fathom the mind of a true artist. I cannot play an instrument; I can barely draw a circle; I don't even take good photos. How cultural artifacts are created is a great mystery to me. And from what I understand, it is often a mystery to the artists as well. I have been told that the layers of meaning in a particular artwork such as a song or a film often are revealed to the artist himself only long after the work is complete. This is the power of art. Its shaping and forming influence is often subliminal, and therefore all the more powerful in the long run. It is precisely because of this power of art that the artists, the creators, need to become more conscious of their influence, particularly on young children. Our artists need to get involved, to help parents ensure that only appropriate artifacts are available to our youth.

For example, the Recording Industry Association of America (RIAA), prodded by the Federal Trade Commission, now stickers music CDs with "parental advisory" labels if they contain content inappropriate for children. I view such stickers as a red light for my kids. The answer is simple if they were to ask about a CD with that sticker: "No." However, nonlabeled CDs don't necessarily have a green light, only a yellow. Those CDs still require discernment and discussion, but at least the labeling weeds out the really bad stuff.

There are a number of technical tools available to parents that help filter out bad language or, with greater sophistication, actually edit/skip certain scenes of sexual activity and over-the-top violence. The industry, however, has responded to these new technological aids with lawsuits and other threats. Rather than trying to take away tools from parents who want to let their kids watch movies (would they rather we just say "No" completely?), the industry should be working with parents to make available to us the "airplane" edited versions of their films. These versions are edited by the directors, and a recent on-line poll at *Parenting Magazine* found that almost three out of four respondents would purchase or rent an airplane-edited version of certain films that they would otherwise choose not to watch at all. Making these films available would be in the economic interest of the industry.

Still, like CD labeling, these edited films could only be at best a "yellow" light for parents, not a "green" one. Some in the industry I have talked to suggest that this would be more confusing for the consumer. I don't know how much more confusing it could be than the current PG-13 rating. What is a parent to do when a film like *October Sky*, with its themes of persistence, hope, and redemption, is rated PG-13, putting it in the same category as *Austin Powers*, in which every joke is sexually suggestive or simply vulgar? While the current rating system is better than nothing, I also believe that making the "airplane" edited versions available to parents would be a giant step in the right direction.

What about television? I am not going to rail at the networks' race to the bottom with cable, or about the negative impact of "reality" shows. But there are two areas in particular where cable and the networks can be more helpful to parents. First, the family hour. This once sacrosanct time slot has slowly been eroded to the point where it now simply does not exist. There is now *no* time of day when parents can be certain that their children will be shielded from inappropriate content. The networks should voluntarily restore the family hour—and that means not only modifying the content of the shows on at that time, but also the advertising and network promotions for other programs (those promos often pack into a few seconds more intense and rapid-fire violence and sex than the shows themselves).

Second, there are the advertisements. Who hasn't been sitting on the couch watching a game with the kids when a sexually suggestive or very violent commercial comes on? I know that sex and shock grab the attention of the otherwise mesmerized viewer whom the advertiser is trying to influence, but we have to remember just who is watching: not just adults, but also children. Advertisers should start to restrain themselves voluntarily from placing inappropriate ads on shows that are aimed at families or aired during times when children are tuned in.

One of the challenges is that the entertainment industry has to produce artifacts that sell: they are a business, after all. And what they think sells is sex and violence. But I am not convinced. The biggest shows on television are often positive. The biggest films are often G and PG rated. The best selling CDs and hit songs are more often than not clean and constructive. So how do you explain the fact that there aren't more socially and culturally redemptive artifacts being created?

One reason, perhaps, is that those of us with traditional values now view arts and entertainment as hostile territory, and so we steer clear of the whole industry. A prominent screenwriter/producer, who happens to be a cultural conservative, recently advertised nationally for an assistant, indicating his interest in hiring someone who shares his values. He got *four* inquiries.

We conservatives have to *engage* the culture. We have to bring our talents and resources into the cultural arena. We also need to encourage our kids to pursue careers in entertainment, the media, and the arts. The only real way to clean up Hollywood is from within. At the end of the day, art is created by a mysterious process within the heart and soul of artists. It reflects some part of them and their worldview. We need more young men and women who hold traditional convictions to see the importance of pursuing careers in the culture industry. We need more artifacts that tell the truth: that beauty is not just in the eye of the beholder, but in truth itself; that goodness really is good and desirable; that wrongdoing has consequences. We need to encourage our children to create *good* art—in every sense of the word. And that does not mean it will all be G and PG. But it will tell the truth. Sure, it will be a challenge for young conservative artists, who will likely be isolated in this field. But the more of them who are there, the easier it will be.

EVEN THE BEST ARTISTIC WORKS can have no impact on culture if no one sees or hears them. The key to the commercial viability of arts and entertainment, therefore, is marketing and distribution. This is both good news and bad news. The good news is that there is a check on access to inappropriate material—the distribution channel. The bad news is that someone is always willing to make a dollar, regardless of the social and cultural cost—and because of advances in technology, especially the Internet, there are more and more ways to get around the checks that are in place. This is where corporate cooperation comes into play. It is critical that corporations be good public citizens and help parents keep their kids away from inappropriate and even harmful material.

Let me tell you about two corporate good citizens—Regal Cinemas and Cinemark. In 2001, the FTC exposed the fact that some Hollywood studios were marketing R-rated films to children under the age of seventeen. The studios were shamed by these revelations, but key to changing their behavior were the efforts of these two theater chains. Both took aggressive steps to make sure that kids were kept out of R-rated movies. They trained their employees, started checking ID, and posted guards at individual screens to make sure that kids didn't sneak in to movies for which they hadn't bought tickets. The result? The type of R-rated films that clearly were targeting adolescent boys began to lose their profitability. Within a year of implementing these new policies, the news from Hollywood was that fewer of these films were being produced. Indeed, the number of R-rated movies decreased from 528 in 2000 to 490 in 2001, while the number of PG-13 movies increased from 146 to 163 over those same two years. I am not a fan of the PG-13 rating, but at least this is a trend in the right direction. And importantly, it was brought about in large part by the actions of two corporate good citizens.

The video arcades I remember from my college years are still around, but the games have grown up since the days of Pac-Man and Asteroids. Now, the games are hyper-realistic in their violence and, in some cases, provocative in their sexual innuendo. I know lots of parents who don't allow their kids to spend any time at arcades because of this stuff: we're among them. But at some movie theaters, a 14-year-old boy can spend an hour at an arcade playing games that are appropriate only for 18-year-olds and older, then go to see an R-rated movie. Again, the fix is pretty easy. There are great video games that don't involve violence and provocative and exploitative images of women. Video arcade owners and movie theaters can fill their arcades with these kinds of games. They'll make just as much money. In fact, they might see more kids playing their machines, because parents will start to feel okay about it.

Some cooperative corporate citizens are reacting to the violence in video games. You won't find any nasty video games at any Disney park, for example. And again, Regal has stepped up and replaced all of its racy arcade games with racing ones.

Another corporate good citizen cooperating with parents to keep kids from inappropriate content has been Wal-Mart. When the Recording Industry Association of America began labeling certain CDs with parental advisory warnings, Wal-Mart decided not to carry *any* of them unless they were edited of offensive language. Wal-Mart's sheer market share obliged the industry to respond, so within months the musical content in many communities was cleaned up. Was this in Wal-Mart's bottom-line interest? Not necessarily. One executive told me that they get more complaints about the "bleeping" than they get compliments. It has also cost them market share and profits, as some kids sneak over to less responsible retailers to buy unedited versions of the CDs. But Wal-Mart has no intention of changing its policy. It has been a good corporate citizen, recognizing the role it plays in fostering the common good.

In addition, Wal-Mart and other retailers have cooperated with parents by instituting register prompts to ensure that certain entertainment content is not sold to children. If a 15-year-old can't buy a ticket to an R-rated movie, why should he be able to buy the same movie on DVD? Stores like Toys-R-Us keep entertainment gaming software in a different area and use the Entertainment Software Review Board (ESRB) ratings to police the sale of Mature-rated games. Wal-Mart has gone even further, kicking soft-porn magazines like *Maxim* out of its stores altogether. This is a critical way for retailers to cooperate with parents.

Seven retailers make up 70 percent of the non-Internet sales of DVDs and VHS videos. Every one of them can and ought to implement a system using register prompts with existing ratings of movies, games, and music to ensure that kids can't buy what even the industry has determined is inappropriate for them.

An emerging area of distribution that requires corporate cooperation with parents is the Internet. With the advent of broadband (cable and DSL), media content is being purchased online and delivered directly to the home through the Internet.

This is especially true with music, which is beginning to make its transformation from retail to online. But movies are not far behind. And online gaming is the rage. It is critical that all of these sites incorporate parental controls. Similar to the way Blockbuster allows parents to keep their kids from renting R-rated movies without their permission, these online services need to give parents the option of preventing their kids from downloading or purchasing inappropriate content.

A quick aside on the Internet: it is a dangerous world out there for kids. The amount of pornography aimed at kids is criminal—and I do mean criminal. The Justice Department must be aggressive in prosecuting, but parents also have to be active in their own policing. I would encourage all readers to check out I-Safe (www.isafe.org) and make sure that they are doing all that they can to protect their children from predators and pornography. This is no time to be asleep at the wheel.

But probably the biggest threat to kids on the Internet is peer-to-peer networks. Countless children and younger teens are downloading music and videos illegally through peer-to-peer (P2P) networks like Kazaa. Most parents have no idea what P2Ps are or how they work. Unlike networks with a central server from which files are downloaded, P2Ps link individual computers with software that makes files available from each to the others. Not only can this make your PC vulnerable to viruses and hacking, it also makes your children vulnerable to pornography and worse. When a child searches on Kazaa for the "Olsen Twins," for example, you would not believe what comes up. The Olsen Twins are charming teenage entertainers who have appeared on TV and in films. What you get on Kazaa is page after page after page of pornography.

Kazaa and other file-sharing software like it are gateways to pornography and possible addiction and worse. I was amazed

when I found out that big, supposedly family-friendly advertisers have ads on these sites where pornography is available to
children. The music and movie industries are fighting these networks because they enable a kind of piracy. We need to join
with these industries in this fight for another reason: so that
parents can have the power to keep this stuff off their home
computers.

Finally, advertisers have another role that they uniquely can
play: using their clout to make sure that television shows aired
during the family hour really are for families and that shows
targeting kids really are for kids. Companies such as Hallmark
should be commended for underwriting high-quality, highly en-
tertaining, and high-minded productions. But there are too few
good corporate citizens who put public health and a healthy
culture above a healthy profit.

A few years ago I met with the CEO of a major beverage
company that spends millions marketing its products to kids.
He told me he had good news and bad news to report about
what he had discovered about his company's advertising strategies. The good news was that his company advertised on six of
the ten top family shows. The bad news was that they advertised on eight of the ten worst. Then he gave me better news: he
had told his advertising buyers to change their purchasing pattern. Several major corporations such as Proctor & Gamble,
Hallmark, Campbell's, and H. J. Heinz have adopted family-
friendly advertising policies to guide their ad buys. We need
more corporations to join them to create a marketplace motive
for the broadcast and cable networks to protect the family hour
and protect our kids by underwriting with their advertising dollars only appropriate content.

The marketplace needs to demand the creation of better,
healthier media content. But even if we do see the creation of

more options for our kids, I fully expect that the entertainment industry will continue to produce R-rated movies, Mature-rated video games, and music fully warranting those "Parental Advisory" labels. The last element in the culture cycle, therefore, is us—the consumers.

ULTIMATELY, THE POWER TO CHANGE the culture and to protect our children rests with every parent. *We* are the market, and people will produce and sell what sells. So don't buy the junk culture, and don't let your kids buy it either. If we all did this, we would soon enough discover that there was much less junk for sale. By demanding good culture, we can create an environment in which those who lead the pop culture industries are people who care, not hucksters of cynicism. If we do this, not only will each of us be protecting our own family, the market will begin to supply more of the goods that are demanded. Soon enough we will find ourselves with a choice between good and better rather than with a choice between bad and worse.

I talked earlier about the concept of subsidiarity, the idea that decisions and actions affecting the common good should be undertaken at the level of the smallest social unit possible, the one closest to the immediate consequences. In the case of cultural consumption, this is the family. Building strong families that can critically engage the culture is how we build a strong society and a healthy culture. Building up our cultural capital starts inside our own homes.

Perhaps the most radical action we parents can and should take is to create within our families our own "popular" culture. Turn off the television, gather your children, and tell family stories. Children, no matter what the age, from 4 to 17, love to hear stories of what life was like when their parents were kids. They love to hear about grandma and grandpa. They want to know what it was like when you were their age. Stories that may seem old, silly, or trite to you are the best kind of history and entertainment to your children. Too often we are focused on the commercially produced culture that pours down on us from the Bigs. But culture can also bubble up from below, from within the heart of the family. This is how a genuine folk culture, a culture of the people, is created—by communicating to your kids the values that matter to you and the stories that illustrate those values.

We like stories in our house. We make them up, tell old tales, and read even more. We often have movie nights with the kids. It is harder and harder to find good films that interest all of our kids at their various ages, I have to admit, but the point is we aren't entertainment Luddites. Still, parents do need to persevere in their effort to set limits on the entertainment content their kids consume. Limit time on the Internet. Don't let your kids tune out the world with their MP3 player at dinner. Only let them watch one show a day, max. Video gaming is fun, but it should be a reward only after schoolwork and chores are completed.

Communication with your own children is where the decision point really is with regard to media consumption. Is the violence in that television or video game appropriate? What was the message behind that movie about the role of family? Does that music video demean women? When you drive back from the theater or concert, talk about what you've just seen and heard. You need to help teach your kids to be discerning about the messages targeted at them. You won't always be there to make decisions for them: you need to equip them to make good choices on their own.

It is also important that parents take measures to ensure that their children's consumption of cultural content is *public*, open to inspection by parents. Having a television in a child's bedroom is asking for trouble. The same is true with the Internet. If you want to protect your kids from Internet porn, don't put a PC in their room with unrestricted online access. The temptation is too great.

I know what I just recommended runs contrary to what a huge proportion of American families are currently doing, and it will strike many parents as extremist and even somehow wrong. After all, they will say, don't children have rights too? And among their rights, don't they have a right to privacy, just like adults? Isn't it the case that good parents respect their children by respecting their rights? That's how at least one of the arguments goes. And here we see a good example of how the court decisions of the village elders have had an impact on the common culture reaching into every American home.

Thinking about the relationship between parents and children in this way reflects the liberal understanding of a society entirely composed of abstract individuals. In fact, one of the great intellectual achievements of the village elders has been to push the logic of liberal individualism into the heart of the family with the concept of "children's rights"—including in some truly extremist views the right of children to "divorce" their parents. For a generation, the village elders have been attempting to revise our laws so that children are no longer treated as members of their families but as rights-bearing sovereign individuals. Parts of this new jurisprudence have become the law of the land and parts have not. But the spirit behind this legal agenda has succeeded wildly and has embedded itself in our common culture: liberal parenting advice has become the common coin of public discussion when it comes to children.

A culture built around the idea that children are sovereign individuals is a culture of lies. Parents need to return to common sense: children are children and adults are adults. We do not "respect" our children when we treat them as if they had a right of privacy shielding them from our supervision. Rather, creating such privacy for them is a kind of abandonment. It is not respect at all; it is neglect.

Beyond the family, there is also a lot of work for voluntary associations to do. One of the benefits of nonprofits is that they can apply nonlegislative pressure on entertainment purveyors. The nonprofits that are most effective are usually the ones that work quietly and discretely. After all, there is a fine line between effectively condemning bad culture and providing free publicity for the same. There needs to be a check on destructive culture, but that operation must be done with a scalpel, not a machete.

There is also a role for nonprofits and schools in training our kids about how to navigate the culture critically. The Boy Scouts and Girl Scouts, for example, understand the importance of media literacy—so do the Boys and Girls Clubs. Schools should likewise be making use of the best cultural content in class and making sure that junk is not in the curriculum. I applaud the new program championed by Dana Gioia of the National Endowment for the Arts that is making live Shakespeare available in communities across the country that are too small to support a local theater group. I am a supporter of the NEA because it can be a vehicle for promoting good culture, for fostering our founders' vision of an American high culture that is second to none. As we all know, the NEA has not always fulfilled this role. Often, the NEA has been a bad steward of public funds. But thanks to public outcry and congressional action it is now a positive cultural force.

But when it comes to culture, I keep returning to the family: family is the key. A child usually cannot buy a $49 video- game without his parents knowing it—or go to a movie without her parents driving her to the mall. Parents are the gatekeepers. We have to empower parents to do the work that only they can do. At a time when technologies are racing ahead in such a way that our children are exposed to too many cultural messages behind our backs, we need to build up a "parent culture" that is at least as strong as our youth culture.

XXXIV

Culture and Public Policy

I have talked a great deal here about what parents can do and what industry can do voluntarily in shielding children from harmful cultural messages. What about government? What role can government play in building up cultural capital? As I said before, I am a strong advocate of freedom of speech when it comes to any political or public policy discourse—even if I don't like some of the speech directed at me! Freedom of political speech is one of our country's first principles, one of the distinctive foundations of a healthy democracy. But I am less an absolutist when it comes to commercial speech. And when it comes to rank pornography and violence, to mere titillation, I am entirely willing to weigh the public good in the balance against "personal expression."

A good example of this delicate balance came in 2000, when one of my colleagues, Senator John McCain, put forth the Children's Internet Protection Act (CIPA), which would require public libraries that receive federal funds (which virtually all do) to implement Internet-filtering devices to protect kids from pornography and other harmful content. I was and am very supportive of this effort in broad terms.

But Senator McCain's approach, while well intentioned, was certainly headed to a constitutional challenge; his bill was also opposed by most of the civil libertarian organizations, including the library associations. My additional concern was that filtering technology is never foolproof, and although useful in blocking pornography, it is a blunt instrument that also blocks appropriate sites while doing little to protect kids from predators in chat rooms. I proposed instead the Neighborhood Children's Internet Protection Act, which allowed libraries to opt for community Internet monitoring as an alternative to filtering technology. I believed that this approach reinforced community standards, further fostered civil society, and encouraged parental and community involvement in the "training up" of their children.

Some conservatives thought this approach was too weak, but others understood that it actually would enhance the protections afforded our children. Still, this example illustrates my preferred public policy approach to questions of culture. Government has a role to play in promoting the common good, but it should do so by equipping and empowering families and communities: it should follow the path of subsidiarity.

One of the roles that government is uniquely capable of playing is providing parents and the pop culture industry with research. I am a strong advocate of federal investment in research in general, and research regarding the impact of media content on children in particular. I stood with Senators Brownback, Lieberman, and Clinton to introduce a $90 million federal grant program to support research into the effects of viewing and using all types of media—including television, computer games, and the Internet—on children's physical and psychological development. The Children and Media Research Advancement (CAMRA) Act would establish a program within the National

Institute of Child Health and Human Development aimed at
energizing research into the role of all forms of digital, analog,
and print media on the cognitive, social, emotional, physical,
and behavioral development of children from infancy through
adolescence.

There have been thousands of studies conducted over the
years, many of them funded by the federal government, investi-
gating the impact of media violence on kids. But little such research has been conducted in the area of sexually explicit media. I suspect this lack of research interest in sexually oriented
media is attributable to the prejudices of the village elders who
direct much of the social science research: although they seem
very concerned about the impact of violence, they are fiercely
protective of No-Fault Freedom when it comes to sexual liberation. However, the consequences of the sexual revolution are so
profound that we cannot afford a research policy of "don't ask,
don't tell." We need more research here and on a whole range of
questions that have arisen because of the unprecedented explosion of media. Government has a role here.

Recently, I found my attention glued to the pages of a *National Geographic* article describing the latest scientific evidence
about the physical process of brain development. The article made
a compelling case that the human brain is not able to fully balance the consequences of risk and reward until the age of 24. It is
not coincidental that rental car companies don't rent cars to people
under that very age of 24: they have discovered the same relationship between age, risk, and reward—not through brain mapping
and CAT scans, but through the analysis of accidents. I am sure
that there are many college-age students who have thought it unfair
that they could not rent a car, just as our teenage children think it
unfair when their parents restrict their access to certain media. It
is research like this which demonstrates that our instincts and the

common wisdom of tradition are often exactly right in what they tell us about how best to raise our children.

There is another role for public policy when it comes to cultural content: to protect the creators of cultural artifacts against theft. We readily understand that this is the government's responsibility when it comes to stealing your purse or your car— but too many Americans fail to see that the same principle is involved when it comes to intellectual property.

As I indicated earlier, protecting these property rights is also valuable in our efforts to protect our kids. Nonprofits and politicians can work with legitimate businesses to push for safeguards on content and for technologies to empower parents. But the people who steal content are not interested in protecting kids from it; in fact, hooking kids is probably their objective. So no matter how many controls Wal-Mart puts in place to restrict the retail sale or rental of an R-rated film, for example, if that film is pirated and distributed illegally, our children are put at risk. This is true also with music and is likely to become so with gaming as Internet broadband allows for larger files to be transferred.

It is because of this that I support legislation that would outlaw the use of camcorders in movie theaters and punish the distribution of pirated movies and songs. I favor aggressively negotiating and enforcing trade agreements that eliminate the international market for illegally pirated entertainment content, which is often made available to our kids through the Internet. I have also called for our Justice Department to aggressively prosecute illegal domestic pirating and distribution, and I am all for throwing the book at those trying to sell or distribute unhealthy violent or sexually explicit content to our children.

Sometimes industry responds to parents' concerns and produces tools to help them navigate the pop culture and protect their kids—and sometimes industry doesn't like competition and tries to litigate their rivals out of business. Some of these "rivals" include the technical tools and options being marketed to parents to allow them to screen or offer edited versions of content. An example of this is CleanFlicks, which offers online rentals of "family edited" movies for in-home use.

Technology has now moved forward, and perhaps you have heard of a movie-filtering technology called ClearPlay that blocks out sexually graphic, violent, and profane content. ClearPlay provides a digital filter that works in a specially designed DVD to delete offensive content from DVDs that you own and play. Similar to this is "cure-free TV" technology, available as an add-on unit for your television or as technology embedded in some DVD/VCR players. TVGuardian offers technology to read closed captioning, and mutes the sound when offensive words are about to be spoken, displaying closed captioning with the offensive words replaced with inoffensive ones. A third technology that parents are finding useful is TIVO, which allows parents to record a program and play it back at their convenience. Although the technology does not embed filtering tools, it allows parents to fast-forward through offensive scenes. These technologies, as well as others, are valuable tools that the market is producing in response to parents' desire to protect their kids. I support legislation that would protect companies that make such devices from copyright infringement lawsuits by film studios.

We also need to do more when it comes to offensive content being broadcast over public airwaves. There are already laws on the books that allow for the federal government to regulate obscenity on the airwaves. A laissez-faire approach by regulators only emboldens certain bad actors in the industry to push the limits. I fully support aggressive enforcement of existing standards by the Federal Communications Commission (FCC), and I support increased fines for violations of existing obscenity laws and regulations. I must also say that I am very impressed with the website that the FCC has created to assist parents in navigating broadcast media, and, if necessary, to register complaints regarding indecency and obscenity (www.fcc.gov/parents/).

Similarly, I support the good work of the Federal Trade Commission (FTC), which has been monitoring marketing and retailing practices aimed at children. It was the FTC that uncovered the movie industry's focus-group testing of R-rated movies with children as young as 13. That discovery started a firestorm of complaint about industry practices and led to changed behavior. The annual report issued by the FTC summarizes initiatives by the film, music, and gaming industries that limit (or fail to limit) marketing efforts aimed at kids. This scrutiny has been an important tool to keep the industry accountable, and, happily, progress has been reported in all sectors since the FTC started its annual effort. The FTC also offers a very useful website that makes it convenient for parents to lodge complaints about inappropriate marketing practices (www.ftc.gov/ratings/).

Beyond these efforts, however, we need a ratings system—for films, television, and video games—that really works for parents. What we have now is helpful, but not helpful enough. I defy anybody to give me an explanation of the difference between R and PG-13 that parents could actually use in making decisions for their children, for example.

Dr. Rich and his colleagues at Harvard are trying to create just such a system:

> One of our goals is to be able to analyze and research the effects of violent images, for example, and translate them into an assessment system. This is not one that is applied and designed by the guys trying to sell you this media. We want a

system applied more like the system for inspecting food—an impartial body that can give you the best assessment of what's there, one that is user-friendly for parents. What we are trying to do is give parents the tools to make informed and accurate decisions based on known health outcomes. We're not trying to create any kind of censorship system. We are more interested in providing an objective set of criteria by which consumers can be informed about the nature of a product and what its likely effects will be on their children.

Government has a role to play here, just as in food safety inspections and drug certification.

Finally, I believe that the diversity and growing complexity of entertainment media lends itself to a unique opportunity for each of the pop culture sectors (television, film, music, distribution, retailing, etc.) to work together to encourage parents to take control. The same message machine that sends pop culture into every nook and cranny of our lives can also serve as a machine to get the message to every parent that they do have tools available to them to engage the culture critically.

I have encouraged all the media sectors to make each June "Parental Media Literacy Month," when each of them can jointly and separately equip parents to navigate around the cultural landmines. For example, stores could take advantage of the month to remind their clerks to monitor the sale of media, and to place more signage at their point of purchase. Theaters could run trailers before PG-13 and R-rated films to remind parents in the audience that content has consequences. Pediatricians could give out fliers that summarize the different rating systems and an update on research that provides insight into the effects of media content on kids. You get the idea. If they work together to remind us parents that *we* are ultimately responsible, and take the extra steps to empower us in our role, the industry can be transformed from adversary to ally.

So government certainly does have a role when it comes to cleaning up our culture, but that role is not the role of censor. We must be good stewards of our cultural patrimony no less than our other inheritances. We have not been very good stewards of that patrimony in recent decades, but that is not cause for shouting gloom and doom. Rather, there are steps we really can take that will build up a healthy culture, steps that will restore cultural capital. And those steps all begin with the family.

Part Six
EDUCATIONAL EXCELLENCE

XXXV

Knowledge, Truth, and Education

Ihave been discussing our stewardship of America's general welfare, our common responsibility for replenishing, in every generation, various forms of "capital" that are the foundation of the common good. I have focused particularly on the family as the "foundation of the foundation" for the common good, and I have tried to address the difficult time parents are having today in their efforts to raise good kids. What about our schools? Our children spend a huge portion of their young lives in school, and so schools have an enormous impact in shaping our children, and thus our society and culture.

In fact, after the family and religious congregations, schools may be the most fundamental institution of society—for three reasons. First, like the family, schools are directly involved in the raising of children, which is always the central task of any society. Second, because it is impossible to raise a child in a genuinely value-neutral way, schools are—like churches—value-laden and value-transmitting institutions. Third, schools are enormous generators of social capital, bringing parents, families, and whole communities together in a common endeavor with common ideals, and thereby building ties of solidarity. So

we must ask: How well are our schools doing their job of raising young people to be mature adults capable of self-government? How well are they transmitting our values? And how
well are they cooperating with parents to build up the family as
the basis for a strong society?

Our founders considered education of crucial importance
when they looked to the future of the newly founded American
republic. James Madison, for example, asked, "What spectacle
can be more edifying or more seasonable, than that of Liberty
and Learning, each leaning on the other for their mutual and
surest support?"

Similarly, George Washington wrote eloquently about the
importance of education:

> Knowledge is . . . the surest basis of public happiness because
> it teaches the people themselves, to know, and to value their
> own rights; to discern and provide against invasions of them;
> to distinguish between oppression and the necessary exercise
> of lawful authority, between burdens proceeding from a disre-
> gard to their convenience and those resulting from the inevi-
> table exigencies of society.

And as I pointed out in a previous section, Article 3 of the
Northwest Ordinance of 1787 states, "Religion, morality, and
knowledge, being necessary to good government and the happiness of mankind, schools and the means of education shall forever be encouraged." Public provision of schooling was thereby
written into the social fabric of the new states of the Midwest,
becoming in time a model for America as a whole.

But we also cannot help but noticing that schools are not
once mentioned in the federal Constitution. This is so despite
the fact that Thomas Jefferson was a long-time advocate of a
"national" university, and despite the fact that some of the states,
such as North Carolina, had and have constitutional provisions

concerning education, including their state universities. There might well have been a national university written into the U.S. Constitution, with its chancellor a constitutional office, just like the president and Supreme Court justices—but that did not happen. Given our founders' emphasis on the importance of education in a republic, what is the meaning of this absence?

I would contend that while our founders fully recognized the importance of education, they nonetheless agreed that the education of children is best accomplished by the family and voluntary associations, not by the state. The system we have today, therefore, is something of an anomaly.

WHAT I PROPOSE TO DO NOW is to look at the question of what I call "intellectual capital" as a component of the common good: What is it? Who is responsible for building it? How can we best do that? Equally important, what are the threats to our intellectual capital? And how may intellectual capital be restored if it is lost?

Let's first consider the most basic question: What is intellectual capital? One way to think about this is in terms of the classical distinction that Scholastic philosophers used to make between intellect and will in the human person. Our will is the part of us that makes choices. We are drawn to things that seem good to us, and we avoid or shun things that seem bad. However, it is possible that we can make mistakes about that—some things that seem good at first may turn out actually to be bad for us, and vice versa. So *knowledge* of the *truth* of things is critically important in the formation of our will. We have to be able to tell what something really *is* before we can make moral choices—choices of right and wrong—about it.

And just as knowledge of the truth is important in the formation of the will, so good moral character is important in the formation of the intellect. For example, if we choose to cheat (to do a morally wrong thing) then the process of learning goes awry and our intellects are not properly formed. By cheating, we may know "the answer" to a problem, but we don't have the intellectual skills to figure out the answer on our own, and so our intellectual development is shortchanged. Moral and intellectual rights and wrongs go hand in hand.

So while we can distinguish between them in abstract theory, in fact there is a close relationship between intellectual growth and moral growth. This is something that parents understand intuitively. Parents *know* that even the most intellectually oriented education can never be "value-free." Too often in our public schools, however, the educational village elders claim that schools are morally neutral zones and that schools exist only for intellectual development or the "acquisition" of "skills." But if classical philosophy is right, then this distinction is itself an untruth: and it is an untruth that we have in some cases built into the very foundation of our educational system.

By intellectual capital I mean the health and vitality of *learning* in a society: everything from basic skills to the highest reaches of scientific research—and also everything from knowing right from wrong at the playground to knowing right from wrong in the most complicated issues of bioethics. Intellectual capital also involves the extent to which our society is dedicated to intellectual development or self-improvement, to life-long learning, the best use of leisure—as opposed to mere entertainment. (The Greek word for leisure, scolê, is the basis of our word "school"—learning *is* leisure.) Intellectual capital also concerns, as a matter of direct public policy, the health and adequacy of our formal institutions of education.

A society rich in intellectual capital is one in which the love of learning is widespread and carefully cultivated, where standards are high, where new discoveries are made, and where a rich heritage of old truths is kept alive through critical study. A society low in intellectual capital is one sunk in complacency, where learning is not honored, where educational standards are allowed to fall, and where ancient wisdom is lost through simple neglect. Where does America stand with respect to its account of intellectual capital? It is a complicated question, with both good news and bad news. But I think all of us can agree that we need to do better. We must work for a renewal of our intellectual capital.

The first of three major building blocks of intellectual capital is, of course, the family. Education begins and ends in the family. It begins in the family because the raising of children is first and foremost the duty and the right of parents, and because from the earliest stages of life children are picking up the habits and attitudes of their parents in how they approach the world. Are parents interested in new things and curious about them? Do they constantly teach their children informally? Do they explore and explain the new things they experience each day? Do the parents model education through life-long learning, by turning off the TV and engaging in creative hobbies and pastimes? Do they prepare their children well for formal schooling and work diligently to support their children's learning process? Whether we think about it this way or not, we parents are inevitably, by nature, the primary educators of our children.

Education ends in the family because there is nothing more important we will do with our own intellectual gifts than to use them within our own families to raise up a new generation of curious, eager thinkers and learners who can hand on the hard-won wisdom of our civilization's tradition and build creatively on that foundation. Education also ends in the family because forming a family of our own is, for almost everyone, the most important thing we will "accomplish" in our lives: I always say the most important job I have is being a husband and father. A good test of an educational system, therefore, is how well it assists us in this fundamental task.

Some of the *implementation* of this duty can be delegated by parents to others, but parents cannot and should not try to escape that basic responsibility. They should embrace that role and be empowered to fulfill it. Government for its part must never forget that its role in education is to serve *parents*, to aid and support them in fulfilling a role that is uniquely theirs.

Too often, we don't think of education in this way. Based on the liberal model of a society of individuals, schools think of themselves as providing a public service to *students*, not as assisting in the private obligations of *parents*. Many of the educational elite, in fact, think of parents as a nuisance or a hindrance. How often do we hear from liberals that education is the answer to every social problem? Why? Because the village elders, the "experts," too often think of education as a form of *re*-education, "liberating" students from the "prejudices" and "superstitions" of parents. That is why, for example, the village elders would like to have earlier and earlier public schooling: best to get the children out of the home and into school as soon as possible, at age four or even three, so that the wisdom of the experts looms larger in a child's life—and parental authority looms smaller. In other words, these social engineers are involved in a kind of genteel war against the family.

(There is a legitimate argument that some parents neglect their children and that therefore early education must be provided as an intervention. But I would suggest spending our resources on helping parents better provide for their children at home rather than removing them from home. Remember, we are often taking these young children out of a virtue-rich environment into a value-neutral atmosphere.)

I know this will be seen as a harsh slap at the whole education system. It is not. I readily admit that across America, most of our schools are staffed with tens of thousands of men and women of good will who are doing their best for our children. I admire those teachers on the front lines, in the classroom, who day after day are giving the best of themselves for the students they encounter. They are confronting problems in school that we have never seen before, often in heroic ways. Not to mention that all of us have memories of a teacher who changed our lives for the better—by serving as a moral example or by introducing us to the sheer joy of learning. But I also have to say that the village elders who sit atop our educational systems—from the faculty of the education schools to the leadership of the National Education Association (the teachers' union)—have a clear liberal agenda that is much more concerned with imposing the will of experts than it is respecting the values and wishes of parents.

We need to reorient our thinking about education and the family entirely. We have to relearn the basics: that parents, faults and all, know better than anyone else what is best for their children, and that's as true in intellectual formation as it is in other aspects of life. The primary role of an educational system is to serve parents, not students.

The second major building block of intellectual capital is this: In addition to the usual checklist of learning skills, sciences, and humanities, the orientation of education toward truth should include *moral* truth as well. I know this will strike some readers as either dangerous or impossible for a public school system in a pluralistic democracy, but that's because we all tend to focus on a few highly contentious areas of morality in our culture, mostly revolving around human life and sexuality. But what about honesty and loyalty? What about self-control and self-sacrifice? Aren't these true values that we can agree to teach our children as being part of an objective moral reality?

What I will argue is that even the most skeptical and liberal of my readers must agree that for his or her values to be maintained in society, we must provide our children with a grounding in the objective reality of moral truths. Instinctively, every parent does this. Our educational system must reinforce rather than undermine the work parents are doing in the moral formation of their children.

I hope to show that a relentlessly "value-free" education, or one based only on "neutrality" and "tolerance," will undermine and eventually destroy everything that we hold dear about goodness, fairness, and rights—and that's the case whether we're liberal, conservative, or something else. The ongoing moral debates in our country must be grounded in the idea that we are engaged in a common project of searching for the truth, not just seeking power to wield over one another.

Third and finally, I believe our contemporary educational system has been built on the basis of some bad philosophical ideas that have passed themselves off as "scientific." In order to restore intellectual capital in America, we need to overcome these philosophical mistakes.

For example, we find ourselves stuck with an absolute distinction between facts and values. Facts, we are told, are real and objective, the realm of science and quantitative analysis. Values are entirely subjective and personal, having nothing to do with the idea of objective truth. "Facts" are understood in a reductionist way—things that can be observed, measured, quantified, broken into parts by analysis. If it cannot be measured, it's not a fact. "Values," on the other hand, are understood as mere preferences, the products of whimsy or prejudice, and because of this, values have no *truth* to them. This view arises from a misunderstanding of what knowledge is, what science is, and from a flawed understanding of nature and our relationship to it. It matters, because with such a distinction, education sets for itself the goal of teaching only "facts" and leaving "values" entirely aside. This is a philosophical mistake that has serious public consequences.

This may sound like an obscure complaint, but bear with me when I make the case. I think you'll agree that there is an important problem lurking here that should be confronted as we work to replenish our country's intellectual capital.

XXXVI

Who Rules the Schools?

Who exactly is in charge of the education of the young, and what is the primary purpose of that education? There are two conflicting approaches to these questions that we see played out in Western civilization.

In premodern times in the West the answers to the questions of the who and why about education were simple for most people: children were educated by their parents (or those selected by parents) for the good of the parents, the family, and the children themselves. In other words, children were educated by the family to serve the needs of the family as defined by the family. As a result, education was usually practical and religiously focused—training in the family's religious faith, family agriculture and business, apprenticeships in crafts and trade, and so forth. This is how most people were educated in the West from antiquity through the late eighteenth and early nineteenth centuries.

What is more, man is a social animal, and no family is an island. So from the time of the Greeks a preparation in things that served the needs of the "city" was also an important part of education, of growing up into responsible adulthood. So the needs of the political community have been and can be served by a family-centered approach to education. Since families exist within a larger social context, they will naturally take into account the needs of society when educating their children. This is common sense, and it is the way of subsidiarity.

But a totally different focus—a focus on the needs of the city or regime above all else—gave rise from the earliest times to another view of education quite different from the bottom-up, family-centered approach. As far back as Plato's *Republic* the visionaries of the good society have talked about taking away from parents the responsibility for the education of their children and giving it to the experts, the social engineers, the village elders. For social visionaries, the idea of shaping and molding children not for the children's sake or the sake of their families but for the needs of the government and the larger community has been almost irresistible. What better way to create and maintain a fixed and "superior" social order than by careful cultivation of the citizens needed to serve and obey? So in various utopian visions from Plato to Rousseau a case was made for muscling the family aside and giving the state firm control of all education.

The first modern attempt to implement this utopian vision of state-centered education was during the French Revolution. It failed, as parents courageously refused to send their children to the revolutionary schools. In the 1830s, however, under more moderate liberal and reforming governments, a statist, top-down model of education was introduced in France and also in the Netherlands, Prussia, and the United States.

In his important book *The Myth of the Common School*, Charles L. Glenn Jr., a Massachusetts state education official himself, surveys the fascinating story of the emergence of the anti-family, pro-state liberal model of schooling in Europe and

the United States, a model championed in our country especially by the well-meaning Horace Mann and other promoters
of the "common school" in Massachusetts.

According to Glenn, by the middle of the 1800s three factors converged to make the case for paternalistic, state-domi-
nated education overwhelming. First, the village elders of the
day, especially in New England, tended more and more to be
deists and unitarians who saw nothing but trouble for society
and government in the divergent and strongly held religious beliefs of their fellow citizens. They were convinced that a lowest-
common-denominator version of "Christianity" (unitarianism,
basically) would provide a common moral and spiritual basis
for social harmony in America. The only way to create a common spirituality and morality was to take away from parents
the duty of educating their children and to vest that duty in the
apparatus of the state. It is clear from the writings of the period,
by the way, that the primary concern of these reformers was *not*
to provide intellectual skills and training, but rather to mold
young people "morally" into ideal citizens for a "progressive"
social-democratic state.

Second, Glenn contends that the increasing urbanization and
industrialization of society created pressure for a new "factory
model" of schooling. The children of working-class families had
to be kept out of trouble and off the streets. What better way to
do that than to create a "learning factory" where the whistle
blows, children sit, knowledge and "progressive" values are
poured in, religious and family-based "prejudices" are driven out,
and a perfectly molded "democratic man" comes out on the other
end of the assembly line?

In other words, the educational leaders of the time saw it as
their role to modernize, centralize, streamline, and deliver according to a routinized formula a better "product" (the fully in-

doctrinated democratic citizen) at the same time and in the same way that business leaders were doing in their respective industries.

Third, Glenn argues that the increasing influx of poor and vaguely threatening Catholic immigrants was the final blow. Even traditional Protestants who had resisted the statist reforms in the first few decades of the nineteenth century eventually capitulated when faced with the perceived threat of a huge number of ignorant people with, it was thought, political loyalties divided between country and church. Catholics, it was claimed, could not be good citizens of a republic. It was simply more important to educate these superstitions out of the children of Irish and Italian immigrants than to maintain any kind of Protestant doctrinal purity.

Yet despite the powerful liberal impulses present in the founding of compulsory education in our country, the common sense of the American people has over the past 150 years kept the most extreme forms of top-down liberal educational philosophy at bay. We can be thankful that, contrary to the wishes of the village elders, our system is still based on such conservative principles as local control of schools by local school boards funded by local taxes, and staffed in most communities by decent people with common sense and traditional values. As a result, across most of America a bottom-up family orientation has remained an important principle of American education from the beginning of compulsory education to the present day. Nationwide, our present system of mass education is a hodgepodge of top-down statist and bottom-up family-centered impulses, all mixed together without a controlling model. You might say that American public education is better in practice than it is in theory. And thank heavens for that!

WHATEVER THE MERITS of the liberal model in the nineteenth-century context, the big factory model has changed in the economy and such a model needs to change in education, too. We need, particularly in our cities, a bottom-up, family-centered model for public schooling. Schools must be run as a service to parents and families, helping them to fulfill their responsibility as the primary educators of their children.

The liberal model for schools has several fatal flaws. It assumes, for one, that families don't understand democratic values and so those have to be force-fed to children in order for democracy to flourish. And it assumes that rather than having a real democratic discussion based on differences in fundamental values, it's the job of the government to create a like-minded citizenry with the "correct" values.

And just who comes up with that "correct" set of values to instill in our children in the top-down educational model? Well, the village elders of course! Why can't we just trust them? After all, they are "neutral" and "scientific" and "only want what's best for our children." Do Americans really want educational elites, school bureaucracies, and teachers' unions to educate our children according to *their* idea of "neutral" values?

On the other hand, can we just trust parents to always make the best choices for their children? What about the children who live in dysfunctional families? Of course those children and their parents will need help, and even supervision, from various kinds of social support networks, including the educational system. But good policy is not built on dealing with the abnormal and the unusual. In the vast majority of cases we can trust parents to know what's best for their children and to have a much better idea of what their children need than any impersonal governmental institution.

A shift to family-focused education with schools in the role of service provider will reinvigorate both families—as they reassume responsibility for something that they have long been too passive about—and also educators, as they become more responsive to the needs of their customers.

Using family-focused education to renew our intellectual capital has many implications. There is one obvious policy implication: school choice. There are also several important implications for parents—their jobs don't get easier in a family-focused educational system, they get tougher. And a focus on family-centered education also opens up all kinds of new educational possibilities, such as homeschooling, a fine option for those willing to make the commitment.

LET'S TALK ABOUT SCHOOL CHOICE and educational scholarships. We already have school choice in this country, actually. The problem is that we've only got school choice for people who can afford it.

School choice today takes two forms. The most obvious form is the choice exercised by those who can afford to pay both the cost of an *unused* public school education for their children (which everyone pays directly or indirectly through property taxes) *and* the cost of a private school education for their own children.

Second, there's a more subtle but very common and affordable form of school choice that does not involve paying for private schools. This kind of school choice happens every day in every community in America. It's called *moving*. People who have children and have the means always—that's *always*—look at the schools in the community when deciding where to live. Families often pick up and move when their children get to school age so they can be in a community with better public schools. We can call this "residential school choice."

So we've got residential school choice already. And you know what? The same hysterical criticisms made by those against making school choice viable for low-income families already apply to residential school choice. It creams off the best students! Families concerned about their children's education move to communities where the schools are better! More resources go to schools that are already better because property values increase when demand increases! All of that is true.

So we have plenty of school choice today already. But it's inefficient and unfair. It's disruptive and costly to move. And it's inequitable. Low-income families *can't* move, so they are stuck; their children are stuck. We must empower *all* our children with scholarships if we are to achieve the common good.

The village elders of the educational establishment, however, claim that educational scholarships will destroy public education. So let's examine the criticisms of school choice to see if they really hold any water.

First of all is the argument that allowing school choice for all will somehow undermine democracy, that if low-income parents are allowed to use public dollars to move their kids to parochial or private schools then the notion of universal education and an American common purpose will crumble. Do we ever hear that America's common purpose is in jeopardy when rich folks send their kids to Andover or Exeter?

The weakness of this argument should be clear: it's a very slightly disguised version of the old argument that the state really needs to be in charge of bringing up our children in order to have a "healthy" democracy. But democracy thrived in America before we had universal public education. And American democracy would be healthier today if every child growing up in this country had the choice to attend a school reflecting his or her family's values. Why? Because one of the big threats to American democracy today is the growing disconnect between the values of the majority of America's families on the one hand, and the "progressive" values being imposed by the public schools on the other. The educationists say their values are "inclusive," but in fact, they are alienating a growing number of Americans.

This objection that school choice threatens democracy often turns around questions of race: the critics contend that giving up on the "common school" means in practice assisting "white flight" into schools of their own, overturning a half century of racial reconciliation. That is a legitimate concern. But the best measure of racial progress is not the sheer percentages of students of various racial backgrounds in a school: after all, students in a mixed-race school may still segregate informally within the school. Dr. Jay Greene of the Manhattan Institute conducted an innovative study to try to find out how informal integration was playing out in schools of various kinds. What he did was measure, by race, who sat next to whom at lunch tables—in schools that were public, private, and parochial. After all, the choice of whom to sit with is a free one: it's a good measure of real racial reconciliation. What he discovered was that voluntary integration was *lowest* in the public schools he studied—and *highest* in the parochial schools. His hypothesis is that the best way to overcome racial prejudices is through a strong and clear message about common values—something the parochial schools are good at, while the public schools head for the hills at the thought of violating values "neutrality." It turns out that school choice could very well be a significant *contribution* to racial reconciliation in America: the exact opposite of the village elders' contention.

Next we find the argument that school choice which extends to parochial schools violates the establishment clause of the First Amendment to the U.S. Constitution. Now, as you know, I think those people running around trying to keep God out of public sight are way off base.

I've already written about how our founders never meant to keep God out of the public square and would shudder at how our courts have perverted the establishment clause. The same holds true when it comes to school choice. The federal government already awards Pell grants to low-income students to go to college, including religious colleges. So why is giving low-income parents public dollars so they can send their children to a Catholic, Jewish, evangelical Protestant, Muslim, or nonreligious primary or secondary school a problem? Obviously, the federal government is not endorsing any particular religion with Pell grants, nor would it with scholarships for primary and secondary education. There is no constitutional principle at stake here. No, the real reason that the village elders dig in their heels at the thought of scholarships is that they want to protect their exclusive control of the primary- and secondary-school education factories so that they can form your children while they are still "lumps of clay" and can be molded into the shape of their choosing. It's as simple as that.

Finally, there's the argument that school choice will decimate public education by taking needed dollars out of the public schools. There are two problems with this argument. First of all, who's to say that under the new market pressures the public schools won't reform in such a way that they begin to deliver a compelling product? After all, they have a huge jump on the competition—a vast infrastructure built with public funds, expensive science lab facilities, big libraries, lots of sports facilities. The covering of some operating expenses for private schools through a scholarship program won't begin to erase the enormous lead the public schools have in taxpayer-funded resources and sunk capital for many years to come.

But perhaps more fundamentally, this argument assumes that lack of dollars is what's wrong with our failing public schools and that more dollars are what's needed to fix them. The evidence against this argument is overwhelming.

Over the last three decades we have more than *doubled* per-pupil spending in real dollars (that is, taking inflation into account). And yet student achievement, by nearly any measure you pick, has flatlined. Today's students are learning and achieving at about 1970 levels—for *twice* the real cost!

The National Assessment of Educational Progress (NAEP), administered by the U.S. Department of Education, has been tracking students' achievement for 30 years in math, science, and reading. Every four years they test students at ages 9, 13, and 17. A graph of the 17-year-olds' performance—basically telling us whether high school graduates of today are doing better than those of the past—is, yes, a flat line. In 1971, the average reading score for 17-year-olds was 285 and in 1999 it was 288. The average math score in 1973 for 17-year-olds was 304 and in 1999 it was 308. And the average science score for 17-year-olds in 1969 was 305; in 1999, it was 295.

Or we could look at graduation rates. According to another study by Jay Greene, graduation rates peaked at about 76 percent in 1969. In 2001 they were about 70 percent. So we doubled the per-pupil spending on students in public schools in the last generation. And what did we get for that? Nothing.

The problem with our schools is not resources. Rather, we must deploy the vast resources we already expend in smarter, more effective ways. The only hope of that happening is through the time-proven economic formula of competition and choice.

Dr. Greene says that research is showing that there has been great improvement in places where the choice idea has been given a chance. In communities in Florida where school choice was implemented, for example, he reports that many of the *public* schools actually improved. Rather than being decimated by school choice as critics predicted, the educators at these schools responded and improved their schools. And in Milwaukee, Dr. Greene shows, public schools that were most impacted by school choice—that is, those which had the most parents in the community taking advantage of school choice—actually improved the most.

Let's be honest. The motives for the attacks against school choice don't really have much to do with how we educate our children. It's about who will have the power and control: parents or experts. The village elders don't want to lose control of your children's formation, and the teachers' unions don't want to lose some public school teaching jobs.

The village elders and the teachers' unions have convinced Americans that the answer in education is simply to throw more money at schools that don't work. But we cannot abandon low-income Americans to educational mediocrity. And we cannot abandon all our children for seven hours each day, 180 days each year, to a values-free zone that calls itself education. It's wrong. It's unfair. It's flatlining the educational progress of America's children. We need school choice.

XXXVII

Not Raising Children, but Raising Adults

All right then, parents: welcome to the new family-centered model of publicly financed education. Instead of you hovering around the fringes complaining ineffectively while the schools do all kinds of things to your children that you really don't like, now you are in control. The professionals are now in your employ and they treat you as a valued customer rather than patronize you as their ward. You are in charge of the educational process and you hire and fire experts to help you achieve what's best for your children and your families as a whole. If you don't like the educational services provided by a given school, you take your scholarships and business elsewhere. If the schools in your neighborhood aren't to your liking, then drive a little further (or use your transportation voucher for the multischool bus system) to a school you prefer. If you don't like any of your school options you can homeschool your kids instead.

Sounds like a great deal, right? What is there not to like? Think again. If you're in control of your children's education, then it's up to you to make sure things turn out right. That means that in a family-centered model parents have a tougher job, not an easier one. Parents know what's best for their kids, and they are empowered to achieve that. But parents must also step up to the plate and assume full responsibility. (By the way, I know a lot of terrific front-line teachers who would love to see parents do just that, instead of showing no interest in their child's education until there is a big problem.)

So parents, you not only need to know what grade your kids are in, but what the school's goals are for that year. What are they planning to teach your children, and why? What kinds of techniques and lessons will they use to achieve those educational goals? Why are certain topics studied at one grade level and not at another? You not only have to help your children with their homework, you need to be in dialogue with their teachers about why they are doing homework at all, and why this particular homework. This level of parental involvement would blow many teachers away, but the good teachers tell me they would love being part of a family team.

Of course, if you pick a good school—a good educational support system—then you can rely on its educators to deal with many of the details. But if you really want to be a good parent, an informed parent, and a loving parent, then you can no longer just mentally check out when it comes to the details of the educational process for your children.

We've been talking about education, but all this has much broader implications for what it means to be a parent, for what it means to be a family, and for raising children so that they are ready to take full advantage of the educational opportunities afforded them.

Having just spent time condemning much of public education, let me agree with many public educators: the fundamental problem with our school system today is that children are coming to school unprepared to learn. They are getting neither the intellectual nor the social and personal formation they need to succeed in school. My wife Karen often reminds me that we are not raising children, we are raising adults. And the first and most important step on the path to adulthood is training children in basic responsibility and social skills so that they get to school ready to learn.

So many parents are so busy doing what they think is parenting that they're not doing what children need. Parents often work two jobs. They rush their children to soccer practice. They eat fast dinners, never together. Middle- and upper-class parents are often pursuing distractions that have nothing to do with raising kids, with raising healthy adults. (At least lower-income and single parents have an excuse, but even that doesn't fly very far because I'm not talking about anything that costs much money.)

I know I'm coming down hard on parents and I know that these are strong statements to make. So let me tell you what I mean by getting your children ready for school. First of all, understand what I'm *not* talking about. I'm not talking about flash cards. I'm not talking about addition worksheets with preschoolers or drilling four-year-olds in spelling. I'm not talking about insisting on classical music instead of "Veggie Tales." In fact, anybody who thinks this is how to get their child ready for school is making a big mistake. Pushing children too early can actually discourage them from learning, especially if they find the exercise frustrating.

Children need a few things to be ready for school. They need to be basically healthy and happy, reasonably respectful and obedient. They need good language and communications skills so they can understand what is going on and make the most of the learning environment. (Help your children build language skills by reading to them when they are young, and by encouraging them to read to themselves once they are able. Turn off the TV—better yet, never turn it on—and hand your children some books.)

But most of all, what your children need is a sense of their place in the world and a healthy respect for authority. They need to know—despite the commercial and entertainment messages with which they are bombarded in mainstream culture that tell them they are autonomous little "miniature adults"—that they are *not* in charge of their lives; their mission in life is *not* to satisfy their immediate desires and impulses. Instead, they are being slowly drawn into the world of adults in which they must consider others' needs before their own, sacrifice some of their own desires for the common good, and make choices that are harder in the short term but healthier and better in the long term.

Through loving guidance and external discipline, children are brought gradually into the world of real adulthood, the world of self-discipline—which is to say, a world in which you make a disciple of yourself. Adulthood is the stage of life when we are no longer dominated by our immediate impulses and appetites. Instead, we weigh what is best for ourselves and those we love in order to make good choices—no matter how hard—and then stick with them. By that definition, it sometimes seems that a considerable number of our fellow Americans never quite make it to adulthood. Children must be constantly taught, encouraged, cajoled, and guided to move from infancy, in which life is nothing but a fulfillment of impulses, to adulthood, in which impulses are guided and channeled by virtue—the habit of doing right things—and reason. Intellectual formation—the building of intellectual capital—is an important part of raising a child. But it is not the most important part. And it will only be successful if the child has the right basic attitudes: a sense of his place in the world, and deep respect for the authority of both parents and teachers.

Our parents' generation took all this as a given. But today, so many parents have become misguided about what parenting is that they aren't parenting anymore. Children don't need more "stuff." They do not need more trips to the "Stuff-Mart." They need their parents making *time for them*. And that's what too many of us parents—including this busy senator—aren't giving the way that we should.

Look, I understand that there is a difference between being a parent in an upper- or middle-class neighborhood and being a parent in a low-income community. I understand that financial resources matter. And I recognize that my criticism about consumerism being a sorry replacement for real parenting applies more to middle- and upper-income parents, and probably more to two-parent families than single-parent homes. I think the discussion in this book to this point paints a compelling picture of a strategy to ease the economic burdens on low-income and single-parent families. But what I'm talking about here is a problem that affects every community and every socioeconomic category—the problem of diminished parenting. Parents of all kinds are failing to give their kids the basics they need to make it in life. Parents must make a serious commitment of their time, of their values, and of their knowledge of right and wrong.

Earlier I said that we were becoming a "society" of individuals, that our social capital is consequently being depleted. We celebrate the individual over the common good. And that tendency has infected our parenting, too.

Bill Doherty is a professor of Family Social Science at the University of Minnesota. He says that "parents are much less confident in their authority now as compared to just a generation ago. This has its pluses and minuses. Today's parents are more sensitive to their children's feelings. If their children have an upsetting experience, parents are much more likely to listen to their children and talk to them about what they are feeling. But they are far less confident in their ability to say no or set limits."

Social scientists like Professor Doherty talk about three parenting types. One is authoritarian. These parents are short on nurture and long on discipline. The second type is permissive. These parents are short on discipline and long on expressing love. The third type is referred to as authoritative. These parents give their children lots of love but also demand good behavior. They give "love and limits," as Professor Doherty and other scholars put it. The research is very consistent: children who grow up with authoritative parents grow up the healthiest, happiest, and most successful. These children have a stronger self-image, get along better with other children, are more likely to stay out of trouble, and do better in school.

"Nobody is doing annual surveys of parenting styles," Professor Doherty says, "but everybody I've ever talked to who works in this field agrees that parenting is moving away from authoritative and more toward the permissive, or indulgent, style."

When I asked the professor what accounts for this change, he pointed to society. "It really reflects the reevaluation of authority that began in the 1960s. Parents raising kids now are part of the post-Vietnam, post-Watergate generation that believes few institutions have as much moral authority as they used to. It's part of a wave that emphasizes the individual." Professor Doherty says that today's parents are much more interested in nurturing unique personalities than in teaching adherence to shared standards of behavior.

Go to any Bob Evans, McDonald's, or Outback and you'll see what he's talking about. You're practically guaranteed to see misbehaving children and parents unwilling or unable to control them.

Yes, things have changed. And these problems inside families are externalized into the educational system. If we want to build intellectual capital in American society, we as parents must take charge of our lives, our families, our children. Each and every parent must make a new commitment to childrearing as a high, if not the highest, priority. From that commitment will flow countless benefits, both to the family itself and to society at large.

LET'S TALK ABOUT an important implication of a family-centered model of education: the importance of teaching children good manners. Manners are a microcosm, and a crucial one, for the way in which children are trained and loved into maturity, self-discipline, and self-reliance.

When I say manners, I'm not talking about which fork to use with the salad, though that is important in its own place. And I know that whenever somebody stands up and says, "It's time to teach America's children manners," people sneer, scoff, and snicker. To them, talking about manners seems a trivial matter when this country is dealing with so many bigger issues: teen pregnancy, drug abuse, school violence, to name a few. Well, have you ever thought that if we started with manners when children are young, maybe some of those big issues wouldn't be so big?

By manners, I'm talking about the basic civilizing lessons that need to take place within every family. I'm talking about lessons that should be taught to every American about how we are expected to act toward one another: with respect and self-restraint. I'm talking about understanding the social order of things, what it means to respect authority, why it's important that someone be in charge and all that entails—and doing that from the time children are very young all the way through the university level. Permit me to quote an expert on manners, my wife Karen, in her book *Everyday Graces: A Child's Book of Good Manners:* "[Manners are] the mirror of a person's heart and soul—an outward expression of inner virtue." That's why manners matter.

It starts with teaching young children how to address someone older than themselves—teaching them "Yes, ma'am" and "Yes, sir," as opposed to "What?" It's teaching them to speak to adults with some title of respect such as "Miss Walker" or "Mr. Mike," rather than "Hey, you" or even "Hey, Mike." The trend of parents letting their children address them by their first names or other adults by their unadorned first names may seem trivial but it is far from harmless. First of all, it's a subtle but very real example of the erosion of parental authority and the drive toward permissiveness that Professor Doherty talks about. It's also a small but important way by which we desecrate the social order. Children who are allowed to call adults by their first names lose a bit of that sense of their own place in the world. They get the message that they are equal to adults. Basic respect for authority and adult competency gets lost, including the notion that adults are the teachers and children are the learners.

I know that today's generation of parents—at least many of them—cringe at the thought that they are molding their children. Professor Doherty talks about how this notion of "molding" flies in the face of the individualism that Americans now embrace and, specifically, how today's parents are much more interested in helping the unique individual in their child blossom than with instilling in their children respect for the norms of social life. But here's the problem: If you don't mold them, somebody or something else will. Growing up is all about formation: the question is, formation into what kind of person? If parents don't take leadership in forming their children, the mass culture and our education factories will be more than happy to step in and mold your child into a politically docile, easy-to-manipulate consumer who defines himself or herself in terms of material acquisitions and the quick satisfaction of appetites.

More specifically, if we don't raise our children to respect others and to respect, for example, their teachers, then what kind of individualism are we really nurturing? Certainly not one that makes it more likely that their intellects will expand and be sharpened. I mean, which child is really blossoming into an individual: the boy who sits quietly in class, addresses his teacher with respect, and focuses on his lessons, or the girl who is disruptive and ill-mannered toward her teacher? Yes, the boy was molded—that is, taught—by his parents. Anyone have a problem with that?

My wife and I have put a lot of work into molding our six children, and we're convinced that it's the best investment we'll ever make. Let's be honest: for parents, it's a lot easier, day in and day out, to let children be "individuals" who are free to do as they please than to demand respect, manners, and good behavior. There have certainly been many times when I've returned home from the Senate bone-tired and one of my kids says or does something wrong. I'm quite tempted to ignore it. It can be tiring dealing with a child's misbehavior, teaching him that showing respect to adults is important, even when he is angry. But I do it because I know it's important. Parents need to put at least as much energy into teaching their children basic manners when they are young as they do in getting their kids to computer clubs or art classes or travel soccer leagues.

So manners education starts and ends with parents. But when children enter preschool, daycare, Early Start, Head Start, or kindergarten, manners should also be a standard part of the curriculum. From making sure good sportsmanship is taught as part of recess and physical education to ensuring that how children talk to each other and talk to adults is part of the daily instruction, manners need to be right up there with reading, writing, and arithmetic.

Manners should be infused into the entire curriculum. Stories should be chosen not only because they promote reading ability, but because the tales they tell depict children and adults dealing with exciting, challenging, or trying circumstances while maintaining self-control and treating others with the respect and dignity that they deserve. Yes, "See Dick be polite" is important!

Manners curricula are not just for elementary school. They need to continue through middle school and high school. I'm not talking about "character education" as that is currently taught in some of our schools. I'm talking about continuing to teach students how to interact politely and respectfully with each other and with the adults in their midst.

And really, it doesn't stop with high school. Our colleges and universities desperately need an infusion of good manners. Political correctness continues to be rampant on college campuses, and many of the worst effects of political correctness are simply the result of the total lack of respect shown for people with "incorrect" ideas. I have had many firsthand experiences on campus with extremely rude and even violent behavior from students who disagree with my views. Obviously, no one taught these young people manners growing up, nobody taught them how to disagree with another person with the appropriate degree of civility. As a result, they know nothing else but to shout down the people they disagree with. That's what passes for intellectual debate in far too many, and perhaps most, college classrooms today. The majority shouts down the minority. Unfortunately, the faculty often reinforce this intolerance. Recently I gave a commencement address at a Catholic college in my state and three-fourths of the faculty walked out as I stood up to deliver my address. (To the students' credit, very few of them followed suit. In fact, while some applauded, most booed the faculty as they walked out.)

Several years ago, the Foundation for Academic Standards and Tradition published *The Diversity Hoax*, a collection of essays written by students at the Law School of the University of California, Berkeley. Here's an excerpt from an essay written by one of the contributors, Jim Culp. (He starts his essay by going out of his way to note that he is not politically conservative, by the way.)

> The professor invited commentary from the class in regards to disallowing intentional inflictions of emotional distress claims in the domestic arena. . . . "How do you feel about this Mr. Culp?" he asked. . . . "Well," I said, "I have five sisters, a mother, two grandmothers and a wife, and I don't feel that men have a monopoly on inflicting emotional distress. In fact, I have come to believe that women are better at it than men. Hence, unlike physical abuse, inflicting emotional distress is not an issue specific to women, as men and women are equally perpetrators and victims of it."
>
> There was a roar of scorn from many women in the class. Many stood up screaming unintelligible insults. Some even threw objects at me.

From kindergarten through law school, you can't have intellectual and personal growth without manners and civility. A mind is a terrible thing to waste—on barbaric behavior or unrestrained anger.

One final comment on all this: when I talk about manners I'm not talking about being hypocritical. You really can deeply and energetically disagree with somebody and still be polite. You can be nice to somebody whose behavior you don't approve of or whose views are completely opposed to your own. That doesn't mean you have to accept every person's behavior. You have a right, and sometimes an obligation, to challenge people. But you also have an obligation to act with civility.

Senator Edward Kennedy and I seldom agree on anything. But we treat each other with courtesy. Indeed, that's what the rules of the Senate demand. It's why one of the rules of the United States Senate is that one senator cannot directly address another senator. This ensures that what is supposed to be a constructive debate doesn't become personal and vindictive. So I can say, "Mr. President, the senator from Massachusetts is wrong, and is misinterpreting the data," but I can't say, "Senator Kennedy, you are wrong." If I do that, I get hammered with the gavel.

We need more virtual gavels in America.

XXXVIII

Bringing the Lessons Home

Shifting the way we build intellectual capital from a top-down, liberal model to a bottom-up, family-centered model has another interesting implication. Once we see compulsory education in its broader social context and recognize that mass education is to a large extent the product of the nineteenth century and the industrial revolution, we may start to wonder if the "factory model" for schooling is really the best thing for our kids after all.

In the nineteenth century most teachers had far more formal education than the average parents of the kids in their classrooms, but that is no longer true. A high percentage of parents today have as much if not more education than most teachers. This has made many parents stop and wonder: Why shouldn't I school my own children?

A growing number of families are choosing to pursue various alternatives to public schools and traditional private or parochial schools. Some are founding new, small, extremely family-centered schools. Others are deciding not to delegate the job of intellectually forming their children at all, but rather to take it on themselves in their own homes or in very small schooling cooperatives that involve no more than a handful of families.

Let me talk a bit about how my wife and I are educating our six children. The ones who are school aged are being home-schooled. My wife Karen is both a loving mother and a brilliant person. She is trained as a nurse and a lawyer, and our kids are lucky to have such a talented and well-trained person as their primary educator. (Yes, I help out too, but for most families it makes sense for one parent to take on the primary educational role.) However, research done by the National Home Educa-tional Research Institute suggests that there is no correlation between the educational level of parents and the educational success of their homeschooled children.

We didn't set out with any grand plan for homeschooling. It just happened rather naturally, when we couldn't find a kinder-garten for our oldest child that we were happy with. A friend of ours suggested we give homeschooling a try and suggested a curriculum. It worked great with our oldest daughter, so we tried first grade, and that too was a success. Eventually, we took the same approach with all of our children. But we did it one year at a time, each year making a decision as to what was the best course for each child.

The greatest thing about homeschooling is that, though it's hard and stressful at times, you develop this amazingly close relationship with your kids. The educationists always talk about the importance of small class size. But even in small classrooms, children only receive a few minutes of individual attention dur-ing a typical day. The home school is the very smallest class-room: one-on-one or one-on-three. Home-schooled children basically have a full-time tutor who just so happens to uncondi-tionally love them and knows their needs better than anyone. The curriculum is tailored and paced according to the needs of each individual child. There is plenty of opportunity to pursue special interests such as music, sports, and field trips. I don't pretend for a moment that homeschooling is for everyone. It requires a time commitment that many parents, especially single parents, cannot afford. In spite of this commitment, according to the Department of Education there are almost *two million* children being homeschooled in America today. Obviously, many parents realize that we owe our children the best path to success, not the easiest path.

I know that the main criticism of homeschooling—we've heard it hundreds of times—is that children who are home-schooled don't have the opportunity to build the same social skills as other kids; in a word, they are not properly "socialized." That may sound like a serious criticism, and some homeschooling families make the mistake of not really thinking about the criticism very carefully. Instead, they take it at face value, responding with a long list of all the opportunities their children have to interact with other children and therefore, according to the logic of the criticism, to be properly socialized after all.

What nonsense!

Children are *all* socialized into *some* kind of society. A frontier family in the American West might have gone weeks or months between the times that the children in the family ever saw another family or another non-sibling child. Yet they were fully socialized within the context of the nuclear family, and from what we know, frontier children would generally become adults of excellent character. The pickpocket boys of Fagin's gang in *Oliver Twist* were socialized into a "criminal family," with bad results. So the question is not *whether* children are socialized, the question is: socialized into *what*? What kind of company do children actually keep during the "working hours" of their day, and how does that form their habits of interaction and communication not only with other children of their own age and class, but also with adults and teenagers and toddlers and babies?

By asking the right question, we can see that when it comes to socialization, mass education is really the aberration, not homeschooling. Never before in human history have a majority of children spent at least half their waking hours in the presence of 25 to 35 unrelated children *of exactly the same age* (and usually the same socioeconomic status), with only one adult to keep order and provide basic mentoring. Never before and never again after their years of mass education will any person live and work in such a radically narrow, age-segregated environment. It's amazing that so many kids turn out to be fairly normal, considering the—by historical standards—unusual socialization they get in public schools.

In a home school, by contrast, children interact in a rich and complex way with adults and children of other ages all the time. In general, they are better-adjusted, more at ease with adults, more capable of conversation, more able to notice when a younger child needs help or comfort, and in general a lot better socialized than their mass-schooled peers. Ask those who have spent much time with homeschooling families and they will generally confirm all of this.

My pitch isn't designed to convince other parents to homeschool—although, according to the Department of Education, homeschooled children scored over 30 percent higher than public school children in national achievement tests. Rather, I'm explaining why my wife and I have chosen homeschooling, and why I feel strongly that we need to make some changes so that more families who want to choose homeschooling can do so more easily. For starters, the public school systems need to be more open to the part-time participation of homeschooled children on a sports team or in the band or chorus. They should even be allowed to use the public school's library or take a course.

My state of Pennsylvania is one of the most progressive in the nation when it comes to a new, technology-driven innovation in education: cyberschooling. Cyberschooling blends the best of traditional schools with homeschooling. Cyber–charter schools are an innovation in public charter schools. They bring the local elementary school into your home. Cyberstudents take some or all of their courses using a computer and live interaction by voice, video, and a "virtual chalkboard" with a teacher and other students. This kind of flexibility and empowerment is definitely the wave of the future. We liked the idea so much that we had some of our children enrolled in some of these public cyberschools—until the increasingly uncivil world of partisan politics extended its venom into our home and into our children's education.

Yes, I'm something of a salesman for homeschooling and for cyberschooling. It is the logical extension of the new parent-centered and family-centered model for education that will lead our country into the formation of more intellectual capital than we've had before. But homeschooling is not for everyone: it's a unique, individual choice for some families only. What I'm pushing for right now are some changes that will make it possible for more parents to choose home- and cyberschooling if they want to. It is one viable option among many that will open up as we eliminate the heavy hand of the village elders' top-down control of education and allow a thousand parent-nurtured flowers to bloom.

XXXIX

Moral Truth and the End of Man

Intellectual formation—building intellectual capital—is all about conforming our minds to the truth. But as I said at the start, truth and goodness go hand in hand. So we also have to talk about how morality fits into the formation of intellectual capital. To do that, please permit me to dig a little deeper into philosophy than is usual in a book on public policy.

Truth and goodness go together. This sounds abstract, and in some ways it is; but at the same time, it's very practical too. If you think about it, to really learn anything, you have to accept and be governed by certain values and certain moral truths. Those include things like the value of hard work (the learning process), of doing your own work when called to demonstrate your knowledge (not cheating on tests), and of respecting others and not disrupting the learning process (good behavior during class), to name a few.

Even the most "value-fearing" village elder can't really avoid facing the question of moral truth and its place in the learning process. In fact, liberals are just as eager as I am to teach morality to schoolchildren. They are eager to teach them lessons about racial and sexual equality, for example. I agree with them; such moral lessons about equality of opportunity and the intrinsic dignity of every human person before God and the law *should* be taught. But equality is not a "fact" in any narrow scientific sense—in fact, the more scientifically we look at human beings, the more *dissimilar* and *unequal* they are. No, equality is not a "fact," but rather a moral judgment, a moral commitment— one that I strongly support our schools teaching. Similarly, we should teach our children to make other kinds of proper moral judgments, such as the importance of tolerance, properly understood, of fairness, of proper respect for people, and of proper respect for the natural world.

As I mentioned before, the most heated arguments about values and morals in our society come from strong disagreements over a fairly narrow range of issues, mostly having to do with sex and human life. So let's put those aside for a moment and talk about the values that have made William Bennett's *Book of Virtues* a bestseller with American families: kindness, honesty, loyalty, friendship, charity, promise-keeping, and self-sacrifice for the good of others. Can anyone seriously doubt that we will more effectively educate our children and build our nation's intellectual and moral capital (as well as all the other kinds of capital I've been discussing) if we include this basic moral formation in our educational system?

Well, yes, in fact, it is possible to doubt this, and a very small minority will. But if you as a parent seriously do not want your child to be educated in these basic moral truths, then in our new family-focused educational model you can take your educational scholarships and head over to the Moral Relativism Academy, or for that matter the Church of the Golden Calf Elementary School, or wherever else you can find someone teaching the values that are important to you. Welcome to the Land of Freedom and Opportunity Version 2.0!

Now, you may not find that pragmatic answer completely satisfying, so let's talk a little more about the basic truths involved
here. Facts are one thing and values are another, it is said. In Philosophy 101 we may have learned that you can't derive an "ought"
(value) from an "is" (fact). That is one of the fundamental claims
of modern philosophy. But is it true? Can there be an *objective*
moral reality? Is there a way that, even if we had to educate all
our children together, we could agree on some basic moral truths
that should be the basis of their education?

Let's try to answer that question by listening to a great thinker
of the twentieth century (who's still going strong in the early
twenty-first, by the way): Alasdair MacIntyre. MacIntyre himself
is a kind of microcosm of—and object lesson for—our times.
Raised in the tradition of philosophical liberalism, as a young
man he became a Marxist ethicist. But he began to think hard
(always dangerous!) about what it would mean for a Marxist to
make an ethical critique of Stalinism (something many Marxists
wanted to do). And that raised a whole series of problems, which
led him back to the historical roots of ethics and philosophy,
where he found the answer he was seeking.

As described in his classic book *After Virtue*, what he found
was this: it is *not* true that there is a fundamental distinction
between facts and values. To start with, some kinds of evaluative
claims (notice the "value" in the center of the word "evaluative")
are clearly factual. For example, if you say, "This is a good car,"
or "This is a good horse," or "He is a good sea captain," you are
making an evaluative claim—saying that something is good or
bad. But those are (or can be, given sufficient context) factual
claims as well—you can make a clear judgment that everyone
must agree with after examining the facts of the case.

The reason evaluative judgments can be true or false is because in each such situation there is (or can be) a known pur-

pose or role that the thing or animal or person does or does not fulfill properly. If I say, "A good car is one that is reliable, gets good gas mileage, and is safe in crash tests," then I can make true or false judgments about whether any particular car is a good car. Similarly, a sea captain can be understood as a person who fulfills a certain role—he has good leadership abilities, is calm under difficult conditions, knows a lot about ships and navigation, understands his crew, and so forth. Given that context and set of purposes, we can determine if someone is or is not a good sea captain—and that determination is every bit as factual as determining the sea-worthiness of a ship.

After making this analysis, MacIntyre asked the question: Why does it seem to us that we cannot make evaluative judgments about moral goodness in the same way? The answer he gives is that in the modern era human nature is viewed as something arbitrary and self-created. Personal autonomy—the right to "create" myself by defining my own "concept of existence, of meaning, of the universe, and of the mystery of human life"— has been given the highest value. In fact, it has become something like a supervalue, throwing every other human good into the shadows of mere opinion. Because of the autonomy ideal, we no longer agree in principle about the *purpose* of a human life, what a human being is *for*. Nor, consequently, do we agree on the answers to follow-on questions, like what a husband or wife are *for*, what children are *for*. If, on the other hand, we could agree about the purpose of human life or some aspect of human life, we could make moral judgments that are completely objective by simply comparing the character and activities of a given person to his or her purposes or ends.

So the autonomy ideal of philosophical liberalism is at the root of our tendency to fall into nervous silence when we try to *reason* about moral questions. It is why I hear so often from liberals that we can't "legislate morality." Obviously, those of us coming to basic questions of human existence from a Judeo-Christian perspective can simply reject the "pure self-created autonomy" notion of human nature, readily answer many of the important questions about the purpose of human life, and thus ask and answer moral questions. But what about nontheists in our pluralistic society? What do we do in the case of, say, public schooling, when we must educate our children together without agreement on religion or other sources of value?

It seems to me that, once again, there is still much we *can* all agree on, and we can educate our children accordingly. We can agree that friendship is a good and honorable thing; that true friends treat each other with respect and dignity; that kindness is the better way when faced with a challenging person or situation; that love involves desiring the good of the other above our own good, and that sacrificing self-interest for the good of the beloved is always right and proper; that human life is valuable and important; that honesty builds up the human family.

These are truths we can agree on, whatever our religious or political views. And with those we can form a fairly complete picture of the purpose of human life and how it should be lived. An educational system can thus be grounded in the natural moral law embodied in these judgments, and our human lives can be fairly and "factually" judged according to whether or not they meet the standards that we have set for ourselves. Morality, far from being an arbitrary projection of wishes and urges, derives from the objective reality that lies at the very heart of being human.

MacIntyre also helps us to see that liberalism's autonomy ideal is not really "neutral." That is the claim liberalism makes for itself. From liberalism's point of view, all other moral teachings are simply someone's particular moral judgments being imposed on everyone. But with liberal autonomy, it is said, everybody gets an equal shot at his or her project of self-creation: what could be more fair? That sounds convincing at first, but when we look into it a bit more closely, we see that having autonomy as our public standard of justice carries its own particular moral judgments, which are every bit as much an imposition on those who do not share them.

For example, liberalism is intolerant of moral commitments and ways of life that are not understood as self-created. Think of the Amish: almost every contemporary liberal moral and political theory is hostile to the Amish. But think also about marriage. Marriage brings to human beings an extraordinary range of human goods and trains us in many virtues, but marriage also limits our autonomy. Liberal theory is therefore skeptical about marriage, more or less unwilling to give it public support. And the same is true about friendship. Deep friendship carries with it obligations, and those obligations are also a limitation on autonomy, which is the liberal supervalue. But would anyone choose to live a life without friendship?

The philosophical village elders thought we could get out of the is/ought problem by saying that what a human being *is* is an autonomous being, whose only permanent and unchanging nature is the freedom to choose. If that is true, then the only permanent and unchanging *ought* is that society ought to equally accommodate everyone's No-Fault Freedom. MacIntyre shows us that this liberal solution doesn't work, even on its own terms: a society constructed on the autonomy ideal still ends up systematically favoring some ways of life and disfavoring others. But we haven't yet absorbed this lesson about liberalism's biases, and so too often we still talk as if autonomy is the one thing everyone can agree on, while every other moral claim is subject to radical doubt.

We have to get back to a fuller, more complete understanding of human nature as the basis for our educational system. We need not agree on every detail of the moral law to agree that we can't live together without a binding moral code, grounded in the facts of human nature itself. And on that basis we can educate our children together and have a democratic polity as well.

After all, without some kind of basic moral consensus, is democracy even possible? Our founders didn't think so. Public education isn't the only thing at stake in this question of objective moral standards.

MacIntyre's investigation leads us to the key question: Whatever happened to the idea of purpose in human nature? What MacIntyre notices is that there is an even bigger question lurking there: Whatever happened to the idea of purpose in nature *as a whole*?

During the second half of the twentieth century, many major thinkers were drawn toward the perennial truths of natural law, toward the idea of an objective moral order. This whole way of thinking got a huge boost in the aftermath of World War II, when the Allies put Nazi leaders on trial for crimes against humanity, only to be faced with the quintessential modern problem: who's to say that what the Nazis did is really *wrong* in some absolute, universal sense? After all, there were no "laws on the books" outlawing the Nazis' crimes, and after all, some of the Nazis were "just obeying orders," just obeying the Nazi law. How can we recognize when the Nazi law, or any law today, is itself unjust? How could the conviction and execution of the Nazi criminals be something more than an act of vindictive force by the victors? How could the Nuremberg trials be an act of *justice* rather than an act of *power*? Only by renewing the tradition of natural law could the Nazis be brought to justice.

Some of the best thinkers in the restored natural law tradition, however, recognized a major problem lurking just below the surface. The tradition of natural law can discern purpose in human nature only because it sees purpose in the whole of nature itself. Human beings have a purpose or "end," a *telos*, only because the whole of creation has an end or *telos* as well. The problem is that modern natural science has rejected the notion that nature has an end. If nature has no end, no goal, no destiny, then neither can human nature. But if human nature has no end, then our judgment of Nazi war criminals has nothing to do with justice, only with power.

The human mind rebels against such a conclusion. Modern science seems to tell us that there is no purpose in nature, only the mindless movement of matter in conformity to the unchanging laws of physics. But somehow we also *know* that human life has a purpose or set of purposes, and as a result we can reason ethically about it. We seem to be in a dilemma.

BUT WHAT IF THE UNIVERSE had a purpose after all? Well, this seems to be exactly the trend of certain developments in modern science in the late twentieth and early twenty-first centuries—contrary to the movement of modern science from its inception in the seventeenth century until the twentieth. The interpretation of these developments is highly controversial: it seems that many scientists, clinging to their picture of a universe without a creator, simply "don't want to go there" when confronted by these new arguments. But we have to go there, we have to follow the evidence to its logical conclusion.

The first powerful indication of "teleology" or purpose in

nature was the gradual establishment of Big Bang theory in cosmology during the twentieth century. Unlike the steady-state theories that preceded it, Big Bang theory gives precise mathematical form to a mass of evidence that the cosmos had a beginning (of some sort) and thus will have an end (of some sort). The point of this is not the crude one that the Big Bang somehow confirms a traditional theistic doctrine of creation out of nothing. The point is simply that, contrary to the best modern science up through the nineteenth century, the cosmos seems to be "going somewhere"—to have an "end" in the most general sense of the term.

The next major indicator that the universe might have some sort of design was the gradual discovery starting in the 1950s of dozens of "fine-tuned" parameters in physics and cosmology that were of seemingly arbitrary values; yet if those values were varied by even the tiniest amount, the universe simply wouldn't "work" in anything like that way it actually does. The Big Bang would have been followed immediately by a Big Crunch. Or atoms and molecules could not have formed. Or galaxies, stars, and planets could not have formed. Or carbon and other heavier atoms—all necessary for life—could not have formed. There is a long list of such parameters that have been identified, and the probability of getting the "right" values for all of these by blind chance so as to enable life as we know it on our planet is so astronomically high that it raises some obvious and weighty questions about whether the cosmos bears the mark of design.

Interestingly, in response to this scientific case for cosmic design many—probably a large majority—of working cosmologists have accepted an ad hoc escape valve called the "multiverse" hypothesis. The idea is that there must be an infinite number of universes (multiverses), each with a random set of physical laws, constants, constraints, etc. We just happen to have "won the lottery"—we're sitting in a single one of these trillions of universes (and I do mean trillions, because the odds are at least that remote) that just happens to have the right conditions that make life possible. Now, doesn't it take a lot of "faith" to believe in this multiverse hypothesis?

And speaking of winning the lottery, the final major area in which design or purpose in nature has been reemerging from science itself is in the life sciences, especially with the molecular revolution in biology and biochemistry. While it might have been plausible in the mid-nineteenth century of Charles Darwin to imagine that complex biological things were made up of simple, quivering blobs of "protoplasm" that required little explanation, the biomolecular revolution has changed all that. Scientific criticisms of Darwin's theory of variation and natural selection have been around from the beginning, but those criticisms have become much stronger in recent years as the evidence of the complex circuits, miniature self-repairing machines, sophisticated feedback loops, and digital information inside the cell piles up.

But what many people may not realize is that, from the start, Darwinism has been something more than just a scientific theory. As anyone who has studied the life of "Darwin's bulldog" T. H. Huxley knows, the theory quickly took on the sociopsychological role of the creation myth of modern atheism, and it has been used as a club against the beliefs of traditional theists ever since.

Moreover, among modern scientific theories, Darwin's theory is almost unique in being *explicitly* anti-teleological—that is, it functions to *deny* the natural inference that the complexities of nature must imply a designer. Other modern scientific theories such as Newton's laws of motion or Einstein's relativity theory provide mathematical *descriptions* of the workings of nature while simply ignoring the question of purpose or design. Atheists accept these "laws of nature" as brute facts that simply *are* and cannot be explained. Theists draw the natural inference that these "laws" require explanation, like anything else, and the only reasonable explanation for the laws is some kind of lawgiver.

But Darwinism is totally different. It is not a mathematical descriptive theory that allows for different explanations (or nonexplanations) of the origins of the laws of nature. Darwin's theory contains only the "law" of natural selection and specifically denies the possibility of a lawgiver or a designer, claiming that what appears to be design in nature is only an illusion. Being anti-teleological, of course, does not in itself disqualify Darwinism as a scientific theory. It is important to neither exclude nor include any theory of origins because it has teleological or even theological implications. We must follow the evidence where it leads, without preconceptions that either include or preclude the notion of design and a designer.

I said that Darwin's theory was "almost" unique in being anti-teleological. We've already discussed the other major anti-teleological theory of modern science: the multiverse hypothesis. Did you notice that both Darwinism and the multiverse invoke *chance* as the real cause of something that appears to be designed? They substitute a spontaneous, random, luck-based explanation for an explanation based on order, plan, and purpose.

Given this history and recent developments in scientific knowledge, there's little wonder then that many scientists aren't buying full-blown Darwinism anymore. Criticisms of Darwin's theory and a new understanding of purpose in biological nature are coming on strong from various schools or camps. "Intelligent Design theory" led by William Dembski, Michael Behe, and Stephen Meyer, among others, claims to be able to scientifically detect in natural things the unique signatures or hallmarks of an intelligent cause. "Self-organization theorists" like Stuart Kauffman claim that not random mutation and natural selection but certain mathematical laws or principles underlie the development of biological complexity. Teleologists like Michael Denton in his book *Nature's Destiny* and Simon Conway Morris in his book *Life's Solution* see powerful evidence for a built-in purpose or striving in biological evolution towards certain preordained patterns or forms, ever increasing in complexity, that are crowned by human life.

In short, the question of whether nature shows evidence of a plan or purpose is very much alive and well within modern science—long after such questions had been thought to be banished into the nether realms of philosophy and theology.

At this point it should be obvious why I have taken a public stance on the question of how evolution should be taught in public schools. I authored the only legislation on this matter ever passed by the federal government. My amendment on the teaching of biological origins,[†] which passed in the Senate by a vote of 91 to 8, became part of the Conference Report of the No Child Left Behind Education Reform Act of 2001. It has in turn sparked many spirited debates among both state boards of education and local school boards as both review their curricula.

Let me emphatically state that schools should teach everything there is to teach about neo-Darwinian evolution, which is certainly held to be true by most modern biologists. But teaching *everything* includes teaching the weaknesses and problems

---

[†]"It is the sense of the Senate that—

"(1) good science education should prepare students to distinguish the data or testable theories of science from philosophical or religious claims that are made in the name of science; and

"(2) where biological evolution is taught, the curriculum should help

as well as the strengths of the theory. Our children should be exposed not just to the historically dominant view of such an important topic, but also the cutting-edge and persistent question: Is there evidence for any kind of design or purpose in nature? This is a scientific question, no doubt, but not necessarily one that can fairly be answered by a cramped, reductionist understanding of science.

I know what skeptics are saying at this point: "What in the world are you, a U.S. senator (a lawyer by training, not a scientist), doing talking about all this? Why are you getting into these issues well beyond your area of expertise?" Well, for three reasons.

First, these issues are not too difficult for the average person to understand in a basic and useful way. In particular, I find young people are fascinated by this subject and are eager to learn more about it. What child doesn't want to know where she comes from and where she is going?

Second, I am encouraged by the fact that men of science whom I respect and admire have come to similar conclusions. Take for example Dr. Leon Kass, a medical doctor, PhD in biochemistry, long-time University of Chicago professor, and most recently chairman of the President's Council on Bioethics. In a brilliant essay titled "The Permanent Limitations of Biology" at the end of his book *Life, Liberty, and the Defense of Dignity*, Dr. Kass shows how modern biology has achieved its astounding results while at the same time suffering from a profound myopia about the real nature of living things. Much in the same way that Alasdair MacIntyre returned to the wisdom of classi-

---

students to understand why this subject generates so much continuing controversy, and should prepare the students to be informed participants in public discussions regarding the subject."

cal philosophy to understand how modern ethical discourse can be regrounded, so Dr. Kass returns to the wisdom of classical philosophy to understand the limits of modern science itself, and to show us a way that we can restore the older wisdom *about* nature without giving up the benefits of our new technical mastery *of* nature.

Among the fundamental limits that Dr. Kass identifies in modern biology are its emphasis on mechanism (living things viewed as machines) and its consequent denial of teleology (final causation) as a real element of the science of living things. But goal-oriented teleology can be found literally everywhere in the world of the living: it takes years of indoctrination and training to turn out biologists who cannot see it.

The third and final reason I have taken up this cause to open up our educational system to evidence of design in nature is because these cosmological ideas have real-world moral consequences. When our imaginations are filled with the prospect of a purposeless universe of blind chance and insensible matter and nothing else, is it any wonder that moral respect for the universal dignity of every human being is eclipsed? The Nazis built their pseudoethics with its grim logic on precisely this Nietzschean cosmological view. Aided in no small part by the horrific negative example of the Nazis, Americans have avoided sliding down this slippery slope. But when we look at the movement for biotech "research" that would require the killing of the smallest and most marginal members of the human family for the harvesting of their cells, I wonder if we have merely been momentarily delayed in our slide.

Intellect and will, truth and morals, cannot be separated. The Darwinian universe has no room for the unique dignity of the human person, for in that universe we are nothing but the result of purposeless chance; moral consequences are eventually drawn from that. But the reverse is also true. The *moral* commitment of modern scientists to a world entirely conquerable by science has led many scientists to a very unscientific rejection of any possibility of a designed universe. It is almost as if they will go to any theoretical length so long as they can hold on to the principle of blind chance as the ultimate explanation for the wonders science has allowed us to see.

As a basis for sound education, what could be better than to explore the great questions of purpose in both nature and human life in a sober, modest, and scientific way? Our nation is not well served by an educational establishment, led by the village elders, that is so intent on driving any recognition of God or a Creator out of the public consciousness that it requires, to the exclusion of all else, the teaching of the dogma of blind chance as the fundamental truth of the universe. No-Fault Freedom has even infected the world of science. *Veritas. Quid es veritas?*

XL

Higher Education and Liberal Education

So far, I've focused on K–12 education. Beyond that, how are America's colleges and universities faring? How well are we sustaining and renewing America's intellectual capital at the top of the educational ladder, in the universities?

It's a very mixed picture. On the one hand, America's universities are the envy of the world. We have the highest percentage of our young people going on to college of any country on earth. Our higher education system is also incredibly diverse, including both huge state universities and small liberal arts colleges, both secular institutions and an array of religiously affiliated schools. Schools like Harvard, Yale, and Princeton are astoundingly wealthy, with endowments in excess of $10 billion. And our elite schools dominate the world in scientific discovery, garnering year after year the bulk of Nobel Prizes.

On the other hand, ever since Allan Bloom's runaway bestseller *The Closing of the American Mind*, we have become increasingly aware of some deeply worrying developments in our universities: including postmodernism, multiculturalism, and political correctness. Core curricula that used to ensure that all students became familiar with the best that has been thought and said in the Western tradition have been abandoned; some schools have experimented with the complete elimination of all requirements. Academic departments like English literature seem to have given up on their *raison d'être*—reading good books with critical care—and have rebuilt themselves as "cultural studies," a kind of jargon-filled, semi-Marxist assault on American society and middle-class mores. Whole new academic "disciplines" have emerged that are explicitly oriented not toward dispassionate scholarship and the increase of knowledge but rather toward the radical transformation of society and the advancement of No-Fault Freedom—"disciplines" such as women's studies, gender studies, and gay and lesbian studies. Grade inflation in the humanities and social sciences has galloped ahead to the point that virtually everyone who graduates from Harvard, for example, does so with honors. And in the name of diversity, universities have created speech codes, smothering the lively debate on controversial topics that most people thought was a crucial aspect of liberal education.

It's a mixed picture, but the overall outlines are easy enough to see, and they map exactly with the fact–value distinction I was discussing earlier. In the hard-fact world of the natural sciences, American universities are simply second to none. This is, once again, a testimony to the hard work and investment of generations of Americans into the building up of a huge range of quality colleges and universities. In scientific fields, our intellectual capital is *strong*. But in the "soft" world of values—in the humanities and the softer social sciences—we see something approaching a wholesale collapse of our intellectual capital, a dumbing down of standards disguised as "advances" in education. This should be a major concern for all Americans.

The first sentence in Allan Bloom's famous book is this: "There is one thing a professor can be absolutely certain of:

almost every student entering the university believes, or says he believes, that truth is relative." That is itself an indictment of our elementary and high schools, since relativism is an elementary error. But rather than challenging this false opinion in higher education, most of our humanities departments have for some time been dominated by postmodernism, which as we have seen is a "sophisticated" philosophical view that rejects the very possibility of truth—there are only opinions; it even rejects the possibility of facts—there are only interpretations.

You can gauge how far the postmodern mindset has advanced when you notice how often words like "truth," "fact," and "justice" appear with scare quotes around them. Those scare quotes signal the postmodern, "ironic" standpoint—the approved standpoint of today's village elders. They indicate that the student or professor (or journalist or politician) cannot bring himself or herself to take seriously the possibility that we could ever *know* what the truth is, what justice is: we can only speak of my "truth" or your "truth." What may seem like an objective standard of justice is only a particular structure of *power*. An education in postmodernism, therefore, is not an education that seeks to develop the intellect so that it can grasp *the* truth. Truth, as opposed to "truth," isn't even a possibility.

I am reminded of the conclusion of C. S. Lewis's *Abolition of Man*, which is worth quoting at length:

> You cannot go on "seeing through" things forever. The whole point of seeing through something is to see something through it. It is good that the window should be transparent, because the street or the garden beyond is opaque. How if you saw through the garden too? It is no use trying to "see through" first principles. If you see through everything, then everything is transparent. But a wholly transparent world is an invisible world. To "see through" all things is the same as not to see.

That is where the academic vogue for postmodernism has led our institutions of higher learning in the past generation: to a kind of blindness that is all the worse because it cannot *see* itself as blind.

The elementary error of relativism becomes clear when we look at multiculturalism. Sometime in the 1980s, universities began to champion the importance of "diversity" as a central educational value. At first, this may have appeared to be a development from some very traditional notions of liberal education: the idea that a liberal education is all about an exposure to a *broad* range of knowledge. Multiculturalism was more than a mere development of that theme, however. For multiculturalism included an explicit relativist premise: that all cultures are equal—equally worthy of esteem, and equally worthy of study.

Now, it may well be true that the traditional curriculum, the traditional "canon" of great books, did not do full justice to great works outside the Western tradition such as the *Analects* of Confucius. On the other hand, America is part of Western civilization, not Eastern, and the ancient command is: "Know thyself." There are very good reasons why education should be centered on our own civilization's heritage. As I have argued in various ways in the course of this book, however, the liberal ideal is the abstract individual who is perfectly autonomous, free to create himself. From this abstract standpoint, we can no longer say that the Western tradition is "our" tradition—since no tradition is "mine" (much less "ours") unless I, as an autonomous individual, decide to make it so. (You see, the village elders not only want to separate you from your family and your faith, but from the mores of Western civilization and particularly from the American heritage.) The liberal standpoint is "the view from nowhere." And from this impossibly abstract view, what seems like common sense can only be bias.

Multiculturalism would not be so destructive if it limited itself to opening up the canon of great books to Eastern master-pieces. However, its relativist premise also rejected the distinc-tion between high culture and low culture. According to the postmodern theory that underwrote multiculturalism, the dif-ference between a great book and an ordinary book is not some-thing real: it is merely the result of an exercise of power by the establishment culture. The canon of great books was rejected as an ideological prop for "dead white European males," as the saying went. The latest mystery novels and even comic books were just as worthy of study as Tolstoy or Shakespeare.

But there was one thing more about multiculturalism: namely, a moral *fervor* for the inclusion of heretofore excluded voices in the curriculum. The postmodernists and the multiculturalists were driven to deconstruct the traditional cur-riculum out of a sense of outrage at what seemed to them to be *injustice*. This reveals the error of relativism. Moral fervor, af-ter all, is the result of a sense of justice—the "exclusion" has been unjust. But by the principles of postmodern relativism, we cannot speak of justice (without the ironic scare quotes). As I explained in detail in the last chapter, there is no ground for a sense of outraged justice if there is no justice in the first place. The sense of injustice that motivated the multiculturalists shows that relativism is self-refuting.

The postmodernists and multiculturalists did not learn this lesson in logic, however. In the absence of truth and justice, we are left only with power. Seeing the world of values as an exer-cise of pure power, these radical leftists on the faculties decided to exercise the power they had to achieve the results they wanted. And that brings us to political correctness. This term refers to the new morality, the new values, that the faculty radicals—the village elders with tenure—have worked to instill in their students. Once again, there is a real irony here. The radicals' critique of the traditional curriculum was that it was not really liberal education, only a kind of indoctrination into the biases and prejudices of Western civilization. But their response has been nothing less than a wholesale embrace of the idea of indoctrination—into the moral enthusiasms of the village elders.

The tools of political correctness have ranged from curricular revolution (for example, "gendering" the study of history) to politicized grading (marking down students whose papers do not come to "correct" political conclusions) to freshman counseling sessions (in which traditional sexual morals are ridiculed and sexual liberation is celebrated) to politicized hiring and tenure decisions (eliminating conservative or religious faculty) to campus codes concerning speech and "community standards" (under which, for example, a student who does not buy into political correctness and says so publicly in a forceful way may face disciplinary procedures). The university, which should be a cosmopolitan forum of free discussion and free inquiry, has become something of a totalitarian village in our otherwise free society.

In the most recent example of political correctness in action, Larry Summers, the president of Harvard University and a liberal who worked in the Clinton administration, faced a firestorm of criticism when he suggested that one reason (among several) that women may be underrepresented on the math and science faculties at the most elite universities could have something to do with biological differences between the sexes. (It is known that on standardized tests, while men and women have about the same average math ability, the "tails" of the bell curve, both at the top and at the bottom, are "longer" for men: meaning that while on average men and women are the same, there should be more men than women who are math geniuses—and more men than women who are math dunces.) According to the canons of political correctness, however, gender is nothing but a "social construct." Summers was therefore vilified, he issued a series of abject apologies, he was subject to a no-confidence vote of the Harvard faculty—the first in history—and it is not yet clear that he will be able to retain his prestigious job.

The liberals sometimes say that political correctness is a myth, carefully cultivated by conservatives in a kind of power game. Tell that to Larry Summers. If even the president of Harvard can find himself ostracized for the most polite and balanced questioning of postmodern dogma, imagine what it is like for a junior professor working toward tenure. Imagine what it is like for an undergraduate writing a paper.

They say that academic politics is so fierce and bitter because the stakes are so small. If all this were only a question of the philosophical ruminations of a few intellectuals in an ivory tower, I wouldn't care very much. But there is more at stake here: what is at stake is the American mind, America's intellectual capital. So how well is the postmodern, multiculturalist approach to higher education doing? Are the universities leading their students, America's future leaders, to higher levels of understanding and mastery of knowledge? Recent surveys of college seniors at some of America's most elite colleges and universities give us the answer:

- 66 percent could not identify George Washington as the American general at the battle of Yorktown;

- 53 percent thought that Abraham Lincoln was president prior to 1860;

- 32 percent did not know who the Axis powers were in World War II.

Now remember, these are *college seniors* at some of our nation's best schools.

In 2002, the National Association of Scholars commissioned the polling firm Zogby International to ask, once again, *college seniors* a series of questions that the Gallup Organization had asked recent *high school graduates* in 1955. The results?

- 79 percent of the 1950s high school graduates knew that Lindbergh made the first nonstop trans-Atlantic flight. Only 49 percent of the 2002 college seniors knew this.

- When asked, "What profession do you associate with Florence Nightingale?" only 53 percent of today's college seniors knew to answer nursing or medicine, while 87 percent of high schoolers in 1955 got the answer correct.

- While 78 percent of 2002 college seniors knew that the decoration given to members of the United States armed forces wounded in action is called the Purple Heart, fully 90 percent of the high school seniors of the 1950s knew.

There is only one way to interpret these findings. This is not progress; it is decline. When it comes to knowledge outside the natural sciences, our universities are not building up our nation's intellectual capital.

Why this decline in what American students know? Well, it has a lot to do with what they are taught. The Independent Women's Forum (IWF) recently published a study that looks into this question. They titled the result *The Death of Liberal Arts?*, and perhaps that question mark was just wishful thinking. The researchers at IWF scrutinized the freshman offerings and requirements at the top ten undergraduate liberal arts colleges as ranked by *U.S. News & World Report*. They looked at three fields: English, history, and political science. Departments that required or offered a comprehensive introductory course for freshmen were given a passing grade. Failing departments on that score were looked at more closely to see if freshmen, by choosing electives, could still get a good basic liberal arts education.

"Davidson, Middlebury, Haverford, and perhaps Pomona—colleges that give their students a relatively strong dose of comprehensive curricula—are exceptions," the report concluded. "At the other top colleges, though, 'liberal arts' has been defined disappointingly downwards. Tuition has soared over the same period. We don't see this as merely ironic—it's highway robbery." The other six top liberal arts colleges—Amherst, Carleton, Bowdoin, Swarthmore, Wellesley, and Williams—were all given failing grades.

Other highlights from *The Death of Liberal Arts?*:

- "A freshman at Bowdoin cannot take a course in Shakespeare."

- "A freshman at Amherst isn't offered a single overview of European or English history."

- "A freshman at Williams will find that what few courses review U.S. or European history focus on "race, ethnicity and gender," rather than the given period's main developments."

- "A freshman at Wellesley will find that the few broad English courses offered to freshmen focus on gender and not the books' themes and styles."

At Williams College, a freshman English course called "Green World" explores "man's desire to transform chaos into civilization and art" while "humanizing, plundering, and destroying the environment."

And at Wellesley College, there's a history course on "Gender and Nation in Latin America" that covers "patriarchal discourses of state and feminized representations of nation, the idealization of motherhood as a national and Christian value [and] the role of military regimes in promoting masculine ideologies."

Outrage has replaced intellectual inquiry, the pursuit of the truth. Actually, better put, on many of our campuses outrage is dressing up and calling itself intellectual inquiry.

IWF runs a Campus Project, by the way. Its purpose is to get alternative ideas (read: ones that are not doctrinaire liberal) into the discussions on campus. Kristen Hellmer is the young woman who runs the project. In the year following the Iraq war she went to about a dozen campuses to speak. One campus newspaper, the *Dartmouth*, flat-out refused to publish a paid advertisement that IWF tried to place. The ad was designed simply to inform students about the organization. It did criticize feminist orthodoxies, but said nothing outrageous or obscene. Still, the student editors of the *Dartmouth* concluded that the IWF ad was beyond the pale, too politically incorrect.

PART OF THE PROBLEM lies in who the faculty are. The members of the "destructive generation" of the 1960s, as Peter Collier and David Horowitz labeled them, have become today's "tenured radicals." The same people who wanted to bring "the system" down in their youth are now firmly lodged in the privileged institution of academic tenure. They simply never left campus life to get a dose of the real America, and it shows.

Recent research has shown just how homogeneous university faculties are when it comes to political views, party affiliations, and voting behavior. One study by California economist Dan Klein and Swedish social scientist Charlotta Stern is titled "How Politically Diverse Are the Social Sciences and Humanities?" Among their findings:

- Anthropologists vote Democratic over Republican at a rate of 30 to 1;

- That balance is 28 to 1 for sociologists;

- Even in the "hard" social science of economics, which some might be tempted to think of as a conservative discipline, the faculty vote Democratic at a rate of three to one.

Similar findings appear in a large study coauthored by Stanley Rothman, S. Robert Lichter, and Neil Nevitte, "Politics and Professional Advancement Among College Faculty." Relying on data from the 1999 North American Academic Study Survey, they found that in the fields of English literature, philosophy, political science, and religious studies, 80 percent of faculty identified themselves as liberal, only 5 percent as conservative. And more remarkably, even in the sciences the balance remains lopsided. Democrats outnumber Republicans four to one in biology, and ten to one in physics.

In a separate study by David Horowitz's Center for the Study of Popular Culture, researchers looked into the voter registration of faculty in six fields at 32 schools (voter registration is a public record). The findings? Democratic registration outstripped Republican ten to one.

In yet another study coauthored by Dan Klein and focusing on the two most prominent California universities, a still more troubling finding was that most of the Republican professors are close to retirement. The ratios are more extreme among assistant and associate professors than among full professors. Klein concludes that "[a]t Berkeley and Stanford, the Republican is an endangered species."

I admit that voter registration is a crude measurement, but these studies do tell us something important. They tell us that "diversity" is a sham in these universities in which it is purport-

edly championed. They tell us that the academy is a monocul-
ture, and it is increasingly closed off to dissenting voices. They
give us more than a notion that the prospects are not good for a
return to a higher education system that has truth as its end.

HOW DO WE REFORM higher education, so that it becomes an engine for generating intellectual capital rather than
an engine of destruction? How can we transform our universities so that truth is pursued and taught in the humanities at the
same high level that it is pursued and taught in the natural sciences? Those are tough questions, especially for a U.S. senator.
After all, contrary to the wishes of Thomas Jefferson, there is
no federal university over which Congress has direct authority.
Many of America's best universities are private foundations, and
because of the principle of subsidiarity I respect their independence. But from the sidelines, I can cheer on worthy initiatives.
And state legislators who oversee public university systems surely
have a role to play in ensuring that tenure does not become
simply the most egregious form of No-Fault Freedom.

One promising initiative is being promoted by David
Horowitz. He calls it the "Academic Bill of Rights." This is a
document that outlines the purposes of a university ("the pursuit of truth," "the study of . . . cultural traditions," "the teaching and general development of students," "the transmission of
knowledge and learning to a society at large") and articulates a
definition of "academic freedom" that is as sensitive to the
student's right to learn as it is to the professor's right to teach.
Political opinions are fine—I obviously have a lot of my own—
but they are not the substance of a liberal education, and students should not be graded for their conformity to their professors' views. The most controversial element of the proposal con-

cerns the value of "intellectual diversity" in a university community, which amounts to a call for universities to take action to break open the closed guild that many departments have become.

Horowitz has been focusing his efforts on public universities, meeting state legislators across the country to advance legislation that would affect state universities, with the hope that such legislation might have a spillover effect, shaming private universities into taking similar action. As he puts it,

> We don't go to our doctor's offices expecting to get political lectures. That is because doctors are professionals who have taken an oath to treat all, regardless of political belief. To introduce divisive matters into a medical consultation would injure the trust between doctor and patient that is crucial to healing. Why is the profession of education any different? It isn't.

Horowitz's greatest adversary is the American Association of University Professors (AAUP), who claim that the Academic Bill of Rights would infringe upon the free-speech rights of faculty members. Ironically, much of the language of the Academic Bill of Rights is taken straight from older statements by . . . the AAUP itself! The 1967 AAUP Joint Statement on Rights and Freedoms of Students, for example, admonished, "Students should be free to take reasoned exceptions to the data or views offered in any course of study and to reserve judgment about matters of opinion." In 1940, the AAUP had warned, "Teachers . . . should be careful not to introduce into their teaching controversial matter which has no relation to their subject."

Why the change in the AAUP, which once insisted on the inseparability of "the freedom to teach and the freedom to learn"? Well, one big reason is the rise of the tenured radicals; another big reason is postmodernism, which holds that there *is* no truth, only opinions. If there are only opinions, then opinions are the proper subject of teaching. As a result, you can be graded down for not regurgitating such opinions on your test.

Postmodern theory is so jargon-filled and convoluted that anyone outside the academic elites who takes it on is likely to be patronized as someone who "just doesn't understand." I know I'm risking that here, but I think I understand postmodernism well enough to see how it has poisoned our institutions of higher education, robbing America of the true liberal learning that is the crown jewel of our intellectual capital.

IN RECENT YEARS there has been another positive development that I'd like to cheer on: the growth on some campuses of independent and semi-independent centers, institutes, or programs that focus explicitly on more traditional bodies of knowledge and modes of inquiry, such as the American founding or Western civilization. One such center, and perhaps the most successful, is Professor Robert George's James Madison Program in American Ideals and Institutions at Princeton University.

Professor George is a stellar scholar at the top of his field, with degrees from Swarthmore, Oxford, and the Harvard Law School, and several books published by the most prestigious university presses. He also served on the United States Commission on Civil Rights, was a Judicial Fellow at the Supreme Court, and is currently a member of the President's Council on Bioethics. On top of that, he has won teaching awards for his performance in the classroom. With a record like this, you would think even as grand an institution as Princeton would hail George as one of its best and brightest. In fact, however, his tenure decision was hotly contested. You see, Professor George is publicly conservative, and some of his faculty colleagues and some administrators seem to have believed that there was no room on the Princeton faculty for people with views like his. It's a story that could be told by literally hundreds of conservative academics.

But however rocky the process, however many attempts were made to scuttle his chances, in the end—unlike so many others—he made it through to the prize of academic tenure. Beyond his high-powered scholarship (which focuses on natural law), Professor George is also what is called an academic entrepreneur, someone who looks for ways to make changes in university curricula and governance. When Princeton appointed Peter Singer—the philosopher who favors infanticide—to a prestigious chair in 1999, conservative alumni and supporters were appalled and the university came under pressure. Professor George seized the opportunity to champion a place within the administrative maze of Princeton for more traditional scholarship and teaching that could be funded by otherwise disaffected donors: the Madison Program was born.

The program, raising its own funds, now hosts visiting faculty and sponsors conferences and lectures at Princeton—and not all of these are conservative. Because of the Madison Program, Princeton students are exposed to real intellectual diversity, younger scholar-fellows have a chance to advance their research, and the whole of the university community is enriched. So successful has been Professor George's initiative that faculty at dozens of other colleges and universities are using it as a model for their own projects. I wish them success.

But notice what a half-victory even this outstanding program is. Unlike the women's studies, gender studies, and gay and lesbian studies programs at countless universities, for example, the Madison Program does not grant degrees—a student cannot major in the Madison Program. Also unlike those

other politically correct advocacy departments, the Madison
Program cannot hire full-time, permanent members of the
Princeton faculty: the visiting scholars associated with the program have something like the status of resident aliens, with no
prospects of ever becoming full citizens of the faculty. What's
more, with the speakers the Madison Program provides for campus lectures the university gets a public relations coup: it can
trumpet to alumni that there is intellectual diversity and balance in the campus programming. But this is only true because
the university is taking credit for the barely tolerated work of
the program: in the rest of the university, commanding infinitely
more resources, the same politically correct line is followed on
who to invite and who to exclude. And in the end, what happens to the Madison Program when Professor George eventually retires? He is the black sheep of the Princeton faculty: Will
there be anyone even remotely like him to take his place? Will
the program be taken over by the post-modernists? Or will it
simply disappear, becoming nothing but a fading memory, a
rumor of what once was?

Still, as those of us in politics understand very well, a half-
victory is better than no victory at all. And who knows what
the future may bring? University alumni and donors hold one
of the very few levers that may be brought to bear against the
entrenched interests of the tenured radicals in our universities.
New centers such as the Madison Program are beacons of hope,
promising to at least partially redeem our universities, against
their will. I hope those with financial means among my readers
who are interested in reforming our universities will investigate
these initiatives further.

THE LATIN MOTTOS of both Harvard and Yale speak of *veritas*, truth. Yet as we have seen, universities today cannot speak of the truth without putting it in ironic scare quotes. Our nation's Latin motto is *E pluribus unum*: Out of many, one. Yet as we have seen, multiculturalism rejects the possibility that we could ever be *one*; its motto would be something like, "Out of many, many more."

What goes on in the university has civic consequences. Will an American citizen who has been through a postmodern education stand up to injustice or defend the rights of others? How can she, when she has been taught that there is no authentic justice, only various "structures of power"? Will an American citizen who has been through a multicultural education come together with others to advance our common good? How will he, when he has been taught that American culture is not his, but someone else's?

What goes on in the university also has educational consequences all the way down the educational ladder. Progressive educational theories often opt for a style of education that stresses "approaches to knowledge"—teaching students "how to think"—without actually transmitting to students anything they might think *about*. This approach has trickled down into our high schools and even into our elementary schools, and whether or not it is successful at teaching "how to think" (I doubt it), it ensures that our students know less and less about their history, their literature, and the great ideas that went into the making of America. Our intellectual capital takes another hit.

We need to put the "higher" back into higher education. From the very first learning at home before schooling ever starts and on through higher education, we have to get back to the business of building up our intellectual capital. We have to see once again that man, the rational animal, is a creature with certain ends or purposes and that therefore moral education is not only possible, but necessary. We have to reexamine the question of science and whether it conflicts with or reinforces our understanding of purpose in human existence. And we have to once again recognize that right and wrong, civil discourse, what great minds in the past thought and wrote, and even manners not only matter, they are irreplaceable.

Finally, we need to reorient our educational system and educational philosophy toward truth. Because truth, held in common, offers the most solid intellectual foundation for genuine liberty.

Conclusion

This book has covered a lot of ground, and I have made a lot of proposals for both public and private initiatives that will make us better stewards of our inheritance as Americans, reweaving the ties that bind and building up the various kinds of capital that constitute the common good. I suspect some will dismiss my ideas as just an extended version of "compassionate conservatism." Some will reject what I have to say as a kind of "big government" conservatism. And some will say that what I've tried to argue isn't conservatism at all. But I believe what I have been presenting is the genuine conservatism our founders envisioned, one that fosters the opportunity for all Americans— not just those of privilege—to live as we are called to live: in selfless families that contribute to the general welfare, the common good.

I said at the outset that the focus of this book was originally intended to be on the poor; it obviously has ranged well beyond that scope. Yet I hope I have demonstrated that my treatment of other aspects of our society and culture was not irrelevant to the condition and prospects of poor families. There's an old frontier saying that comes to mind: "Don't drink downstream from the herd." Poor families in America live downstream from the rest of us. They are the ones who suffer the most from the actions of the Bigs, who have structured society to benefit themselves and their lifestyle choices without thinking about how their No-Fault Freedom will affect others.

In the economy, I have argued that the village elders have treated the poor as disabled victims who need to be permanently attached to government life support. The village elders believe in the treadmill economics of income transfer, which simply freezes people in poverty. On the contrary, I believe in helping Americans build up an ownership society, with policies to promote home ownership, small business creation, financial knowledge, savings, and stable families. Unfortunately, most of the government programs that liberals have created in years past to achieve their worthy ideals have not worked. Worse, they have in many places undermined the natural family and left in its wake isolated individuals in disconnected communities. I have laid out a plan for changing welfare policy to focus more on responsible fatherhood, healthy marriages, and family wealth-building. Poor families, after all, will most likely be healthier if they are wealthier.

At a recent hearing of the Senate Finance Committee I learned that the federal government currently provides incentives for Americans to save $120 billion per year. Yet we only get $85 billion of new net saving from that public investment. Why? Because the incentives mostly allow high net-worth individuals to move their money from taxable savings and investments into subsidized, non-taxable savings. It's a great deal for the Bigs—and it is meaningless to everyone else. That is why we need IDAs and KIDS accounts, which would encourage savings for life-changing initiatives like starting a small business, getting a higher education, or buying a home.

I wrote of the depletion of social capital and how its consequences most dramatically affect the poor. A wealthy person
has the resources to survive and prosper (at least economically)
out in the world alone. But without a network of family, church,
neighbors, and friends, the poor will struggle in every aspect of
their lives. A poor young girl without such a network is today
immersed in a community, a school, and a culture that all preach
No-Fault Freedom. Young girls in that position cannot afford
to "do whatever feels good as long as you don't hurt someone
else"—because they have no way to buy themselves out of the
hurt *they* will experience. The village elders' paradigm of pulverizing the American family so that we are all unconnected,
self-sufficient (with government aid) individuals may work for
the Hollywood/Harvard crowd. But downstream, it is creating
a frighteningly empty, lonely world where nothing can fill the
void created by a "freedom" that has no purpose and no hope.
We can clean up the stream—by rebuilding the network of family, faith, and community across America. Renewing our social
capital will benefit all Americans, but it will bring the most hope
to those who have suffered the most from No-Fault Freedom.

The corrupting of our moral and cultural capital by the village elders has had devastating effects on the poor. The cultural
artifacts of the village elders teach us the lie that there are no
negative consequences and no alternatives to the self-centered
pursuit of pleasure. The moralists of the village elders teach us
that there is no truth, that, therefore, we are "free" to put our
wants (our "truth") above everyone else's. Here too the poor
suffer much more than the village elders, simply because they
usually don't have strong families and networks to fall back on
and have fewer resources to recover from the consequences of
their actions. When a son of the Bigs lives the self-indulgent life
the village elders prescribe and ends up with multiple addic-

tions, there is always rehab and a second, third, and fourth chance. When the son of the poor single mom does the same thing, he ends up either in a gang, on the street, in jail, or dead. Being downstream from No-Fault Freedom is hazardous to your health.

The most obvious area where the liberal ideal has failed the poor is in education. The wealthy have often been able to escape the education factories created to produce the new "progressive man," but even they have now fallen victim to the emptiness of the liberal doctrine advanced in all but the most traditional schools. The educational elite has failed poor parents by failing to give their children the tools they need to succeed in this economy and as good citizens. In the process, they have also abandoned the very reason for education—the search for, and communication of, the truth.

THIS BOOK HAS BEEN filled with policy proposals, but I have also introduced you to a lot of private initiatives whereby social entrepreneurs are breaking new ground, creating new methods for replenishing America's social, economic, moral, cultural, and intellectual capital. Those private initiatives are at least as important as the public policies, because as I said at the beginning, the general welfare, the common good, is not something that government can *secure* or *establish* directly. As the Preamble of our Constitution indicates, government can only *promote* the efforts of active, virtuous citizens who every day participate in building up the ties that bind us together as Americans, *E pluribus unum*, one family at a time. It's up to us, *We the People*. We need a revolution of civic participation and community leadership in America, and we need a government that recognizes, honors, and works *with*—not against—the efforts of families, churches, and local communities. That is the conservative way.

When the village elders hear conservatives talk about "a thousand points of light" or about unleashing America's "armies of compassion," they say that we are talking in code words, employing a feel-good rhetoric that masks the "real" conservative agenda of shrinking the welfare state and throwing vulnerable people into the street. I hope that this book has demonstrated that our concern about and respect for America's intermediate associations, local organizations, churches, and families are not code words: they are the real agenda. And that agenda is not a recipe for insecurity: it is a platform for hope, opportunity, and the human decency that is only put into action one person, one family, at a time.

The village elders sometimes talk the talk about civil society and social capital, using terms like "civic participation" and "community leadership." But when they do, they have something very different in mind from what I have been talking about. To them, those words mean left-wing activists working to bring more "government services" (and government bureaucrats) to impoverished areas, or filing lawsuits to make "them" pay—whoever "them" is. To me, "civic participation" and "community leadership" mean something entirely different. They mean fathers volunteering time to build ballparks, grandmothers sitting on front porches or stoops to keep an eye on the neighborhood children, local school boards respecting community standards, Boy Scout and Girl Scout leaders modeling responsible adulthood for their young people, church people feeding the hungry and rescuing lives trapped in addiction or crime, Lions Club and Rotary Club and Knights of Columbus members working together to meet local needs— and yes, also the new breed of social entrepreneurs who are devising the tools to give people who are "broke" a lift up onto the ladder of opportunity.

So, yes, sometimes conservatives and liberals use the same words, but behind those words are very different visions of America. For the village elders, in the end society is just a collection of individuals with the government at the center, the only thing holding it all together. Once those individuals step beyond themselves, if they ever do, it can only be as *consumers* in the marketplace or as *clients* of the government. For a generation, the village elders have been hard at work constructing a government (and reconstructing a society) fit for consumer-clients. They have catered to the individualism that Tocqueville saw as the deadly temptation of modern societies. And as a result, America's common good has been slowly trickling away into the sands of atomized liberalism.

In the conservative vision, people are not autonomous abstract individuals, nor are they consumers and clients. They are *workers* and *citizens*. As workers, they are literally building up our nation's capital, day by day, through their dedicated labor and entrepreneurial ingenuity. As citizens, they are making the common good happen right where they are, by taking responsibility, together with their neighbors, to solve their common problems and to seize their common opportunities. *We the People* are at the center, not the government.

And *We the People* are not a heap of sand. In the conservative vision, people are first connected to and part of families: the family, not the individual, is the fundamental unit of society. Without strong families, nothing else is possible; with strong families, the sky's the limit to what we can achieve. Yet in the sophisticated theories of the village elders, the family is often seen as a potential obstacle to the common good, since devotion to the family can eclipse concern for others. For liberals, public spirit and family spirit are thought somehow to conflict. But that is not the lived truth of American life. In America's experience, strong families are the seedbed of virtue, and that includes public virtue. American citizenship is strongest where the American family is strongest.

In light of America's tradition of strong families as the basis of a strong civil society, the village elders respond, "That's fine in practice, but it just doesn't work in theory." Well, that may be true of liberal theory. But conservative theory, from the very beginning, has always understood the central importance of the family for the common good. In the eighteenth-century words of Edmund Burke, "We begin our public affections in our families. No cold relation is a zealous citizen. We pass on to our neighbourhoods, and our habitual provincial connexions. These are inns and resting-places. . . . The love to the whole is not extinguished by this subordinate partiality." We cannot build up a civil society of active citizens participating in the common good unless we start with strong families. It takes a family.

As I FINISH THIS BOOK, I think back to my hometown of Butler, Pennsylvania. Like so many of the small towns and urban neighborhoods of my state, Butler was brimful of social capital, with hard-working moms and dads doing their best to get ahead and to raise their children to be responsible adults. Those strong families supported each other, neighbors supported each other, and the whole community lent a hand: I can't tell you how many civic and fraternal organizations there were (and are!) in Butler, each working to advance our common good and taking special care to look out for those in need. Sure, we had our problems—chief among them the changing economic climate—but we also had respect, common decency, hope, trust, love, loyalty, piety, patriotism, and public spirit. The people of Butler, by focusing on being good parents and good neighbors, together created a great place in which to grow up.

That is what every town and neighborhood in America should be. That is what *America* should be: a great place to grow up. The ancient philosophers said that raising children is the central political problem, and that is just as true in America today. That means we can't just take for granted that we will always have a society of mature and responsible adults, fit for the American experiment in ordered liberty. Rather, we have to *think* about what it takes to raise our children well, and we have to *do* something about the obstacles standing in the way of bringing the promise of America to every home.

Like every father, I want to pass on to my own children something more than I received. As an American, I want to hand on to all our children a country renewed in social, economic, moral, cultural, and intellectual capital. Of course, every politician has a plan for building a better America. But too often, politicians' plans focus on one big thing—more prosperity, more liberty, more security—and neglect everything else, all the "small stuff." But as my eighth-grade basketball coach Harry Leyland used to tell me, "You want to be good? Focus on doing the little things well." He was right. The small stuff isn't small: in fact, it's the foundation for everything else, the precondition for every other aspiration. Family, faith, and civic involvement: they are the building blocks of the real American dream, and they are too often ignored. They are the things we must all do well, if we are truly going to be good.

Bibliographical Note

Throughout the writing of this book, I debated with myself about how extensively it should be footnoted. I am not a scholar, and personally I often find footnotes a distraction; on the other hand, citations allow the reader to follow up on ideas that I may not have developed fully, and they allow the reader to see where my figures and statistics are coming from. My completed manuscript was fully footnoted, but in the end my publisher argued that these hundreds of notes would make an already very long book just too long. And so it was decided that this bibliographical note would be a good alternative.

First of all, at various points in the book there are extended quotations from individuals, usually social entrepreneurs such as Scott Syphax or Jeremy Nowak. Unless otherwise indicated, these are taken from interviews conducted either by myself or by Jeffrey Rosenberg. There are also numerous quotations from American founding fathers. These can be found in *The Founders' Constitution* (five volumes), Philip B. Kurland and Ralph Lerner, eds. (Indianapolis: Liberty Fund, 2000) or in *The Founders' Almanac*, Matthew Spalding, ed. (Washington, DC: Heritage Foundation, 2001). Sometimes I have also briefly quoted from journalistic sources: in nearly every case, these quotations can be found on the Internet.

In Part One ("It Takes a Family"), I cite Russell Kirk's notion of conservatism as "stewardship of a patrimony," and this becomes a major theme in the book. Kirk's most famous work is *The Conservative Mind* (Chicago: Henry Regnery, 1953), but a more accessible illustration of the stewardship approach to political and social questions is offered in the essays collected in Kirk's *Redeeming the Time* (Wilmington, DE: ISI Books, 1999). I also cite Mary Eberstadt's *Home-Alone America* (New York: Sentinel, 2004).

This first section is swarming with statistics, and unfortunately, these come from a swarm of sources. Among the important sources for comparative data on outcomes for children in various family forms, I have learned in particular from work by Sara McLanahan. For example, her book, with Gary Sandefur, *Growing Up with a Single Parent: What Hurts, What Helps* (Cambridge, MA: Harvard University Press, 1994). Also her study, with several coauthors, "The Fragile Families and Child Wellbeing Study Baseline National Report," and her study, with Cynthia Harper, "Father Absence and Youth Incarceration," both prepared for the Center for Research on Child Wellbeing at Princeton. Other statistics first appeared in L. Edwards Wells and Joseph H. Rankin, "Families and Delinquency: A Meta-Analysis of the Impact of Broken Homes," *Social Problems* 38 (1): 71–93; Douglas A. Smith and G. Roger Jarjoura, "Social Structure and Criminal Victimization," *Journal of Research in Crime and Delinquency* (February 1988): 27–52; Kathleen M. Roche, et. al., "Neighborhood Variations in the Salience of Family Support to Boys' Fighting," *Journal of Adolescent & Family Health* 3 (2): 55–64; Seth J. Scholer, Edward F. Mitchel Jr., and Wayne A. Ray, "Predictors of Injury Mortality in Early Childhood," *Pediatrics* 100 (1997): 342–47; and John P. Hoffmann and Robert A. Johnson, "A National Portrait of Family Structure and Adolescent Drug Use," *Journal of Marriage and the Family* 60: 633–45.

Data on cohabitation comes from work by the Center for Research on Child Wellbeing, the Urban Institute in Washington, D.C., and the National Marriage Project in Piscataway, New Jersey—and from Larry Bumpass and L. Hsien-Hen, "Trends in Cohabitation and Implications for Children's Family Contexts in the U.S.," *Population Studies* 54: 29–41; and Alfred DeMaris and K. Baninadha Rao, "Premarital Cohabitation and Subsequent Marital Stability in the United States: A Reassessment," *Journal of Marriage and the Family* 54: 178–90.

The discussion of fertility rates in Europe relies in part on the United Nations publication, *World Population Prospects: The 2002 Revision: Highlights* (February 26, 2003). Also cited are John C. Caldwell and Thomas Schindlmayr, "Explanation of the Fertility Crisis in Modern Societies: A Search for Commonalities," *Population Studies*, 57 (3): 241–63; Joseph Chamie, "Low Fertility: Can Governments Make a Difference?" which was a paper presented at the Annual Meeting of the Population Association of America, Boston, Massachusetts, April 2, 2004; and Patrick Festy, "Looking for European Demography, Desperately?" a paper presented at the U.N. Expert Group Meeting on Policy Responses to Population Aging and Population Decline in New York, October 16–18, 2000.

In Part Two ("Social Capital and the Ties that Bind"), the key text is Robert D. Putnam, *Bowling Alone: The Collapse and Revival of American Community* (New York: Simon & Schuster, 2000). I quote Robert L. Woodson's *The Triumphs of Joseph* (New York: Free Press, 1998), and Bob Woodson appears again in Part Three. Allan Carlson's observations about the family-friendly New Deal are found in *The "American Way": Family and Community in the Shaping of the American Identity* (Wilmington, DE: ISI Books, 2003).

Statistics concerning incarceration were drawn from published data by the U.S. Justice Department's Bureau of Justice Statistics. Statistics on marriage and children come from G. Gibson, K. Edin, and S. McLanahan, "High Hopes but Even Higher Expectations: The Retreat from Marriage Among Low-Income Couples," Center for Research on Child Wellbeing Working Paper #03-06-FF, June 2003; Joanna K. Mohn, L. R. Tingle, and R. Finger, "An Analysis of the Causes of the Decline in Non-marital Birth and Pregnancy Rates from 1991 to 1995," *Adolescent & Family Health* 3 (1): 39–46; James T. Bond, E. Galinsky, and J. E. Swanberg, "The 1997 National Study of the Changing Workforce" (New York: Families and Work Institute, 1998); and from work by Robert Rector appearing in *The Heritage Foundation Backgrounder* (nos. 1533 and 1713).

I would also like to share the titles of several books that Karen and I have personally found helpful in raising our own family: James C. Dobson, *Bringing up Boys* (Wheaton, IL: Tyndale House Publishers, 2001); Philip C. McGraw, *Family First: Your Step-by-Step Plan for Creating a Phenomenal Family* (New York: Free Press, 2004); James B. Stenson, *Compass: A Handbook on Parent Leadership* (New York: Scepter Publishers, 2003); and Laura Schlessinger, *Parenthood by Proxy: Don't Have Them If You Won't Raise Them* (New York: HarperCollins, 2000).

In Part Three ("The Roots of Prosperity"), I quote from Adam Smith, *The Wealth of Nations*, which is available in multiple editions and is also on the Internet in fully searchable form. Statistics are drawn from Charles Murray, *Losing Ground: American Social Policy, 1950–1980* (New York: Basic Books, 1994); June E. O'Neill and M. Anne Hill, *Gaining Ground? Measuring the Impact of Welfare Reform on Welfare and Work* (New York: Manhattan Institute for Policy Research, Civic Report #17, July 2001); Brady E. Hamilton, Paul D. Sutton, and Stephanie J. Ventura, "Revised Birth and Fertility Rates for the 1990s and New Rates for Hispanic Populations, 2000 and 2001: United States," *National Vital Statistics Reports* 51 (12), August 4, 2003; Stephanie J. Ventura and Christine A. Bachrach, "Nonmarital Childbearing in the United States: 1940–99," *National Vital Statistics Reports* 48 (16), 2000; and from published data from the U.S. Census Bureau.

In Part Four ("Moral Ecology") I refer to Gertrude Himmelfarb,

*Roads to Modernity: The British, French, and American Enlighten-
ments* (New York: Knopf, 2004). The poll results illustrating a decline in perceptions of moral capital are drawn from another book
by Himmelfarb, *One Nation, Two Cultures* (New York: Vintage,
2001). When characterizing the claims of Steven Pinker, I have in
mind *The Blank Slate: The Modern Denial of Human Nature* (New
York: Viking, 2002). I also refer to Peter Singer's *Rethinking Life
and Death: The Collapse of Our Traditional Ethics* (New York: St.
Martin's, 1995). The quotation from Edmund Burke both here and
in the conclusion are drawn from his important 1790 book, *Reflections on the Revolution in France* (New York: Oxford University
Press, 1999).

This section includes numerous references to Supreme Court decisions. In virtually ever case, these can be found on the Internet. A
useful compendium of relevant religion cases is also Terry Eastland,
ed., *Religious Liberty and the Supreme Court* (Washington, DC: Ethics and Public Policy Center, 1993). My quotation from Mary Ann
Glendon is taken from an essay of hers appearing in an appendix to
Eastland's collection: "Religion and the Court: A New Beginning?" I
am also indebted to her book *Rights Talk: The Impoverishment of
Political Discourse* (New York: Free Press, 1993).

The second half of Part Four concerns abortion. I quote from Karen
Santorum, *Letters to Gabriel* (Irving, TX: CCC of America, 1998), and
from Kenneth L. Garver and Betty Lee Garver, "Historical Perspectives, Eugenics: Past, Present, and the Future," *American Journal of
Human Genetics* 49: 1109–18 (1991). The extensive quotations from
the Congressional Record can be found on the Internet at http://
www.gpoaccess.gov/crecord/index.html. The voices of women who regret their abortions appear in Melinda Tankard Reist, *Giving Sorrow
Words* (Sydney: Duffy & Snellgrove, 2000). Polling data on women's
attitudes about abortion are taken from work by the Center for the
Advancement of Women.

Figures for the incidence of abortions are taken from Lawrence B. Finer and Stanley K. Henshaw, "Abortion Incidence and Services in the United States in 2000," *Perspectives on Sexual and Reproductive Health* 35 (1), January-February 2003, and from *Morbidity and Mortality Weekly Report* 53, No. SS-9, Centers for Disease Control, November 26, 2004.

I mention that that the number of children born with Down Syndrome has declined thanks to prenatal screening and the availability of abortion. I want to recommend a book about a Down Syndrome child that may open your mind and heart to these at times challenging yet loving gifts to our society: *Expecting Adam: A True Story of Birth, Rebirth, and Everyday Magic,* by Martha Beck (New York: Times Books, 1999).

In Part Five ("Why Culture Matters") a key text for me was Michael Medved, *Hollywood vs. America* (New York: Harper Collins, 1992). It is from this book that I found the comments of David Puttnam, Richard Grenier, and Irving Kristol. A good introduction to just how the culture industry works is the PBS Frontline episode, "Merchants of Cool." The quotation from Martha Bayles is from her article, "The Perverse in the Popular," *Wilson Quarterly* 25 (3), 2001. Also quoted is Naomi Wolfe, "The Porn Myth," *New York Magazine*, October 20, 2003. Walker Percy's comments on good books and bad books are from an article by Steven Garber in the January-February 2003 issue of *Breakpoint Worldview*, available online. I reference Joseph Pieper's *Leisure: The Basis of Culture* (South Bend, IN: St. Augustine's Press, 1998 [50th anniversary edition]). And you can find out more about William Wilberforce at the Wilberforce Forum, www.wilberforce.org.

Data on the media-consumption habits of children and on the sexual content of music and television aimed at teens are from S. Liliana Escobar-Chaves, S. Tortolero, C. Markham, and B. Low, *Impact of the Media on Adolescent Sexual Attitudes and Behaviors* (Austin, TX:

The Medical Institute for Sexual Health, 2004). The dollar figures for public health costs of sexually transmitted diseases also come from the Medical Institute. The Ad Council figures for where teens get their news comes from their report, "Turning Point: Engaging the Public on Behalf of Children" (2004). The polling on attitudes toward moral absolutes was done by the Barna Group. The figures for teens' desire for greater parental guidance can be found in the report, "Portrait of Adolescence," by the Institute for Youth Development (1999). The RAND report quoted is Rebecca L. Collins, et. al., "Watching Sex on Television Predicts Adolescent Initiation of Sexual Behavior," *Pediatrics* 114 (3) September 2004: e280–e289.

For parents struggling with how to talk to their children about sex, I personally would recommend the "theology of the body" developed by the late Pope John Paul II. There are several books now available which summarize this teaching in easily understandable terms.

In Part Six ("Educational Excellence") my account of the history of public education in America depends on Charles L. Glenn's *The Myth of the Common School* (Amherst, MA: University of Massachusetts Press, 1988). I cite my wife Karen's book *Everyday Graces: A Child's Book of Good Manners* (Wilmington, DE: ISI Books, 2003). I also cite *The Diversity Hoax: Law Students Report From Berkeley*, David Wienir and Marc Berley, eds. (New York: Foundation for Academic Standards and Tradition, 1999), Allan Bloom, *The Closing of the American Mind* (New York: Simon & Schuster, 1987), and C. S. Lewis, *The Abolition of Man* (London: Oxford University Press, 1943).

I discuss the thought of Alasdair MacIntyre at some length. His classic book is *After Virtue: A Study in Moral Theory* (Notre Dame, IN: University of Notre Dame Press, 1981). Also helpful is that book's sequel, *Whose Justice? Which Rationality?* (Notre Dame, IN: University of Notre Dame Press, 1988).

On the subject of Darwinism and Intelligent Design, I have found valuable *Uncommon Dissent: Intellectuals Who Find Darwinism Un-*

convincing, William A. Dembski, ed. (Wilmington, DE: ISI Books, 2004), and John Angus Campbell and Stephen C. Meyer, eds., *Darwinism, Design, and Public Education* (Lansing, MI: Michigan State University Press, 2003). I also refer to Stuart A. Kauffman, *The Origins of Order: Self-Organization and Selection in Evolution* (New York: Oxford University Press, 1993); Michael Denton, *Nature's Destiny: How the Laws of Biology Reveal Purpose in the Universe* (New York: Free Press, 2002); Simon Conway Morris, *Life's Solution: Inevitable Humans in a Lonely Universe* (New York: Cambridge University Press, 2004); and Leon Kass, *Life, Liberty and the Defense of Dignity: The Challenge for Bioethics* (San Francisco: Encounter Books, 2002)

The study of lunch-table integration in schools is "Integration Where It Counts," by Jay P. Greene and Nicole Mellow, a paper presented at the annual meeting of the American Political Science Association, Boston, Massachusetts, September 1998. The study of graduation rates is Jay P. Greene, "High School Graduation Rates in the United States," Manhattan Institute Report, November 2001, revised April 2002. The information on improvement in public schools affected by vouchers is from Jay P. Greene and Marcus A. Winters, "When Schools Compete: The Effect of Vouchers on Florida Public School Achievement," Manhattan Institute Working Paper, August 2003. The NAEP figures for educational achievement by year can be found on the website of the U.S. Department of Education.

The figures on the knowledge of college seniors come from two studies, one by the American Council of Trustees and Alumni (Jeremy L. Martin, *Losing America's Memory: Historical Illiteracy in the Twenty-first Century*, 2000) and one by the National Association of Scholars (*Today's College Seniors and Yesteryear's High School Grads: A Comparison of General Cultural Knowledge*, 2002). I cite faculty registration figures from Daniel B. Klein and Charlotta Stern, "How Politically Diverse Are the Social Sciences and Humanities?" (Sweden: Ratio Institute, 2004) and Stanley Rothman and S. Robert Lichter, "Politics and Professional Advancement Among College Faculty," *The Forum* 3 (1) 2005. The full text of David Horowitz's "Academic Bill of Rights" can be found at www.studentsforacademicfreedom.org/abor.html.

Index

A

AA. *See* Alcoholics Anonymous
AAUP. *See* American Association of University Professors
Abington v. Schempp, 231
Abolition of Man, The (Lewis), 405
Abraham, Spence, 104
Academic Bill of Rights, 414–16
Achilles, 205
Acquired Immune Deficiency Syndrome. *See* AIDS
Adams, Abigail, 197, 272
Adams, John, 43, 44, 48, 197–98, 199, 204, 272–73
Adams, Samuel, 43
Ad Council, 277
Adolescent and Family Health, 89
AFDC. *See* Aid to Families with Dependent Children
AFL-CIO, 18
Africa, Africans, 17
African-Americans, 62, 109, 139, 141, 159, 161, 184–88, 189–91, 212, 293–94, 311
After Virtue (MacIntyre), 390
Agenda of Opportunity, 112

AIDS (Acquired Immune Deficiency Syndrome), 89, 90, 313
Aid to Families with Dependent Children (AFDC), 69, 104, 128, 133, 135
Alcoholics Anonymous (AA), 84
Alternative Minimum Tax (AMT), 96–97
Altman, Robert, 285
America, 3–10, 13, 15–16, 35, 43, 44–45, 50–52, 61–62, 86, 99, 103, 105, 115, 119, 122, 129, 135, 191, 197, 232, 248, 351–52, 362–68
American Association of University Professors (AAUP), 415
American Community Renewal Act of 2000, 104, 176–77
American Dream: Three Women, Ten Kids, and a Nation's Drive to End Welfare (DeParle), 82
American Dreams, 318
American Revolution, 43–44, 202, 273
Americans with Disabilities Act, 260
Americans United for Life, 252
America Saving for Personal Investment, Retirement, and Education (ASPIRE) Act, 152

AmeriCorps, 63–64
Amherst College, 411
Amish, 393
AMT. *See* Alternative Minimum Tax
Analects (Confucius), 406
Andover, 366
Antioch Baptist Church, 171
AP. *See* Associated Press
Arizona, 79
Arkansas, 79
Ashcroft, John, 104
ASPIRE Act. *See* America Saving for Personal Investment, Retirement, and Education Act
Associated Press (AP), 254
Atlantic, 311
Austin Powers, 328
Austria, 36
Axis powers, 410

B

Bachelorette, The, 300
Bane, Mary Jo, 134
"Banking on Our Future," 164–65
Baptists of Danbury, 229
Barcelona, 280
Barna Research Group, 299
Baumgardner, Julie, 73–75
Bayh, Evan, 81
Bayles, Martha, 299
Baylor University, 114
Behe, Michael, 399
Bennett, Elayne, 90
Bennett, William, 90, 389
Berkeley, California, 293, 414
Best Friends Foundation, 90–91
Best Men program, 91
Bible, 4, 114, 244
Big Bang theory, 396
Big Crunch theory, 396
Bill of Rights, 47–48
Black, Hugo, 225

Blackstone, Sir William, 272
Blockbuster, 333
Bloom, Allan, 287, 403, 405
Bono, 14
Book of Virtues (Bennett), 389
Bordlee, Dorinda, 252
Bourque, Kelly and Karen, 59–61, 72
Bowdoin College, 411
Bowling Alone (Putnam), 54, 61, 64, 102
Boxer, Barbara, 255–57
Boys and Girls Clubs, 338
Boy Scouts, 67, 108, 338, 427
Braveheart, 283
Bringing Up Boys (Dobson), 98
Britain. *See* England
Brookings Institution, 127
Brown, Janice Rodgers, 107
Brownback, Sam, 341
Brownson, Orestes, 48–49
Brown v. Board of Education, 238, 293
Bryant, John, 149, 163–67, 170, 192
Bulgaria, 35
Bunning, Jim, 304
Burke, Edmund, 216, 275, 429
Bush, Barbara, 78
Bush, George W., 6, 38, 64, 69, 76, 104, 105, 106, 107, 122–23, 207; administration of, 22
Butler, Pennsylvania, 429–30

C

California, 107, 112, 147, 162, 255, 413
California, University of at Berkeley, 316, 381
California Supreme Court, 107
Campbell, Ben Nighthorse, 258
Campbell's, 334
Campus Project (Independent Women's Forum), 412

CAMRA Act. *See* Children and Media Research Advancement Act
Canada, 37–38
Capra, Frank, 300
CARE Act. *See* Charity Aid Recovery Empowerment Act
Carleton College, 411
Carlson, Allan, 66, 211
Cash, Johnny, 284
Cash, June Carter, 284
Catholic Charities (CC), 107–8
Catholic Church, Catholics, 28, 68, 99, 107, 108, 239, 296, 363, 368
CBS News, 248
Census Bureau, 135
Center for the Study of Popular Culture, 413
Center on Media and Child Health, 307
Centers for Disease Control and Prevention, 86, 252
Chamie, Joseph, 36
Chariots of Fire, 291
Charitable Choice, 104
Charity Aid Recovery Empowerment (CARE) Act, 152
Charles, Marvin, 83–85
Charles, Ray, 302
Chattanooga, Tennessee, 73–74
Chaucer, Geoffrey, 299
Chester, Pennsylvania, 184–88
Chicago, University of, 401
Child Protective Services (CPS), 84
Children and Media Research Advancement (CAMRA) Act, 341–42
Children's Hospital of Boston, 307
Children's Internet Protection Act (CIPA), 340
China, 223–24
Christianity, 296, 362
Cinemark, 330
CIPA. *See* Children's Internet Protection Act
CitiBank, 164

City Year program, 63–64
Civil Rights Act of 1964, 71, 105
civil rights movement, 211–12
Civil War, 12, 310
CleanFlicks, 344
ClearPlay, 344
Clinton, Bill, 64, 70, 105, 131, 134, 176, 209, 243, 244, 267
Clinton, Hillary Rodham, 65–67, 101, 209, 258–62, 266, 341
Clinton administration, 408
Closing of the American Mind, The (Bloom), 287, 403, 405
Coats, Dan, 103, 104
Cobb, Ty, 305
College Republicans, 20
Collier, Peter, 293, 412
Colson, Chuck, 110–11
Commentaries on the Laws of England (Blackstone), 272
Community Reinvestment Fund, 171, 177, 178, 181–83
Community Service Block Grant, 104
Compass: A Handbook on Parent Leadership (Stenson), 98
Confucius, 405
Congress, U.S., 39, 69, 81, 105, 107, 108, 122, 127, 132, 136, 155, 156, 200, 220–21, 229, 232, 238, 242, 248, 255, 414
Congressional Budget Office, 137
Connecticut, 225
Constitution, U.S., 33, 38, 43, 47–48, 50, 57, 115, 116, 197–203, 221–22, 224–25, 229–35, 264, 352–53, 368, 426
Constitutional Convention, 44, 46–47
Contract with America, 112, 131
Corporation for Economic Development, 152
Cortes, Luis, 173–75
Corzine, Jon, 152
Cosby, Bill, 293, 311

Costner, Kevin, 304
Council of Europe, 35
Covenant Marriage Act, 80
Cowper, William, 244
CPS. *See* Child Protective Services
Crozer Chester Medical Center, Pa.,
    187
C-SPAN, 266, 267
Culp, Jim, 381
Czech Republic, 36

D

D.A.D.S. (Divine Alternatives for
    Dads), 85
Dartmouth, 412
Darwin, Charles, 397–400, 402
Darwinism, 397–400, 402
Daschle, Tom, 152
Davidson College, 411
Deadwood, 302
The Death of Liberal Arts? (Indepen-
    dent Women's Forum), 411–12
Declaration of Independence, 230,
    240
Delany, Tom, 181
Dembski, William, 399
Democracy in America (Tocqueville),
    51, 53
Democratic Party, Democrats, 39, 70,
    71, 101, 107, 141, 145, 249, 413
Demographic Yearbook 2003 (Coun-
    cil of Europe), 35
Denton, Michael, 399
DeParle, Jason, 82–83
Department of Health and Human
    Resources, U.S., 134
Department of Health and Human
    Services, U.S., 22
Department of Housing and Urban
    Development (HUD), 148, 160
Depo-Provera, 87
Desperate Housewives, 295, 315

Destructive Generation (Horowitz
    and Collier), 293
Disney, 331
Diversity Hoax, The (Foundation for
    Academic Standards and Tradi-
    tion), 381
Divine Alternatives for Dads. *See*
    D.A.D.S.
Divine Providence, 265
Dobson, James, 39, 98, 209
Doherty, Bill, 375–79
Dole, Bob, 132
Down Payment Assistance Act, 162
Dred Scott decision, 240
Drexel University, 142
Durham, North Carolina, 190

E

Earned Income Tax Credit (EITC),
    136, 149–50
Eastwood, Clint, 282
Eberstadt, Mary, 16
Edelman, Peter, 134
Education Department, U.S., 369,
    385, 386
Einstadt v. Baird, 225, 236
Einstein, Albert, 398
EITC. *See* Earned Income Tax Credit
Eli Lilly, 147
Ellis, Ray, 76–77
Eminem, 291
Empowerment Zones, 176
England, 200, 205, 234, 271–72, 289,
    411
Enlightenment, 197, 199, 204, 205
Enterprise Communities, 176
Entertainment Software Review
    Board (ESRB), 332
Environmental Impact Statements,
    217, 220
Epperson v. Arkansas, 231
Equal Rights Amendment, 252

Erie, Pennsylvania, 91
Esperanza USA, 173–75
Estonia, 35
Europe, 35–37, 54, 101, 115, 229, 286, 361, 407, 411
Evanescence, 302
Evans, Christina Duncan, 92
Everson v. Board, 230
Everyday Graces: A Child's Book of Good Manners (K. Santorum), 378
Exeter, 366
Expert Group Meeting on Policy Responses to Population Aging and Population Decline (2000), 36

F

Fagan, Pat, 103
Families Northwest, 26
Family First (McGraw), 98
Family Planning Perspectives, 87
Father Knows Best, 300
Federal Communications Commission (FCC), 345
Federal Housing Administration (FHA), 160, 161
Federalist, 203, 222
Federal Labor Standards Act (1938), 94
Federal Reserve, 122, 179
Federal Thrift Savings Plan, 158
Federal Trade Commission (FTC), 327, 330, 345
Feingold, Russ, 257
Feinstein, Dianne, 162, 245
Feminists for Life, 252
Festy, Patrick, 36
A Few Good Men, 145
FHA. *See* Federal Housing Administration
Fifth Amendment, 224, 234
Finding Nemo, 301

First Amendment, 33, 199–200, 224, 229–35, 368
First Call, 182
First Things First, 73–74, 77
Florida, 134, 370
Ford Motor Company, 185
For the Love of the Game, 304
Foster, Serrin, 252
Foundation for Academic Standards and Tradition, 381
founding fathers, 119, 202, 204, 216, 353, 394
Fourteenth Amendment, 224, 234
Fourth Amendment, 224
France, 51–52, 202, 205, 289, 290, 361
Franklin, Benjamin, 119, 271–72
Frederick, Maryland, 59
French Revolution of 1789, 52, 202, 361
Freud, Sigmund, 282, 285
Friends, 283, 317
Friess, Foster and Lynn, 188
Frist, Bill, 39
FTC. *See* Federal Trade Commission
Fukuyama, Francis, 211

G

Gallagher, Maggie, 39
Gallup Organization, 410
Garver, Ken, 261
GDP. *See* Gross Domestic Product
George, Robert, 416–19
Georgia, 87
Georgia, University of, 191
German Democratic Republic, 35
Germantown, Maryland, 59, 59–60
Germany, 35, 36
Gettysburg, 310
Gibbons, Sam, 133
Gibson, Mel, 283
Gingrich, Newt, 112, 131

Gioia, Dana, 338
Girl Scouts, 67, 338, 427
Giuliani, Rudy, 311
Glendon, Mary Ann, 218, 234
Glenn, Charles L., Jr., 361–63
God, 52, 79, 84, 93, 112–13, 170, 231, 260, 289, 295–96, 300, 368, 389, 402
Goin, Andrew, 266
Goldberg, Whoopi, 291
Golden Rule, 48, 99, 263, 268
Gooding, Cuba, Jr., 304
Goodrich v. Department of Public Health, 30, 237
Grady Memorial Hospital, Atlanta, Georgia, 87
Great Depression, 12, 61, 66, 190
"Great Disruption," 211, 293
Great Leap Forward (China), 223
Great Society, 45, 69, 104, 109, 125, 129, 133, 178, 193
Greco, El, 299
Greece, 36
Green, Darrell, 305, 306
Greene, Jay, 367, 369–70
Grenier, Richard, 299
Griffin, Larry, 91
Griswold v. Connecticut, 224, 235, 236
Gross Domestic Product (GDP), 126, 155
Guild Theatre, Sacramento, California, 171–72
Guinness, Os, 201–6, 216

H

Habitat for Humanity, 114
Hallmark, 334
Hamilton, Alexander, 222
Hannity, Sean, 209
Harvard University, 54, 206, 293, 307, 345, 403, 404, 408–9, 417, 419, 425

Haskins, Ron, 127, 128–29, 131, 135–36
Hastert, Dennis, 176
Haverford College, 411
HBO, 302
Head Start, 81, 380
Hellboy, 297
Hellmer, Kristen, 412
Heritage Foundation, 103
Hill, M. Anne, 137
Himmelfarb, Gertrude, 205
Hispanics, 109, 173–74
HIV (Human Immunodeficiency Virus), 89, 90, 314
H. J. Heinz, 334
Hollywood, 3, 18, 20, 206, 283, 291, 292, 298, 329, 330, 425
Hollywood vs. America (Medved), 301
Home-Alone America (Eberstadt), 16
Home Depot, 170, 171, 181–82
Horn, Wade, 22, 26
Horowitz, David, 293, 412, 413, 414–15
House of Representatives, U.S., 39, 104, 130, 145, 217, 242
House Ways and Means Committee, 127, 130
HPV. *See* Human Papilloma Virus
HUD. *See* Department of Housing and Urban Development
Human Immunodeficiency Virus. *See* HIV
Human Papilloma Virus (HPV), 314
Hungary, 35
"Hurt" (Cash), 284
Huxley, T. H., 397

I

Iacocca, Lee, 185
Iceland, 35
Ice Storm, The, 283

IDAs. *See* Individual Development Accounts
Ideas Have Consequences (Weaver), 287
IFI. *See* InnerChange Freedom Initiative
Incarcerated Fatherhood Programming, 111
Independent Women's Forum (IWF), 410–12
Indiana, 103
Individual Development Accounts (IDAs), 151–52, 424
Information Age, 286
InnerChange Freedom Initiative (IFI), 113, 114
Institute for Youth Development, 316, 323
Intelligent Design theory, 399
Internal Revenue Service (IRS), 32–33, 97, 162
Internet, 208, 233, 276, 277, 315–16, 330, 333–34, 336, 340–41, 343, 387
Iowa, 113
Iraq, 202, 207
IRS. *See* Internal Revenue Service
I-Safe, 333
Italy, 36
It's a Wonderful Life, 300
It Takes a Village (Clinton), 65–67, 209
IWF. *See* Independent Women's Forum

J

Jackson, Janet, 302
James Madison Program in American Ideals and Institutions, 416–19
Japan, 36
Jefferson, Thomas, 43, 203, 223, 229, 273, 352, 414

Jerry McGuire, 304
Jesus Christ, 107, 113, 275
Jim Crow laws, 189
Joe Millionaire, 300
John Paul II, Pope, 286, 299
Johnson, Byron, 114–15
Johnson, Kevin, 171
Johnson, Lyndon B., 71, 129–30
Journal of the American Medical Association, 87
Judaism, 108
Judeo-Christianity, Judeo-Christians, 14, 15, 44, 48, 52, 99, 212, 214, 240, 265, 282, 392
Justice Department, U.S., 62, 110, 333, 343
Justice Fellowship, 112

K

Kansas, 113
Kant, Immanuel, 199
Kass, Leon, 399–400
Kauffman, Stuart, 399
Kazaa, 333–34
Kelling, George, 310–11
Kemp, Jeff, 26
Kennedy, Anthony, 227
Kennedy, Edward, 133, 382
Kennedy, John F., 48, 49, 71
Kenya, Kenyans, 17
Kerrey, Bob, 152
Kerry, John, 18, 103, 207
Keystone Opportunity Zones (KOZs), 185
Kids Investment and Development Savings (KIDS), 152–53, 424
King, Martin Luther, Jr., 193, 213–14
Kinko's, 166
Kirk, Russell, 7
Klein, Dan, 413–14
Knights of Columbus, 427

Koran, 105
KOZs. *See* Keystone Opportunity
    Zones
Kristol, Irving, 37, 300, 301
Krofsky, Jason, 26
Kuo, David, 246
Kurtz, Stanley, 39

L

Lasch, Christopher, 265
Latinos, 27, 173–74
Lawrence v. Texas, 235–37
Learned, Nicole, 159–60
Lee, Ang, 283
Lemieux, Mario, 305–6
Leo, John, 296
Letters to Gabriel (K. Santorum), 246
Lewis, C. S., 405–6
Leyland, Harry, 430
Library of Congress, 273
Lichter, S. Robert, 413
Lieberman, Joe, 151, 152, 341
Life, Liberty, and the Defense of Dignity (Kass), 401
Life's Solution (Morris), 399
Limbaugh, Rush, 209
Lincoln, Abraham, 206, 410
Lindbergh, Charles, 410
Lions Club, 427
Lochner v. New York, 238
Long Distance Dads, 112
Lord of the Rings, The, 283, 301
Los Angeles, 166
Lott, Trent, 244
Louisiana, 59, 79, 80
Loving v. Virginia, 32
Lowry, Rich, 254
Lusk, Herb, 77

M

McCain, John, 340–41
McCain-Feingold campaign finance
    bill, 233
McGraw, Phil, 98
MacIntyre, Alasdair, 390–91, 393–94, 401
Madison, James, 43, 203, 352
Malcolm X, 170
Manhattan Institute, 367
Mann, Horace, 362
Mansfield, Harvey, 51
Mao Tse-tung, 223
Marriage Movement, The, 74
Marriage Protection Amendment, 38, 39, 79
Marshall, Thurgood, 124
Marxism, 208–9, 282, 285, 390, 404
Maryland, 59
Massachusetts, 30, 33, 37, 197, 225, 229, 237, 361, 382
Maxim, 332
Medicaid, 75
Medicare, 66, 75, 96, 154
Medved, Michael, 300–301
Melendez, Tony, 266
Memphis Belle, 291
Meyer, Stephen, 399
Michelangelo, 299
Michigan State University, 267
Middlebury College, 411
Middle East, 207
Midwest Catholic Conference (2003), 99
Milch, David, 302
Miller, Zell, 243
Milwaukee, Wisconsin, 91, 370
Minnesota, 113
Minnesota, University of, 375
Missouri, 253
Monroe County, New York, 87
Moore, Thomas, 186–87

Moral Impact Statements, 218, 220, 237
Morris, Simon Conway, 399
Morton, Billy Jo, 139–40
Moseley Braun, Carol, 179
Mother Teresa, 56, 268
Moynihan, Daniel Patrick, 133
Mr. Rogers' Neighborhood, 322
Mr. Smith Goes to Washington, 300
MTV, 284, 295, 314, 321
Museveni, Janet, 89–91
Muslims, 105, 368
Myth of the Common School, The, (Glenn), 361

N

NAACP. *See* National Association for the Advancement of Colored People
NAEP. *See* National Assessment of Educational Progress
NASCAR, 68
National Abortion Rights Action League, 253
National Assessment of Educational Progress (NAEP), 369
National Association for the Advancement of Colored People (NAACP), 141
National Association of Scholars, 410
National Campaign to Prevent Teen Pregnancy, 92
National Center for Neighborhood Enterprise (NCNE), 62, 191–92
National Education Association, 357
National Endowment for the Arts (NEA), 279, 296, 338–39
National Fatherhood Initiative, 81–82, 111
National Geographic, 342
National Home Educational Research Institute, 384

National Institute of Child Health and Human Development, 342
National Press Club, 82
National Youth Risk Behavior Survey, 86
Nature's Destiny (Denton), 399
Nazis, 394–95, 401
NCNE. *See* National Center for Neighborhood Enterprise
NEA. *See* National Endowment for the Arts
Nehemiah Project, 147–48, 158, 159–62, 169, 170–73, 177, 183
Neighborhood Children's Protection Act, 341
Netherlands, 361
Nevitte, Neil, 413
New Deal, 66
New England, 45, 362
Newton, Isaac, 398
New York, 36, 87, 298
New York City, 36, 262
New York Diamond Market, 58–59, 72
New York Times, 82, 248
Nicholson, Jack, 145, 291
Nietzsche, Friedrich, 401
Nightingale, Florence, 410
Nineteen Eighty-Four (Orwell), 276
Ninth Amendment, 224
Nisbet, Robert, 55
NIX Check Cashing, 166
No Child Left Behind Education Reform Act of 2001, 399
No-Fault Freedom, 14, 15, 17, 44, 50, 53, 56–57, 88, 125, 137, 201, 205, 210, 252, 264, 278, 279, 281, 283, 284, 293, 321, 342, 393, 402, 404, 414, 424, 425–26
Nolan, Pat, 112–14
North American Academic Study Survey (1999), 413
North Carolina, 190, 352–53

Northwest Ordinance of 1787, 200, 230, 352
Norway, 35
Nowak, Jeremy, 177–80, 183, 187, 192
Nunn, Sam, 64
Nuremburg trials, 395
NYPD Blue, 302

O

O'Connor, Sandra Day, 231–32, 235
October Sky, 328
Ogilvie, Lloyd, 244
Ohio, 219, 238
Oklahoma, 103
Olasky, Marvin, 103
Oliver Twist (Dickens), 385
Olsen, Mary-Kate and Ashley, 333–34
O'Neill, June E., 137
O'Neill, Mike, 186
One Percent Solution, 62
Ontario, Canada, 37–38
Operation HOPE, Inc., 164–67, 192
Orthodox Jews, 58–59, 105
Orwell, George, 276–77

P

Packwood, Bob, 132
Parenthood by Proxy (Schlessinger), 98
Parenting Magazine, 328
Parents Television Music Council, 295–96, 317
Passion of the Christ, The, 283–94, 301
Paterno, Joe, 13
Paul, Alice, 252
Pediatrics, 316
Penn State University, 13, 20

Pennsylvania, 62–64, 91, 139, 169, 173, 184–88, 201, 240, 387, 429–30
Pennsylvania, University of, 183, 230
Pennsylvania Abortion Control Act, 53
Percy, Walker, 282, 285, 296
"Permanent Limitations of Biology, The" (Kass), 401
personal retirement accounts (PRAs), 154–58
Philadelphia, 46–47, 62–64, 77, 141–42, 165, 180
Pieper, Joseph, 272, 304
Pileggi, Dominic, 184–85
Pilgrims, 101
Pinker, Steven, 212–13, 228
Piss Christ (Serrano), 296
Planned Parenthood, 106, 224, 253, 254
Planned Parenthood v. Casey, 53, 56–57, 222, 227, 236, 264
Plato, 361
Player, The, 285
Pledge of Allegiance, 231
Plessy v. Ferguson, 189, 238
PNC Bank, 165
Poland, 59
Polybius, 203, 205
Pomona College, 411
Population Association of America, 36
Powell, Colin, 193
PRAs. *See* personal retirement accounts
Preamble to the Constitution, 47, 48, 50, 116, 426
Preferred Real Estate Investments, 186
President's Council on Bioethics, 401, 417
President's Council on Service and Civic Participation, 306
Primus, Wendell, 134

Princeton University, 403, 416–19
Prison Fellowship Ministries, 111, 112, 113
Proctor & Gamble, 334
Protestantism, Protestants, 108, 296, 363, 368
Prussia, 361
Puritans, 198, 229
Putnam, Robert, 54–55, 61, 64, 102
Puttnam, David, 291

R

Radanovich, George, 62
RAND, 316
Rangel, Charles, 140
Reagan, Ronald, 121, 149
Reaganomics, 121
Recording Industry Association of America (RIAA), 327, 332
Regal Cinemas, 330, 331
Religious Freedom Working Group, 103
Rembrandt, 299
Renewal Communities, 104, 176, 186
Republican Party, Republicans, 6, 20, 57, 69, 71, 104, 127, 130, 131, 135, 240, 413, 414
Republic (Plato), 361
Resnick, Michael, 87
Rethinking Life and Death (Singer), 228
Return of the King, The, 8, 283
Reverse Commuting Program, 179
Rice, Condoleezza, 193
Rich, Michael, 307–10, 345–46
Richard Allen Public Housing Project, Philadelphia, Pa., 62–63
Ridge, Tom, 173
Ritalin, 322
Roads to Modernity (Himmelfarb), 205
Roaring Twenties, 12
Rodgers, Mark, 240

Roe v. Wade, 128, 222, 226–27, 236, 238, 240, 250
Rogers, Fred, 322, 323
Rome, Republic of, 205
Roosevelt, Franklin D., 150
Röpke, Wilhelm, 55
Rotary Club, 427
Rothman, Stanley, 413
Rousseau, Jean-Jacques, 212
Rowry, Shervonda, 90
Russia, 36, 202

S

Sacramento, California, 147, 158–59, 169–73
St. Hope, 171
Sammartino, Bruno, 298
Sandler, Adam, 294
Santorum, Gabriel Michael, 245–47
Santorum, Karen, 23, 98, 240–41, 244, 245–47, 258–61, 266, 274, 283, 307, 308, 323–24, 373, 378, 379, 384
Santorum, Rick, 246–47, 255–57
Schlessinger, Laura, 98, 209
Scientology, Scientologists, 103
Scott Paper, 185
Seattle, 83–84
Securities and Exchange Commission (SEC), 122
Selig Center for Economic Growth, 191
Senate, U.S., 39, 63, 70, 71, 107, 130, 133, 217, 238, 242–44, 265–66, 382, 399
Senate Finance Committee, 73, 424
Serrano, José, 296
Sesame Street, 322
Seventh-day Adventists, 103
Sex in the City, 283, 314
Sexual Revolution, 283
Shakespeare, William, 299, 407, 411
Shaw, Clay, 134

Sikhs, 103
Singer, Peter, 228, 417
Sixties, 210–12, 280, 376
Smith, Adam, 119–20
Smith, Bob, 242–43, 244
Social Security, 66, 70–71, 96, 154–58
Soviet Union, 4
Spain, 36
Spanglish, 294–95
Spawn, 297
Specter, Arlen, 243
Spiderman 2, 301
Sputnik, 12
Stalinism, 390
Stanford, 414
Star Sexual Trauma and Recovery program, 315
Steel, George "The Animal," 298
Stenson, Jim, 98
Stern, Charlotta, 413
Stewart, Jimmy, 291
Stewart, Potter, 225
Stillman, Whit, 280
Stinnett, Bobbie Jo, 254
Streisand, Barbara, 291
Stuart, Charles, 111–12
Summers, Larry, 408–9
Sun Shipbuilding, 185
Supreme Court, U.S., 30, 32–33, 53, 56–57, 221, 222, 224–38, 248, 249, 264, 293, 353, 417
Swarthmore College, 411, 417
Sweden, 35
Switchfoot, 302
Switzerland, 36
Syphax, Scott, 146–49, 150, 159–62, 170, 192

T

Templeton, Jack, 188
Temporary Assistance to Needy Families (TANF), 104, 135, 138, 152

Ten Commandments, 48, 221
Tennessee, 73–74
Texas, 113, 114
Thrift Savings Account, 153
TIVO, 344
Tocqueville, Alexis de, 51–55, 68, 115, 167, 203, 428
Tolstoy, Leo, 407
Tommy D's Home Improvement Centers, 181–82
Tragedy of American Compassion, The (Olasky), 103
Tripodi, Cara, 315–16
Triumphs of Joseph, The (Woodson), 189
Turkey, 35
Turner, Michelle, 141–42
TVGuardian, 344
Two Towers, The, 38

U

U2, 14, 265
Uganda, 89–90
United Nations (UN), 36
United States. *See* America
United States Commission on Civil Rights, 417
Urban Institute, 135
USA Freedom Corps, 64
USA Today, 300
U. S. News & World Report, 411

V

Vagina Monologues, The, 68
Veggie Tales, 373
Verizon, 59
"Vertigo" (U2), 14
Victoria, Queen, 289
Victorian era, 44
Victoria's Secret, 274

Vietnam War, 62, 376
Virginia, 204, 273

W

Wallace, William, 283
Wallace v. Jaffree, 231–32
Wal-Mart, 332, 343
War on Terrorism, 207
Washington, D.C., 59, 82, 92
Washington, George, 43, 198, 271, 352, 410
Washington Post, 246
Washington State, 26
Watergate, 376
Waters, Maxine, 145, 146, 163
Watts, Donna Joy, 266
Watts, J. C., 103, 163, 176
WB network, 300
Wealth of Nations, The (Smith), 120
Weaver, Richard M., 287
Welfare Reform Act of 1996, 46, 104, 127
Wellesley College, 411, 412
Wells Fargo, 164
West, 360, 385, 406–7, 408
Widener University, 187
Wilberforce, William, 280, 289–90, 303, 312

William Penn High School, 62–64, 77
Williams College, 411, 412
Wilson, Aaron, 184
Wilson, Alan, 181
Wilson, James, 230, 310–11
Wisconsin, 91, 257, 370
Wizard of Oz, 96
Wofford, Harris, 64, 242
Wolf, Frank, 94
Wolfe, Naomi, 318
Woodruff Hotel, Sacramento, California, 171
Woodson, Robert, 62, 189–93
Workplace Religious Freedom Act, 103
World War II, 155, 394, 410
World Wildlife Fund, 106

Y

Yale University, 403, 419
Youth Life Foundation, 306

Z

Zogby International, 248, 410

About the Author

Rick Santorum has served in the United States Senate since January 1995, where he is serving a second term as Republican Conference Chairman, the party's third-ranking leadership position in the Senate. As Conference Chairman, Senator Santorum directs the communications operations of Senate Republicans and is a frequent party spokesman. He is the youngest member of the leadership and the first Pennsylvanian to hold such a prominent position since the 1970s.

While Senator Santorum is proud of his accomplishments as a lawmaker and public servant, he is most proud of his role as a husband and father. Senator Santorum and his wife, Karen Garver Santorum, are the parents of six wonderful children: Elizabeth, John, Daniel, Sarah Maria, Peter, and Patrick.